# Believing in Cleveland

In the series *Urban Life, Landscape, and Policy*, edited by David Stradling, Larry Bennett, and Davarian Baldwin. Founding editor, Zane L. Miller.

J. MARK SOUTHER

# BELIEVING IN CLEVELAND

*Managing Decline in "The Best Location in the Nation"*

TEMPLE UNIVERSITY PRESS
*Philadelphia • Rome • Tokyo*

TEMPLE UNIVERSITY PRESS
Philadelphia, Pennsylvania 19122
*www.temple.edu/tempress*

Library of Congress Cataloging-in-Publication Data

Names: Souther, Jonathan Mark, 1971– author.
Title: Believing in Cleveland : managing decline in "the best location in
the nation" / J. Mark Souther.
Description: Philadelphia : Temple University Press, 2017. | Series: Urban
life, landscape, and policy | Includes bibliographical references and
index.
Identifiers: LCCN 2017010551 (print) | LCCN 2017027075 (ebook) |
ISBN 9781439913741 (e-book) | ISBN 9781439913727 (cloth : alk. paper) |
ISBN 9781439913734 (paper : alk. paper)
Subjects: LCSH: Community development—Ohio—Cleveland. | Economic
development—Ohio—Cleveland. | Urban renewal—Ohio—Cleveland. |
Cleveland (Ohio)—Economic conditions—21st century. | Cleveland
(Ohio)—Social conditions—21st century.
Classification: LCC HN80.C6 (ebook) | LCC HN80.C6 S68 2017 (print) |
DDC 307.1/40977132—dc23
LC record available at https://lccn.loc.gov/2017010551

9  8  7  6  5  4  3  2  1

*For Keely*

# Contents

# Believing in Cleveland

# Introduction

In 2005, the *Plain Dealer*, Cleveland's last surviving daily newspaper, launched a slogan campaign that called on Clevelanders to "Believe in Cleveland." The campaign emerged from a plan hatched by *Plain Dealer* publisher Alex Machaskee and Stern Advertising head Bill Stern. The "Believe in Cleveland" slogan appeared on red-and-white bumper stickers, billboard signs, and newspaper, television, and radio ads that featured stimulating messages by Cleveland Clinic chief Toby Cosgrove, Cleveland Orchestra director Franz Welser-Möst, former Browns cornerback Hanford Dixon, and Case Western Reserve University president Edward Hundert. The slogan suggested a need to combat civic malaise, as though believing in the city were a simple but powerful step toward effecting its transformation.[1]

How quickly the Forest City had lost its way! Only a decade earlier, Clevelanders seemingly had been brimming with civic spirit. National media lavished attention on Cleveland as America's "Comeback City." Sellout crowds filled the new, retro-modern Jacobs Field for a record 455 consecutive home games and, in 1995, cheered the Indians to their first World Series appearance in nearly fifty years. In 1996, civic leaders illuminated bridges over the Cuyahoga River and choreographed pageants to commemorate the bicentennial of the city's founding moment: Moses Cleaveland's landing near where the Cuyahoga emptied into Lake Erie.

The "Believe in Cleveland" initiative was not the first time the *Plain Dealer* had found it necessary to bolster local morale with an image campaign following two decades in which Cleveland's fortunes had slid. In 1978, in fact, Machaskee, then an assistant to the newspaper's publisher and editor, Thomas Vail, had worked with Vail to activate a similar effort called the "New

Cleveland Campaign." And, in 1981, the *Plain Dealer* had given subscribers purple bumper stickers that read, "New York may be the Big Apple, but Cleveland's a Plum." The very existence of a "Believe in Cleveland" campaign suggests how short-lived Cleveland's tenure as the "Comeback City" turned out to be, calling into question any assumption that urban revitalization was the logical, inevitable next step in the evolution of cities that had experienced decline in the decades that followed World War II.

Cleveland boosters' efforts to will their city to renaissance, exemplified in the rhetoric surrounding Mayor George V. Voinovich's seemingly pivotal election to office in 1979 and amplified by the "Plum" campaign, was hardly unique. The last quarter of the twentieth century was a time marked by great faith in so-called "messiah mayors." Cleveland's good press mirrored that of Mayor William Donald Schaefer's Baltimore, where the James Rouse–designed Harborplace and the National Aquarium symbolized not only an enlivened waterfront but also a city on the rebound.[2] The vaunted role of public-private partnerships seemed to offer a blueprint for the salvation of cities wracked by more than a decade of urban crisis. Although late-1970s and early-1980s urban comeback narratives served as a balm for frayed nerves amid unresolved urban problems, these narratives failed to maintain their potency and therefore obscure more than they reveal about fundamental turns in the trajectory of postwar American urban history.

*Believing in Cleveland* proceeds from the premise that undoing the notion of decline and comeback as a sequential, unidirectional phenomenon requires closer attentiveness to how comeback efforts and metropolitan change unfolded in tandem and how, on numerous occasions, zealous boosters were too quick to declare victory. *Believing in Cleveland* removes the emphasis on decline and renewal as a linear process and treats decline and renewal as two simultaneous forces in constant tension. Focusing on the act of "believing" in the city's future in no way denies the presence of an opposite outlook: that of doubting the prospects for progress.[3] The reader will discern a similar tug between sanguine booster rhetoric and expressions of pessimism, not only between people but also within the same individuals whose private admissions sometimes do not match their public professions.

Put a different way, this book seeks to complicate understandings of "growth coalitions," a term sometimes employed by urban historians to describe various amalgams of municipal and business leaders committed to catalyzing economic development in metropolitan areas.[4] Commonly depicted as sharing a unified vision of the urban future, these so-called coalitions may have shared a general common purpose, but they did not always attain the degree of cohesion that marked Pittsburgh's midcentury coalition that advanced along multiple fronts to attack that city's urban problems. I find in Cleveland what was, at best, an uneasy alliance of widely varying interests, often riven with internal dissension. Thus, the reader should understand my use of "growth coalition" as a convenient shorthand to describe development-oriented leaders and their organizations rather than as an implication of unanimity on approach or in support of specific endeavors.

Although this book does not relate a successional narrative of decline and renewal, "decline" is nonetheless a word that begs unpacking, for the concept, no matter how murky, recurs frequently in discussions about the metropolitan future, as a fate to be averted or reversed. To be sure, some forms of decline are indisputable, because they are measurable. Population, household income, tax valuation, number of commercial or industrial firms, and value of retail trade can rise or fall. Yet there is no simple metric to apply to perceptions. Some observers sense downtown decline in the replacement of high-end stores by discount stores. Others conflate demographic changes with neighborhood decline and, if pervasive enough, with a city's decline. If perceived decline is simply part of a spectrum of metropolitan change, I argue that perceptions are nonetheless important triggers for actions that shape the courses of cities.

Likewise, the reader should understand at the outset this book's use of the term "managing decline." I employ this concept to refer to efforts to manage, or modulate, citizens' attitudes toward their city during times of real or perceived decline. Available sources offer plenty of evidence about how Clevelanders responded to efforts to characterize the city in a positive light. Did civic boosters "believe" in the city, or were they merely doling out rhetoric, imagery, and high-profile projects to combat undeniable decline, or at least to make distasteful change more palatable? Although the historical record does not always enable parsing the degrees to which boosters truly believed in a bright future for Cleveland, organizational meeting minutes, personal correspondence, internal memoranda, and a trove of confidential interviews offer revealing glimpses of what civic leaders uttered when their microphones were switched off.

Many scholars have examined the subject of urban decline in its various forms. We know much about how suburban growth siphoned business away from downtown retailers, leading to widespread store closings in most American downtowns. Likewise, the suburbs offered attractive new single-family houses on affordable terms, which drained populations away from older city neighborhoods. Suburbia also provided the space that manufacturing firms needed for plant expansions. The departure from cities of retailers, households, and industries left behind shuttered storefronts, deserted homes on overgrown lots, and hulking shells where machinery once hummed.[5] Decentralization depleted the central-city tax base, leaving fewer and less-affluent people to subsidize the services a city needed. For cities in the Northeast and the Midwest in particular, growing Sunbelt competition only added to the challenges of more localized metropolitan change.[6] In addition to spatial and structural changes that produced urban problems, scholars have been very attentive to the ways in which racial discrimination and responses to it re-shaped the metropolitan landscape after World War II.[7] We also know much about the prescriptions, some of them flawed, that politicians, planners, devel-opers, and boosters deployed in response to measured and perceived de-cline: urban renewal, highway construction, tourism promotion, downtown beautification, historic preservation and adaptive reuse of obsolete commercial and industrial buildings, formation of community development corporations (CDCs), the use of tax abatements, code enforcement, managed integration, policing, and appeals to attract growth industries, such as health care and high technology, among others.[8]

Few historians, however, have focused on how concerns about cities' im-ages shaped responses to metropolitan change. Likewise, few have moved beyond the assumption of a periodization of urban growth, decline, and renaissance to consider the tension between decline and renewal.[9] None have done so through a detailed examination of a single city. Apart from a grow-ing preoccupation with problematizing so-called ruin porn, few have de-voted much attention to the role of image apart from its utility in building the tourist trade.[10] *Believing in Cleveland* builds on understandings of how civic leaders employed rhetoric, imagery, and actions geared toward "selling" a city to tourists as a means of revitalizing it by considering the ways that boosters "sold" a city—seldom dissociated from its metropolitan area—to its own residents. The book posits that concerns about image were inseparable from those about the actual or perceived state of the city and surrounding metropolitan area but finds that managing image itself emerged as a key preoccupation in the 1970s. Even so, *Believing in Cleveland* demonstrates that this fixation grew out of problems that predated the oft-cited Cuyahoga River fire of 1969 and built on image-making efforts that, despite evolving to meet changing circumstances, were themselves decades in the making.

Why Cleveland? The answer is counterintuitive. Cleveland is an ideal subject for this type of inquiry precisely because it is not the textbook ex-ample of failure or success—or reinvention.[11] Detroit's extreme hardship and creative ploys to reverse its course, in addition to a generation of scholars inspired by Thomas J. Sugrue's seminal book *The Origins of the Urban Crisis* (1996), have in recent years made the Motor City likely the most deeply stud-ied American city outside New York, Los Angeles, and Chicago.[12] Cleveland did not endure a collapse as thorough and stultifying as that in Detroit. It was not a city like Chicago, sufficiently large, diversified, and globally connected to foster resiliency. It also did not match the tourism-driven reboot of Balti-more. Nor was Cleveland a city like Pittsburgh, where an almost complete demise of the steel industry, paired with eds-and-meds and tech-oriented investments, provided a clear template for reinvention, although not unal-loyed success.[13] Rather, Cleveland is among the largest of the nation's old industrial cities whose histories of postwar difficulties have been detailed far less in existing scholarship.

*Believing in Cleveland* resists the temptation to assign too much weight to the onset of either "decline" or "comeback." Indeed, rather than dwell on when—or whether—the city halted its slide, this book focuses on statements, depictions, and actions that evinced faith in Cleveland's future as well as how such portrayals or deeds played out and how they were contested at moments when no one could agree whether the city was improving or worsening. The symbolic bookends for my study are the advent of the longtime popular slogan for Cleveland, "The Best Location in the Nation," which the city's leading electric utility coined during World War II in the hope of postwar expansion of the market for its services, and the election of Mayor Voinovich thirty-five years later, which prompted local boosters to proclaim the arrival of a "New Generation" in a "New Cleveland." The electric company's 1940s slogan was less a response to decline than an effort to assure citizens of the city's enduring stature as an industrial center. The company's image campaign provides a useful prologue to concerns about decline, in part because the "Best Location" slogan soon became a target of derision as Cleveland's fortunes deteriorated. Similarly, although the narrative of renaissance surrounding Voinovich's rise took such firm hold that national commentators dutifully dubbed Cleveland the "Comeback City" for years, it, too, ran out of steam as the city's difficulties again overtook hopefulness. This book demonstrates that neither slogan described reality as much as aspiration. Just as Cleveland was never truly the best location, it also never truly came back.

*Believing in Cleveland* is organized into two sets of three chapters, with an intervening chapter that bridges the two sets. The first three chapters, which cover roughly the two decades after World War II, find a city and metropolitan area that were deeply divided, with the former generally suffering at the expense of the latter's continuing growth. Even in the mid-twentieth century, long before the infamous river fire, image concerns suffused efforts to deal with the problems of the central city. The book's middle chapter covers the four-year mayoralty of Carl B. Stokes, the nation's first African American mayor of a large city, who campaigned in 1967 using the slogan "I Believe in Cleveland." It views the metropolitan area as lying at a significant crossroads under the leadership of a man whose own symbolic power lifted hopes higher than circumstances would permit fulfilling. The second set of chapters picks up the story in the 1970s, during which Cleveland's city-suburb division was wider than ever. These chapters explain why image concerns took on a life of their own. Taken as a whole, the book's organization permits one to gain insights into why the city's familiar 1980s comeback story obscures a long, difficult history of attempts first to avert and later to reverse or at least manage reactions to the problems of a major city in the emerging Rust Belt, as a large swath of the Northeast, the Great Lakes region, and the Midwest came to be known in the 1980s.

The book's first three chapters examine three concerns about the state of the postwar city, focusing on efforts to reinvigorate downtown, rehabilitate neighborhoods, and fight deindustrialization from the mid-1940s through the mid-1960s. As the reader will discover, in all three chapters, the shift from expectations of ongoing growth toward concerted actions to reverse decline occurred in the late 1950s as the realization set in that Cleveland proper was losing ground relative to other cities and in absolute terms. Each chapter examines initiatives that boosters believed would play catalytic roles that might prove transformative at the city level. Chapter 1 concentrates on three downtown projects that were imbued with great potential to strengthen downtown and improve the city's image: a downtown circulator subway that was under consideration between 1943 and 1959, new convention and hotel facilities in the vicinity of the Mall planned in the late 1950s, and Erieview, the nation's largest federally backed downtown renewal project, which was unveiled in 1960. Promoters billed these projects as investments that would not simply bolster downtown but also ensure metropolitan growth. Nevertheless, as they watched downtown change in the 1950s, municipal and business leaders recast downtown redevelopment as a tool for reversing downtown decline rather than simply preserving a strong city center. The initial chapter also offers the book's first exploration of the doubts that needled even some outwardly bullish downtown boosters. Seen in this light, downtown projects were not merely facets of an economic development strategy but also exercises to lift downtrodden civic spirit. Regardless, the projects covered in this chapter ultimately faced sufficient public opposition to nix them or so delay them that they lost whatever transformative properties they might have possessed.

Chapter 2 introduces the concept of what I call "bellwether neighborhoods"—those parts of the city that growth coalition leaders regarded as a barometer for future urban revitalization. This chapter examines the emergence and evolution of initiatives to renew the city's East Side neighborhood of Hough between World War II and the Hough riots of 1966. Hough's battle with worsening living conditions, which began before its well-known 1950s racial transition, resulted in part from circumstances wrought by the war itself: a massive influx of newcomers seeking industrial work but faced with little available housing, as well as *Cleveland Today . . . Tomorrow: The General Plan of Cleveland*, a product of the wartime inception of a reorganized city-planning commission whose focus on urban renewal in the adjacent Central neighborhood unwittingly displaced thousands of residents, many of whom flooded into Hough. Hough's transformation struck civic leaders as increasingly inseparable from their ability to stage University Circle's growing importance as the city's cultural, educational, and medical district in the late 1950s and 1960s. As overly ambitious and woefully underprepared Cleveland renewal leaders tried to implement fundamentally flawed urban programs, they hastened the destruction of the city's most vulnerable East Side neighborhoods. Amid their floundering, they and other growth-focused stakeholders worked to cultivate the image of progress in Hough, but they were too late. A handful of ballyhooed "demonstration projects" only accentuated how far short the grandiose plans had fallen. The Hough riots prevented the onetime bellwether neighborhood, which through the 1950s had seemed a crucible in which Clevelanders might produce a cure for the "disease" of blight, from becoming the envisioned axle connecting the city's two hubs—downtown and University Circle.

Chapter 3 turns to industrial promotion amid the loss of manufacturing jobs from the central city to the suburbs and, increasingly, from the metropolitan region itself. Although the Cleveland Electric Illuminating Company (CEI) launched a Cleveland booster slogan, "The Best Location in the Nation," in 1944, it was more concerned with expanding electricity consumption by encouraging development throughout its 1,800-square-mile northeastern Ohio service area. The chapter closely examines the actions of the Greater Cleveland Growth Board (GCGB), which formed in 1961 to combat the newly discovered local problem of deindustrialization. The GCGB's efforts to brand the metropolitan area as the "Greater Cleveland Growthland" mimicked those of CEI. The Growth Board filled a void in the city government by meeting with heads of firms who, for a variety of reasons, were thinking of leaving the city. In doing so, the GCGB, like CEI, knowingly facilitated the suburbanization of industry. The chapter also juxtaposes the unabashedly metropolitan preoccupation of CEI and conflictive city-and-suburbs approach of the Growth Board with the city government's Gladstone urban reindustrialization project, whose 1955 inception produced disappointing results through 1966, the same year that the GCGB dissolved. The internal tension between conserving industry in the city and facilitating its drift to suburbia demanded an outward appearance of steering a dynamic "Growthland" in which plant openings, expansions, or retentions (whether in situ or through relocation within the region) might be scripted categorically as success stories, regardless of where they occurred in the metropolitan area.

Chapter 4 pulls together these three strands (downtown, neighborhoods, and industry) during the mayoral administration of Stokes in 1967–1971. Stokes's tenure began at a moment when many Clevelanders believed their city had reached its nadir, with the Hough riots symbolizing the depths of Cleveland's own urban crisis. His campaign rhetoric and mayoral initiatives aimed to renew Cleveland in every sense, making his tenure an important time to examine the tension between decline and revitalization. Chapter 4 argues that Stokes's program for civic renewal—which he branded *Cleveland: NOW!*—was an attempt to reframe Clevelanders' and outsiders' sense of how Cleveland was performing. It was also a way to buy time while Stokes pursued more difficult, substantive change that was sometimes politically challenging or even impossible to effect. The chapter diverges from the previous focus on one of three single topics over the course of several mayoral administrations in a two-decade span, instead taking a deeper look at all three topics during a four-year period. Doing so recognizes that, for all the challenges he faced, Stokes embodied and pursued a significantly different approach to advancing a city during a time of urban tribulations. The contrast between the relatively minimal attention given to previous mayoral administrations and that of Stokes may seem jarring, but it reflects my agreement with contemporary critiques of the so-called caretaker mayors who preceded him, none of whom seems to have shared the sense of urgency that Stokes brought to city hall. While Stokes was certainly not the first Cleveland mayor to view the city's image with concern, I argue that he was the first to be so attentive to image while also taking more earnest steps to redress the actual conditions that contributed to Cleveland's image problems.

The remaining three chapters continue to propel the chronology forward by examining the three broad initiatives introduced in the first three chapters, again proceeding from downtown to neighborhoods to industry in the 1970s. Chapter 5 resumes the story of downtown, tracing a notable shift from relying on large-scale infrastructure and physical redevelopment projects to creating targeted urban entertainment draws and vibrant corridors to link them. To be sure, these inclinations were not absent earlier, as suggested by recommendations in the 1959 and the 1965 downtown plans, but rather than remaining in books that gathered dust on planners' shelves, such ideas were finally put into practice. To relate this story, Chapter 5 introduces two concurrent efforts that emerged in the early 1970s, one launched in grassroots fashion from the cavernous ruin of a closed theater by a school district employee from Seattle and the other from the boardroom of a leading downtown department store. Both of them—one to restore four historic 1920s Playhouse Square theaters and the other to incorporate historic buildings and new in-fill development into a Settlers' Landing attraction in the Flats—reflected attempts to harness existing resources to recast downtown as a fun, exciting symbol of a renewed Cleveland. The chapter also examines the *Concept for Cleveland* plan of 1974 by Lawrence Halprin and Associates, the Bay Area firm responsible for remaking San Francisco's Ghirardelli Square. Although never fully implemented, the Halprin plan attempted to stitch the Playhouse Square and Settlers' Landing projects into a people-friendly downtown that could entice suburbanites and tourists to take a fresh look at the city. As was true of downtown in the 1950s and 1960s, new efforts in the 1970s to create an atmosphere of excitement in the city center after the evening rush hour not only failed to offset the continued decline of retail trade but also struggled against the push of concerns about safety and diversity and the pull of comforting, easily accessible suburban experiences. At best, the latter half of the 1970s saw downtown hold ground as its office growth and efforts to match the entertainment-driven attractions in cities from Boston to San Francisco partially offset its declining importance as a place with central appeal to Clevelanders who already were atomized across the broadly drawn "Best Location in the Nation."

Chapter 6 returns to the concept of the bellwether neighborhood, exploring a shift from redevelopment to historic preservation and from the city's riot-scarred, increasingly black East Side to its comparatively tranquil, heavily white West Side. In the 1950s and 1960s, civic leaders concentrated on remaking the deteriorating stretch between downtown and University Circle, a focus that persisted in the 1970s. However, starting in the late 1960s and continuing in the following decade, suburbanites began returning to a section of the Near West Side, which had been the separate municipality of Ohio City in the mid-nineteenth century. Attracted by its historical sense of place and impressive housing stock, people invested sweat equity and grassroots sensibility in an effort to translate their own restoration of Victorian houses into what they hoped might be a transformative back-to-the-city movement in the spirit of Beacon Hill, Society Hill, and Georgetown. However, the Ohio City renaissance had limited capacity as the prototype for an expanding back-to-the-city movement that might enable Clevelanders and outsiders to see beyond the city's troubled East Side neighborhoods. Beyond the drag exerted by a nationally lagging local economy, those who saw Ohio City as a bellwether for reshaping Cleveland's future were frustrated by the fact that not everyone in the neighborhood shared their vision or cared about the city's image. At best, in the 1970s, Ohio City was a fictive overlay of upper-middle-class white homeowners seeking to conjure an imagined Victorian past in a larger neighborhood whose mostly Appalachian or Puerto Rican renter residents continued to call it the Near West Side. Local media used the moniker "Ohio City" when touting new investment in revitalization, but they called it "the Near West Side" when engaging in frank discussions of such problems as drug abuse, arson, poverty, and interethnic strife. The Ohio City renaissance catalyzed neither a convincing reversal of Cleveland's neighborhood struggles nor of the Near West Side's ongoing population loss.

Chapter 7 returns to the problem of deindustrialization in the 1970s. Municipal and business leaders continued to try against growing odds to attract and retain manufacturing plants, but they also tried to adapt to the sort of economic transformation that was occurring in many older cities of the Northeast and the Midwest as a result of foreign competition and increasing corporate pressures to seek cheaper sources of labor and modernized plants with labor-saving innovations. Concurrently, Cleveland leaders saw the need to reshape how Clevelanders dealt with these wrenching changes, encouraging them to embrace a future dominated by the service sector. Hoping to bolster the city's lingering heavy industrial presence and third-ranked Fortune 1000 headquarters concentration, boosters greatly expanded their promotion of the city's arts, culture, and recreation as hooks to entice corporate headquarters and high-technology research labs.

Doing so, however, required escaping the gravity of more than an ossified business establishment and its deep enmeshment in an old economy dominated by iron-ore shipping, steel, and heavy machinery in a time when nimbler competitors on the coasts offered "brainpower" for space-age electronics and the South beckoned with nonunion labor and other cost-saving inducements for basic manufacturing. To attract or retain headquarters, offices, and research centers also required grappling with Cleveland's worsening national image as a city beset by problems. Of course, most of Cleveland's problems also were the problems of most older cities, but Cleveland emerged as the object of cruel jokes, especially following the 1969 river fire, and struggled against a seemingly endless onslaught of embarrassments over the ensuing decade.

As Chapter 7 demonstrates, image rehabilitation became an important activity for business leaders. Cleveland boosters crafted a new ad campaign in 1974 that proclaimed that "The Best Things in Life Are Here," a considerable departure from the self-assured boast of being "The Best Location in the Nation." The chapter considers this campaign, aimed at both corporate decision makers and Clevelanders, in the context of the city's ongoing economic slide and image struggles. It also shows how boosters had to adjust their approach by 1978 to offset the deleterious effects of a nationally publicized clash between big business interests and Dennis J. Kucinich, a brash mayor whose populist, David-versus-Goliath appeal was rooted in his distaste for business-dominated development agendas and a seeming willingness to disrupt them at any cost. By the late 1970s, any Cleveland image campaign that promised the best of anything was untenable, so boosters began to craft the image of a "New Generation" of public-private cooperation to propel the city forward. However, as the closing chapter argues, such a message struggled amid a continuing downward spiral of problems ranging from corporate headquarters' departures to the first municipal default since the Great Depression.

The Epilogue briefly surveys the so-called comeback during Voinovich's mayoral administration and its unraveling late in his successor Michael White's tenure. It also circles back to the problem of searching for a pivot point in the city's fortunes. It notes the limits of the 1980s turnaround and ends with a cautionary note in connection to the most recent spate of good news surrounding Cleveland's downtown boom, sports successes, unprecedented investments in arts and culture, burgeoning health care sector, and neighborhood renewal driven by millennials and food culture.

*Believing in Cleveland* is, in net, a retelling of the recent history of a city that entered the postwar period as America's "Sixth City," then lost ground to its suburbs, and ultimately (with its suburbs) fell back as a metropolitan region during a period of robust national growth. Like many cities across the Great Lakes region, Cleveland was a city whose leaders faced broad challenges that forced them to manage its decline or, perhaps more accurately, to manage perceptions of metropolitan transformations that produced spatially differentiated outcomes—winners and losers. Rather than a story of decline, it is a story of resilience. Whether Clevelanders learned to "believe" in Cleveland, they consumed a steady stream of assurances that their city was still great. And, whenever Cleveland fell short, boosters were there to sell glimpses of a future worth believing in.

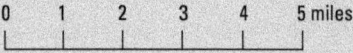

*LAKE ERIE*

0 1 2 3 4 5 miles

*St. Clai*
*Superi*

*Ho*

*Downtown*

*Central*

*Ohio*
*City*

**Cleveland**

*Detroit*
*Shoreway*

*Tremont*

**Lakewood**

**Rocky**
**River**

*Clark-*
*Fulton*

*Warszawa/*
*Slavic Villag*

I-71

*Old Brooklyn*

**Fairview**
**Park**

**Brooklyn**

**Cuyahog**
**Heights**

I-77

*CLEVELAND-*
*HOPKINS*
*INTERNATIONAL*
*AIRPORT*

**Brook**
**Park**

**Parma**

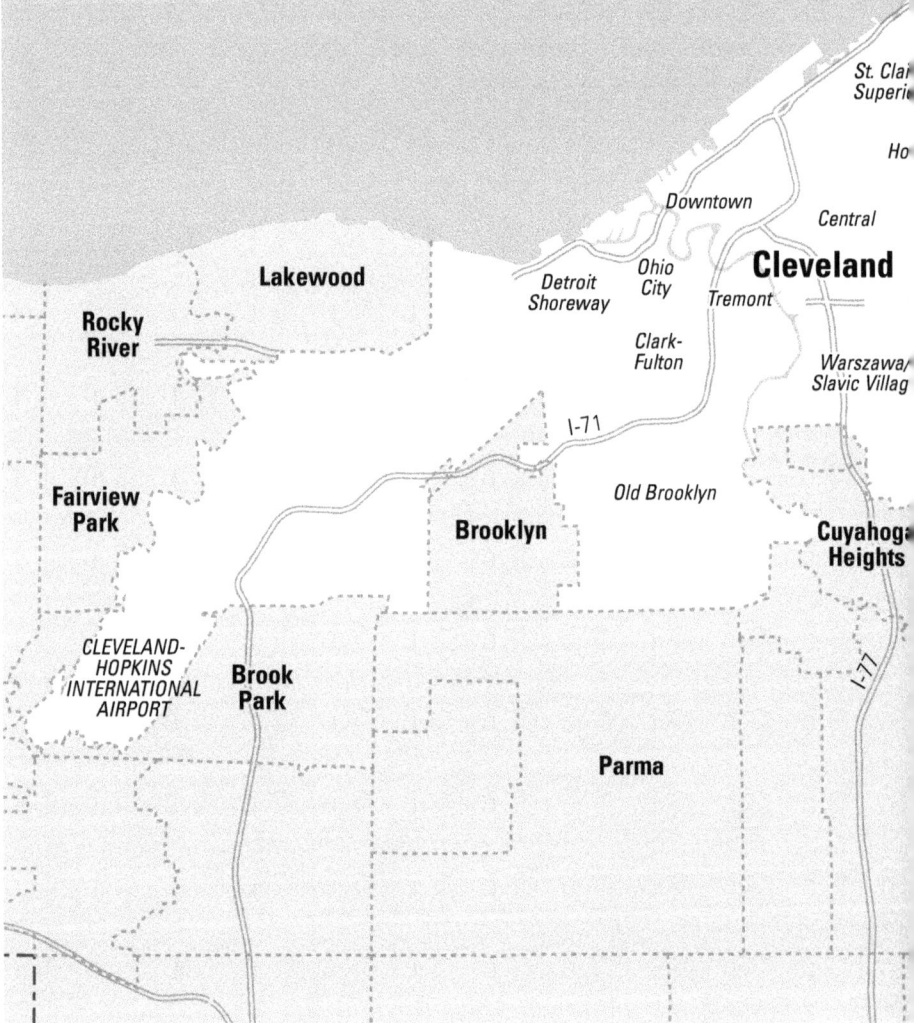

Cleveland Metropolitan Area. (Map by Nat Case, INCase LLC. Municipal boundaries derived from data © OpenStreetMap contributors.)

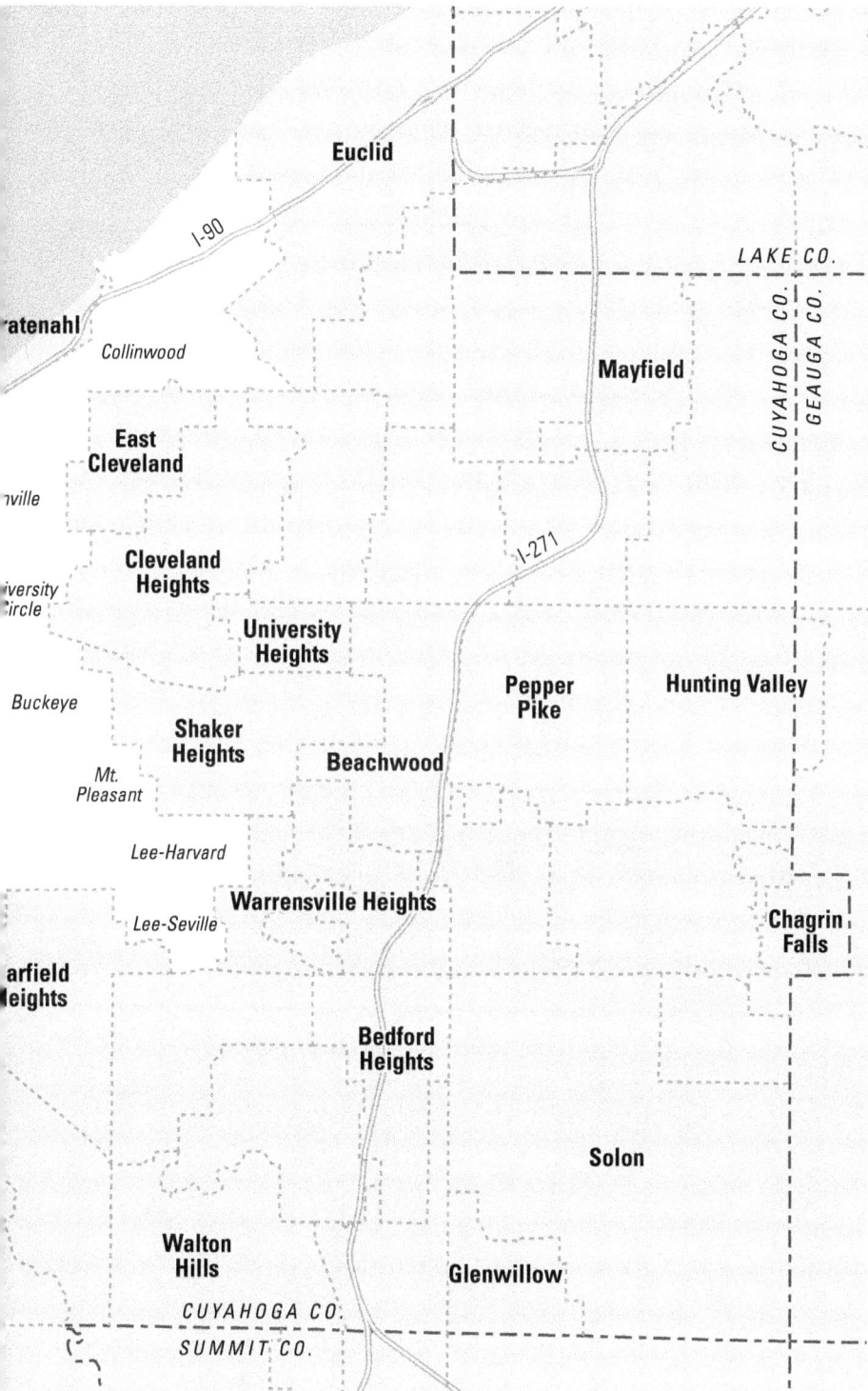

Euclid

I-90

LAKE CO.

atenahl

Collinwood

Mayfield

CUYAHOGA CO.
GEAUGA CO.

East
Cleveland

ville

Cleveland
Heights

iversity
ircle

University
Heights

I-271

Buckeye

Pepper
Pike

Hunting Valley

Shaker
Heights

Mt.
Pleasant

Beachwood

Lee-Harvard

Warrensville Heights

Chagrin
Falls

Lee-Seville

arfield
eights

Bedford
Heights

Solon

Walton
Hills

Glenwillow

CUYAHOGA CO.
SUMMIT CO.

## DOWNTOWN CLEVELAND

CLEVELAND
MUNICIPAL STADIUM

*Erieview*

ERIEVIEW
TOWER

East 17th St

Cleveland Memorial Shoreway

East 9th St

Chester Ave

MALL

Superior Ave

THE CHESTERFIELD

Ontario St

PUBLIC
SQUARE

Euclid Ave

HALLE'S

PLAYHOUSE
SQUARE

SETTLERS'
LANDING

Prospect Ave

HIGBEE'S

CLEVELAND
UNION
TERMINAL

LAKE ERIE

0          .5 mile

0          1 mile

Shoreway

Cleveland Memorial

Superior Ave

East 55th St

*Erieview*

East 17th St

Innerbelt Freeway

East 9th St

Chester  Ave

Downtown

Euclid Ave

Prospect  Ave

Carnegie Ave

Central

Superior  Ave

I-77

East 55th St

Woodland Ave

West 25th St

Ohio
City

I-71

Cuyahoga River

Gladstone

Carnegie Ave

Tremont

I-77

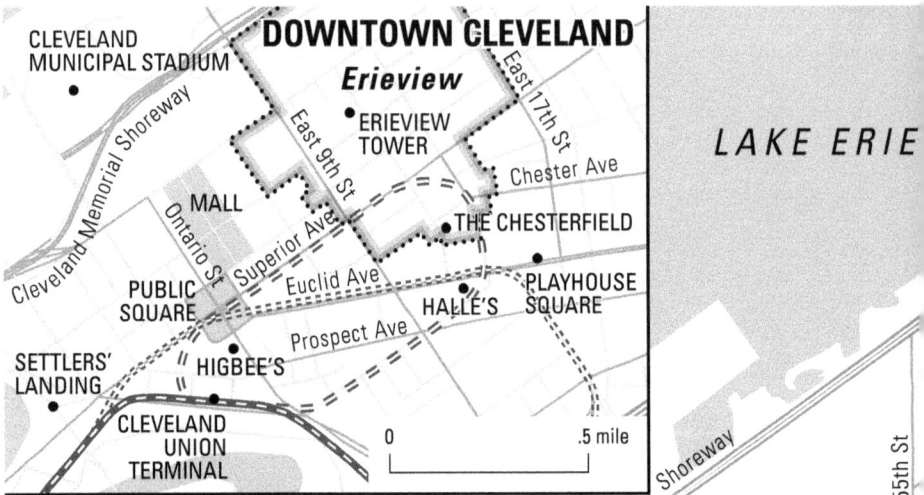

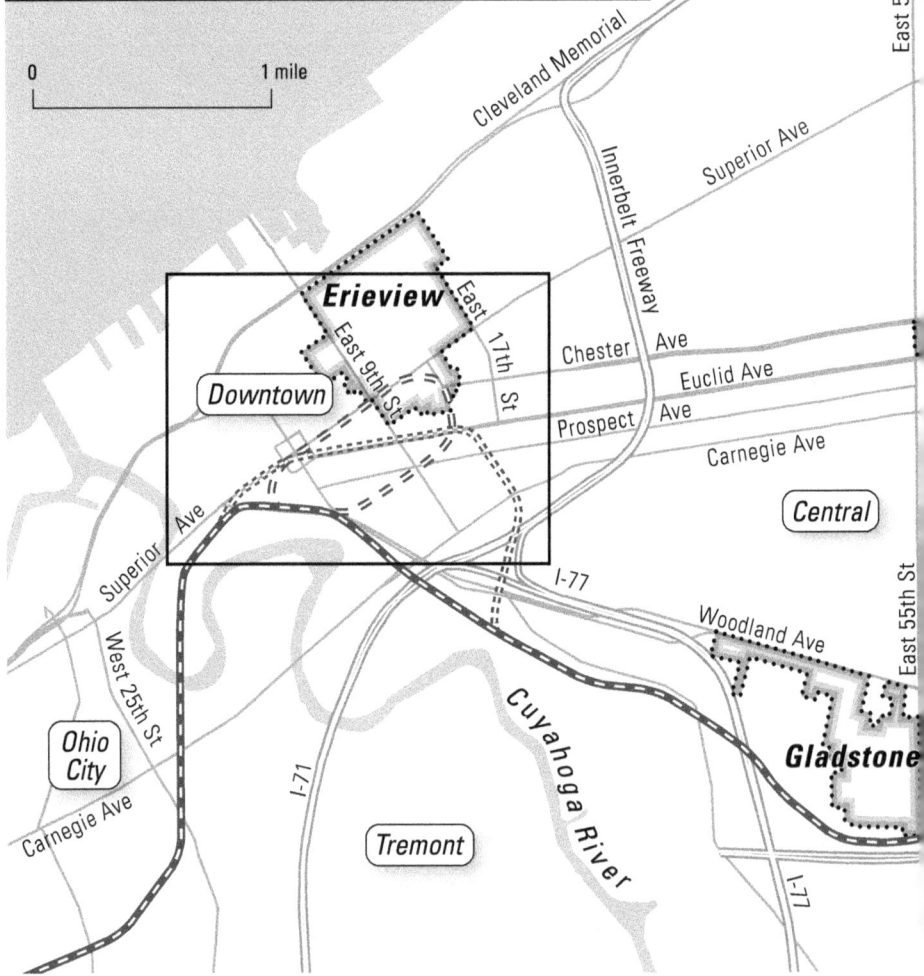

Cleveland—Central City. (Map by Nat Case, INCase LLC. Municipal boundaries derived from data © OpenStreetMap contributors.)

# Bratenahl

I-90

St Clair Ave

East 79th St

East 105th St

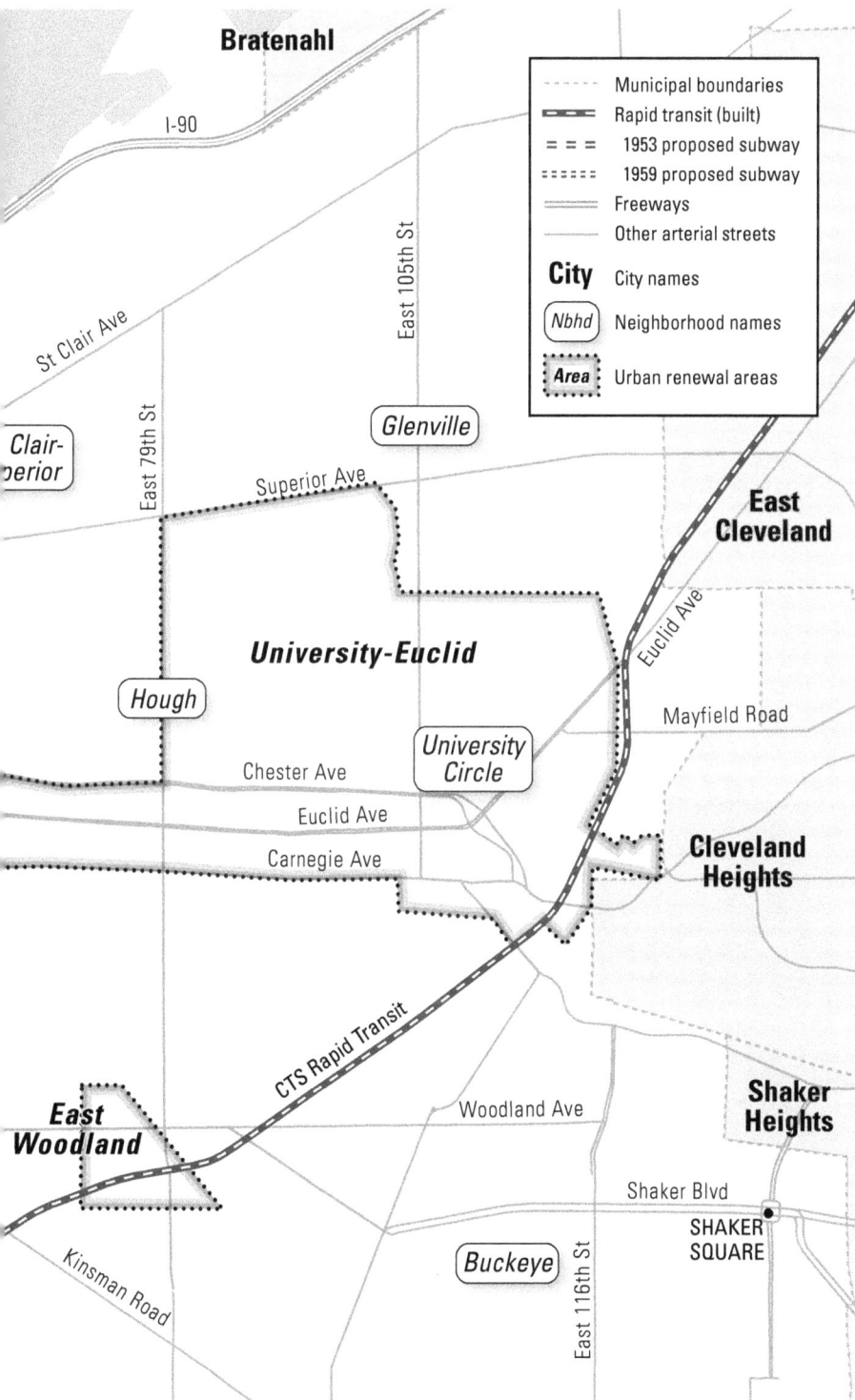

Clair-
perior

Glenville

Superior Ave

East
Cleveland

Euclid Ave

*University-Euclid*

Hough

Mayfield Road

University
Circle

Chester Ave

Euclid Ave

Cleveland
Heights

Carnegie Ave

CTS Rapid Transit

Shaker
Heights

*East
Woodland*

Woodland Ave

Shaker Blvd

SHAKER
SQUARE

Kinsman Road

Buckeye

East 116th St

# 1

## Rewinding Cleveland's Mainspring

*Downtown Renewal, Urban Image,*
*and the Metropolitan Future*

On December 9, 1958, Boston developer and real estate investor Theodore W. Berenson addressed the thirty-eighth annual meeting of the Euclid Avenue Association in the Statler-Hilton. Berenson's invitation to speak resulted from the announcement a few months earlier of his partnership with Cleveland investor Sydney Galvin to develop a twenty-four-story apartment tower called the Town House on East 13th Street just north of the Sterling-Lindner department store on Euclid Avenue. Titled "Rewinding Cleveland's Mainspring," Berenson's talk aimed directly at a growing concern among merchants, hoteliers, theater operators, and property owners that business was slipping on the city's main thoroughfare. Berenson's audience surely applauded the implicit message in his title. Like a mainspring—the spiral metal ribbon used to power a mechanical watch—downtown powered the city and, whenever slowed down or stalled, it might simply be rewound by such projects as the Town House. Berenson pointed to the move of several corporate offices from outlying areas into the new twenty-two-story Illuminating Building on Public Square (the first new office building erected downtown in nearly thirty years) and observed that such offices contributed to a growing demand for downtown living. At a time when downtown retail sales were slumping, Berenson claimed that his development would "bring new life to Euclid Avenue, in the same way that city dwellers do in Manhattan and on Chicago's near North Side. . . . With a couple of thousand people moving in and out of the Town House every day," he assured, "there won't be much danger of East 13th Street looking like a ghost town."[1]

Berenson's bullish rhetoric typified the manner of downtown boosters in Cleveland and in every other major city in the sixth decade of the twentieth century. This chapter explores what it meant to "believe" in Cleveland through a close examination of downtown. Faith in the future of downtown was never simply a commonly held sentiment reflecting some monolithic booster perspective. "Downtown" itself was merely a euphemism for more focused interests of competing stakeholders. Into the mid-1960s, downtown—like Cleveland more broadly—lacked truly unified leadership. Competing or, at best, complementary organizations, such as the Euclid Avenue, Public Square, and Prospect Avenue Associations, looked after their own constituents' interests and often differed in their reactions to various downtown initiatives. Projects to revitalize downtown produced particular benefits for some downtown interests even as they undercut those of others.

Like downtown merchant groups, the broader business community, the city government, and the press promoted downtown development in their own manners. Dominated by powerful leaders of Cleveland's iron-and-steel sector, the chamber of commerce and the Cleveland Development Foundation (CDF)—a committee of top business leaders formed in 1954 in echo of Pittsburgh's celebrated Allegheny Conference on Community Development—wanted to preserve and enhance the existing makeup of the metropolitan area's economy. For them, downtown was an important seat for industrial management and a showcase for the region. City hall reflected the influence of dozens of council members more concerned about constituents in their wards than in downtown as well as a weak mayor system in which two-year terms kept mayors pliable. The mayors during most of the 1950s and 1960s, notably Anthony J. Celebrezze (1953–1961) and Ralph S. Locher (1961–1967), deferred to ward-level concerns while also endorsing key downtown development projects that they were often unable to "sell" to Clevelanders. The city's dominant newspaper, the *Cleveland Press*, and its vociferous editor, Louis B. Seltzer (often called "Mr. Cleveland"), also endorsed business leaders' development agendas and pushed municipal officials to fall into line, but even Seltzer could not force cooperation amid competing visions. In such an environment, CDF aspired to powerful, unified leadership, but in the absence of leadership consensus, it relied on planning behind the scenes and repeatedly rolling out flashy projects for which it struggled to win public support. In addition, even some of the most active boosters' professions of confidence in some particular project often concealed their fundamental doubts about downtown's future. Close observers gradually became unable to ignore the impact that metropolitan decentralization was exerting on downtown and often believed that no renewal project was capable of reversing the trend.

The subject of postwar downtown renewal has received ample historical attention. We know much about the general scope and direction that urban renewal took, broadly and in relation to downtown. We know the structural reasons for decline and the predilection of public and private boosters for economic growth strategies over social investments. We also know that renewal was never simple or assured but rather was a series of successes and failures as cities sometimes muddled their way toward "renaissance." And we understand the promises made (and often broken) by promoters and the arguments lodged by opponents of renewal.[2] This chapter adds to the conversation on postwar American cities by profiling the hesitancy, doubt, and, sometimes, outright disapproval that even downtown stakeholders felt but rarely expressed openly toward big-ticket projects touted as panaceas.[3] By drawing on their views recorded in sources ranging from quoted statements in newspaper articles, to the letters and memos they wrote to each other, to the concerns they confided through private interviews, it is possible to reconstruct a more complicated story of inner conflict within individual boosters and fractures within the growth coalition to which they ostensibly pledged their support. Perhaps some truly believed that downtown Cleveland might continue on the path it had taken during its initial half-century rise, but many more said what they were expected to say publicly while expressing serious concerns behind the scenes. In this respect, I argue that the act of "believing in Cleveland" was, in fact, often a sign of "managing decline" by providing the opportunity for showcasing exciting developments that deflected local and outside attention from the city's uneasy experience of its own metropolitan transformation.

Long before urban image became unhinged from the specific symptoms of the urban crisis and morphed into almost a self-driven obsession with reversing decline, it served as a rationale for promoting development that would maintain growth. In downtown Cleveland, as in many other American downtowns, the 1950s were a pivotal decade that saw slippage in relation to the booming suburbs as people's discretionary visits became fewer and further between. Through its exploration of a prolonged battle over building a downtown subway that came to a head in 1957 and again in 1959, efforts to build a civic center and convention hotel in 1957–1959, and the nation's largest downtown renewal project in the 1960s, this chapter traces how boosters' expressions about improving downtown's image transformed from being a part of a pattern of assuring growth to, variously, a key to reversing downtown's perceived decline or a mask for growing skepticism that anything could be done to preserve the city's "mainspring."

From 1943 to 1959, a downtown subway plan as the heart of a metropolitan rapid transit system ranked as the primary vehicle for strengthening and, eventually, rehabilitating downtown Cleveland. The focus on transportation initially reflected the prevailing contention that downtown remained strong but merely needed a means of reducing traffic congestion and fostering accessibility to keep it attractive amid swelling suburban retail competition. Over the course of the 1950s, however, determined opposition to the subway appeared. Emboldened by pro-freeway, anti-transit county engineer

Albert Porter, opponents balked at the subway. These opponents included suburbanites and residents of outlying neighborhoods, who preferred that attention be given to their own needs rather than those of downtown. Yet even downtown interests could not agree that a subway was desirable. Reflecting a longtime division, merchants and property owners close to Public Square and the Cleveland Union Terminal—which together composed the hub of public transportation—did not want to build a subway that whisked workers and shoppers to competing office buildings and stores away from Public Square. Following the failure to construct a subway and similar defeats of concurrent plans for a civic-convention center and a major new convention hotel in the late 1950s, the city of Cleveland, spurred by CDF, turned to urban renewal as the preferred tool for downtown revitalization. In doing so, it sidestepped a downtown master plan developed in 1959 by some of the nation's leading urban planners. Placing their hopes in Erieview, the nation's largest downtown urban renewal project, these leaders sought to redevelop a large swath of land just north of the city's most intensely developed downtown corridor along Euclid Avenue. As with the subway plan, Erieview faced concerted opposition that revealed not only disagreements over whether to privilege downtown in the larger enterprise of revitalizing Cleveland but also fissures within what was anything but a unified downtown establishment.[4] Throughout these years, concerns over the image that downtown projected sometimes illuminated and sometimes obscured these differing outlooks.

## The Downtown Subway, Cleveland's Chicago Loop

Although Cleveland's downtown subway plan became the first major response to the perceived need for downtown revitalization, it began as one element within a general transit modernization initiative launched in 1942 by the newly formed Cleveland Transit System (CTS). With the city near its zenith as an industrial center, public-transit ridership was at an all-time high. CTS board chairman William C. Reed and CTS general manager Walter J. McCarter's blueprint for a loop subway to distribute riders throughout downtown rather than deposit them in the Cleveland Union Terminal appeared in 1943 as part of a full complement of radial lines.[5] The transit plan evolved over the ensuing years, leading to a favorable public vote in 1949 on a charter amendment required to undertake construction of the new system.[6] The time between the 1942 formation of CTS and the charter passage seven years later mirrored the same interval between the creation of the City Planning Commission and the release in 1949 of its *Cleveland Today . . . Tomorrow: The General Plan of Cleveland* to guide the city's future development. City if not metropolitan planning was the order of the day during and after World War II, as leaders raced to position their cities to be competitive after conversion from wartime production. A few assertions that rapid transit service would revitalize an already fading downtown were the exception to the rule of emphasizing the importance of mass transit for downtown and metropolitan growth.

In 1953, with the first rail line in the rapid transit system under construction, CTS proposed a $35-million county bond issue to fund a downtown subway, which transit officials began to argue was a precondition for extending rapid transit service across the metropolitan area, because it would distribute an expected increase in transit riders throughout downtown rather than dump all of them in Cleveland Union Terminal's lower concourse. The subway plan garnered almost immediate support from Mayor Celebrezze, the city's three daily newspapers, the chamber of commerce, and a range of civic organizations. The *Plain Dealer* editorialized the sentiments that guided subway backers: A subway would remediate downtown congestion, bring more people into downtown, enhance tax valuations, and serve as a stimulus to urban renewal, but it was not yet a tool for reviving a declining downtown. Rather, the editorial stated, it was essential to "the preservation of the downtown area."[7]

More than just a boost to downtown, backers contended, the subway would be a shining token of metropolitan prosperity. Subway promoters, who claimed to speak for the entire metropolitan area, hailed the subway as a demonstration "to the world that Cleveland has faith in its own future."[8] Harnessing the power of the image of Chicago, the Midwest's largest metropolis, *Cleveland News* reporter Harry Christiansen called the subway Cleveland's version of the "Chicago Loop" and argued that, in making downtown more accessible to suburbanites, the project would boost home values countywide.[9] On the day before the bond referendum, Halle Brothers department store, which would benefit from a nearby subway stop in the vicinity of Euclid Avenue and East 14th Street, announced it was repurposing its normal *Plain Dealer* ad space inside the front section to urge support for the subway. Rather than "dresses, coats and furniture," Halle's devoted its ad space "to the 'best buy' Cleveland homemakers can make tomorrow" by pointing to how the subway augured easier access to downtown for women shoppers, higher home values, and metropolitan progress. According to the ad, a subway would "keep Cleveland the Best Location in the Nation" (see Figure 1.1).[10] Convinced by the pitch, 65 percent of Cuyahoga County voters approved the subway bond issue in November, which set in motion a series of steps necessary to clear the way for the project.[11]

Even in the mid-1950s, despite decades of metropolitan decentralization and periodically voiced concerns that the central city might lose its luster, few Clevelanders could envisage downtown decline on the horizon. Some 116,000 workers poured into downtown office buildings every weekday morning.[12] Few bothered to comment on the sooty film, a telltale residue from the city's many belching smokestacks, that blackened their stone or

Figure 1.1. On November 2, 1953, Halle Brothers department store devoted its newspaper ad space to this call for women to vote for the downtown subway bond issue to ensure metropolitan prosperity and to preserve "The Best Location in the Nation." (*Cleveland Press*, November 2, 1953.)

terra-cotta facades. Through plate-glass windows lay enticing worlds of colorful and varied merchandise that, all tallied, constituted the nation's sixth-largest shopping center.[13] Euclid and Prospect Avenues, four arcades, and numerous side streets were flush with hundreds of retailers. Indeed, consultants hired to study the feasibility of using the bond issue to build a downtown subway drew on data that pegged downtown department store sales in 1954 at 103 percent of the volume in 1949. The consultants based their recommendation for the subway on the assumption that Cleveland's downtown area could remain robust and that it simply needed improved accessibility to relieve an expected increase in auto traffic congestion and an overreliance of rapid transit on the single downtown station in the Terminal.[14]

When county engineer Porter received the consultants' report in late winter of 1956, he wasted no time in contradicting its vision of an expanding metropolitan region with a vibrant downtown core. Skeptical of the future of rail transit, Porter, a strong freeway partisan who had no direct stake or interest in being a downtown cheerleader, believed that no amount of transit infrastructure could separate people from their automobiles and overcome their growing affinity for car-friendly suburban shopping centers. In his own report, he argued that downtown Cleveland's future was as "a local service center for adjacent residential areas."[15] Porter listed only nearby, majority-black East Side neighborhoods while omitting any mention of nearby, largely white neighborhoods to the west of the Cuyahoga River, a veiled race-baiting tactic that underscored his suggestion that downtown would become a place of necessity for those whose presence in growing numbers might unsettle whites. Not only would a subway fail to deliver downtown from this fate, Porter argued; it would also hasten the demise of the city center as a premier destination for suburban shoppers. He conjured a scene of severed utility lines, a din of jackhammers and bulldozers, and a giant, deep trench ripping through downtown for three years.[16] Although Porter's doomsday scenario was his own fiction (Toronto had successfully undertaken a similar cut-and-cover excavation for its Yonge Street Subway without crippling downtown interests only a few years earlier), just days later, the *Plain Dealer* got hold of a letter by Cleveland Trust Company president George Gund that echoed Porter's concerns. Gund's Pantheon-like banking house anchored the southeast corner of Euclid Avenue and East 9th Street, so if Porter turned out to be right, Gund would be in for difficult times. Regardless of whether Gund's controlling interest in the Forest City Publishing Company (the *Plain Dealer*'s owner) played a role, the *Plain Dealer* now reversed its position on the subway and called for its defeat.[17] The paper's new stance was an overt example of its long-standing competition with the *Cleveland Press*, a rivalry that was another example of how ruptures in the growth coalition shaped the potential for situating downtown improvements within an image of civic progress.

As they waited and hoped for a subway to provide a major stimulus, the plan's biggest supporters—merchants and business owners along Euclid Avenue to the east of East 9th Street—saw some signs for hope. CTS general manager Donald C. Hyde commented in 1957 that in the last four years, investors had sunk some $30 million into new downtown buildings, alterations, and improvements—hardly a sign of decline. Halle Brothers had undertaken a $1-million renovation of its flagship store at 1228 Euclid Avenue and initiated free express bus service between Public Square and its store to ferry shoppers as a stopgap measure until the subway came. In the words of the store's president, Walter M. Halle, this renovation was a "carefully calculated investment" in downtown, although, in fact, its actions masked Halle's growing fear of a Darwinian retail future in which only the fittest (and most profitably located) stores would survive.[18] Its latter move was necessary because, with the opening of the initial rapid transit line, CTS had stricken express bus service to downtown on several East Side routes to funnel riders onto the new rail line, which bypassed Euclid Avenue on its way to the Terminal station. To Citizens League director Estal Sparlin, Porter's claim that downtown was destined to become nothing more than a local service center was indefensible. As evidence of downtown's viability, Sparlin pointed to plans by printing equipment manufacturer Harris-Seybold to move its headquarters from suburban Cuyahoga Heights to the Illuminating Building on Public Square.[19] Such moves, no matter how anomalous, assumed symbolic power, because they cut against the grain of the inexorable spread of suburbia.

On June 13, 1957, two of three county commissioners voted against building the downtown subway, and the project failed to win approval.[20] Two years later, retail and theater interests in Playhouse Square, the section of Euclid Avenue located between East 12th and 17th Streets, decided to make a renewed push to build the subway before the 1953 bond issue expired in 1960. Represented by the Euclid Avenue Association, this time they persuaded the City Planning Commission to include a simpler, less-costly subway plan in *Downtown Cleveland 1975*, its downtown master plan prepared in 1959 to steer future development. Commissioned with $100,000 contributed by CDF, the Cleveland Foundation, the Leonard C. Hanna Jr. Fund, and the Louis D. Beaumont Foundation, the plan was prepared by city planning director Eric A. Grubb in association with a cadre of nationally significant planners, including Edmund Bacon of Philadelphia and Walter Blucher of Chicago.[21] The subway was an integral piece of a plan that acknowledged that the downtown portion of Euclid Avenue "was a curiously constituted creature with a head at each end of a long, weak body." Between pairs of large department stores clustered at each end—Public Square and Playhouse Square—was one half mile marked by "dead spots" that discouraged pedestrian flow between each cluster. The plan also proposed spot redevelopment of marginal properties within a block or so of Euclid Avenue for new office towers, apartment buildings, and parking lots as well as a redesign of Public Square and the creation of a pedestrian plaza at the Euclid/Huron/East 14th intersection. In keeping with the plan's emphasis on building on Euclid Avenue's dominant position in downtown, the new subway route would avoid the Union Terminal station, instead jogging to the north under East 14th Street and then west under Euclid Avenue, with stations beneath East 14th, East 9th, and Public Square.[22]

In 1953, boosters had urged a subway's construction as an antidote to traffic congestion and inadequate downtown parking, and their campaign reflected at least their public stance that downtown's future, like that of Cleveland writ large, was one of growth. Six years later, the mood had changed, but not all downtown interests envisioned the same future. Thanks to their advantageous position near the lone rail transit station in the Terminal, Higbee's and the May Company, two of the city's three largest department stores, continued to enjoy robust sales and believed that they could ride out any slump. Their outlook—one of self-satisfaction with retaining their existing positions as dominant retailers and an unwillingness to support projects that might expand the downtown economy—was hardly unusual and mirrored efforts by longtime hoteliers in many cities to block new competitors.[23] To the east, however, Playhouse Square interests, including the other top-three department store, Halle's, had seen a noticeable drop in business, despite operating free buses to and from Public Square. Timothy W. (Tim) Grogan, a leading downtown property owner and building manager based in the Hanna Building at 1422 Euclid Avenue, noted the departure of most physicians' offices and many other office tenants in Playhouse Square, who either wanted to move closer to the Terminal or, more commonly, to the suburbs. Grogan lamented that Cleveland's "best street is now taking in discount houses in desperation to fill . . . vacancies."[24] Across from Halle's, Sterling-Lindner, another department store that was feeling the pinch of suburban competition, used one of its windows—usually reserved for lavish Christmas displays—to show a scale model of the subway with continuous-loop narration.[25]

With downtown interests divided over whether a subway was necessary and even whether downtown (or at least their little part of it) was declining, subway backers knew they needed to return the debate to the metropolitan level. CTS general manager Hyde and the *Cleveland Press* both contended that the subway was the key to building future extensions of the rapid transit system to serve Cleveland's many suburbs.[26] Euclid Avenue merchant Harry Jacobson argued that it was critical to maintain downtown property values, which he claimed accounted for 12 percent of the value of the Cuyahoga County tax duplicate, or else suburban residents would face a growing tax burden. Federation of Realty Interests president Henry DuLaurence Jr. even connected the subway to the effort to combat deindustrialization. Noting that industries were beginning to exit the region, DuLaurence argued that a subway would bolster downtown, "the showroom of the City of Cleveland" and an amenity for corporate decision makers.[27]

Ultimately, the subway lost in the arena of public opinion in 1959. A popular concept only a few years before, the subway now looked riskier and less important to many Clevelanders. While the original bond issue had failed only in one reportedly thrifty "nationality ward" (the predominantly Polish Ward 13, located about three miles southeast of downtown), Porter's warnings, amplified by a pair of *Plain Dealer* reporters, now resonated with many working-class Clevelanders. Rather than a bulwark against tax increases, as proponents claimed, the subway appeared to many observers more likely to become a new excuse to squeeze more money from the public, particularly if

Porter was correct in his insistence that subway construction would produce tremendous cost overruns. *Plain Dealer* reporter Philip W. Porter (the county engineer's brother) accused Playhouse Square merchants of selfishly favoring "any proposal no matter how nebulous to bring potential customers to their front doors," especially when "other people would be paying for it."[28] Mayor Kenneth J. Sims of the working-class suburb of Euclid, eleven miles northeast of downtown, argued that the subway did nothing to solve the ongoing problem of efficiently moving twenty thousand people daily to and from Euclid's many factories.[29] Several council members in largely working-class wards of Cleveland proper also appealed to tax-averse constituents by depicting the subway as a dangerous waste of taxpayer dollars that would implicitly benefit mainly wealthy Shaker Heights residents, who had enjoyed an enviable twenty-minute rail commute from their East Side suburb to the Terminal since the late 1920s.[30] As in 1957, two years later, only one of three county commissioners supported the downtown subway.

Concerns that the subway might turn out to cost too much were inseparable from the growing distance—physical and psychological—that removed many Clevelanders from the historic urban core. On average, they lived farther from downtown than they had earlier in the decade. The last of the city's streetcar lines, which once tethered Clevelanders to downtown along the city's many radial boulevards, ceased operation soon after the 1953 subway referendum. Although buses replaced them, they failed to match the experience of the trolleys. With middle-class and affluent Clevelanders embracing the drive-in culture of the suburbs, and with more department stores and medical and dental offices chasing them into the "crabgrass frontier," fewer people each year were left to ride the bus downtown. Likewise, in a scene that played out in cities from St. Louis to Pittsburgh, downtown's image slumped as venerable hotels and stately theaters aged ungracefully, losing their hold on metropolitan leisure seekers.[31]

## "Civic Progress" in the "Heart of Cleveland": The Civic Center and Mall Hotel Plans

The subway failure was one of several setbacks for downtown Cleveland in the late 1950s, a time when expressions of confidence in downtown's future increasingly became semantic covers for pessimism. Boosters lauded two new aluminum-and-glass office towers, although some of them worried that both buildings had been spearheaded by local utility companies, in contrast to some other cities' construction of new corporate headquarters or regional branch offices. Not only did downtown boosters lament the seeming aversion that local investors showed toward funding new downtown towers to attract new offices; they also watched helplessly as voters showed a similar aversion to public spending that might support an expansion of the city's convention trade. Although perhaps they should have questioned their own blind presumption that the public felt a stake in downtown's future, boosters relied too heavily on beautiful front-page artists' renderings of sleek new buildings and zestful newspaper reporting to sell their plans.

Such was the case in 1957, when the Heart of Cleveland Committee, composed of ten city council members, led a $15-million bond drive for an elaborate convention center that would double as a "civic center" calculated to appeal to Clevelanders, although it was particularly aimed at tourists and suburbanites who often criticized downtown's dullness. It was no accident that boosters in postwar American cities chose "civic center" as a name when pushing new convention centers to try to appeal to suburbanites by filling the void left when downtown hotels and clubs lost their hold as social centers. As Aaron Cowan argues, the term "referenced an earlier generation of urban buildings that had—at least ideally—served as centers of community pride and public dialogue." It was also telling that civic center backers adopted the name "Heart of Cleveland" for their committee. Like Berenson's characterization of downtown as the city's mainspring, the plan implied that the entire metropolitan area's lifeblood emanated from this vital organ. The commissioned planning firm proposed a northward extension of the Daniel Burnham–designed Mall to the lakefront. In addition to a large new convention hall, there would be a thirty-four-story office building, a ten- to twelve-story hotel, a rooftop restaurant, an ice-skating rink, an all-season arboretum, an exhibition swimming pool for aquacades and water ballet, a high-end shopping plaza, a museum of science and industry, and a permanent "This is Cleveland" display. The firm's principal, Franklin Outcalt, argued that the plan answered the call "to create a symbol of civic vitality, progressiveness, and accomplishment." The decision to build a collection of attractions rather than simply expand the city's existing convention center would, in short, help remedy Cleveland's reputation as "uninteresting" by "making it appear that the heart of Cleveland is something more than a couple of streets."[32]

The plan's bold scale and its location near the city's long-neglected lakefront reflected boosters' hope to take advantage of the expected 1959 completion of the St. Lawrence Seaway, a system of locks, canals, and navigable channels on the St. Lawrence River intended to facilitate the movement of oceangoing freighters between the Atlantic Ocean and the Great Lakes. Visions of becoming a world port filled the heads of downtown boosters. One of them, downtown architect Howard B. Cain, even floated plans to rename East 9th Street (whose northern terminus was Cleveland's main pier) "Seaway Boulevard" and build an international bazaar in a redesigned Public Square to sell goods from around the world.[33] New York developer William Zeckendorf, whom Cleveland leaders hoped to interest in developing the project's hotel and office tower, was noncommittal. In his effort to persuade CDF and other representatives of the growth coalition to push for the subsidies that he claimed he would require before investing in Cleveland, Zeckendorf urged, "The St. Lawrence Seaway is coming and now is the time to take advantage of it."[34]

Two bond referendums, in 1957 and again in 1958, failed to win public support. Pitched narrowly as a municipal project, the civic center bond issues seemed extravagant to many Clevelanders, who saw their own neighborhoods losing ground to the suburbs while boosters were crowing about the "Heart of Cleveland." More than a few also viewed the plan as an expensive subsidy for Zeckendorf. If they could not sell Cleveland voters on the need for a convention center to boost downtown's fortunes, city boosters—feeling a growing sense of desperation to show fast progress—decided to try instead to build a major convention hotel. CDF and city hall wooed hotel baron Conrad Hilton by promising to give him the southern end of the Mall and a $6-million bond subsidy to erect a one-thousand-room, twenty-five-story Hilton that would give Cleveland its first major new hotel since the Great Depression.

Clevelanders learned of the hotel-on-the-Mall plan on Christmas Eve, 1958, when the *Cleveland Press* broke the story in an editorial. Seltzer argued that the Mall hotel would reinvigorate the local convention trade, lighten homeowners' tax burden, and "become an exciting symbol of progress, reassuring evidence that downtown Cleveland is holding its place among the other big cities of America." Seltzer's point about reassurance is revealing, for it offers another sign that downtown's health was in some doubt. As with the downtown subway plan, the Mall hotel plan reflected the tendency among the city's newspapers to place their rivalry ahead of unified support for downtown development. The *Plain Dealer*, by some accounts miffed that City Planning Commission chairman Ernest J. Bohn had leaked the story to the *Press* first, argued that the plan was a misuse of public land and an unfair subsidy.[35]

Opponents seized on the *Plain Dealer*'s characterization of the Mall hotel plan and set out to foil it. Ward 13 councilman Ralph J. Perk introduced legislation in city council to ensure that voters would have the final say on the plan.[36] In an echo of the concurrent push against the downtown subway that was heating up for the second time in 1959, Philip W. Porter pointed out that Mayor Celebrezze would "have a big selling job to persuade the horny-handed workers of Fleet Avenue, Broadway, Storer and Scovill Avenues that the public's property is not being used as a pawn to help some wealthy blokes make money." Porter understood the sentiments of many ethnic Clevelanders, who were reputedly frugal, tax averse, and more interested in the affairs of their parishes and wards than in downtown revitalization. As one prominent downtown attorney pointed out, "You can't tell someone down on [East]

55th and Broadway that . . . building a Mall Hotel and bringing more people into Cleveland is going to help him." Likewise, city utilities director Bronis Klementowicz, something of a folk hero in the heavily Polish Warszawa neighborhood where he had served six terms as a city councilman, captured well the distaste among the city's so-called cosmopolitan groups for delivering such a gift to downtown boosters: "Who in the Sam Hill in the 14th Ward cares about what happens on the Mall?"[37] The vote in city council on whether to support the leasing of part of the Mall to Hilton reflected the conflict that council members felt. Under great pressure to demonstrate faith in downtown from Mayor Celebrezze, who was allied with CDF in staunch support of the hotel plan, and facing a groundswell of opposition in their own wards, the city council voted 27–3 in favor of the plan—but privately, a number of council members expressed their distaste for it. Some "salved their consciences" by rationalizing that hotel boosters would fail in their efforts to actually raise the $6 million.[38] Despite council members' reluctant support for the Mall hotel, the plan faced further setbacks. City planning director Grubb omitted the project from the planning commission's *Downtown Cleveland 1975* plan in defiance of sponsor CDF's wishes, and Republican mayoral candidate Tom Ireland succeeded in collecting 19,647 signatures on a petition, thereby forcing the Mall hotel question to be posed to voters on the November 3 ballot.[39]

With opposition to the hotel on the Mall swelling, backers hurried to sell the idea that the development, more than just a needed spur to the city's convention business, was also a much-needed boost to Cleveland's sagging image, especially as rival Pittsburgh was receiving national acclaim for remolding its once-dingy downtown into the "Golden Triangle" (see Figure 1.2). CDF chairman and Republic Steel president Thomas F. Patton told the Heart of Cleveland Committee that by building the hotel, "we will be able to go around the country holding our heads high and say, 'We're from Cleveland.'"[40] The long-standing and influential Citizens League of Greater Cleveland urged approval of the Hilton's construction as a way of recapturing the city's "receding national reputation." Much like the earlier pitch for the civic center, the league argued that the Hilton would be more than just a convention hotel; with "its outdoor skating rink like that in Rockefeller Center" and other amenities, it would reinforce "the best location in the nation" and "give us something to show and be proud of when our friends and relatives from Pittsburgh, St. Louis and other cities, come to visit or start bragging about their wonderful new buildings."[41] Clearly, the Mall hotel was as much a civic symbol as an economic need. To take this sort of message to the public, hotel backers formed the Committee for Civic Progress, yet another tellingly named entity that, like the Heart of Cleveland Committee, sought to portray downtown's needs as inseparable from those of the entire metropolitan area. The Committee for Civic Progress was a who's who of the growth coalition.

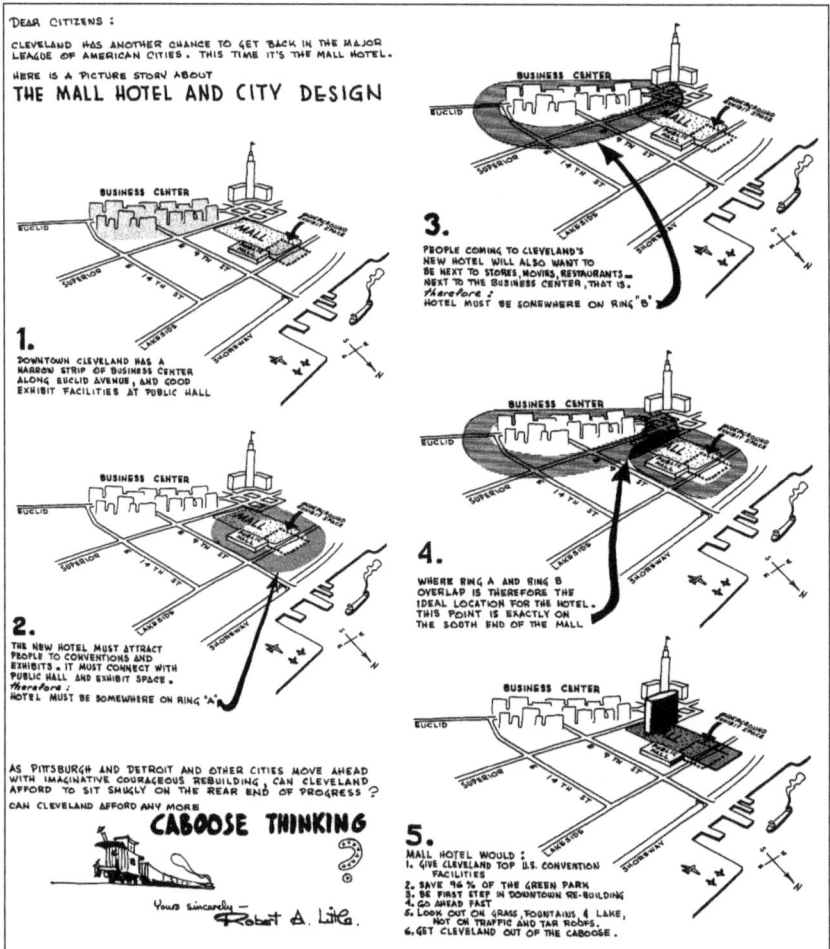

**Figure 1.2.** This 1959 cartoon by Cleveland architect Robert A. Little reasoned that a Hilton hotel on the Mall might enable Cleveland to take its place alongside purportedly more "progressive" cities, such as Pittsburgh and Detroit. (Cleveland Press Collection, Cleveland State University.)

Chaired by Higbee's president John P. Murphy, its leaders included Patton of Republic Steel, National City Bank board chairman Sidney B. Congdon, chamber of commerce president Curtis Lee Smith, Standard Oil of Ohio (Sohio) president Charles E. Spahr, and managing partner John W. Reavis of the Jones, Day, Reavis and Pogue law firm. To bolster support among the city's working-class voters, representatives of the AFL-CIO Building and Construction Trades Council and the Cleveland Federation of Labor rounded out the Committee for Civic Progress.[42]

If Mall hotel opponents needed a little help to defeat city hall's Hilton dream, they got it just six days before the election, when Hilton rival Sheraton Corporation of America chief executive Ernest Henderson of Boston presided at a grand party in the ornate lobby of the Hotel Sheraton-Cleveland, which with one thousand rooms was one of the city's two largest hotels. The party provided Henderson, who had made no secret of his opposition to Hilton's plan to enter the downtown Cleveland market, the occasion to unveil his plan to build a two-thousand-seat banquet facility, a parking garage, and potentially hundreds of additional guest rooms. With Mayor Celebrezze in attendance, Henderson made oblique but clear reference to the planned Mall hotel when he commented, "Now all of this is, of course, unless some new serious event comes to change the picture."[43] As it turned out, that is precisely what happened. Fifty-one percent of voters rejected the Hilton Hotel on the Mall, even as they voted overwhelmingly to return Celebrezze, its biggest cheerleader, to city hall for a fourth term. Although there was considerable opposition to the hotel plan, there was arguably even more apathy, hearkening to Klementowicz's observation. Nearly twenty-five thousand more people cast votes in the mayoral contest than on the Mall hotel issue.[44] Zeckendorf and now Hilton had come and gone after Clevelanders refused to subsidize their developments, and downtown Cleveland still had no new hotel or convention center. Four weeks after the "No" vote, Hilton dedicated the 815-room Pittsburgh Hilton, which overlooked Point State Park in the heralded Golden Triangle, leading one Cleveland reporter to lament, "If the spirit is willing in Cleveland, the cash is weak."[45]

The mood among growth coalition leaders, developers, and many downtown merchants was one of defeat and, behind closed doors, bitterness. Even though CDF had helped fund the *Downtown Cleveland 1975* plan, correspondence between its president Upshur Evans and real estate executive and City Planning Commission member H. Horton Hampton in the days before the final defeat of the subway plan reveals impatience with allowing downtown to enter the 1960s without concrete action. Evans confided to Hampton that Berenson's Town House was "dead as a dodo," a casualty, he claimed, of city planning director Grubb's "ineptitude if not willful lack of adequate reporting" on the feasibility of downtown living to the Federal Housing Administration (FHA). Evans surely was also angry with Grubb for having disapproved of the Mall as a site for the Hilton, whose glaring omission from the planning commission's downtown plan was a precursor to the hotel's eventual voter defeat. Evans also complained that the subway fight had split CDF's board of directors "right down the middle" and that, after the defeat of the Mall hotel and a charter amendment for metropolitan government, he had to talk Smith and Patton out of resigning their respective posts in the chamber of commerce and CDF.[46]

## Erieview, Cleveland's Rockefeller Center

The defeats of the late 1950s created a sense of desperation to ameliorate downtown's sagging fortunes.[47] The city's business and government leaders had had an opportunity to pursue downtown renewal in the early 1950s, when Cleveland architect Richard Hawley Cutting tried to interest civic leaders in an elaborate plan, devised at his own expense, for luxury apartments and office buildings between Euclid Avenue and Lake Erie. When several dozen leading industrialists had formed CDF, however, they opted not to follow Pittsburgh's lauded downtown-first renewal strategy, choosing instead to launch urban renewal in Garden Valley on marginal land donated by Republic Steel Corporation, whose president Patton served as CDF's executive committee chairman.[48] Their decision largely left downtown revitalization to chance. Individual downtown interests undertook many small, piecemeal investments, and only the subway plan offered a semblance of systemic change.

Even before the subway and Mall hotel defeats in late 1959, Evans, Cleveland Urban Renewal and Housing director James M. Lister, and chamber of commerce president Smith had been "quietly working" in the spring of 1959 on "something comparable to the Lower Manhattan Project." Hoping to interest deep-pocketed outside developers, they corresponded secretly with John D. Rockefeller's grandson, David Rockefeller of Chase Manhattan Bank, who had chaired a committee in the mid-1950s that led to the construction of a sixty-story bank headquarters that was a major catalyst in reviving downtown New York at a time when it was all but eclipsed by Midtown Manhattan.[49] Rockefeller warned against ad hoc redevelopment and recommended creating a clean slate as close to the lakefront as possible.[50] When he showed no commitment to investing in Cleveland, the Cleveland leaders tried next to interest Newark-based Prudential Insurance Company of America in opening a Midwest regional headquarters in Cleveland. Evans and Lister drafted a letter that CDF chairman Patton sent to the president of Prudential, but the response they received was disappointing.[51]

Evans, Lister, and Smith purposely kept the City Planning Commission in the dark until their downtown renewal plan was ready to announce, likely because Bohn had expressed public opposition to the Mall hotel plan after its backers had negotiated with Hilton, thereby contributing in their minds to the defeat of a key downtown project.[52] The secretiveness of their endeavor created a problem for General Electric (GE). On the advice of the Cleveland Electric Illuminating Company's (CEI's) area development department, GE took an option to acquire land on Lakeside Avenue next to the *Cleveland Press* building to relocate its industrial electric equipment service division away from Woodland Avenue and East 49th Street, which stood in the midst of the rapidly deteriorating Gladstone neighborhood, where many employees felt unsafe. Knowing that an urban renewal project was in the offing,

Lister asked GE to wait, creating an embarrassing situation for the city.[53] The City Planning Commission remained completely unaware of the secret scheme right up to the public announcement of the Erieview urban renewal project at CDF's annual meeting on January 14, 1960. Indeed, just days earlier, planning commission vice-chairman George B. Mayer had remarked that downtown development was likely to proceed "a bit at a time."[54]

Located on the tattered northeastern flank of downtown, the renewal project—christened Erieview—was slated to occupy 125 acres (later revised to 163 acres and divided into two phases) generally bounded by East 9th Street on the west, East 17th Street on the east, Lake Erie on the north, and Chester and Superior Avenues on the south. A hodgepodge of older storefronts, low-rent residential hotels, warehouses, small manufacturing plants, parking lots, and vacant tracts, the project area garnered designation as "blighted" largely because Cleveland municipal and business leaders imagined a more profitable—and symbolic—use of the land.[55] Such use was possible only by leveraging federal matching funds to give developers an incentive to take a risk, and reaping urban renewal funds entailed demonstrating blight. It was a wholesale departure from the carefully considered *Downtown Cleveland 1975* plan that Evans's own CDF had underwritten. Unlike the 1959 plan's assumption that many investors would spearhead its various elements, Erieview's plan favored using broad condemnation of marginal property to leverage federal funding. To place Erieview's size in perspective, it dwarfed Pittsburgh's Gateway Center (twenty-three acres), Baltimore's Charles Center (thirty-three acres), and Boston's Government Center (forty-four acres).[56] The scope of Erieview reflected Evans's and Lister's belief that downtown had stalled long enough and that nothing short of the nation's largest downtown renewal plan was worthwhile.

The Erieview site plan was designed at the drafting table of the eminent Chinese American architect I. M. Pei, who was known for his work on Philadelphia's Society Hill Towers, Washington's L'Enfant Plaza, and Montreal's Place Ville Marie. For Cleveland, Pei devised an international-style complex of low-slung, interlocking building blocks punctuated by several skyscrapers. Pei's presentation to Cleveland leaders played to their dreams of placing Cleveland in league with New York and Chicago. To help them imagine how a set of buildings and plazas built from scratch on the fringes of downtown could generate a new sense of place, Pei asked them to imagine the Terminal area as Cleveland's Wall Street and Euclid Avenue as its Fifth Avenue. Then he asked them to envision Erieview as Cleveland's answer to Rockefeller Center.[57] Placing Erieview in the context of Rockefeller Center called to mind NBC's studios, the swank Rainbow Room, and the famous Rockefeller Plaza Christmas tree and ice rink.

For many Clevelanders, the November 1960 passage of the bond issue to undertake Erieview seemed a panacea for downtown. One common complaint it seemed to address was the belief that downtown was unappealing. Many believed that downtown Cleveland lacked the vitality found in other large American cities. One city official lamented that downtown Cleveland had less life at night than any other major city he knew. Contrasting a recent Detroit Tigers game that drew fifty-one thousand and a recent Cleveland Indians game that mustered only eighteen hundred, he supposed that Clevelanders would rather stay home or go to country clubs than spend time downtown.[58] City councilman John F. Kovacic regarded Erieview as a remedy for downtown's dullness, which he explicitly contrasted with New York, Chicago, and Philadelphia—all much larger, despite Cleveland's number-eight population rank in 1960. Noting his dissatisfaction with fading attractions, such as Captain Frank's Lobster House on the East 9th Street Pier, "girlie-girlie acts" on Short Vincent (a block of burlesque clubs just north of Euclid Avenue), and Herman Pirchner's Alpine Village supper club in Playhouse Square, Kovacic saw in Erieview the promise of the cosmopolitan excitement he believed that downtown needed.[59] Echoing his view, Jeanette Dempsey of the tony lakefront suburb of Bratenahl wrote Mayor Celebrezze to exclaim that the issue's passage would end her embarrassment about the state of downtown compared to that of Detroit and Pittsburgh.[60] Republic Steel president Patton congratulated the mayor for moving the city "off dead center" and remarked that Cleveland should soon see the greatest building boom since Shaker Heights developers Oris and Mantis Van Sweringen erected Cleveland Union Terminal in the late 1920s.[61] In public talks, the mayor himself pointed to Erieview as evidence "that Cleveland has broken away from the self-doubt and hesitancy that held back earlier plans."[62]

No one was more excited about backing Erieview than Seltzer. Although technically Seltzer had to answer to the *Cleveland Press*'s parent company, Scripps-Howard in New York, the company allowed its editor free rein to champion local projects or causes, which Seltzer employed to the utmost. To understand Seltzer's support of Erieview, one needed only to look around his new building on the northeast corner of Lakeside Avenue and East 9th Street, which he had located "at the very gateway to the St. Lawrence Seaway." As a reporter from the competing *Plain Dealer* pointed out, "There he is, as soon as they come up the hill off the freeway or from the harbor there's the Scripps-Howard lighthouse." In the immediate vicinity were a 1920s Sunoco station; the county morgue; the neglected, fortresslike Central Armory; and gritty rooming houses, such as the Alva Apartments. Concerned about his newspaper office's immediate surroundings, Seltzer had every interest in Erieview's success.[63] Seltzer's self-interested advocacy of Erieview, like that of Playhouse Square's leaders' earlier pleas for a subway, became inseparable from his claims of wanting what was best for downtown as a whole.

Regardless of whether Seltzer conflated what was good for downtown with a project situated in his portion of it, the increasingly worrisome state of downtown animated considerable discussion by the early 1960s. One sign of how rapidly conditions had eroded appeared in a downtown merchant's letter to the editor of the *Plain Dealer* in 1962. Saul F. Keeti, the president of Bon Kay Fashion Shop at 411–413 Euclid Avenue, recalled how, five years earlier, he had "displayed confidence in the downtown" by remodeling his store. Since that time, he pointed out, two department stores had closed, and banks were replacing retailers. He blamed inaccessibility for the drop in business and doubted that building Erieview would be nearly as helpful as replacing a number of old buildings with city parking lots, as Pittsburgh had done.[64] Soon after, Bailey's became the second major downtown department store to close. Its president blamed the failures of the subway, the Mall hotel, and the convention center expansion for conditions that produced a 6 percent decline in sales between 1960 and 1961.[65] Some observers understood that downtowns throughout the United States were undergoing a transformation away from retail and toward offices. However, stakeholders whose interests varied from improving sales volume to creating more cosmopolitan flair to boost Cleveland's image felt concerned—a clear demonstration that decline was in the eye of the beholder.[66]

For the city's urban renewal leaders, Erieview's symbolic value was tremendously important. Even if they failed to woo any Fortune 500 executives to move their headquarters to downtown Cleveland, the principals behind Erieview understood the need to obtain commitments from at least a sampling of prominent local companies to validate Cleveland as a city on the move and to convince everyday Clevelanders that downtown might overcome the pull of the suburbs. Erieview Tower, developed by John W. Galbreath of Columbus and designed by the architectural firm of Harrison and Abramovitz (which was also responsible for the United Nations headquarters and the last four buildings in Rockefeller Center), was to be the renewal project's forty-story modernist centerpiece bounded by East 9th and East 12th Streets and Saint Clair and Hamilton Avenues (see Figure 1.3). Evans effused that Harrison and Abramovitz "have outdone themselves," adding that Erieview Tower "is even greater and finer than their job in Rockefeller Center." Yet after repeated failures to find out-of-town firms willing to locate their headquarters or regional offices in Erieview Tower, CDF had to twist arms to get major local companies, including Ohio Bell, M. A. Hanna, White Motor, and Eaton, to lease floor space for the greater civic good. Thus Evans could point out with feigned pride in 1961 that the proposed tower was 90 percent leased, even though nearly all of its major tenants would have simply relocated from other downtown buildings.[67] Even in 1964, as the tower was nearing completion, a regional office of Pittsburgh-based U.S. Steel Corporation stood alone as a confirmed out-of-town tenant. Nonetheless, and unsurprisingly, representatives of the Cleveland-based firms locating in Erieview Tower dutifully took the opportunity to connect Erieview to the welfare of the metropolitan

**Figure 1.3.** Cleveland urban renewal director James Lister (right) and colleagues examine a scale model of Erieview Tower. Erieview offered hope for the success that had eluded recently failed ventures, such as the Civic Center plan (whose renderings are visible on the wall behind the men). (Cleveland Press Collection, Cleveland State University.)

area. Claude M. Blair, the president of Ohio Bell Telephone Company, which leased three-eighths of Erieview Tower, remarked that the utility's six-block move reflected "a commitment of faith in Erieview and Cleveland." In a full-page newspaper advertisement, Ohio Bell, of course, made no mention of having been cajoled into committing to Erieview. Rather, it echoed its president's boosterism and described the move as necessary, because the utility was forced out of its building at 750 Huron Road by its own ever-expanding, "intricate maze of electronic equipment," another sign of Cleveland's expansion.[68]

Just as the subway plan had prompted myriad downtown businesses to profess their confidence in downtown's future, Erieview elicited a similar response. Even before the Erieview bond issue passed (and possibly as an implicit endorsement of it), Stouffer's announced it would completely remodel its Stouffer's Midtown Restaurant at 725 Euclid Avenue as "further evidence of our company's complete faith in the future rebirth of the downtown area."[69] Although it did not specifically cite Erieview, Bailey's reconsidered its decision to leave downtown only six months after closing its Ontario Street store and reopened five blocks away on Prospect Avenue.[70] Each of the other surviving downtown department stores also made upgrades, reflecting the belief that downtown remained a safe investment. In contrast to the grim assessments of some downtown property owners, whom Mayor Celebrezze's successor Locher called the "gloom and doom boys," Higbee's president Herbert E. Strawbridge boasted in 1963 that even the soon-to-open, nine-hundred-thousand-square-foot Severance Center shopping mall in Cleveland Heights was only nine-tenths the size of Higbee's store on Public Square. Strawbridge claimed that Cleveland's downtown decline, which he surely judged in retail terms, was five to seven years less advanced than that of many other cities.[71] At the time, Higbee's was working through a complete renovation of its flagship store under the direction of Raymond Loewy, known for his design work for Macy's, Westinghouse, and Studebaker, among others. Nor were Higbee's competitors resting on their laurels. In 1964, the May Company opened a ten-story parking garage on the site of the former Bailey's store. May Company president Francis A. Coy remarked that the garage "will demonstrate our faith and confidence in downtown Cleveland." That same year, Sterling-Lindner ran an ad that included a drawing of its store with Erieview Tower looming behind it, justifying the store's "modernization program" as a reflection of "our confidence in the continuing progress of downtown Cleveland." In 1965, Halle's described its latest remodeling in part as a response to the anticipated boon of "the new high-rise apartments within a short walk of the store."[72]

Thus, downtown stakeholders, like the daily newspapers, played their expected public roles as Erieview cheerleaders. Despite its supporters' painstaking boosterism, however, Erieview raised serious concerns in the minds of many Clevelanders interested in the city's future. Following on the heels of several years of poorly realized renewal plans in the city's East Side neighborhoods, the project produced an unsurprising critique, especially as attention to Erieview appeared to account for the sidelining of much of the University-Euclid urban renewal plan in Cleveland's troubled Hough area, described by some as a powder keg (see Chapter 2).[73] Opponents rightly saw in Erieview a zero-sum game in which lavishing money on downtown to protect its actual and its symbolic value came at the expense of much-needed resources in the city's neighborhoods. Less clear to those who based their assessment of Erieview's popularity only on what they read in the newspapers was the undercurrent of doubt and even hostility that existed toward the project from within the growth coalition, particularly among those in the fractured downtown establishment.

Those who doubted that Erieview could succeed in strengthening downtown seldom translated their skepticism into formal opposition to the project, but their perceptions are important, because they demonstrate that even avowed proponents of downtown urban renewal sometimes harbored the same lack of confidence that smaller downtown merchants expressed in downtown's future. Many of their doubts pertained to the plan for 5,500 to 6,000 new units of housing in Erieview. This aspect of the project acted on a recommendation in the 1959 downtown general plan, which was actually less ambitious than a contemporary study embraced by Mayor Richard J. Daley in Chicago that recommended that at least thirty-nine thousand apartment units be built in the Loop.[74] Nevertheless, one official who represented real estate stakeholders could not and did not want to imagine six thousand new apartments flooding the downtown market. He argued that Cleveland "isn't an apartment house town." When someone could live in the prized suburb of Shaker Heights and enjoy a short commute to downtown, how, he asked, could one expect to fill twice as many apartments as in all of Shaker Heights? One of the CDF directors found himself secretly agreeing. He could not see Erieview competing successfully against Bratenahl or Shaker Heights, a view that he admitted he dared not divulge publicly. Another prominent booster of downtown renewal and of Erieview in particular admitted privately that he was perfectly content with his fifty-minute commute from Cleveland Union Terminal's garage to his home in rural Geauga County.[75]

Not only did Erieview housing have to compete with desirable and conveniently located suburban high-rise apartment districts, such as Shaker Square and Lakewood's emerging Gold Coast; it also suffered potential liabilities in the eyes of some. For one, Erieview's reliance on FHA financing made some Cleveland leaders nervous that racial integration might prove unavoidable. Berenson's Town House proposal in the late 1950s had tried unsuccessfully to obtain FHA support while charging luxury rents. Curtis Lee Smith confided in an interview that the Erieview apartment plan "comes up against the Negro problem," because federal funds might constrain the free hand of management.[76] One city councilman agreed, comparing this situation unfavorably with that of Shaker Square, where discriminatory renting practices maintained the color line. One of his colleagues agreed: "You'll have Negroes in there sure as the dickens," he warned.[77] Although FHA regulations did not yet mandate nondiscrimination, President John F. Kennedy's recent appointment of Robert C. Weaver, the first African American administrator of the Housing and Home Finance Agency (which included the FHA), may have raised the specter of strings being attached to federal funds, an issue not unlike the 1949 legal battle to integrate Stuyvesant Town, a New York City housing development built by Metropolitan Life with public subsidies.[78]

A second liability, some believed, was the ongoing, if slowly improving, problem of air pollution from steel mills and other industries in the Flats along the Cuyahoga River. Fewer than four months after the Erieview proposal was publicly announced, urban renewal chief Lister warned that air pollution could stymie plans to build luxury apartments downtown.[79]

Erieview's importance to the growth coalition provided ammunition for antipollution watchdog groups to step up their demands. When Pittsburgh-headquartered Jones and Laughlin (J&L) Steel threatened to close its Cleveland operations if subjected to further activism, one antipollution activist responded by observing that the prevailing winds would blow J&L's fumes directly into Erieview, imperiling plans for luxury apartments.[80] After city hall issued a permit to Republic Steel in 1961 to convert two open-hearth furnaces to the oxygen process, strong opposition from neighborhood-based antipollution organizations led U.S. Representative Charles A. Vanik of Ohio's 21st District to warn that the federal government might withhold funding for Erieview if the dispute were not settled satisfactorily.[81] Thanks to project delays and gradual steps toward cleaner air that occurred in the interim, neither open housing nor air pollution turned out to impede Erieview housing, but concerns about them were nonetheless important markers of the constraints under which boosters labored to make Erieview the centerpiece for revitalizing downtown and ensuring Cleveland's attractiveness for investment.

While most of those who doubted the value of Erieview concluded that it was doomed to fail, other opponents based their complaints on the fear that it would succeed and thereby undercut their own business interests. In this sense, Erieview, like the downtown subway, became a battleground that exposed rifts in the downtown establishment. In particular, real estate interests—including developers, building owners, and property managers—possessed a fairly narrow sense of downtown. Their interests were deeply rooted in the most valuable properties in a small triangle bounded by East 17th Street and Superior and Prospect Avenues. Therein lay the vast majority of downtown's major office buildings, theaters, restaurants, and retailers, including all of its department stores. But this 150-acre footprint was less than one-sixth of the area outlined in the 1959 downtown plan, which represented the aspirations of CDF, the chamber of commerce, city hall, and the three daily newspapers. Although even this compact core had many aging buildings that invited a number of observers to characterize it as shabby or rundown, its tax valuations remained very high, making it a poor candidate for a large-scale renewal project.[82] Given renewal leaders' ambition and desperation, it is hardly surprising that they looked to the periphery of this expensive core and regarded Lake Erie views from Erieview as an untapped amenity.

The placement of Erieview almost wholly outside what many realty interests considered to be part of "downtown" led to charges that Erieview was almost a surrogate downtown rising parallel to, but in isolation from, what they viewed as the real downtown.[83] In contrast to the 1959 downtown plan's focus on revitalizing Euclid Avenue, Erieview concentrated most of its development activity well to the north between Lakeside and Saint Clair Avenues, where David Rockefeller and Pei believed lake views would entice developers.[84] In one of many insinuations that Lister and Evans purposefully plotted Erieview around the new headquarters of the *Cleveland Press*, one observer commented that "it just doesn't add up to take downtown and relocate it just because Mr. Seltzer happens to have a building down on Ninth and Lakeside."[85] *Cleveland News* editor Nathaniel R. Howard believed that Erieview represented its backers' assumption "that the present downtown is no longer 'exciting' enough and cannot be made sufficiently alluring again." Therefore, Howard noted, they wanted to create "a new and transferred downtown."[86] Howard's sentiment was widely shared by downtown property owners. Karl M. Duldner, a representative of property owners and an outspoken Erieview opponent, demanded to know why the project did not concentrate on replacing substandard buildings.[87] Instead, observed a property owner with interests immediately west of Cleveland Union Terminal, "they're trying to transform the whole face of the city by going . . . way out in left field." He wondered whether office workers in the new Erieview buildings would walk several extra blocks to patronize their usual stores and restaurants on their lunch breaks.[88]

The cloistering effect of Erieview also thwarted the efforts of would-be contributors to downtown's renewal. Renewal leaders urged investment by local developers, but they would not stand for proposals that lay outside Erieview's borders, even when those proposals comported with the recommendations of *Downtown Cleveland 1975*. For example, soon after Erieview was announced, local developer Albert A. Levin introduced a separate plan for an apartment tower on the northeast corner of Euclid and East 22nd Street in place of a parking lot he had acquired. The location fell within one of the recommended apartment zones in the 1959 plan and might have helped fulfill the plan's intent to strengthen the eastern edge of downtown, but it also represented unwanted competition for out-of-town players, such as Galbreath and Berenson. When his permit request was denied at city hall, Levin wrote to CEI chairman and CDF director Elmer Lindseth to express his belief that CDF had not given adequate thought to rescuing Euclid Avenue from "its present doldrums." He argued that CDF's fixation on Erieview neglected the street that had done the most to make Cleveland worthy of CEI's slogan "The Best Location in the Nation." After a series of letters exchanged between the men, Lindseth wrote Evans to recommend that CDF "consider entering into a 'cultivation' program with the real estate interests of which Mr. Levin is typical." Lindseth's letter was a clear admission that the city's renewal leaders had not only kept the planning commission in the dark in 1959 but also held real estate interests at arm's length in the time thereafter.[89] Levin ultimately gave up on his planned apartment tower and sold the parcel for a classroom building at the new Cleveland State University.

Behind charges that Erieview was a shadow downtown was the conviction that its office buildings would empty older buildings of their tenants. Many, in fact, had taken years to recover from the introduction of the Cleveland Union Terminal group, which had a "magnet effect." Between 1928 and 1930, Sohio, Midland Bank, the chamber of commerce, the Builders Exchange, and numerous smaller companies and professional practices flocked to the Terminal, which immediately reduced the attractiveness of dozens of once-prime office buildings.[90] The day after the City Planning Commission dutifully rubberstamped CDF's Erieview plan, Henry H. Eccles of the Cleveland Building Owners and Managers Association warned that Erieview would make Euclid Avenue a "slum." Eccles pointed to downtown's annual 2.5 percent growth rate of office occupancy, which amounted to about two hundred thousand square feet per year, and contrasted it with the roughly three million square feet proposed in Erieview. He observed that the Illuminating and East Ohio Gas buildings, completed two years before, had yet to bring in a substantial influx of out-of-town tenants, so it seemed that Erieview was destined to poach from existing office buildings.[91] The planned federal building in Erieview alone would siphon federal offices from several other downtown buildings, all "to build a monument," in the words of one Cleveland attorney.[92] A disgruntled city council member summed up the sentiments of many downtown property interests, arguing that with Erieview, "we're creating while we're destroying."[93] However, in an interesting counterpoint to realty interests' concerns, one black professional commented privately that when Erieview had emptied older buildings, their owners would "be glad to have Negro tenants."[94]

In the first three years of the 1960s, the downtown renewal supporters effectively muted outward displays of opposition. It helped that Celebrezze and Seltzer spoke with one voice on urban renewal. In confidential interviews, several council members explained why they refrained from open opposition. One admitted that although he had voted to approve Erieview, he had done so "with my tongue in my cheek," because he feared being labeled "an obstructionist to progress," a sentiment shared by a number of fellow council members.[95] Leo A. Jackson, an African American city councilman, explained that political survival dictated why even someone like him, who was witnessing the disintegration of East Side neighborhoods in the absence of timely rehabilitation, would facilitate downtown renewal: Any council member who tried to go against Erieview, he said, would "get cut to shreds real good." As a result, he said, council members would vow, "I'm not going to get in front of a train and let it run over me. . . . I'll speak out and I'll raise questions . . . but when it comes down to a vote, I'm going to be on that train."[96]

Erieview boosters also neutralized opposition by maintaining at least outward support from city hall and the city's daily newspapers. The newspapers painted opponents of the project as obstructionists if, indeed, they even allowed them a voice. Perhaps by the 1960s, they were desperate for any sign of new life downtown. Although the *Plain Dealer* had turned against the downtown subway and fought the Hilton on the Mall, both plans that the *Cleveland Press* had steadfastly defended, the archrival newspapers' editorials and articles spoke in almost perfect unison in their approval of Erieview until 1963, when discordant tones emerged. Mayor Celebrezze, whom many observers claimed was a product of Seltzer's power, could always count on ironclad support in the *Cleveland Press*. When his successor Locher assumed the mayoralty, however, he did not enjoy such support. Under pressure from many downtown interests who were shut out by Erieview, Mayor Locher approached Evans to ask CDF to fund a new downtown plan that might take into account suggestions for improvements outside Erieview's borders.[97]

Meanwhile, Erieview backers' push in 1963 to close a section of East 13th and 14th Streets to provide the calmer environment that Pei believed was necessary to attract suburbanites to the project's envisioned apartments only reinforced the notion among Euclid Avenue interests that Erieview was to be a separate, new downtown built by handpicked developers.[98] When viewing the street-closure plan, Halle's vice president Paul J. Hoover concluded that Erieview was "planned as a separate entity unrelated to the rest of downtown."[99] One Playhouse Square property owner, the former U.S. Senator Robert J. Bulkley, complained that the street closures would prevent Erieview's becoming a credit to "all of downtown." Jacobson, who operated a men's clothing store on Euclid Avenue, agreed, adding that his own interest was not so much in attracting several thousand new apartment dwellers into downtown as in facilitating shoppers who drove in from the suburbs. Grogan went a step further, charging Erieview promoters with trying to cut off Euclid Avenue to help new Erieview businesses capture the patronage of Erieview tenants.[100] Opposition to the plan wrested a compromise from city hall; it would close East 14th Street north of Chester Avenue but maintain East 13th in the block between Chester and Euclid.[101]

Amid the controversy over street closures, *Plain Dealer* reporter Eugene Segal penned a five-part critical series that reminded readers how CDF had completely ignored the 1959 downtown plan it had financed when its members hatched the Erieview plan. Like Mayor Locher, by 1963, CDF leaders seemingly understood that a new downtown plan—one that did not contradict but rather complemented Erieview—might channel dissent toward a new exercise in dreaming of the future downtown.[102] In an internal CDF progress report on the new study was an admission: "We have allowed the physical appearance of our Downtown to deteriorate, and have done little to make Downtown an attractive place to visit or work. Further, although we have made a major step forward in Erieview, we have failed to bridge the gap between Erieview and Euclid Avenue through selective renewal or new construction on Euclid Avenue. Pittsburgh has done a good job in this regard." While suggesting that Erieview was a "step forward," the report also pointed to the lack of local investment by banks, real estate investors, and developers. It had taken an outsider, Galbreath, to lead the way, and no major Cleveland bank had invested—"only little Cuyahoga Savings is sticking its neck out."[103] This latter lament not only contradicted CDF's assertion that Erieview represented "major" progress but also denied the many efforts by local investors who had believed in Cleveland but had been thwarted by renewal leaders in their zeal to adhere strictly to the Erieview plan.

Everyday Clevelanders did not need planners to tell them that Erieview was far from being the salvation of downtown. Its shortcomings were painfully evident. Erieview's sheer scale and boosters' insistence on its centrality to the city's future primed it to be a disappointment, especially when no developers came forth to fill the windswept wastes surrounding its few towers. Moreover, rather than chronicling the realization of a dream, newspaper headlines in the 1960s tracked an unfolding debacle: small business owners' lawsuits to cling to their properties, reticent out-of-town developers, and quarrels over street closures. The gradual addition of new buildings over the next two decades, coupled with the visible slippage of downtown's lively scene (not to mention urban decay on a broader scale), only reinforced the notion that Erieview was a failure. The project failed to produce a dramatic turnaround that might have excited Clevelanders to continue to believe their city was "The Best Location in the Nation."

In the two decades after World War II, American downtowns from coast to coast showed little immunity to the disease of decentralization. As downtowns lost their allure, large new development projects became a favored way of trying to preserve and, eventually, restore downtown vitality. As Pittsburgh demonstrated with its renowned Gateway Center renewal, it was possible to challenge the inevitability of suburban triumph over the central city, but even downtown Pittsburgh proved better at forging an image of a unified response that produced gleaming steel and aluminum totems of urban revitalization than at preventing the metropolitan changes that favored the periphery over the center. Cleveland, in its contrasting civic disunity, diminished whatever chances it might have had to accomplish a series of downtown projects that boosters hoped might answer Pittsburgh's success. With each new downtown failure, its boosters had to work all the harder to manage the perception that Cleveland was losing ground, especially as the nation's urban crisis manifested in dramatic form in the late 1960s.

By 1966, Galvin and Berenson's efforts to build the first new downtown luxury apartments, originally called Town House but now recast as the Chesterfield, were finally moving forward after being stalled for eight years. In May, as leasing began, Galvin pointed to the urgent need for improvements in the immediate vicinity, because future apartment construction in Erieview was "bound to await our own experience in establishing the fact that people want to live in our Erieview apartments. We in The Chesterfield are the guinea pig." He urged swift action "so that the growing numbers of skeptics . . . can regain their confidence in the long-term outlook for the central city."[104] On July 18, as work continued on the Chesterfield, the Hough neighborhood exploded in riots, rattling a city already beset with a growing list of problems. Coming on the heels of a well-publicized spike in violent crime and brazen robberies in the central city, the riots exacerbated the trepidation many suburbanites already felt about going downtown.[105] Ten stories above troubled Euclid Avenue, Halle's department store displayed Chesterfield model suites decorated in Traditional, French Provincial, Early American, and Danish Modern styles, promising that "Park Avenue splendor" had come to downtown Cleveland.[106] When the Chesterfield accepted its first tenants in November 1967, the fanfare seemed muffled. Not only the riots had cast a pall over the city; so had the U.S. Department of Housing and Urban Development's decision to withhold further funding to Cleveland's urban renewal program as a result of the city's dismal failure to meet its commitments to the program. In August 1968, Galvin and his wife threw a lavish housewarming party in their Chesterfield penthouse, for which they left their apartment in the Heights, but too few other Clevelanders joined them. In stark contrast to the earlier assurance that downtown could support thousands of new apartment dwellers, fully one-third of the Chesterfield's 411 units remained vacant two years after the commencement of leasing.[107] The *Plain Dealer* stopped running stories of Shaker Heights couples who traded suburban homes for the excitement of downtown living. Despite the promise of urban renewal, before the decade's end, Sterling-Lindner closed, and the row of four giant Playhouse Square cinema houses went dark. Cleveland's mainspring was broken.

# 2

# City on Schedule

*Fighting Blight to Save Cleveland's*
*Cultural Heart*

On the evening of June 11, 1962, the SS *South American* pushed off from the East 9th Street Pier in downtown Cleveland. The eleventh annual Cleveland Chamber of Commerce Cruise, a four-day, "fun-and-knowledge" Great Lakes cruise to Sault Ste. Marie, Michigan, was underway. As the steamer plied the waters of Lake Huron two days later, some 350 business and civic leaders on board previewed *Cleveland: City on Schedule*, a half-hour booster film produced for the Cleveland Development Foundation (CDF) to highlight urban renewal in the city. Two weeks later, CDF showed the film again at its annual meeting in the Midland Building headquarters of Republic Steel, the city's leading manufacturing firm. At an invitation-only screening at Music Hall, Cleveland Electric Illuminating Company (CEI) chairman and CDF chairman Elmer L. Lindseth exclaimed that viewers would leave "feeling 10 feet tall with pride."[1] After an initial round on the banquet circuit of the growth coalition, the film made its way to local television by summer's end. Hosted by NBC newsman Chet Huntley and produced at a cost of more than $60,000, the film offered a window into the city's business-backed, government-funded solutions to the problems of downtown decline, loss of industry, and neighborhood decay.[2]

*Cleveland: City on Schedule* touted what it called "the bright side" of the city by training the camera on its humming machine-tool and metal-fabrication plants and its prized museums and educational and medical institutions. Then Huntley turned to the city's problems, which he said Clevelanders had the foresight to tackle as early as 1942, when the newly reorganized Cleveland City Planning Commission set out to draft a comprehensive city plan. When

a lack of available land for the relocation of displaced slum dwellers threatened to halt nascent plans for urban redevelopment in the early 1950s, the
city's business community responded to a call for action at a meeting of top
executives headed by John C. Virden, the chairman of the Federal Reserve
Bank of Cleveland. CDF, which grew out of that meeting, came to the rescue
of urban renewal by getting its members to subscribe $2 million for a revolv-
ing fund. CDF acquired a neglected dump along Kingsbury Run, two miles
southeast of downtown, and Republic Steel promised to fill in a ravine with
slag (a by-product of steel production) to provide 105 acres for housing evicted families. In keeping with the 1954 Housing Act's requirement of replacement housing as a condition for clearance, the resulting Garden Valley
housing development freed the city to clear and redevelop crowded, largely
black slums in the nearby Central neighborhood just east of downtown while
discouraging black movement into formerly white neighborhoods.[3]

Even as it undertook redevelopment in Central, the city eyed other areas
for "rehabilitation" based on the assumption that they were salvageable. One
such area was Hough. Named for early Western Reserve settlers Oliver and
Eliza Hough, this 2.2-square-mile swath of Cleveland's East Side developed
in streetcar suburb fashion in the decades following the area's annexation by
Cleveland in 1872. Centered approximately three miles east of Public Square
and bordered on the south by the former "Millionaires' Row" on Euclid Avenue, Hough stretched northward to Superior Avenue between East 55th and
East 105th Streets. Immediately east lay Wade Park, donated to the city by
Western Union Telegraph founder Jeptha H. Wade in 1882 and gradually
developed into a residential allotment and a collective campus of leading
Cleveland institutions. Wade Park eventually became University Circle, a
name originally applied in 1902 to a streetcar turnaround on the edge of the
Case School of Applied Science and Western Reserve University (WRU). By
the 1920s, Hough was already losing cachet, as well-to-do Clevelanders departed for suburban homes in the Heights suburbs to the east of University
Circle.[4] As Cleveland grew into a major industrial city, however, Hough developed into a densely settled district of some forty thousand mostly white
residents by the beginning of World War II.

The neighborhood's rapid transformation in the 1940s coincided with
the gradual withdrawal of the Cleveland Indians baseball team from League
Park, located in the heart of Hough at Lexington Avenue and East 66th
Street, between 1940 and 1946. The Negro League Cleveland Buckeyes used
the field from 1943 to 1950, but their departure anticipated the demolition
of the stadium the following year.[5] Once Municipal Stadium on the downtown lakefront became the sole home of the Indians, few Clevelanders from
outside Hough encountered the neighborhood except while commuting between downtown and their suburban homes in the Heights. If Hough ceased

to be a destination for baseball fans, it became a magnet for industrial job-seekers in need of apartment housing. Pressures accompanying the influx of newcomers made Hough the city's number-one problem and its linchpin in efforts to cultivate Cleveland's image as a livable city.

World War II set in motion the same severe housing shortage that affected other large American cities into the early postwar years. In addition to returning GIs, large numbers of southerners sought industrial work in northern cities. Appalachian whites fled the decline of coal mining in Kentucky and West Virginia, while African Americans left Deep South plantations transformed by the mechanization of cotton harvesting and a region beset by overt racial discrimination.[6] Appalachian whites flocked not only to Hough but also to the Near West Side, located across the Cuyahoga River on the other side of downtown. They continued to do so well into the 1950s, joining smaller cohorts of new Puerto Rican migrants and Japanese Americans relocated from the West Coast during the war.[7] So many southerners arrived that Dunham Elementary School in Hough reached a record 86 percent student turnover in 1955, leading its principal to quip that "it seems everybody from Logan County, West Virginia, is in Cleveland."[8] In Hough and on the Near West Side, landlords converted mansions into rooming houses or turned smaller single-family homes into two- and four-family apartments to accommodate the influx. In Hough, whose proportion of elderly residents had been higher than the city average in the late 1940s, the number of children under age ten doubled in the 1950s, swelling schools to the point that students had to start attending in half-day shifts.[9]

Although the city's overall population growth leveled off through white flight to the suburbs in the early 1950s, Hough continued to add newcomers, including more and more black southerners. Even as Cleveland's African American population almost tripled to more than 250,000 in the twenty years after 1940, available housing for blacks actually declined.[10] The Central neighborhood, which had absorbed nearly all black newcomers through the 1940s as a result of discriminatory banking and real estate practices, now faced massive clearance and redevelopment at lower density under a series of federal urban renewal programs. Additionally, as Cleveland moved forward with urban renewal in Central in the 1950s, it built little publicly or privately financed housing on the crowded East Side. A lone attempt in 1952 and 1953 to build public housing outside the inner city—in the Lee-McCracken area in southeastern Cleveland—produced such a "big rhubarb" over creating "a new Harlem" that the plan was dropped in favor of rezoning the land for industrial use, and a gentlemen's agreement circulated among members of the city council not to locate public housing in any ward lacking its council member's approval.[11] The unrelenting prejudice of the outer neighborhoods and suburbs (and also the city's virtually lily-white West Side) led a

*Cleveland Call and Post* writer in 1954 to lament that "'The Best Location in the Nation' is surrounded by a solid iron curtain of race-hate in its suburbs as bad as anything that can be found in Georgia's hardscrabble cotton-and-peanuts belt."[12] Coupled with the demolition of housing in renewal areas with little attention to helping people relocate, the suburban aversion to open housing funneled an increasingly black population into Hough by the mid-1950s.

This chapter examines how Hough emerged after World War II as a bellwether neighborhood whose future many Clevelanders viewed as inseparable from that of the city itself. Although Central received the preponderance of attention from urban renewal leaders through the 1950s, Hough's renewal sprang first from the grass roots and then, after urban renewal's focus shifted away from slum clearance, became the key neighborhood of concern for city hall and other powerful renewal backers in the 1960s. Neighborhood-based activism, rooted in the belief that Hough could become a model of neighborhood conservation and "a laboratory to deal with the problems of the central city," yielded to a hope that nearby University Circle's dramatic expansion might help underwrite housing rehabilitation in Hough.[13] Thanks to a new provision in the federal urban renewal program, institutional spending in the Circle leveraged the designation of the University-Euclid urban renewal project, which local leaders billed as the nation's largest, most ambitious federally funded rehabilitation project. Although Hough might have remained an intact neighborhood linking Cleveland's two main hubs, fundamental flaws in the federal urban renewal program and in its local implementation doomed the neighborhood to the decline that boosters had hoped to avert. In the midst of Hough's slide, civic leaders touted University Circle as an engine for urban reinvention as they labored to manage perceptions of adjacent Hough through token "demonstration" projects calculated to elicit hope. Given most whites' hostility toward open housing, the prospect of preventing Hough's decline through housing rehabilitation also made the neighborhood the most critical front in the war to preserve suburban racial exclusivity.

Like downtown revitalization, neighborhood renewal was crucial in civic efforts to manage perceptions of metropolitan change. By the 1960s, Hough stood at the center of that struggle, in large part because of its location between downtown and the city's cultural heart in University Circle. However, unlike downtown, this form of civic renewal forced business and civic leaders to grapple with the city's worsening race relations and their explosive potential. Although these leaders could characterize downtown projects as safeguarding Cleveland's enduring greatness, they could not sell the renewal of Hough in the same booster frame without first admitting the failure of this place.

## "You Can Live in a Better Neighborhood without Moving": Grassroots Revitalization in Hough

In 1942, building on its earlier work in response to the problems of the Central neighborhood, the Welfare Federation of Cleveland—an outgrowth of an organization created almost three decades earlier by the chamber of commerce to coordinate charitable and philanthropic activity—started a new citywide campaign that concentrated group work programs at the neighborhood level. Composed of clergymen, school principals, community organization members, and concerned citizens, the resulting neighborhood agencies—called "Area Councils"—planned to address juvenile delinquency, liquor control, zoning, policing, lighting, sanitation, and other matters of neighborhood improvement. Although it stood twenty-four blocks west of Hough, the Goodrich-Sterling Settlement House at East 31st Street and Superior Avenue served as the initial staging area for the federation's activity in Hough. Three years later, after it helped develop neighborhood playgrounds, daycare centers, canteens, and basketball clubs, the project coalesced into the Hough Area Council (HAC), an interracial organization under the coordination of Marjorie Buckholz, the organization's first field worker.[14]

After World War II, conditions worsened in Hough. Exploitive absentee landlords often illegally converted houses into multifamily rooming houses, taking advantage of the city's lax enforcement of housing codes—an artifact of the city's pragmatic, if shortsighted, response to the wartime housing shortage and of an overtaxed building department whose inspectors could not keep up with the rapid changes.[15] Although the City Planning Commission's 1949 city plan, *Cleveland Today . . . Tomorrow*, urged neighborhood conservation in Hough, building-code violations became the norm, and city services, such as street cleaning and garbage pickup, became erratic, filling the air with "the stench of decaying food" and attracting legions of rats.[16] In 1950, more than 2,500 African Americans already lived in Hough, but at that point, they constituted less than 4 percent of the neighborhood's population. Hough's overcrowding and deterioration thus initially affected mainly whites. Over the ensuing decade, however, Hough experienced a net loss of more than forty-four thousand whites as it attracted more than fifty thousand African Americans, bringing the black proportion of the population to nearly 74 percent by 1960. As a former Hough resident, Jacob Rosenheim, later recalled, when friends of the family sold their Crawford Road home to William O. Walker, the black publisher of the *Call and Post*, "as soon as they moved into the house, it seemed as though 'For Sale' signs along the streets in the neighborhood popped up like tulips in springtime."[17]

In the early 1950s, as racial transition added a new dimension to continued overcrowding in Hough, HAC promoted neighborhood conservation, which required managing the social and physical conditions of the neighborhood. The organization found common cause with area clergy, notably Rev. Dr. John Bruere of Calvary Presbyterian Church and Fr. Floyd L. Begin of St. Agnes Catholic Church, who looked uneasily from their Euclid Avenue pulpits at the rising transiency in Hough and the departure of more-affluent white congregants to the suburbs. HAC, which adopted the slogan "You Can Live in a Better Neighborhood without Moving," labored to foster amicable race relations and a sense of stability and calm even as the neighborhood began its demographic transformation. In addition to deflecting concerns away from race and toward the depredatory actions of blockbusting real estate brokers, the organization sponsored street club gatherings and neighborhood festivals that featured African American, Appalachian, Lithuanian, Puerto Rican, and Slovenian music and dance.[18] On September 19, 1951, after working for several months with Hough clergymen, HAC held a meeting attended by more than one thousand people at Calvary Presbyterian Church. At the meeting, HAC revealed a plan to make Hough a model for civic revitalization, leading the *Cleveland Press* to comment that Hough residents were "wise" to see the value of safeguarding what was still "the best location in Cleveland." The plan entailed organizing Hough into four quadrants, in which HAC would encourage the formation of street clubs and other neighborhood groups.[19] These organizations spearheaded cleanup days and petition drives to force rezoning of streets to curtail the trend toward rooming houses, but organizers also understood the need for more symbolic undertakings that could reframe residents' perceptions of their neighborhood and city. Bruere observed that the effort was "a rewarding experiment in effective teamwork in the inner city" whose significance "extends far beyond the area."[20]

In 1952, HAC launched Cleveland's first home conservation demonstration project in cooperation with the *Plain Dealer* and the city's building department and newly formed urban redevelopment department. The plan, which included all or portions of Curtiss Avenue; Olive Court; and East 57th, 59th, and 61st Streets in the southwestern corner of Hough, sought voluntary property owner participation by coordinating favorable financing and an umbrella contract for repair work to minimize costs while relying on the city to make street improvements. Virgie McClendon of Olive Court, a leader in the pilot project, pointed out that "if this neighborhood is going to be saved we've got to save it ourselves." More than merely a pilot project to resuscitate faith in Hough's future among residents, however, the Curtiss-Olive project also represented, in the eyes of its planners, the first chapter in a story of citywide renewal foretold in the 1949 city plan.[21]

Years before city hall and its allies in the business community overcame the obstacles to leveraging federal funds to start Cleveland's first urban renewal projects, Hough residents acted on their belief that neighborhood decay was not irreversible. In addition to carrying out the painting and repair of dozens of houses in the Curtiss-Olive demonstration area, HAC's project inspired residents four blocks north to form the Utica Avenue Improvement League in 1952 with an eye toward a similar goal, and by summer's end, HAC affiliates had painted more than 560 houses across Hough. HAC also obtained a commitment by the city's building department to ferret out code violations to the north of the pilot area and ultimately in the entire area bounded by East 55th and 71st Streets and Superior and Chester Avenues.[22] The organization's early successes led *Cleveland Press* editor and tireless civic booster Louis Seltzer to ask, "Why can't we somehow light the same flame for the whole of Greater Cleveland—and in our time put this city back up where it belongs—'on the hill'?"[23]

Enthusiasm waned considerably by 1954, as it became clear that deterioration was outpacing improvements. Although the city promised to support neighborhood conservation through street improvements and building inspections, it simply did not have resources sufficient to the task. Only seventeen inspectors were responsible for keeping tabs on all buildings in a city of almost one million people. The problem of code enforcement produced deep frustration among those who were fighting the notion that the inner city was doomed to decline. At a public forum at Calvary Presbyterian Church in October 1954, Bruere lamented that the city could approve more than $500,000 to build a new pachyderm house at the Cleveland Zoo and propose a $1-million bond issue to build new zoo quarters for monkeys but could not find money to enforce the housing code in Hough.[24]

The challenge of upholding the building code encompassed more than simply the problem of too many newcomers vying for too few dwellings. As previously suggested, the racial dynamics of the metropolitan area exacerbated the problem of housing. Federal policy steered subsidies for new home construction toward the suburbs, and a combination of discriminatory actions by homeowners, real estate agents, and lending institutions conspired to deny most African Americans the opportunity to purchase suburban homes.[25] As late as 1960, of the 255,310 blacks in Greater Cleveland, 250,818 lived inside the city limits, most of them trapped in several square miles of the East Side by either poverty or racism.[26] Although the Ludlow neighborhood that straddled the border between Cleveland and Shaker Heights undertook a progressive grassroots campaign to foster an integrated community starting in 1957, it was locally and nationally exceptional.[27] Without determined civic activism, expansion of the housing supply open to African Americans occurred only in an environment of panicked selling and rapid turnover from white to black occupancy, a trend that forced HAC to take concerted action starting in mid-1954.[28] In 1950s Hough, many landlords held out for white tenants, enduring months or even years of vacancy to preserve the color line until they could no longer afford to maintain their apartment buildings. Then they had a choice: Sell the buildings or allow them to integrate. Either way, integration tended to be fictive, or at least short-lived, because black demand was so great that it tempted landlords to decree their buildings were going "colored" and to institute across-the-board rent hikes, often of 50 percent or more. City councilwoman Margaret McCaffery, who had lived her whole life in Hough, found herself having to move repeatedly in the late 1950s as integration forced rents to unaffordable levels.[29] In many cases, landlords also divided buildings into more and smaller dwellings to profit further from black desperation, which in turn produced great strain on buildings. Of course, this toleration of illegal conversion of housing for multifamily occupancy meshed with the hope of many influential whites, by this time almost entirely a suburban breed, to contain minorities and the poor through urban renewal and public housing efforts directed solely toward the central city. The very people who dominated the city's growth coalition might have lobbied more effectively for code enforcement (and paid the taxes necessary to support it) if they had not decamped to the suburbs.

As early as 1955, it was becoming clear that the dream of neighborhood conservation was unrealistic in the absence of a larger renewal program, which Hough leaders began to advocate. In September, Bruere and HAC's rehabilitation committee met with CDF president Upshur Evans and Kermit C. Parsons of the City Planning Commission to discuss the potential for obtaining federal funding to redevelop the area bounded by Chester and Euclid Avenues and East 75th and 79th Streets. The following April, HAC leaders met to consider whether all of Hough might be added to the city's urban renewal plan.[30] Out of these meetings emerged a six-month study guided by Parsons. Released in January 1957, the study revealed a startling statistic: Hough had grown to an estimated 83,700 people, which meant the neighborhood's density had swelled from just under thirty thousand to more than thirty-eight thousand per square mile in just six years. The study also set forth many of the features that would be included later in the University-Euclid urban renewal project. It called for dividing Hough into eleven smaller, self-contained neighborhoods, each oriented around a school, a playground, or a shopping center. To accomplish this, the city would rework the flow of traffic through the area by closing or rerouting a number of streets. Finally, a dual program of demolition and rehabilitation would modestly decrease population density and limit commercial land uses.[31] A preliminary plan completed one year later focused on rehabilitation in eastern Hough, which prompted representatives of the League Park Center and several street clubs to insist that western Hough was also worthy of rehabilitation.[32] Although Bruere was pleased to see urban renewal planning for Hough, he warned that without a willingness on the part of white suburbanites to accept African Americans who could afford suburban homes, the entire central city, including Hough, might become a ghetto.[33] Similarly, Cleveland Metropolitan Housing Authority (CMHA) director Ernest J. Bohn—who concurrently chaired the City

Planning Commission and was widely recognized as a national pioneer in
launching public housing in the 1930s—had argued as early as 1953 that the
inner city could not be expected to accommodate all low-income people displaced by the urban renewal and highway programs. However, the notion of
open housing on the suburban fringes of the city produced sharp white opposition.[34]

## "A Project for Mankind": University Circle and Urban Renewal in Hough

As Hough community leaders began to see their efforts hampered by problems too large to solve at the neighborhood level, leaders in University Circle
also grew concerned that Hough's problems might adversely affect their institutions.[35] Their fears were hardly unique. Urban universities and other
large institutions, such as hospitals, museums, synagogues, and churches,
emerged in the postwar era as potent shapers of urban landscape and policy
and became important adjuncts of growth coalitions in many cities. For
example, Columbia University, along with more than a dozen other institutions on the edge of Harlem, founded Morningside Heights Incorporated in
1947 to try to reconcile institutional expansion with nearby neighborhood
needs. Other large institutions, including the University of Chicago and the
University of Pennsylvania, became similarly active in the Hyde Park and
West Philadelphia neighborhoods, respectively, in the 1950s.[36]

Institutional decisions to reinvest in University Circle rather than join the
flight to suburbia were preconditions for stabilizing the district. Most notably,
in 1951, the leadership of Temple Tifereth-Israel, one of the nation's largest
Reform Jewish congregations, decided against leaving its massive Ansel Road
synagogue on the eastern edge of Hough for a suburban home. As Rabbi
Daniel J. Silver recalled a decade later, after the Jewish community had largely abandoned the city proper for the Heights, the synagogue's leaders "were
determined that Cleveland should not be a city without a [Jewish] congrega-
tion. They were determined that The Temple in Cleveland should be involved
in the fate of the city. They were determined that you simply couldn't put
green grass around you and say: 'I'm going to turn my eyes away from slums
and the Hough area next door.'" Silver characterized the decision as a "symbolic" one without which "we would have caved in the western wall [of University Circle]."[37]

In 1952, Temple Tifereth-Israel joined WRU, Case Institute of Technology, University Hospitals, Mt. Sinai Hospital, the Cleveland Museum of Art,
and other nearby institutions to form the University Circle Conference Committee to address matters of common concern. The committee lacked sufficient funds to do more than brainstorm until Elizabeth Ring Mather, the

widow of a Cleveland iron-ore shipping magnate, came forward in 1955 with an offer to underwrite a master plan. Mather's gift spurred philanthropic and corporate support, including $2 million from the Leonard C. Hanna Jr. Fund, named for a director of the iron-ore mining firm M. A. Hanna Company and a longtime patron of University Circle institutions, as well as another $1 million from Republic Steel, Sohio, other corporations, and private individuals.[38] Mather's gift coincided with HAC's initial investigation into the possibilities of an urban renewal solution in Hough.

With funding in hand, Case president T. Keith Glennan and a small cohort of other institutional heads hired the Cambridge, Massachusetts–based planning firm of Adams, Howard and Greeley to study University Circle's needs. The firm's resulting *University Circle General Plan*, released in 1957, was a typical midcentury plan that in some respects resembled the City Planning Commission's preliminary plan for revitalizing Hough (see Figure 2.1). Like the Hough plan, it called for injecting greater order into land use with adjacent nodes dedicated either to academic and medical institutions or public-oriented leisure uses. Just as the Hough plan called for centering several neighborhood mini-units around schools or other focal points, the Circle blueprint recommended a "university center" that would provide a central gathering place for professionals, students, and visitors. Finally, both plans recommended street closures or relocations and targeted demolition of houses to create public spaces, with a WRU "Greenway" roughly mirroring the vision of a central playfield in Hough.[39]

As with the Hough preliminary plan, whose goal was to take a large, impersonal, unknowable urban landscape and fashion small, knowable, self-contained neighborhoods, the University Circle plan involved creating a special destination through careful land-use planning. The Circle, in other words, should not simply blend imperceptibly into its surroundings, whose worsening physical conditions were critical in the decision to commission the plan. However, if institutional leaders could cast Hough's division into small enclaves as a way to humanize what was an alienating urban jumble, they could not afford to allow University Circle to be labeled a retreat for the privileged. Somehow they needed to bolster the Circle's image as a place of central importance in Cleveland's progress without simply buffering the Circle against urban decay. Circle planners hoped that the district's leaders would influence their physical surroundings. They warned that University Circle "is not an entity in itself, but is part and parcel of its surroundings." Their opinion of the condition of the surrounding neighborhoods aligned closely with that of city planners, perhaps a reflection of the influence of Massachusetts Institute of Technology (MIT) professor John T. Howard, who had served on the City Planning Commission before joining the Cambridge firm. Nearby Cleveland Heights and Shaker Heights, among Cleveland's most stable and affluent suburbs, were home to a disproportionate number of representatives

**Figure 2.1.** Neil Carothers shows the University Circle master plan to two members of the Temple Women's Association at Temple Tifereth-Israel. All three were residents of tony Shaker Heights. (Photo by Frank Reed. Cleveland Press Collection, Cleveland State University.)

of the city's growth coalition. These leaders unsurprisingly viewed University Circle not only as an important buffer protecting their homes from the spread of blight but also, like downtown, as a beachhead for urban renewal in the span between the two hubs. If heavily white Cleveland Heights remained "extremely stable," the planners characterized majority-black Glenville to the north of the Circle as being merely worthy of "conservation" and majority-black Hough as needing remedial action.[40]

Central to the implementation of the $175-million University Circle plan and to institutional efforts to remake the Circle's western periphery was the formation of a unified coordinating body. Headed by Neil J. Carothers, with whom Glennan had served on the Atomic Energy Commission, the new University Circle Development Foundation (UCDF) reported directly to the chief officers of WRU, Case, and University Hospitals. UCDF coordinated institutional planning, land acquisition, parking, landscaping, and eventually policing, but in addition to these quotidian responsibilities, it also worked hard to place University Circle at the heart of the growth coalition's efforts to manage Cleveland's image and entice new industry.

UCDF shared with city planners an assumption going back to the 1920s that downtown and University Circle were the two anchors for Cleveland. Having strong anchors, UCDF reasoned, would "give the city an invaluable base for metropolitan planning between the two."[41] Referencing CEI's longtime booster slogan, an article in the *Case Alumnus* extolled UCDF's work, which would "help make Cleveland, more than ever before, 'the best location in the nation.'"[42] Glennan pointed to the success of Boston's "Laboratory Lane" (Route 128) and called University Circle, especially its proposed University Circle Research Center (UCRC), Cleveland's best shot at competing against other cities for "Electronics and Space Age" industries.[43] In the late 1950s and 1960s, UCDF worked tirelessly to persuade the various corporations and organizations responsible for industrial recruitment to highlight University Circle as an amenity and a contributor of "brainpower."[44] In an echo of the Cambridge-based planners' exclamation that the Circle could "become a powerful symbol for urban America" by serving as a modern-day analog to a medieval cathedral square or a colonial village green, a 1959 *Plain Dealer* pictorial magazine feature called University Circle "a brain workers' city within a city."[45]

In addition to creating a symbolic place, UCDF—like counterparts in Chicago's Hyde Park, New York's Morningside Heights, and Philadelphia's University City—also wanted to reshape its periphery, especially Hough. Initially, its actions in this regard were limited to "seeding" residents affiliated with its institutions in housing along its fringes. Circle leaders hoped to encourage white occupancy around the Circle to counter wholesale racial turnover, making University Circle an unlikely counterpart to Ludlow, where the Ludlow Community Association labored to attract new white suburbanites to its transitioning neighborhood to overcome the assumed inevitability of a completely black neighborhood. Unable to acquire properties outside its jurisdiction, UCDF persuaded CMHA to reserve dozens of apartments for Mt. Sinai Hospital and University Hospitals interns and residents in the new Springbrook housing project it planned to build at Hough Avenue and Ansel Road. UCDF argued that doing so would promote "racial balance" in the development and "go a long way towards assuring its stability." Like Morningside Heights Incorporated, UCDF sought opportunities to encourage institutional uses in older hotels and apartment buildings near its collective campus. Although these efforts produced few results, UCDF managed to acquire the Tudor Arms Hotel at Carnegie Avenue and East 107th Street for conversion into graduate student housing.[46]

Renewal efforts in Hough and University Circle became interwoven in 1959, when University Circle leaders and their counterparts at a handful of leading national urban universities succeeded in securing a revision to the federal Housing Act of 1949. Section 112 of the revised bill enabled development expenses incurred by major private institutions, such as universities and hospitals, to be claimed as credits toward a city government's contribution to urban renewal projects that framed those institutions' campuses. Thus, institutional expenditures could substantially reduce a city's responsibility from the usual one-third of the price tag for a renewal project. As Carothers observed, University Circle's expansion could now break the impasse in Hough renewal, which had been "relegated to the mere talking stage," because the city government's necessary contribution was more than it could afford on its own.[47] Section 112 infused Circle leaders with greater confidence. Carothers characterized University Circle as "an essential anchor in Cleveland's whole redevelopment program," whose strengths might "permeate the whole governmental and civic fibre [sic] of the central city."[48] Similarly, UCDF boasted that "the cultural advance represented by Cleveland's University Circle has become a social force, perhaps the most dynamic single force in the future of its city."[49] Tellingly, however, the growth coalition would keep HAC and other community organizations at arm's length, despite the fact that Hough was the lone renewal area where demand for action sprang from the grass roots.[50]

In 1960, the city unveiled its plan for the 1,400-acre University-Euclid urban renewal project alongside Erieview. Together, the downtown renewal plan and University-Euclid, billed as the nation's first use of Section 112 and its largest rehabilitation project, represented a first step in effecting the revitalization of the city's East Side. University-Euclid was to remake an area bounded by Superior and Carnegie Avenues and East 79th and 118th Streets, along with a panhandle that stretched westward to East 55th Street along Chester, Euclid, and Carnegie Avenues. In addition to the ongoing expansion of Circle institutions, the project included plans for high-rise apartments in the Euclid Avenue/Mayfield Road and Euclid Avenue/East 105th Street areas, along with a research park near Carnegie and East 109th and a combination of home rehabilitation and targeted demolition north of Chester Avenue and west of University Circle. Through Section 112, an expected $6 million in spending by Circle institutions between 1955 and 1965 would trigger $12 million in federal renewal funds to go to the city for University-Euclid, thereby reducing the city's share of the total project cost.[51] University-Euclid seemed to offer an answer to critiques such as those by panelists at a 1961 City Club Forum that Cleveland's urban renewal was stuck because of fears that it would "force Negroes into white neighborhoods" and because of suburbs that had placed "a lily white rope around the neck of the central city." Following a CDF board meeting, the *Cleveland Press* gushed that Cleveland's urban renewal lag was in the past and that "a new city" was "beginning to flower, because the seeds were sown by courageous men and women, nurtured by determination and love of their city."[52]

The project, which gained federal approval in 1962, drew mixed responses in Hough. Some residents were pleased to learn that the city finally appeared to be in a position to make good on years of promises to rehabilitate their neighborhood. One resident on East 88th Street even applauded the project for assuming a name that evoked longtime strengths—University Circle and Euclid Avenue—to replace the tarnished Hough name.[53] However, many in the black community wondered whether Circle leaders were simply drawing federal funds to create a buffer against the changing neighborhoods to their north and west. To counter this suspicion, UCDF pointed to the 1957 general plan's call for reaching out to surrounding areas. UCDF claimed "no authority over the University-Euclid project," for which it said municipal government was solely responsible. Not only did UCDF deny responsibility for the project; it also displaced the burden of Hough's future onto the neighborhood's property owners. UCDF insisted that only "truly blighted" homes faced demolition and that concerned property owners' best defense was to keep their properties "in good repair." University Circle, it opined, was "A Project for Mankind."[54]

As the civil rights movement gathered steam in the early 1960s, with growing expectations of substantive moves toward nondiscrimination and racial inclusiveness by such groups as the Congress on Racial Equality (CORE), United Freedom Movement (UFM), and Freedom Fighters, UCDF began to realize that it needed to take seriously the Adams, Howard and Greeley recommendation that the Circle liaise meaningfully with surrounding neighborhoods. Doing so required reconciling its desire to stand apart with its need to reach out. An internal report on public relations in 1962 warned that University Circle needed to be careful not to appear to be "an island, a 'city within a city,' a walled fortress standing against a sea of decay." It suggested that University Circle's boundaries should never be marked by signs or shown on maps, because they would "give people outside something specific to resent, fear, and blame." Likewise, the report continued, UCDF also should avoid calling undue attention to itself as the entity prosecuting Circle expansion. Instead, it should refer more opaquely to "University Circle." In other words, when trumpeting the district's development, the instrument itself should be heard but never seen. Finally, UCDF should take care that institutional spending be presented as the reason for University-Euclid's existence, but University Circle's own agenda should never be conflated with that of the larger renewal area. Although unintended, this recommendation betrayed an implicit paternalism in Circle institutions' role in Hough.[55]

UCDF also conducted a series of interviews with Circle stakeholders to gauge their views on the district's relationship with surrounding neighborhoods. Some of the responses suggested the difficulties inherent in trying to overcome community distrust. In perhaps the most revealing interview, Rabbi Daniel J. Silver of Temple Tifereth-Israel warned that any statement on community relations must be a "flaming liberal document" containing antidiscrimination language to satisfy African Americans. Otherwise, he said, the document should be destroyed, lest it leak and do serious damage to University Circle. On the other hand, Silver believed that a document that was liberal enough to be accepted in Hough would likely be rejected by many of the institutions' boards. As he pointed out, University Circle could not so readily be compared with the University of Chicago or Columbia University. The latter institutions, financed by national money, were not subject to the same pressures from prejudiced suburban leaders. In other words, University-Euclid was not Hyde Park. Silver recommended taking meaningful steps—quietly and without fanfare—to improve community relations, such as starting job placement and scholarship programs, paying fair market value for any black-owned houses needed for expansion, pursuing a policy of open housing in any housing acquired, and razing corner lots to provide community playgrounds. In short, Silver believed that University Circle institutions had the capacity to demonstrate that they believed in Cleveland, and the best way to do so was to avoid promises and instead pursue quick, quiet action.[56]

The most significant expression of University Circle's responsibility to bridge the divide with its neighbors appeared in another internal report released in the winter of 1964. Written by UCDF's recently hired community services coordinator Michael Copperman, the report contained the sharpest critique to date about University Circle institutions' estrangement from their surroundings. Copperman argued that, for people in the nearby neighborhoods, "the Circle represents the summit of power, wealth, and everything else that is beyond their reach. This makes for class hostility and color suspicion. The Circle area becomes a white extension of the suburbs." Copperman disagreed with the 1962 report's contention that UCDF could manage public outcry by hiding behind an imprecise "University Circle." He argued that people considered the motives of any University Circle institution to be inseparable from those of its peers. He lamented the damage that WRU had done in 1963 by allowing its housing bureau to issue a housing list to students in which about half of the included landlords refused to rent to nonwhites. Blame for the action "was not merely laid at the doorstep of Western Reserve University" but rather attributed to the entire Circle leadership, which one person described as "a bunch of racists." Copperman also pointed his readers to the problem of overcoming the popular belief that the institutions "wished to build a wall around the Circle that would keep Negroes out," which he stated was an unfortunate outcome of the decision to designate only the eastern half of Hough (near University Circle) for rehabilitation to provide institutional spending credits to the city for urban renewal. Comparatively worse housing problems in western Hough thus failed to trigger federal assistance and lent the impression that these areas were expendable, because they were not near the Circle. Copperman warned University Circle leaders that they needed to make more than token gestures toward majority-black neighborhoods if they hoped to avoid clashing with UFM, which he worried might jeopardize the Circle's ability to carry out its plans.[57]

The two reports seem to have prompted no action. Perhaps Circle leaders shared Evans's belief that they were unnecessarily "apologetic."[58] Their inaction mirrored a largely stagnant urban renewal program. For a variety of reasons, the very program that CDF asserted was evidence of a "City on Schedule" was, in fact, far behind schedule. Within months of the infusion of federal funds in 1962, the University-Euclid project was creating utter confusion on the part of Hough homeowners, who were eager to fix up their properties but uncertain whether the city intended to buy them out.[59]

University-Euclid was behind schedule in part because Mayor Anthony Celebrezze's administration had opted to start first in Erieview, which redirected the Cleveland urban renewal office's attention from the rest of the city. As early as September 1960, Carothers had complained to Celebrezze that despite being presented to the public as two parts of a cohesive renewal plan, University-Euclid was not progressing in tandem with Erieview. The mayor argued that Erieview must come first, because if city hall started both projects simultaneously, "we could spread ourselves too thin."[60] Increasingly, Clevelanders interpreted University-Euclid as a casualty of Erieview, the mayor's showpiece. In 1962, mayoral challenger Willard W. Brown, who left his country estate in Hunting Valley to establish a Cleveland address on Carlton Road overlooking University Circle, mocked the idea that the city was "on schedule" and castigated the Celebrezze administration for allowing Hough to suffer while downtown renewal proceeded.[61] Several months later, the *Call and Post* offered a more stinging critique. Hough's problem, it editorialized, was that it was "caught between two grindstones of civic redevelopment, Erieview downtown, which is the City Father's [sic] dream of recapturing the heart of the city for whites, and Euclid-University Circle which seeks to build a wall of culture against the spread of the slums."[62] Days before voters' defeat of a bond issue to allocate additional funds for Erieview in November 1963, *Plain Dealer* reporter Philip W. Porter noted that the appearance of organized opposition was a result of the city's preoccupation with "encouraging real estate promoters to put up tall new buildings in a project which has the euphonious name of Erieview."[63]

Despite the fact that by early 1965 the city had renovated only 137 of 2,020 houses earmarked for rehabilitation in University-Euclid, city officials repeatedly promised that the delays would end.[64] While preoccupation with Erieview surely contributed to the delays, it was hardly the lone factor. City hall also greatly overtaxed its renewal staff as it tried to undertake urban renewal on a total of 6,060 acres, by far the largest target area in any American city.[65] Another problem was that until the passage of the Housing and Urban Development (HUD) Act of 1965, the federal government offered little in the way of support for actually undertaking rehabilitation. On the eve of the bill's enactment, Housing and Home Finance Agency Administrator Robert C. Weaver admitted that the federal government had little experience in supporting rehabilitation. Property owners' inability to secure insurance against fire and vandalism also often resulted in FHA denials of loans to rehabilitate dwellings.[66] Others who were locked into exploitive land contracts (in which the seller retained the title until the buyer's final payment was received) could not risk the added uncertainty of having to pay off even a favorable home repair loan.[67] Even after the HUD Act facilitated rehabilitation, local officials complained that challenging federal forms and unresponsive federal officials confounded their efforts to assist homeowners wishing to take advantage of new grants and loans.[68]

Perhaps the most fundamental policy problem that exacerbated the impact of the others was the city building department's quiet retreat from maintaining the building code through inspections after the formal inception of University-Euclid. Although it appeared to the public that this lapse owed chiefly to overburdened building inspectors and an inability to move cases expeditiously through the courts, the city's urban renewal office eventually admitted that it had purposefully avoided code enforcement to drive down property values to levels that facilitated more economical purchase with renewal funds.[69] When combined with property owners' reluctance to spend their own money; almost insurmountable hurdles to obtaining financing; and the strain of overcrowding, landlord neglect, and vandalism, the city's failure to enforce the building code sentenced much of Hough to eventual demolition. Of course, Cleveland was hardly unique in its inability to make real headway in neighborhood rehabilitation. Had they examined Detroit's experience, for example, rehabilitation advocates would have found similar factors impeding conservation efforts in Mack-Concord, a neighborhood that shared much in common with Hough.[70]

Beyond municipal and federal failures lay another stark reality. When University-Euclid was planned in 1960, city officials, University Circle leaders, and neighborhood activists generally believed that Cleveland would remain an industrial powerhouse and that Hough, as a so-called port of entry for migrants, would continue to feel the pressure of a continued influx of "Negroes and Mountain Whites."[71] Instead, the city lost more manufacturing jobs with each passing year, in turn shutting off the flow of newcomers. A Community Action for Youth (CAY) survey on population trends in Hough in 1966 showed that, since 1960, the neighborhood had lost more than twelve thousand residents, more than nine-tenths of them white. Even the black population dipped slightly. Nevertheless, Hough remained overcrowded, packing nearly twenty-seven thousand people, an alarming number of them unemployed or underemployed, into each square mile of worsening decay. The combination, a *Cleveland Press* reporter noted, made Hough a "powder keg as explosive as that which touched off the Watts disaster last summer in Los Angeles."[72]

## "Pockets of Hope": Hough Rehabilitation Demonstrations as Symbolic Renewal

Meanwhile, University Circle's 1957 plan, originally intended as a twenty-year initiative, was going so well that its leaders boasted that it might be fully realized in only eleven years.[73] Although institutional construction spending leveraged millions of dollars in federal matching funds to the city for urban renewal, Lister's office had little to show in Hough. Amid the utter lack of progress in University-Euclid, the *Plain Dealer* scoured the sagging neighborhood for glimmers of hope. It lavished attention on reasons to continue believing in Hough. On Talbot Avenue, for example, the newspaper called attention to a joint effort in September 1963 by the University-Euclid urban renewal field office, the Cleveland Junior Chamber of Commerce (Jaycees), and the Talbot Avenue street club to plant trees, reseed lawns, make minor home repairs, and build a new playground (see Figure 2.2).[74] Two months later, the paper spotlighted Newton Avenue, a close-knit street lined mostly with well-kept, owner-occupied bungalows. If more of Hough were so maintained, the reporter wrote, "Cleveland might have an inner city atmosphere that could be compared with Washington's Georgetown or Greenwich Village before New York went on its current skyscraping spree."[75] The following spring, the paper covered a public demonstration by the Garden Center of Greater Cleveland (the predecessor of today's Cleveland Botanical Garden). Garden Center landscapers transformed the yards of three adjacent homes on Crawford Road, relying on the naïve assumption that because "pride in property can be contagious," merely seeing pretty lawns would spur Hough residents to launch a large-scale beautification drive.[76]

For its part, the city's urban renewal office continued to struggle, with repeated promises to initiate work followed by months of delay. Unable to overcome a range of obstacles at the local and federal levels, by 1964, Celebrezze's successor, Mayor Ralph S. Locher, was under intense pressure to show progress in Hough. In the previous year, CORE had picketed the city's

**Figure 2.2.** The Talbot Avenue Youth Corps, formed in 1963, was one of many grass-roots initiatives to save Hough during a time when the University-Euclid urban renewal project was floundering. (Cleveland Press Collection, Cleveland State University.)

University-Euclid field office to demand action, and Citizens for Better Housing had presented the city with a fourteen-point position paper insisting on a speedup in Hough.[77] Perhaps Locher also felt some guilt for having presided over the city's lax code enforcement during his previous tenure as Cleveland's city law director. In any case, the city awarded Walker and Murray Associates of Philadelphia a $170,000 contract to study its renewal problem.[78] The firm identified the Hough Avenue/East 86th Street/Crawford Road intersection and the Hough Avenue/East 93rd Street intersection as the twin cores of blight in University-Euclid and suggested a targeted approach to counter these deleterious influences. The resulting emphasis on showing token improvements in the most rapidly deteriorating locations in eastern Hough was another example of managing decline.[79]

Either in disregard of the very real obstacles to executing rehabilitation or perhaps because of them, the consultants recommended a pilot demonstration program to create visible progress. In an echo of the frustration that had led CDF and James Lister to plot Erieview five years earlier as a sign of faith in downtown's future, Lister's office now needed a similar symbolic action in Hough to reframe its public image. By May 1965, the situation was acute, because Lister had just received a federal ultimatum to initiate meaningful improvements within thirty days or face possible cancellation of the project. UCDF leaders were deeply concerned. More than a blow to the project their institutions had worked to launch, University-Euclid was critical to the Circle's realization of its own expansion. Although federal funds were not central to campus development at Case and WRU, by accepting earmarked federal renewal funds, the city was committing to constructing new water and sewer lines for University Hospitals, relocating streets, and acquiring houses for demolition to support expansions there and at Mt. Sinai Hospital.[80]

Just in time, Walker and Murray's work enabled Lister to unveil a plan for a $200,000 city improvement program on eleven streets in Hough, which was to coincide with rehabilitation work on segments of East 86th, 90th, and 93rd Streets and Crawford Road that might create a more positive image for the city's most vulnerable neighborhood.[81] Mayor Locher placed these eleven streets at the forefront of city hall's campaign to install extrabright mercury vapor streetlights to "maintain Cleveland's reputation as the lighting center of the world."[82] Unfortunately, although the city managed to repave streets and sidewalks and install new streetlights, even its token home rehabilitation demonstration quickly hit a snag. When the city's urban renewal office announced its plan to acquire and rehabilitate two vandalized houses at 1795 and 1801 East 93rd Street for $34,800, Mayor Locher and some city council members balked at a cost that was greater than that of tearing down and rebuilding them. Lister admitted that the plans for the houses were "elaborate" but insisted that the idea was to "show the city wants to rehabilitate homes."[83] After returning to the drawing board, Lister and his hired consultants responded four months later with a revised pilot rehabilitation demonstration aimed at a blighted and partially burned-out four-story, fourteen-unit, orange-brick apartment building at 1839 East 90th Street between Chester and Hough Avenues. William Seawright and Associates, said to be the first black-owned contracting firm to bid on a major federal project, won the bid to carry out the rehabilitation. The *Plain Dealer* effused that the East 90th Street demonstration would "inspire investors and private homeowners" to undertake rehabilitation.[84]

As city hall worked on its pilot demonstration, it made other key changes to mend Cleveland's frayed image: It accepted the embattled Lister's resignation as urban renewal director, changed the office's name from "Urban Renewal" (a lightning rod) to the more innocuous "Community Development," and appointed Albert A. Levin to chair the mayor's special committee on housing. Soon after, Levin, who just three years earlier had been denied a permit to build market-rate apartments on Euclid Avenue in downtown, announced that he and black millionaire businessman Alonzo Wright, along with an interracial group of investors, hoped to build eighty-four apartments for low-income families in the 9000 block of Hough Avenue.[85]

CDF, among the most active agents in recasting the city's image through its support of urban renewal, now needed an image boost itself. It had been a spark plug driving urban renewal since its inception in 1954, and yet it had remarkably few significant successes to show after more than a decade of pursuing housing renewal.[86] Accordingly, in 1966, CDF created a nonprofit housing organization called University-Euclid Housing Association (soon renamed Hough Housing Corporation, as the name "University-Euclid" became a liability) to amplify the impact of the city's East 90th pilot.[87] CDF's action came after failing to secure a commitment by CMHA director Bohn to rehabilitate one thousand units of existing housing for large families instead of building new housing projects aimed primarily at smaller households. In 1965, CDF had promised to rehabilitate two hundred units if Bohn would make such a commitment, but the public housing director stalled for more than half a year and ultimately refused to cooperate on the grounds that his responsibility was to create new housing. It seemed to matter little that Hough continued to lack the most critically needed kind of public housing that larger, low-income black families could occupy. Instead, CMHA had built just 590 smaller units, all in the high-rise Wade and Springbrook apartment towers overlooking University Circle. Unfortunately, the majority of these units were reserved for "golden agers," and UCDF's agreement with Bohn filled many of the rest with white college students or couples affiliated with Circle institutions, leading one observer to nickname Springbrook Apartments the "White Island."[88] Having failed to secure desperately needed large-family dwellings through rehabilitation of old rooming houses into public housing, CDF decided to act on its own.[89]

While city hall, Levin and Wright, and CDF pursued token, symbolic rehabilitation in University-Euclid, small-scale projects continued in an effort to keep the western part of Hough—or Superior-Chester, increasingly referred to as "Forgotten Hough"—from being left behind in Cleveland's campaign for renewal. The efforts of church-backed organizations were commonly covered in the local press. Housing Our People Economically (HOPE) Incorporated, a nonprofit housing organization headed by Hough Avenue United Church of Christ pastor Rev. Walter Grevatt Jr., identified multifamily brick houses at 6215 and 6303 Belvidere Avenue for rehabilitation. As Grevatt observed, "We are trying to create pockets of hope."[90] As HOPE Incorporated struggled to assemble funds to undertake rehabilitation, another church-based rehabilitation demonstration emerged under the leadership of Our Lady of Fatima Catholic Church. The church's so-called slum priest, Fr. Albert A. Koklowsky, who arrived in Cleveland after years of ministering to the poor in Mississippi and Puerto Rico, was so disturbed by the conditions he found in Hough that he was determined to try to fill the void left by urban renewal. When an unnamed savings and loan company donated an abandoned house at 1694 East 70th Street to the church, Koklowsky launched a public donation campaign to raise the $8,000 needed to refurbish it. The priest cloaked his action in the same cloth of managing decline through cultivation of image found in so many other civic revitalization efforts in the 1960s. "Even if the city has abandoned us," he said, "[w]e can show . . . that there is still hope in the lower Hough area."[91]

Although urban renewal officials and a handful of neighborhood-based organizations were taking small steps to jumpstart rehabilitation in Hough, by 1966, such actions were widely viewed as tokens having little real value in a neighborhood subjected to exploitation and neglect over the previous two decades. They also seemed to underscore the futility of relying on a scatter-shot approach to revitalization amid rapid decline. *Life* magazine's December 24, 1965, issue highlighted the enormity of the problem. Alongside disturbing color photos of ill-clad children, piles of unfolded laundry, overflowing alley garbage cans, and a child forced to stand to eat for lack of a table, it described how, two years earlier, black real estate brokers and civil rights leaders Charles Lucas and Arnold Walker had bought the rat-infested Gordon Towers, a condemned brick apartment building built in 1903 at Hough Avenue and East 73rd Street, and invested enough to reopen it as "part of a small-profit, high-altruism plan to check Hough's plummet to oblivion." But, the magazine concluded, "paint and plumbing stand small chance against the forces of decay in Hough."[92]

On July 18, 1966, when violence erupted outside a tavern at the corner of Hough Avenue and East 79th Street and spread across Cleveland's East Side, it was anything but a surprise. Indeed, the plight of "Rough Hough" was already known not only to its unfortunate denizens but also to Clevelanders and, thanks to *Life*, the nation. For several years, various commentators had pointed to what one University Circle leader termed Hough's "truly explosive racial potentials."[93] Like riot-torn Watts in south-central Los Angeles, Hough was a powder keg waiting for a spark. Although the spark was spillover from an argument following a barkeeper's refusal to serve a black patron in the 79ers Café at East 79th Street and Hough Avenue, the rioting that spread across dozens of city blocks in or near Hough in the days that followed reflected a similar toxic mixture found in poor, black sections of many American cities: rapid demographic change, diminishing opportunities for work, landlord neglect, crime, police brutality, and overcrowding exacerbated by the displacement of residents for urban renewal.[94]

After six days, the Ohio National Guard had restored order in Hough, but the damage wrought by the uprising was only a spike in what was otherwise a slow-burn decline of the city's most troubled neighborhood. Extreme neglect, population loss, vandalism, demolition, and arson began before the riots—sometimes well before—and continued afterward. Nonetheless, the Hough riots laid bare what African Americans had understood for years: Cleveland was not "The Best Location in the Nation." The Eastern Hough

Organized for Action Committee issued a statement suggesting that if city hall had been willing to work more closely with neighborhood organizations, the riots might not have happened. "Why," it asked, "must people have to resort to violence to be heard?"[95]

Two months after the riots, the city held an open house in its rehabilitated apartment building at 1839 East 90th Street. The open house begged the question, who was the audience? Purportedly part of an effort "to demonstrate to residents what can be done," it was more accurately window dressing for the city's benighted renewal program.[96] Upon seeing one of the suites, "elegantly furnished" by Sears Roebuck and Company, contractor William Seawright expressed sadness that most of the people who toured it that day could not qualify to occupy the suites. Commenting that more should be expected from a country "spending $53,000,000 a day in Viet Nam," Seawright concluded that what Hough needed more than these one- and two-bedroom apartments were four- to six-bedroom flats for large families.[97] Indeed, at adjacent 1833 East 90th, five families with twenty-four children crowded into a rooming house owned by an absentee landlord and poorly tended by an absentee custodian. Its "bald lawn" provided a stark counterpoint to the "bright green grass" next door and underscored the enormity of trying to renew a slum one building at a time.[98] However, CDF's Hough Housing Corporation, which it managed in cooperation with the Goodrich Social Settlement, announced a $1-million campaign to build on the city's East 90th Street demonstration project by rehabilitating an additional 106 housing units in nine apartment buildings.[99]

In October 1966, Warner and Swasey, a major producer of machine tools and machinery whose primary factory was located on the western edge of University-Euclid at the corner of Carnegie Avenue and East 55th Street, announced that it would be the first industry in Cleveland to sponsor housing rehabilitation in Hough.[100] With the help of African American community leaders, the company identified the four-story Rosewood apartment building at 1579–1581 Crawford Road that had been subdivided into eighteen apartments and set out to restore it to its original thirteen suites, after which it sold the building to the St. John–St. James Housing Corporation operated by the city's two largest African Methodist Episcopal (AME) churches.[101] Warner and Swasey's action demonstrated company leaders' understanding that projects could no longer be hatched in corporate boardrooms and then presented in final form to the community. Indeed, months before, Daisy Craggett, the first African American head of the Hough Community Council (as the Hough Area Council had restyled itself in 1962), which had found itself sidelined by urban renewal planners, had vented her frustration with white leaders, no matter how well intentioned some might be. Referring to Bruere, Craggett argued, "The day of the Great White Father [has] passed. . . . His voice was once the voice of the Hough community, [but] let us acknowledge that that voice no longer speaks for the residents of Hough."[102] It is difficult to know whether the Hough riots spurred Warner and Swasey's action. The firm's president, James C. Hodge, claimed he had thought about the project for years and had been inspired by his service on an interracial businessmen's committee.[103] Regardless, the decision to announce the project after the riots suggests that Hodge's action also reflected concern for the future of the company's own deep investment in the city.

Whatever its motives, Warner and Swasey's action was very much an exception and not large enough to move much beyond serving as a symbol of civic faith. To some, CDF's expansion of the city's East 90th Street demonstration appeared to be a face-saving measure. A Garden Valley community organizer blamed CDF for undertaking rehabilitation in Hough despite its failure to close out Garden Valley and other "hopelessly behind schedule" urban renewal projects. He suggested that CDF's move was an attempt to deflect attention from its failures and gain the appearance of being a force for revitalization. In other words, in this view, the Hough Housing Corporation was merely another example of the growth coalition's managing the city's decline.[104] Nor was city hall above manipulating public opinion about renewal. Beginning in November 1965, when it launched Operation Demolition as the nation's first federally funded demolition program, the municipal government masked its rehabilitation failures by redesignating hundreds of structures once intended for rehabilitation and stepping up demolitions. In the time that the city completed fourteen units of rehabilitated housing at 1839 East 90th Street, it demolished ninety houses and buildings, which represented a tiny fraction of the nearly twenty-seven hundred structures that Operation Demolition would claim over the next eight years.[105]

Sizeable rehabilitation efforts by smaller nonprofits also resumed after the Hough riots but often faced difficulties. As HOPE Incorporated attempted to speed up its rehabilitation efforts, the Greater Cleveland Council of Churches challenged its more than four hundred member churches to raise funds to help HOPE Incorporated rehabilitate or build "400 Houses for Hough."[106] With $70,000 amassed from some twenty-five suburban churches, HOPE Incorporated began planning a $2-million project to purchase and rehabilitate fifty-three residential structures of varying types on Belvidere Avenue between East 60th and East 65th Streets into a self-contained community situated around a pedestrian mall on a segment of Belvidere, replete with community center, swimming pool, and meeting facilities. Grevatt showed a sense of heightened urgency as he described the project: "The time is late in the ghetto," he said. "We need a symbol to show that somebody cares." HOPE Incorporated obtained Federal Housing Administration (FHA) approval and entered talks with three national lumber industry associations that might contribute $150,000 in seed money. Unfortunately, absentee landlords who held many of the properties designated for the project raised their asking prices to the point that, even with outside help, HOPE Incorporated could not afford them.[107]

As even larger spot-rehabilitation endeavors produced limited results at best, Hough exemplified the ongoing tension between decline and revitalization in the city. To be sure, there continued to be no dearth of ideas for carving out small "pockets of hope." A notable example was a partnership between a suburban businessman and Koklowsky of Our Lady of Fatima Parish that salvaged three thousand yards of sod from the lawns of Rocky River homes condemned for the construction of the Northwest Freeway (I-90) and planted the grass, along with trees and shrubs donated by two nurseries in Lake County, to refresh the landscape of a several-block area just south of League Park.[108] However, in the absence of a workable plan to recast the large, unwieldy Hough area, deterioration and human misery continued in spite of small, well-intentioned demonstrations of hope for the city's future. Where the local press had once seen small nonprofit forays into renewal as heroic offensives capable of repulsing decline, the mood after the riots was decidedly less confident. With only 3 percent of the city's land area, Hough now accounted for 25 percent of all housing vacancies, and vacancies were essentially a death sentence for buildings. As one reporter lamented, spot rehabilitation "won't even scratch the surface."[109]

Five years after CDF paid television personality Chet Huntley to declare that Cleveland was a "City on Schedule," a 1967 episode of the WKYC-TV (formerly KYW-TV) documentary series *Montage* presented a bluntly critical assessment of Cleveland's urban renewal failures. The episode's title, "It's Still Yesterday in Cleveland," suggested not only that the city's renewal campaign was not on schedule but also that it had essentially stood still for more than a decade while other cities had boldly moved forward. The documentary cited successes in combined redevelopment and rehabilitation, such as Philadelphia's Society Hill and Baltimore's Harlem Park. Director of Community Development Barton R. Clausen asserted in the documentary that Hough was in its current dismal shape because the city's renewal office "never dealt with a set of realistic figures" about how much relocation housing was needed to handle displacement from urban renewal projects or considered "whether these [housing units] were available . . . to nonwhites." In a subtle echo of the gloomy "Mistake on the Lake" nickname that was already beginning to circulate in Cleveland, Clausen commented that he saw Cleveland as "a leaky boat. We're trying to patch up the leaks in it and make it a real sailing craft. If it goes down, everybody goes down with it." Therein lay a veiled warning to the city's influential, self-assured suburbanites: The costs of not believing in Cleveland would be borne not just in "Rough Hough" but also in tony Shaker Heights.

Cleveland's experience with urban renewal may have been particularly problematic, but the city was hardly alone in facing sharp public rebuke. Even as Cleveland's renewal leaders—like their counterparts in other cities—were insisting that urban renewal would usher in a bright urban future, a combination of swiftness to demolish, sluggishness to rebuild, and inability to support rehabilitation was hastening the decline of the very places they hoped to save. In the early to mid-1960s, a growing chorus of critics questioned the notion that major federal spending could succeed in remaking central cities for the better. Urban renewal was not up to the task of producing large-scale improvements in the condition of urban neighborhoods; in fact, its backers were unwittingly contributing to the destruction of urban neighborhoods. In Cleveland and across America, the backlash against urban renewal would lead to new approaches that promised greater citizen input and sensitivity to fostering total community development.

Much had changed in the five years since the release of *Cleveland: City on Schedule.* In 1962, there had been enough hope for substantive improvements through urban renewal to support booster claims. By 1967, Clevelanders' skepticism had turned to anger—even violent repudiation. Frank P. Celeste, a mayoral contender that fall, argued that "Cleveland has hit bottom. The only way to go now is up." Surely many Clevelanders hoped he was correct in his prediction. It would require more than merely managing decline to restore people's faith in the city. "Maybe the little printed signs seen around town aren't wrong," the documentary concluded, as it showed a "Pray for Cleveland" bumper sticker. "Unless prayers are answered, and workable public-minded action replaces promises and failure, it will always be yesterday in Cleveland."[110]

# 3

## Greater Cleveland Growthland

*Industrial Flight and Boosterism in*
*"The Best Location in the Nation"*

"Look north out the windows of an office high up in the 55 Public Square Building," advised the narrator of a 1963 promotional booklet, and one would behold the key to Cleveland's enviable industrial position. A typical day would bring "two or three Great Lakes freighters, each delivering 20,000 tons or more of Lake Superior iron ore," and cranes loading or unloading the cargo of "foreign flag vessels from all over the world." From the same windows, one would also see the tracks of the New York Central and Pennsylvania Railroads as well as an emerging freeway system. Finally, not far outside the building's shadow was Burke Lakefront Airport, one of two major local airports. In this hyperbolic narrative, which situated Cleveland as the hub of multiple transportation networks capable of carrying people, materials, and products far and wide, the recently formed Greater Cleveland Growth Board (GCGB) hoped to renew the idea that the nation's eighth-largest city enjoyed an ideal location for manufacturing expansion. Located on "Ohio's and America's North Coast," this metropolis boasted "a population greater than 19 of our states, producing more goods than 34 of them," and stood "within an overnight haul" of 52 percent of the U.S. population.[1] The narrator's choice of 55 Public Square, better known as the Illuminating Building, as a perch from which to survey the metropolitan area was anything but haphazard. Opened five years earlier in 1958, the Illuminating Building not only was the first new skyscraper erected in downtown Cleveland since the completion of the Cleveland Union Terminal group in 1931 but also served as home to its namesake, the Cleveland Electric Illuminating Company (CEI), whose area development department had launched the city's nationally known booster campaign in 1944.

CEI's claim that Cleveland was "The Best Location in the Nation" was an easy civic sales pitch as long as each year brought an upward arc of new business investment to Cleveland. However, as plant closures emerged as a newfound concern in the late 1950s and early 1960s, the slogan begged reinforcement. With more and more firms not simply moving from central-city plants to modern facilities in the suburbs but also abandoning the metropolitan area for other states, especially in the Sunbelt, the Cleveland area also needed active study of problems facing manufacturers and a combination of advocacy and persuasion to prevent their departure. CEI's area development program no longer seemed sufficient to the task. The area needed an organization whose sole mission was to attract and retain industry, which was the economic backbone and an integral part of the image of Cleveland. For five years in the early to mid-1960s, GCGB served these functions and replaced CEI as the leading voice for encouraging industrialization in northeastern Ohio.

This chapter examines industrial recruitment, retention, and boosterism in the two decades after the wartime inception of the CEI slogan. Just as fears of decline in downtown and Hough in the late 1950s prompted a more pointed insistence that major new investments in the central city were crucial to Cleveland's future, this chapter argues that concurrent manufacturing losses galvanized new initiatives to battle decline. Downtown's and Hough's declines were a product of certain facets of midcentury metropolitan change— namely, suburbanization and the accompanying transformation of the central city. Similarly, into the 1960s, the perception of industrial decline was still predominantly the same kind of shift of manufacturers from central city to suburbia that many other older American cities were also facing. To date, much scholarship on deindustrialization has focused on macrolevel economic restructuring and its impact on what came to be known later as Rust Belt cities. More recently, other scholars have examined workers' sense of loss and scarred urban landscapes.[2] In contrast, this chapter emphasizes how boosters viewed the problem and how they asserted Cleveland's ability to leverage its purported natural advantages. The chapter also juxtaposes the often-conflicting motives of boosters concerned about the central city versus those for whom central-city losses were an acceptable, even advantageous result of ongoing metropolitan change.

As in its responses to downtown change, members of Cleveland's growth coalition also did not always march in lockstep on matters of industrial change. CEI, GCGB, and other large, active industrial boosters, such as the East Ohio Gas Company and National City Bank, viewed the problem through a metropolitan lens. To the extent that any of them advocated retention of manufacturing plants inside the central city's boundaries, their intervention was merely part of their larger concern for the overall profile of metropolitan Cleveland. However, unlike CEI, whose economic development interest was inseparable from selling electricity throughout its expansive service area, or the Growth Board, whose leaders represented interests spread across and beyond Cuyahoga County, the Cleveland municipal government naturally placed industrial expansion and retention in the context of augmenting a tax duplicate that suburban development was hollowing out more with each passing year.

As the power of CEI's area development program and the metropolitan image it crafted began to erode, GCGB emerged to revive and rebrand the region. Like "The Best Location in the Nation," the Growth Board's "Greater Cleveland Growthland" slogan was synonymous with a multicounty metropolitan area. Importantly, the Growth Board did not simply assume this area was the "best location" but instead understood that it required a redoubled effort to bring growth. That effort prevented GCGB, like CEI, from fully addressing central-city industrial decline, which in turn left that problem for the municipal government and the Cleveland Development Foundation (CDF) to solve. Each had a strong motive for trying. The city desperately needed to restore its depleted tax base and preserve jobs for its citizens, which it hoped to accomplish in part by attracting and retaining industrial plants. Conversely, CDF wanted to protect the deep investments that many of its directors had in steel mills, refineries, and other relatively immovable heavy industry ensconced in the central city. These allied urban renewal backers looked to Gladstone, a central-city reindustrialization project, as a blueprint for preserving industry within the city proper. Unfortunately, Gladstone became hopelessly entwined with the Erieview project in downtown, whose consumption of most of the city's redevelopment resources and attention impoverished other urban renewal undertakings in Cleveland. Even if it had had a dozen projects like Gladstone, the city of Cleveland would still have had to overcome fundamental changes in the national economy and the overarching metropolitan vision of the Growth Board and leading utilities. In the midst of these challenges, however, even the appearance of investment in the city's industrial future possessed civic and political value.

## "The Best Location in the Nation": Selling Growth to Sell Electricity

On August 6, 1945, the day that the *Enola Gay* dropped its atomic bomb on Hiroshima, the Cleveland Chamber of Commerce circulated its *Headlines from Cleveland* newsletter, which asserted, "Postwar planning seeds, well-planted in Cleveland, now are beginning to sprout and give promise of a bumper crop of jobs after this war has been won."[3] Not only were the city's factories anticipating few if any reconversion problems; many were planning to expand their operations in the city. During World War II, CEI had planted some of these seeds as it stepped up its area development program with an eye toward preparing Greater Cleveland to attract new industries to maintain the momentum stoked by wartime production. CEI's area development department kept a file on all available industrial sites, advertised Cleveland in national business and trade magazines and via direct mail campaigns and booster films, and even purchased and held in reserve rural acreage for eventual resale to industrial firms.

Perhaps most important, CEI had coined the slogan "The Best Location in the Nation" in 1944 to promote the conversion of about thirty major war production plants employing twenty-nine thousand workers to peacetime uses. The slogan was the brainchild of CEI's area development manager Robert C. Hienton and its head of advertising and public relations Frank J. Ryan, who were searching for a catchy name for the Greater Cleveland area. Hienton had recently come to Cleveland from Ashtabula in extreme northeastern Ohio, where he had headed industrial sales in CEI's Ashtabula office and formed a civic committee to promote new industry.[4] Although the slogan became closely associated with Cleveland, where many civic and business interests appropriated it to promote the city, it actually pertained to CEI's entire 1,800-square-mile electrical service area, which stretched eastward from Avon Lake, Avon, and Ridgeville Townships in Lorain County through Cuyahoga, Lake, and Geauga Counties to Ashtabula County's eastern border with Pennsylvania. CEI was not the first to tout Cleveland's prime industrial location to a national audience during the war. In the spring of 1944, National City Bank had run ads in *Business Week* and the *Wall Street Journal* titled "Cleveland—in America's Industrial Heart." It is possible that these ads, which featured a circular map with a radius of four hundred miles drawn around a large heart atop Cleveland and northeastern Ohio, inspired CEI's large and long-standing campaign.[5]

The early postwar years brought exactly the scenario of rapid industrial expansion that CEI's wartime campaign anticipated. After World War II, soaring American purchases of durable goods, such as automobiles, refrigerators, and television sets, accompanied the mass exodus of the "Greatest Generation" from central cities to the suburbs, and industry responded by expanding production. To minimize manufacturing costs, companies increasingly sought modern, efficient, single-floor plants. Their need for a sprawling layout, combined with growing demand for expansive employee parking and truck-loading docks, sent an increasing number of them packing for inexpensive suburban or rural sites. The rise of suburban manufacturing much predated World War II, but the impact of industrial decentralization on the central city mounted considerably after the war.[6] Although the city of Cleveland could boast 32,590 jobs in its ten largest factories in 1959, the ten largest factories in its suburbs accounted for 36,570 workers.[7] Between 1948 and 1959, new factories engulfed well more than two thousand additional acres of suburban land, nearly doubling the area in the suburbs devoted to industry.[8] One such company was the arc-welding equipment maker Lincoln Electric, which transferred its operations in 1951 from the city's northeastern neighborhood of Collinwood to the adjacent suburb of Euclid. In this case, the city was fortunate in that Thompson Products, a major Cleveland manufacturer of aviation parts, quickly moved into the empty Lincoln Electric facilities.[9] Of course, CEI touted investments in new or expanded plants as gains, even though they often represented labor-saving upgrades that reduced employment.

Nonetheless, Cleveland's leading industrialists understood and even embraced the idea that the central city was maturing and should expect a slower pace of development in the future. Speaking at the annual Cleveland Chamber of Commerce luncheon in 1956, Chamber board chairman Thomas F. Patton of Republic Steel remarked, "While there has been and will continue to be extensive expansions of existing industries in the city—witness our own in Republic Steel and that of Jones and Laughlin in their plants in the flats—major *new* industrial developments are far less likely to take place in the city than in the environs anywhere up to 50 miles from the heart of the city." Rather than urge a recentralizing of industry, Patton took a different tack: "Cleveland should strive to be to northern Ohio what Chicago is to 8 million people in Illinois, southern Wisconsin, and northern Indiana—a center of service, supply, commerce, entertainment and culture." With only steady national growth seemingly on the horizon, Patton saw no problem for the city proper. Like downtown, industry inside Cleveland would maintain its strong position through expansions, even as the suburbs absorbed most new development.[10]

Unconcerned about the city's prospects as a home for industry, CEI aggressively facilitated the location of industry in the suburbs and beyond, especially in Avon Lake, Solon, Euclid, and along what it dubbed the "Chemical Shore" in Lake and Ashtabula Counties. Starting in the late 1940s, after they had succeeded in finding firms to repurpose the city's war plants, CEI area development officials ramped up their efforts to help suburbanites soften their view of industry as a nuisance. In 1950, CEI launched a community development section within its area development department for this purpose, leading to the embrace of industrial zoning within a few years.[11] In 1953, the utility reported that it possessed 820 acres of land to market to firms seeking locations in northeastern Ohio.[12] CEI executive vice president Ralph M. Besse noted in 1957 that Lake and Ashtabula Counties, aided by the extension of the Lakeland Freeway eastward to Painesville, were fertile ground for industrial expansion that might bring an eightfold growth in the company's electric provision.[13] Indeed, whenever the company referred to growth, it championed what its president and, later, chairman Elmer L. Lindseth dubbed "thinking regionally." Lindseth's vision informed the company's special report in 1960, *More Land for Industry*, which mapped some eight thousand acres of available land in move-in-ready "industrial districts" and an additional fifty thousand acres in larger tracts. Tellingly, only three of these thirty-two industrial districts were located inside the city of Cleveland, all of them near Cleveland Hopkins International Airport. Eleven were in western Cuyahoga and eastern Lorain Counties, and eighteen were in eastern Cuyahoga, Lake, Geauga, and Ashtabula Counties.[14]

CEI's area development work was hardly unique among electric utilities. The Detroit Edison Company, the West Penn Electric Company (based in Pittsburgh), and the Philadelphia Electric Company also created area development departments by the 1950s that were metropolitan in focus, while larger utilities, such as Niagara Mohawk Power Corporation, whose area development activity stretched across upstate New York, could not associate as closely with a single city.[15] Nor was CEI alone among infrastructure-related companies in promoting Cleveland area development. Railroad companies, such as the Pennsylvania and New York Central, also promoted industrial expansion along the transportation corridors they served, including in northeastern Ohio, but, like Niagara Mohawk, they did not focus industrial recruitment in any one metropolitan area. Similarly, the Cleveland-based East Ohio Gas Company mailed 2,500 brochures every other month to leading manufacturers all around the country to tout relocating or expanding near Cleveland. However, East Ohio Gas seldom overtly conflated local boosterism with development in its service area, which sprawled from northeastern Ohio to eastern Pennsylvania.[16] If CEI's "Best Location in the Nation" campaign was not the only such promotion, it was certainly among the most concentrated and forceful.

Facilitated by CEI, East Ohio Gas, and railroads, many factories left Cleveland in the 1950s, bound mostly for its own suburbs but also for out-of-state locations. For example, Lamson and Sessions, a manufacturer of nuts, bolts, and fasteners, abandoned its longtime West Side plant in 1958 for an expansive new facility in Brooklyn, Ohio, only three miles to the south.[17] In contrast, when General Motors closed two West Side automotive plants that employed about nine hundred workers, it shifted some employees to suburban Euclid and the outlying town of Hudson in northern Summit County but others to LaGrange, Illinois, as part of a consolidation of operations into fewer and larger facilities.[18] The outright loss of jobs from the metropolitan area is reflected in the fact that in the five years following the Korean War, Cuyahoga and Lake Counties experienced a combined net loss of approximately seventy thousand manufacturing jobs, even as suburbs from Avon Lake to Solon lured hundreds of new, mostly small-scale factories.[19] The losses did not prevent CEI's continued assurances to its stockholders that the area's industrial economy remained sound, but they did seem to temper its booster rhetoric. After annually tallying each new height in the metropolitan area's workforce, for the first time in 1954, the company was silent on this point. In contrast to earlier years in which CEI provided annual figures on plant expansions, by 1956, the utility did no more than report that "the number of prospects now studying the advantages of locating or expanding here is greater than at any time in the past." The next year, CEI withheld figures on expansions, noting opaquely that the number "will be lower in 1958 than in 1957." CEI's boosterism became increasingly subdued as the decade drew to a close. In 1958, it acknowledged a downturn but deemphasized it by situating it in a context of national recession. In 1959, the company expressed its commitment to "provide all the leadership we can in helping to solve the problems which today are afflicting this and other major metropolitan centers."[20]

The first plant closure that invited particular scrutiny was that of the Murray Ohio Manufacturing Company. In 1956, some 1,250 Clevelanders lost their jobs or faced transfer when Murray Ohio closed its bicycle, toy, and fan factory in the Collinwood neighborhood in the city's heavily industrial northeastern corner. The company's core business in bicycles, scooters, and wagons suffered with growing competition from Japanese manufacturers after World War II but enjoyed a brief resurgence during the Korean War, when an army ordnance contract for 350,000 shells swelled the company's ranks to 2,800 workers. The end of the contract, coupled with stiffer competition in bicycles, eventually prompted Murray Ohio to forsake Cleveland to preserve its profit levels. Down to 1,250 employees by 1956, even fewer than before the Korean conflict, Murray Ohio transferred most of its Cleveland workforce to its relocated bicycle division, housed in a brand-new plant built and leased by the town of Lawrenceburg, Tennessee.[21]

The loss of the Murray Ohio bicycle works was the first plant closure to prompt coverage in the *Plain Dealer*. However, it elicited a more dismissive response from one chamber of commerce official, who remarked in 1957 that all the factories that had left Cleveland in the previous five years would fit into a corner of just one of the new Ford plants in Brook Park.[22] Through the late 1950s, the arrival of several major automotive-industry plants and the expansion of a number of major industrial firms, including massive steel works in the Flats along the Cuyahoga River, deflected attention from this outflow of plants and accompanying reduction of jobs through automation, making it easier to believe in Cleveland's industrial future. The new auto plants all opened in suburbs, including Brook Park, Parma, Twinsburg, and Walton Hills. Their need for significant additional electrical loads satisfied CEI. For its part, the city of Cleveland, which had no tracts of land large enough to lure these massive plants, was relegated to being a handmaiden for industrial decentralization. In the late 1940s, Cleveland had supplied water service to tracts in the village of Brook Park, later chosen by Ford for a new foundry and engine plant. Likewise, after the Pennsylvania Railroad sold land in Walton Hills for a new Ford automotive-stamping plant in 1953, the city ran a new water line six miles outside the Cleveland corporate limits to the southeastern Cuyahoga County plant.[23]

## Greater Cleveland Growthland: Sugarcoating Industrial Flight

By the early 1960s, the growth coalition was belatedly coming to acknowledge that the Cleveland area faced intense competition for a share of the nation's industrial growth. In his *Plain Dealer* column, Nathaniel R. Howard, also the editor of the sister newspaper *Cleveland News*, pointed out, "If we include the northeast lake shore, the Cleveland area has had good fortune in growth in the post-war years." Howard echoed Patton's observation of four years before when he added that "all industrial centers reach a certain maturity." But rather than assume, as Patton had, that expansions of factories inside the city limits would keep Cleveland prosperous, Howard pointed obliquely to a "record of aloofness, uncertainties, and a few civic undependabilities [*sic*]," by which he surely meant the indifference or even hostility displayed by some business and government leaders toward the plight of industrial firms facing challenges to the expansion of their plants.[24] Previously oblivious, at least publicly, to these challenges, in one of his monthly reports to CEI employees in August 1961, Lindseth pointed to the growing attractiveness of southern communities that were poaching industry from older cities like Cleveland. He noted the recent closure of one of the city's wire-products manufacturers, which had thrown some four hundred Clevelanders out of work when it accepted a generous offer of assistance from the municipal government of Georgetown, Kentucky, in the form of plant financing and tax abatement. Lindseth considered land-use studies such as the one CEI had recently completed for neighboring Lake, Geauga, and Ashtabula Counties and civic investments in Erieview and University Circle as increasingly useful tools for improving the area's image and, consequently, attracting new industry.[25]

Likewise, by 1961, the Cleveland Chamber of Commerce was finally rethinking its confidence in Greater Cleveland's industrial future and preparing to launch the metropolitan area's first formal response to deindustrialization. Heeding the growing alarm about the retreat of industry from the region, CEI helped the chamber form GCGB as a separate organization to grapple with this problem by countering outside lures to local industrial firms and cultivating city council members whose support was needed to solve companies' challenges. The move represented a dramatic departure from the longtime unwritten division of responsibility in which the chamber concerned itself chiefly with industry in Cleveland itself while ceding the suburbs and outlying counties to CEI. In 1951, when Curtis Lee Smith became its president, the chamber of commerce had steadfastly avoided placing plants in the suburbs. A decade later, the Growth Board expanded its progenitor's focus to Cuyahoga and Lake Counties, the U.S. Census Bureau's definition of metropolitan Cleveland.[26] Richard L. DeChant, who for years had headed the area development department at CEI, presided over GCGB, which had a staff of five funded through donations from CEI, Republic Steel, Standard Oil Company of Ohio (Sohio), and several banks and department stores. The Growth Board soon expanded its reach across an eight-county area.[27] Reflecting its core responsibility to attract and retain industrial firms, GCGB planned as part of its 1962 agenda to cooperate in the development of a University Circle research park, encourage transportation improvements, compile timely data about the metropolitan area, and develop and maintain "a 'positive image' of the Greater Cleveland area."[28]

Beginning that year, GCGB undertook an aggressive national marketing plan that included a series of advertisements in the *Wall Street Journal*. The campaign grew out of a brainstorming session in which GCGB leaders compiled a list of thirty-nine "reasons people should believe that Greater Cleveland is the best location in the nation." Building on CEI's campaign, which had for the greater part of two decades built Cleveland's image around the idea of inevitability associated with the city's geographical location, the Growth Board sought to amplify that message while also updating it to reflect an emerging understanding that "brainpower" was just as important as "broad shoulders" in attracting modern industry. Among the thirty-nine talking points were the outlines of the city's future image: the National Aeronautics and Space Administration's (NASA's) Lewis Research Center; the presence of seventeen Fortune 500 headquarters; and a number of renowned philanthropic foundations, hospitals, parks, museums, symphony orchestra, and universities.[29] GCGB's ads continued a longtime focus on the area's large stock of available suburban land, skilled workforce, abundant supply of fresh water, and location within a day's drive of half of the nation's population, but they also touted industrial innovation and quality of life.

GCGB placed particular emphasis on world trade and research, especially as the latter related to the aerospace industry. One ad exclaimed that, thanks to the St. Lawrence Seaway, Cleveland's port was closer than New York City to Copenhagen, Denmark, transforming the Great Lakes into "a new North Coast of America" (a name that later became a tagline for promoting the city). Taking a giant leap further, another ad asked, "Is your quickest route to outer space by way of Cleveland?"[30] Upon learning that NASA would assign responsibility for Centaur, Agena, and M-1 rocket development to its Lewis Research Center in Cleveland, GCGB ran an even bolder ad that called Cleveland the "leading center for propulsion development," soon to be second only to the Marshall Space Flight Center in Huntsville, Alabama, among NASA's facilities.[31] A follow-up ad boasted that, in addition to NASA's work, Cleveland's Thompson Ramo Wooldridge (TRW; formerly Thompson Products) and other companies were also supplying rocket hardware "from nozzles to nosecones," while Case Institute of Technology and Western Reserve University (WRU) were "brain-power generators" that could attract even more space-age industries (see Figure 3.1).[32] The universities not only were sources of brainpower but also served as integral parts of the city's cultural crown jewel, University Circle. Perhaps the most memorable of the Growth Board's ads was one in 1964 that carried the title "What Your Wife Knows about Finding a Plant Site." The ad paired the presumed concerns of a male executive and his wife when considering relocation. It suggested that while he might focus on geography and infrastructure, she would appreciate an art museum "second only to the Metropolitan [and] a symphony second to none," along with "the finest suburban living in the country," a clear reference to Shaker Heights, which had recently been named the nation's most affluent community.[33]

The Growth Board's ads attempted to reframe Cleveland in the national public imagination, but they elided some disadvantages in the city's location. For example, in cultivating the idea that Cleveland was taking its place among the national leaders in foreign trade and research and development, the organization was merely papering over serious rifts in the local growth coalition and weaknesses in "The Best Location in the Nation." First, the promise of the St. Lawrence Seaway, heralded in the late 1950s as a transformative development, was falling far short of its potential only a few years after opening, with Cleveland barely besting Toledo as the fourth-largest port on the Great Lakes. Just as feuding between downtown merchants undermined a subway plan that might have stimulated downtown redevelopment, the rivalry between entrenched shipping companies hurt prospects for industrial expansion. Sometimes a ship had to linger offshore for hours because its contracted shipping company's docks were filled and the company would not send the ship to its rivals' docks. Meanwhile, the Port Authority of New York maintained an office in Terminal Tower, from which it worked to siphon port business away from Cleveland to the East Coast.[34] Mayor Anthony Celebrezze's administration bowed to the will of existing shipping companies, which did not want regulation or new competition, and steadfastly opposed the creation of a port authority. Likewise, powerful railroad and steel interests opposed port development, each for their own reasons. Railroads preferred not to compete with shipping companies for the carriage of freight, while steel manufacturers saw the threat of foreign steel imports via the seaway as outweighing whatever advantages the introduction of iron

NEW
BIG
SHOT

## Hardware for man-on-the-moon now being built in

Shooting a man to the moon is something like launching Cleveland's 52-story Terminal Tower. It takes a vehicle almost that tall to get him there. And more and more of the components for these space monsters are being built right here in Cleveland, by companies like Thompson Ramo Wooldridge Inc.

The new big shot in aerospace is Cleveland. NASA's mammoth Lewis Research Center has already made us first in the nation in propulsion research. Now TRW and others are supplying increasing amounts of the actual hardware, from nozzles to nose cones. For example, TRW Cleveland is the nation's largest supplier of rocket nozzles, including production for Minuteman, Polaris, Scout. A new contract: 120 inch-diameter nozzles for Titan III C space launch vehicle. TRW Cleveland's space systems development work includes Sunflower solar-power conversion system, SNAP 8 nuclear power conversion system and attitude controls for the Saturn V space booster. TRW has 6,000 people in Cleveland working on aerospace-defense projects.

Credit Cleveland's scientific environment. Here are over 350 research laboratories — the nation's fourth largest concentration. Here are Case Institute of Technology with its famous computer center, Western Reserve University with $11 million in new facilities for research, and a full score of other institutions of higher learning. Brain-power generators. No wonder space-oriented industry is looking our way.

*The Greater Cleveland Growthland is one of the world's greatest opportunities for business growth*

## The GREATER CLEVELAND GROWTHLAND

LAKE ERIE

CLEVELAND

For further information, please write or phone Richard L. DeChant, Executive Director, Greater Cleveland Growth Board, Union Commerce Building, Cleveland 14, Ohio. Phone: Area Code 216, 241-4383.

**Figure 3.1.** This 1963 Greater Cleveland Growth Board advertisement superimposes a Saturn V rocket on the Terminal Tower, Cleveland's most iconic symbol. The ad suggests the growth coalition's aspirations for a space-age economy, whose pillars were rooted in University Circle institutions, NASA, and other research centers and defense industry–related firms located mainly in the suburbs. (MS 3471, Greater Cleveland Growth Association Records, The Western Reserve Historical Society, Cleveland, Ohio.)

ore from Labrador had brought. Thus, the Cleveland Chamber of Commerce caved to its shipping, steel, and railroad members and lobbied against building up the city's port facilities.[35]

Second, GCGB's focus on space-age research and development sounded good but ignored weaknesses in Cleveland's ability to compete nationally. Unlike the defense industry of yesteryear, whose production relied heavily on proximity to the city's steel industry along its major railroads and in the Flats, the new, nimble defense industry focused more often on lightweight electronic instruments and components whose manufacture and distribution was better suited to places with more competitive labor rates. For this simple reason, most of the expansion by Cleveland-based TRW, the subject of repeated advertising by CEI and GCGB, occurred not in Greater Cleveland but in southern California. Further, despite the Growth Board's casting of University Circle as a cultural center and "brainpower" hub, Case and WRU did not match the influence of Boston's Massachusetts Institute of Technology (MIT) or the Bay Area's Stanford University.[36]

GCGB not only prospected for space-age industry but also busied itself with the problems of existing industry, including many antiquated multistory factories filled with workers whose relatively high wages curbed competitiveness. The Growth Board regularly tallied the number of industries it assisted. Thanks to a detailed survey of one hundred top executives in 1963, GCGB was well aware that high labor costs and strikes were sources of considerable angst among industrial heads. Also, few could forget how a four-month strike in 1955 had prompted the Cleveland Worsted Mills to dissolve, costing the city 1,450 jobs, plus another 400 at the company's Ravenna, Ohio, plant.[37] Smith commented that local manufacturers often found themselves "caught in the steel complex plus the automotive complex" of wages dictated by the United Steelworkers and United Automobile Workers unions "and just could not pay comparable rates."[38]

Although there was little it could do to mediate labor disputes, the Growth Board was sometimes able to broker deals with city council members in wards where companies were encountering resistance against zoning changes to support factory expansions. For example, GCGB's intervention led Councilman Richard Masterson to sponsor legislation to permit expansion of the V. D. Anderson Company, a manufacturer of nut- and seed-oil extraction machinery in the Cudell neighborhood on Cleveland's West Side, thereby preserving some three hundred jobs. The firm was among dozens that GCGB assisted in 1962 alone. While salvation of jobs in the city was certainly part of GCGB's activity, the organization never demonstrated a difference in how it characterized retention of firms inside the city versus those it assisted in moving to the suburbs. In strict accord with its stated mission, all were successes in its official view and contributed to the Growthland image. Thus, the V. D. Anderson Company's decision to remain on West 96th Street was no more an accomplishment than American Packaging Corporation's choice to relocate from East 45th Street to an industrial park in Boston Hills in northern Summit County rather than move out of the state.[39]

As far as they went, the Growth Board's services provided a way for manufacturing concerns to wrest concessions from reluctant council members. With their eyes trained on the entire metropolitan area, however, GCGB officers were able to devote only part of their attention to retaining industry inside Cleveland proper. When a factory left Cleveland but committed to expand in a nearby suburb, GCGB counted that as a victory, but inside the city limits, it provoked a sense of defeat. Understanding that the Growth Board's multicounty mandate prevented its being a total advocate for industrial retention inside the city limits, Councilman Anthony Pecyk introduced an ordinance in 1961 that proposed forming a municipal department for industrial and economic development, but the plan languished. Two years later, after National Castings Company closed its factory on Platt Avenue at East 79th Street, citing high labor costs, Pecyk blamed Mayor Ralph S. Locher and city council president Jack P. Russell for having failed to support his plan, which he implied might have preserved the 850 jobs lost at National Castings. Pecyk also acknowledged that GCGB had "a multicounty problem and cannot give the attention or time to the city of Cleveland."[40] Like "The Best Location in the Nation," which was as far-flung as CEI's service area, the Growth Board's eight-county "Growthland" evolved into another vehicle for managing decline as the prospects for significant industrial recruitment dimmed amid stiffening competition. Both taglines masked the presence of winners and losers and undercut the efforts of those who favored industrial recruitment and retention in the central city. From its peak of 341,700 in 1953, the number of manufacturing jobs in Cuyahoga and Lake Counties plummeted to 273,700 in 1958. With the assistance of GCGB and other industrial boosters, the number grew a modest 12 percent (33,100 jobs) between 1958 and 1967. During the same time frame, however, the suburbs registered a robust net gain of 42,600 (46 percent), while the city of Cleveland recorded a net loss of 9,500 jobs (–5 percent). Of these lost jobs, incidentally, 430 resulted from Sohio's decision in 1964 to close its century-old Cleveland Refinery No. 1 and rebuild in Toledo. The fact that Sohio president Charles Spahr was also GCGB's president demonstrated that economic considerations trumped emotions and loyalties. Even Cleveland's biggest boosters were on some level managing decline even as they promoted growth.[41] The city would have to fight deindustrialization largely on its own, at times battling the Growth Board's abetment of industrial flight to the "crabgrass frontier."[42]

The loss of industry from the central city coincided with the continuing influx of African Americans into Cleveland. Between 1950 and 1965, Cleveland's black population nearly doubled to 279,352, as about 128,000 African Americans arrived from the South and close to 242,000 white residents fled the city, causing the proportion of the black population in the city limits to soar from 16 to 34 percent. As historian Leonard N. Moore has demonstrated, the majority of the newcomers arrived between 1952 and 1958, just as tens of thousands of manufacturing jobs were disappearing.[43] In a letter to the editor of the *Call and Post* in 1959, a black resident of Longwood Community Homes, one of the city's first urban renewal housing developments, commented that "if your name is Jaizebowski, Kazhalov, or if you can with deep Ozark accent, speak of your mountain folk ancestry, you will find a door open to you," but African American workers could not expect the same.[44] Indeed, into the 1960s, the restriction of blacks to the most menial unskilled industrial jobs was widespread in Cleveland.[45] Presaging what scholars would later dub "spatial mismatch," the *Call and Post* editorialized in 1962 that the city's growth coalition, seeing the rising black presence, "read the handwriting on the wall" and "in seeming good conscience advise[d] industry to settle in places like near-rural Geauga County." It asked what Cleveland boosters planned to do about deindustrialization, "besides issuing another bright brochure about 'The Best Location in the Nation.'"[46] To be sure, GCGB's metropolitan spread reflected a range of considerations, among them an understanding of the city proper's well-known shortage of available land for development or expansion as well as industries' preference for modern one-floor plants with ample parking. However, although the available record offers no direct official mention of a racial calculus by GCGB, its staff must have been influenced by industrial leaders' association of the growing black population on the city's East Side with heightened security concerns ranging from vandalism to employees' personal safety.[47]

## Gladstone: "Junk Is the Only New Product"

Just as the chamber of commerce understood the need for greater attentiveness to meeting the needs of industry, the city of Cleveland and CDF—which had favored allocating federal urban renewal grants to accelerate housing redevelopment through the second half of the 1950s—began to realize by the early 1960s that their efforts to lure industry simply by acquiring and reselling central city property were inadequate to stem the tide of industrial decline inside the city limits. As the chamber of commerce was preparing to launch the Growth Board, the city of Cleveland finally acknowledged the need to direct federal subsidies to incentivize industrial development in the central city.

When CDF formed in 1954 and joined with the city administration to seek renewal funding, deteriorating neighborhoods had seemed to pose a more immediate threat to the city's future than either the stagnation of downtown or a lag in central-city industrial development. As previously noted, the Korean War marked a high point in industrial output in Greater Cleveland, and

the arrival of tens of thousands of automotive industry jobs with new investments by Detroit's "Big Three" in the mid-1950s temporarily offset the loss of
factory jobs to other regions. In this context, the decision to undertake a single, relatively small-scale industrial redevelopment project on an experimental
basis initially seemed a sufficient investment. At an assembly of Cleveland
architects in 1953, New York, Chicago, and St. Louis Railroad (Nickel Plate
Road) vice president H. Horton Hampton referred to the paradox of the almost completely African American Gladstone neighborhood two miles southeast of downtown, then designated as "Section L" in the city's 1949 master
plan. Here, he noted, one could find some of the finest food-handling terminals anywhere surrounded by some of the most deteriorated housing. "When
a part of a machine wears out, it must be replaced," he argued. For Hampton,
Cleveland's industrial machine simply needed routine maintenance.[48]

Only after Hampton's insistence did the city agree in 1955 to take more
decisive action in Gladstone, promising to transform what the commission
labeled "a slum" into a "food industry and warehousing district."[49] Gladstone, relabeled "Area O" in the city's revised blueprint for urban renewal,
was a ninety-seven-acre patchwork of "warehouses, junkyards and slum
dwellings" from East 34th to East 55th Streets southward from Woodland
Avenue to the Nickel Plate Road and New York Central Railroad, close to the
city's food-wholesaling district. It was thus a seemingly prime locale for future expansion of food-related industries. Ironically, despite the fact that
thousands of people had once lived adjacent to such businesses near Broadway and Woodland Avenues, planners now claimed that an encroachment
of food businesses, packing factories, and scrap yards made Area O "unfit for
raising children." Removing the scrap yards and housing, they contended,
would create a model park filled with food producers that would entice new
development and strengthen the city's tax duplicate.

Given the growing outcry against the rapid and complete clearance of
Area B (framed by East 30th and 40th Streets and Quincy and Woodland
Avenues), which displaced thousands of residents to make way for the Longwood housing development, Urban Renewal and Housing Development director James M. Lister promised in 1957 that the city would move several
hundred families out of Area O incrementally as replacement housing became
available in Longwood and in Garden Valley.[50] Lister believed that city hall
could acquire property on an as-needed basis, sell it at cost to industrial firms,
and assess the companies for expenses for new streets, sewers, water lines, and
streetlights. Echoing CEI's rose-colored view of industrial growth, Lister appeared sure that Gladstone's central location near railroads and new highways
would make it so attractive that it would fill with factories and warehouses
without federal subsidy.[51] Cleveland's foray into industrial renewal was hardly unique: Philadelphia, Cincinnati, Buffalo, and St. Louis attempted much
larger industrial renewal projects along their own railroads and freeways.[52]

One week before CDF unveiled Erieview in January 1960, the city of Cleveland issued a legal notice in local newspapers requesting proposals for either expansion by industries already located inside Gladstone's boundaries or relocation by firms facing displacement by urban renewal or other publicly funded projects elsewhere in the city. It was already too late for some. In 1958, construction of the Inner Belt Freeway ousted a group of wholesale florists on Woodland Avenue that had long served one of the nation's leading concentrations of greenhouse cut-flower producers.[53] Along with Erieview land acquisitions, freeway projects claimed dozens of manufacturing, warehousing, and wholesaling businesses in the central city. Although twenty-two industrial firms responded with proposals soon after the ad's publication, the property appraisals made four months later were sobering. To break even, the city would have to expend $3 to $3.50 or even more per square foot for acquisition and clearance of properties, far more than the typical $1.50 to $1.75 per square foot that industry usually expected to pay for land. Marvin Bilsky, the president of the Cleveland-Sandusky Brewing Company, which was located inside the renewal area at 2764 East 55th Street, was shocked by the price range and averred that he would rather sell and move out of the city than pay that much. Also, contrary to the oft-repeated assertion that Gladstone was the city's "worst slum," when inspectors finally conducted a thoughtful survey of housing, they found that less than 10 percent of the 460 buildings there were unfit for habitation. Although the rest could be brought up to code through rehabilitation, for years thereafter, the *Plain Dealer* persisted in calling it the city's worst slum.[54] Just as Erieview was born of desperation to reverse the slippage of the 1950s, Gladstone bore the signature of haste. In both cases, city leaders gambled that Cleveland truly was "The Best Location in the Nation," when, in fact, it was clearly not even the best location in the county from an economic standpoint.

The gap between booster hope and economic reality was the space in which the city's urban renewal office discovered it needed Uncle Sam's aid. Lister understood the odds that Gladstone faced. Cleveland had already received $12 million in federal urban renewal commitments and awaited approval of an additional $56 million for renewal projects. Mayor Locher's predecessor, Celebrezze, had hoped to accelerate Gladstone so that it might absorb some of the light industry being driven out of the Erieview urban renewal area in downtown. From there, however, little happened. Cleveland was attempting to administer 6,060 acres of renewal projects citywide, the largest such undertaking in the nation—a point of civic pride until it proved unmanageable. Erieview, which quickly became the flagship of Cleveland's urban renewal enterprise, siphoned funds away from other renewal projects, including some of the amount the city was supposed to allocate to Gladstone as its match for the federal subsidy. At one point in 1962, Mayor Celebrezze tried to pull the plug on Area O clearance even as work proceeded on downtown renewal, but he relented after intense pressure from organized Gladstone property owners, guided by Councilman Warren Gilliam, and GCGB's assurance that several industries were ready to locate in Gladstone if the city could make land available. In 1963, the federal government earmarked almost $4.2 million for Area O, delivering newfound hope for the reindustrialization of the central city.[55] However, city hall's urban renewal officers dragged their feet in assembling industrial properties in Gladstone. With a planned expansion of the Northern Ohio Food Terminal into Gladstone stalled by the city's inaction, Seaway Foods relocated to a new warehouse on twenty-two acres in the suburb of Bedford Heights, eight miles to the southeast.[56]

With Gladstone mired in delay, Lister's office decided to attempt a parallel industrial renewal project one mile to the east near the intersection of the Pennsylvania Railroad and Nickel Plate Road. Originally conceived in the mid-1950s as one of several housing-based urban renewal areas along Woodland Avenue, the East Woodland urban renewal project (Area P) was a forty-six-acre triangular pocket of aging workers' houses and small factories flanked by two cemeteries on the west and separated by railroad tracks from a third cemetery and several large foundries, including National Castings and Van Dorn Iron Works. Its location had led the Federal Housing Administration (FHA) to refuse to insure a residential mortgage there in 1954, but CDF, determined to forge ahead, worked with a group of building and loan associations to finance the low-cost, 148-unit Community Apartments as relocation housing for some of the residents forced out of Area B. The rest of the renewal project was to consist of the rehabilitation of existing houses and new construction.[57] Councilman Bronis Klementowicz condemned the idea of housing "under a railroad bridge" on what he saw as land better situated for industry. Residential redevelopment not only prevented an opportunity to open up precious space for new industry but also ended up driving out what little industry was sandwiched between its small houses, including the Empire Varnish Company on East 76th Street in 1963.[58] After the city's plans had prompted dozens of residents to pour thousands of dollars into renovating their homes, the city suddenly announced in 1964 that East Woodland, due to its proximity to cemeteries and railroads, was not consonant with residential development and should instead become an industrial renewal area. On Lister's pledge that industry was "waiting in line" for land in East Woodland, the City Planning Commission approved amending land use in Area P, but, as in Area O, the change produced no results apart from generating a resumption of hopeful newspaper headlines that made it seem as though the city still had a bright industrial future.[59]

Meanwhile, under pressure to show progress in the listless University-Euclid urban renewal project in Hough, in 1965, Mayor Locher stepped up the city's pace of home demolition, removal of abandoned cars, and cleanup of trash and debris. Five years after the commitment of federal funding, Uni-

**Figure 3.2.** The city government, which warned against dumping in urban renewal areas, turned a blind eye to dumping and even burning debris hauled from other renewal areas into Gladstone, shown here in 1966. (Photo by Glenn Zahn. Cleveland Press Collection, Cleveland State University.)

versity-Euclid had almost nothing to show for the investment beyond university and hospital expansions in University Circle that had subsidized the city's match for federal money under the Housing Act of 1959.[60] As part of his attempt to "make the area brighter," the mayor forbade the burning of debris from wrecked houses in University-Euclid, banishing incineration to Area O. One Gladstone warehouse owner complained that flames from piles of debris hauled in from other renewal areas had leapt more than 150 feet skyward on one occasion, igniting some abandoned homes and prompting firemen to race to the scene (see Figure 3.2). Ironically, even as the city trucked rubble from Hough to Gladstone for disposal, it relocated Gladstone residents whose apartment houses it bought into already overcrowded Hough, where they joined displaced residents driven out of Erieview and other renewal areas. Thus, as pieces of Hough went up in smoke in Gladstone, renewal refugees from Gladstone arrived in Hough just in time to witness its explosive riots in the hot summer of 1966.[61]

Besides its dubious distinction as an emerging city dump, Gladstone began once more to generate proposals that kept alive some hope of reviving its bullish image of the late 1950s. Three unrelated ideas were hatched in the spring of 1965. First, a private firm called the Central Cleveland Corporation approached the city administration with a proposal to purchase Gladstone for use as a trucking freight terminal. Days later, the Norfolk and Western Railroad, having recently acquired the Nickel Plate Road, also indicated it might be interested in taking charge of industrial development in Gladstone.[62] After only a few more days, the Greater Cleveland Growth Corporation (a financial arm of GCGB formed after state legislation opened the way for specially chartered agencies to issue bonds to finance industrial expansion) announced its intent to investigate taking over Gladstone's redevelopment from the city. Even as it eyed Gladstone, however, the Growth Board was also considering purchasing eight hundred to a thousand acres, much of it owned by the Austin Powder Company, an explosives manufacturer, for an industrial park in the firm's company town of Glenwillow, located more than fifteen miles southeast of Area O.[63] None of the three investments came to fruition.

Mayor Locher finally could seemingly point to a kernel of success when American Poultry Company decided in 1965 to move its processing plant to a two-acre site in Gladstone instead of moving to the town of Middlefield in rural Geauga County, some thirty-five miles east of downtown Cleveland.[64] Over the next two years, however, the city still had not given the green light for construction to begin, forcing American Poultry to consider a suburban industrial park in Beachwood as an alternative. While American Poultry mulled its options, the city suffered a further setback when Councilman Leo A. Jackson, the chairman of the city council's urban renewal committee, refused to support the purchase of a tenement building in Gladstone whose owner had illegally converted its nineteen suites to forty-seven and now asked $110,000 to cover what he claimed was $75,000 in remodeling to the building. The building was part of the ten-acre parcel that the city had failed to secure more than a year after promising it for sale to REA Express for a truck terminal, leading REA to go instead to suburban Brook Park.[65] By the winter of 1967, the city had spent more than $5.2 million to acquire more than four hundred properties in the Gladstone area, but the only visible activity was the continued burning of debris from other renewal areas. To make matters worse, when General Electric (GE) left its facility on Woodland Avenue to move into Erieview in downtown Cleveland, it left a large, obsolete building that the city feared it might have to purchase if GE could not lease or sell it.[66] More than a year after signing its first new industrial construction, Gladstone finally got a second commitment, this time from Crayton's Southern Sausage Company, a black-owned meatpacking firm that planned to triple the size of its plant. Leroy Crayton believed in Cleveland, building his sausage plant on East 53rd Street in 1954, soon after Gladstone was originally announced. Thirteen years later, his remained the singular private investment in Gladstone.[67]

A decade of delays in urban renewal exacted a toll in neighborhoods across Cleveland's East Side. Gladstone was no exception. For the merchants in the once-bustling retail node at Woodland Avenue and East 55th Street on the northern edge of the renewal area, the announcement of Area O in the mid-1950s was the equivalent of a death sentence for their businesses. Although the area's largely Jewish population had long since moved eastward into the suburbs and been replaced by African Americans, some businesses, including Bender Shoes, remained until the demolition of thousands of units of housing through urban renewal emptied their neighborhood of customers. One by one, retailers left Woodland and 55th as their clientele departed, leaving behind blocks of boarded-up storefronts.[68] The Woodland–55th Market, which once housed about sixty vendors but had since dwindled to a dozen, went so far as to sue the city for effectively taking its property by forcing out its customer base and eliminating all nearby parking lots.[69] When *Plain Dealer* reporter Donald Sabath surveyed the landscape exactly seven years after the city had advertised Gladstone for proposals, he found nothing remotely approximating the orderly industrial parks that dotted suburbia—only packs of dogs roaming an urban wasteland, littered with junked cars and appliances and dotted with crumbling remnants of the one-time neighborhood: casualties of the city's mismanaged, piecemeal approach to land acquisition. In what was once touted as the pilot project of Cleveland's urban renewal campaign, "junk is the only new product," Sabath concluded.[70]

Hampered by local mismanagement and the challenges of negotiating the labyrinthine bureaucratic complexities of the federal urban renewal program, Gladstone offered little realistic hope of conserving the food-processing industry inside the city limits, let alone stopping the flood tide of broader industrial losses from the central city. Gladstone's ninety-seven-acre renewal area paled in comparison to the nationally recognized Philadelphia Industrial Development Corporation's (PIDC's) reindustrialization enterprise, which benefited from its consolidated city and county's success in placing close to two thousand acres into a land bank.[71] Ninety-seven acres simply was not enough to make more than, at best, a symbolic impact. Yet even as a symbol of Cleveland's ability to retain its industrial base, Gladstone failed. Not only was it too small; it was also surrounded by a "shabby patchwork" of cleared properties dotted by "small islands of three or four homes"—hardly enough to enable much cultivation of a campuslike setting to match that of suburban industrial parks.[72] Unwilling to privilege industrial redevelopment over downtown revitalization, the city government put up little defense in the face of the active efforts by booster organizations and zealous suburban and out-of-state competitors to transplant industry. Unfortunately for Clevelanders, the "Growthland" not only lay mostly outside the city limits but also effectively extended across the Sunbelt, whose enticements contributed to a Cleveland industrial diaspora.[73]

Gladstone's failure was an extreme example nationally, but Cleveland was not alone in its disappointing experiment with industrial renewal. In most cases, cities underestimated the amount of cleared land necessary to attract industry and overestimated the attractiveness of the central city for industry, particularly in light of the abundance of affordable, ready-to-build land that lay on the outer fringes of metropolitan America. Cincinnati's Kenyon-Barr/Queensgate project promised to create an industrial park on 296 acres along Mill Creek, but in the city's haste to show progress, it sold off small parcels to an array of industrial, wholesaling, and distribution firms and ultimately fell far short of producing the sixteen thousand manufacturing jobs originally promised. Likewise, in St. Louis, interminable delays in redeveloping cleared land in the 454-acre Mill Creek Valley project led St. Louisans to dub it "Hiroshima Flats." Even in Philadelphia, which was exceptional in the sheer size of its undertaking, the best that may be said, as Guian McKee has argued, is that PIDC's reindustrialization projects "slowed the progress of deindustrialization."[74]

In the summer of 1964, as Gladstone languished and the food industry abandoned the city little by little, Stouffer's, a longtime Cleveland food business, opened its Top of the Town restaurant on the thirty-eighth floor of the new Erieview Tower. Stouffer's fancy dining rooms sported English, Scotch, French, Italian, and Scandinavian décor to evoke the glamor of international trade that the St. Lawrence Seaway had substantively failed to deliver as a result of local industrial and shipping interests' unwillingness to accept new competitors in the production and carriage of iron ore. Two miles away, the company's frozen-foods division was outgrowing its Woodland Avenue processing plant. Ten years earlier, after patrons of Stouffer's Shaker Square restaurant had urged freezing menu items for takeout, Stouffer Foods had opened its frozen-food processing plant in the newly designated Area O.[75] Stouffer's, which had shown its faith in Cleveland by committing to Erieview at a time when much of the area remained a wasteland of parking lots, also hoped to support Gladstone by expanding beyond its five-acre site there. The company waited as long as it could for the "uncertain politics" of urban renewal to be sorted out. As one Stouffer's executive later recalled, Gladstone's transformation into a virtual city dump ultimately became a deal breaker for a company whose "food process is associated with cleanliness. . . . How could we bring visitors in and say, 'Now isn't our plant wonderful?'"[76] Unable to expand and fed up with its deteriorating surroundings, the company began looking for a new plant site in 1966. James M. Biggar, the vice president of the company's frozen foods division, spotted a bumper sticker that read, "Who Cares About Industry? Solon Does." Soon he was inquiring about a Solon parcel for Stouffer Foods and selected a forty-acre site.[77] While Cleve-

land allocated only 143 of its 6,060 acres of urban renewal projects for industry, after World War II, Solon had rezoned some 2,000 acres for industrial
use. In the 1960s, as Cleveland's industrial climate seemed to worsen with
each passing year, "Solon became something of a suburban Klondike for
industry." It also remained almost completely white, with only a single African American family in residence as late as the mid-1960s. If Solon was
Cleveland's "Klondike," Gladstone, in the eyes of one *Call and Post* reporter,
was its "Ghost Town."[78]

# 4

# Believe in Cleveland

*Carl B. Stokes and the Struggle*
*to Redeem the City*

On the afternoon of July 24, 1968, following a night of violence in which eleven people died in a gun battle between police and black nationalists in Cleveland's Glenville neighborhood, Mayor Carl B. Stokes held a press conference to announce his decision to reassign white policemen and leave their African American counterparts to work alongside National Guardsmen to help quell the disorder. That night, black policemen manned twenty-one patrol cars in support of neighborhood leaders who worked to calm tensions inside a cordoned area that included all of Hough and Glenville. Looting and arson continued, but the area suffered no further casualties. Although the mayor permitted white policemen to return to Glenville the next night, the decision to interfere with the police, he later recalled, "meant the end of Carl Stokes as hero." Indeed, Stokes's response to the Glenville incident crushed any illusions of a unified city and removed whatever latitude his political opponents had allowed him to chart a new course for Cleveland.[1]

The city's second destructive major riot in three summers also dampened hopes that Cleveland was embarking on a bright new future in which civic activism, inspired by the nation's first elected black mayor of a major American city, could bring transformative change amid the national urban crisis. Just three months before the violence, Stokes had elevated such hopes by launching *Cleveland: NOW!*—a ten-year, $1.5-billion program to remake the city. However, not even Stokes's charisma and ambition could overcome the inertia of municipal politics, the drag exerted by suburbanization and economic restructuring, and the devastating blow of the Glenville violence. Like previous chapters, this chapter demonstrates a continuing tension between decline and revitalization. Focusing on Stokes's two mayoral terms (November 1967 to

November 1971), it draws together three preoccupations of the city's growth coalition—the state of downtown, neighborhoods, and industry—and examines how Stokes managed these concerns in the context of his *Cleveland: NOW!* program. This four-year period also saw concern about urban image begin to pivot from being an unsettling by-product of Cleveland's emerging urban crisis to a vexing preoccupation in itself. More than booster slogans placed in national publications, boosterish reporting in local dailies, or comments made by Clevelanders responding to civic successes or failures, the invocation of image found its way into municipal policies packaged with an eye toward reframing Clevelanders' perception of their changing metropolitan area. This chapter shows how Stokes—himself an embodiment of civic hope—used symbolic actions to manage the urban crisis and public perceptions of a changing Cleveland. Stokes might even be considered a prototype of the "messiah mayor," a term that historian Jon C. Teaford coined to describe the "new wave" of municipal executives of the 1970s and after who "preached a message of revival."[2] Stokes's mayoralty disrupted the city's smug, ossified leadership and heralded the rise of a politics of image that would mark the coming decade.

## "A Doomed City—Destined for Oblivion"

The Hough riots in 1966 deeply scarred not only Cleveland's most troubled neighborhood but also the city itself. The riots brought to a head years of festering racial antagonism that had plagued the city's labor unions, public schools, and urban renewal program. Mayor Ralph S. Locher had managed to weather the first two challenges, but Hough's eruption hastened a referendum on his leadership. His combative response—blaming outside agitators—did nothing to calm the anger that many African Americans and, increasingly, the business establishment felt toward a callous, indifferent city hall. As long as business prospects were good, suburbanites who dominated the growth coalition were content to cede city hall to the likes of Romanian-born Locher, a man who understood and abetted fears and aversions that typified Cleveland's "cosmopolitan wards." After January 1967, however, when the U.S. Department of Housing and Urban Development (HUD) served notice to the Locher administration that it would withhold further funds from Cleveland's urban renewal program, the city's plight provoked handwringing in the business community and a barrage of stinging criticism from local and national media. The Cleveland Electric Illuminating Company (CEI), ever defending "The Best Location in the Nation," sought to counter negative press by placing ten pages of ads in the July issue of *Fortune* in which it extolled the city's virtues, including its universities, museums, and the revered Cleveland Orchestra, as reasons why Cleveland ranked fourth nationally as home to blue-chip headquarters. Hoping to draw a different kind of response at the local level, Cleveland's daily newspapers now labeled Locher "a civic disaster."[3]

Perhaps the most damning assessment came in the John Skow article that appeared in the July 29, 1967, issue of the *Saturday Evening Post*, "The Question in the Ghetto: Can Cleveland Escape Burning?" Characterizing Hough as "a 50-block-by-10-block infection," Skow portrayed the entire city as being in crisis—a place, he noted, that the poor now called "the mistake on the lake." The reporter laid blame for Cleveland's condition not merely at the doorstep of city hall. The problem, he argued, came from a quarter century of "non-mayors" who were "elected not to lead and especially not to tax." The same tax-averse white ethnic constituents who opposed big downtown projects, such as the subway and Erieview, similarly contested the cost of maintaining basic city services, including code enforcement in struggling areas, such as Hough. Skow concluded that Cleveland's problem was rooted in the fact that it had devolved into "a loose and rancorous federation of walled villages." Neither suburbanites nor so-called cosmos (ethnic whites) inside the city limits wanted anything to do with Central, Hough, and Glenville, rendering this roughly eight-square-mile area a ghetto with "gates barred from the outside."[4]

The campaign to unseat Locher in the Democratic primary included bids by former Lakewood, Ohio, mayor Frank P. Celeste and Ohio state senator Stokes, the great-grandson of slaves and a onetime resident of the Outhwaite Homes public housing project. Seth C. Taft, the grandson of President William Howard Taft and an attorney at Jones, Day, Reavis and Pogue, prepared to face the winner of the Democratic primary in the November general election. Following a literally and symbolically well-worn path that previous suburbanites had taken to "save" the city, Celeste moved one block across the Lakewood border into a Cleveland apartment building, while Taft left tony Pepper Pike for a small house one block inside Cleveland from the Shaker Heights border. On the campaign trail, Locher remarked condescendingly that his opponents were "aware of the crabgrass and cricket situation of the suburbs." He characterized Celeste and Taft as "carpetbaggers" who "have been more concerned with Lakewood and Pepper Pike than Cleveland."[5]

These opponents, nevertheless, knew enough to identify Cleveland's problems and attribute them to the mayor, and the local press amplified their message. Celeste conjured the city's beleaguered image in a campaign advertisement. Speaking of Mayor Locher, the ad observed:

His 5-year record is all around you. It's in dirty, dimly-lit, unsafe streets and in decaying neighborhoods. It's in our sagging population figures. It's in the conversations and the faces of those people who haven't moved to the suburbs—yet. It's in businesses and factories that have pulled out. It's in 6000 empty, trash-covered acres of

urban renewal land, worthless as tax producers. It's in broken promises, unfulfilled plans, secret meetings and do-nothing committees.
His record is all around you. Look.[6]

Although it endorsed Stokes, the *Plain Dealer* editorial board agreed with
Celeste and situated Locher at the end of a string of caretaker mayors. It argued that because of their indifference, "a lot of old chickens have come home
to roost—deteriorating neighborhoods, sagging police forces, drooping
downtown business," and, perhaps worst of all, "a creeping grayness."[7] Not
only was Cleveland suffering from the urban crisis; it had become dull and
worn out—*gray*.

In a city whose population was now about two-thirds black following
decades of white flight, the incumbent Mayor Locher did his best to hold on
to white ethnic support. He had some help from Cuyahoga County Democratic party chairman Albert S. Porter. Ever controversial, Porter, who had led
the crusade against a downtown subway in the 1950s, now sent a missive
urging white voters to turn out for the October 3 Democratic primary to "save
Cleveland" from black control by reelecting Locher.[8] But Locher appeared
increasingly out of touch. As he denied his opponents' worthiness to seek office as true Clevelanders, Locher defended his record by invoking concerns
about the city's image. Referring to a speech from a year before in which he
had urged citizens to accentuate the positive rather than denigrate their city
for its problem, the mayor dismissed negative national coverage as "slander-
ous attacks and downright lies." "Cleveland was depicted as a doomed city—
destined for oblivion," but, Locher insisted, such smears "made the people of
this city mad and aroused a new spirit and a new determination to show the
world that Cleveland plays second fiddle to no one."[9]

Indeed, negative reportage on Cleveland aroused new determination, but
not with the results Locher wanted. Two years earlier, Stokes had narrowly
missed election as mayor. This time, he enjoyed strong backing from a committed cadre of "housewives from high-toned Shaker Heights, lawyers and
businessmen, college professors and young people . . . who help[ed] direct an
army of Negro volunteers." Many in the city's business establishment seemed
to regard Stokes as "insurance" against the recurrence of violence, such as
that in Hough in 1966.[10] Determined not to be seen as only a candidate for
blacks or a protector of business interests, he struck a chord with many voters as he circulated widely throughout the city in the months before the
Democratic primary. Stokes's tone and rhetoric were from the outset calculated to mobilize a new "spirit" and "determination." Unlike Locher, Stokes
situated these impulses as reactions to real failures rather than merely to
accusations from afar. In a *Plain Dealer* ad to launch his campaign, Stokes
proclaimed that his slogan would be "I believe in Cleveland." He called for a
"renaissance, a resurgency [*sic*] of faith in ourselves, a renewal of spirit and

morale as well as a renewal of buildings and other physical facilities." Stokes said his campaign had "no room" for "unclean peddlers of bigotry and hatred"—only "room for everyone who *believes* in Cleveland."[11] Stokes won the Democratic primary, taking more than 52 percent of the vote. Locher captured more than 43 percent, while Celeste managed only 4 percent. Just over one month later, on November 7, 1967, Stokes overcame the Republican challenger Taft in the general election by a razor-thin 1 percent margin.[12]

## "Cleveland: NOW!" as an Image-Rebuilding Tool

As Teaford has noted, Stokes stood among a small cohort of dynamic, youthful newcomers to municipal politics in the 1960s. Like other so-called glamorboy mayors—notable among them John Lindsay of New York, Jerome Cavanaugh of Detroit, and Kevin White of Boston—the vigorous, engaging Stokes contrasted sharply with his "dreary" predecessor.[13] Stokes's arrival in office just over sixteen months after the Hough riots, along with the reorganization of the chamber of commerce and the Greater Cleveland Growth Board (GCGB) into a new, unified Greater Cleveland Growth Association (GCGA) just over a month later, produced a sense of impending renaissance in Cleveland. In the words of one of his staffers, Stokes was not afraid to "pull the covers off the problems of the city . . . to let Cleveland know that it was not the 'Best Location in the Nation,'" but he also offered a restorative vision.[14] Stokes had amassed tremendous political capital by the time he took office. As just one example, in the winter of 1968, a local public relations firm spent almost $57,000 of its own funds to launch a "Brag a Little about Cleveland" promotional campaign to encourage Clevelanders to maintain an upbeat mood about their city. Although Stokes politely ducked participation, the campaign captured the imaginations of many. General Electric's (GE's) Lamp Division at Nela Park in East Cleveland adopted the "Brag a Little" campaign, while a Lakewood woman sent Mayor Stokes a self-composed "Brag a Little" song.[15]

Indeed, a new light seemed to burn in the city following Stokes's election, and it shone like a beacon throughout the country. The mayor's executive assistant, Henry Matt, took pleasure in the fact that wherever he traveled, people now showed real interest in Cleveland.[16] However, Stokes quickly found that it was easier to articulate a compelling civic vision than it was to implement it. The new mayor faced high hopes for immediate signs of progress but had considerable work ahead just to fill his cabinet with new administrators. By January, Stokes was exhausted and slipped away for a two-week vacation in the U.S. Virgin Islands. The city's struggle to clear its streets in a major snowstorm that hit during Stokes's absence brought grumbles that he was already falling short of his promise.[17]

Despite his early challenges, Stokes filled his cabinet with young staffers whose energy matched his own, notably thirty-six-year-old Richard R.

Green, whom the mayor named community development director. Within two weeks of Stokes's appointment of Green, who had served as the assistant to Boston's urban renewal director Ed Logue, HUD secretary Robert C. Weaver announced a "thaw" on funds for Cleveland urban renewal projects that had been frozen for more than a year.[18] Although maverick journalist Roldo Bartimole questioned the decision to restart urban renewal by building new high-rise housing aimed at graduate and medical students, institutional employees, and retirees at the corner of Euclid Avenue and Mayfield Road in University Circle, the action was a huge boost to Stokes, who had campaigned on a promise to restore Cleveland's commitment to building and rehabilitating housing.[19]

Stokes also found opportunity in tragedy. In the days following the assassination of Martin Luther King Jr. in Memphis on April 4, 1968, black leaders worked to maintain calm in Cleveland, in contrast to outbreaks of violence in many American cities.[20] The mayor hoped the city's success in avoiding rioting might generate momentum for effecting major community improvements of the sort he had pledged to make. Seizing on an idea presented to him by Irving Kriegsfeld, a local housing advocate and later the director of the Cleveland Metropolitan Housing Authority (CMHA), Stokes approached key figures in the city's business community with Kriegsfeld's plan for a community-wide drive to tackle Cleveland's most pressing problems.[21]

Such an initiative required a major public relations and fundraising plan. With a $68,100 grant from the Greater Cleveland Associated Foundation, Stokes hired William Silverman, a *Cleveland News* reporter and prominent public relations counsel who had run Taft's mayoral campaign and worked on Nixon's 1960 presidential campaign, to manage city hall's communications with citizens. Charged with packaging Stokes's major new initiative, Silverman chose the name *Cleveland: NOW!* to convey the sense that the city was making visible progress.[22] GCGA president George J. Grabner promised business backing to raise $10 million in corporate support for a long-range plan to leverage federal funding. Harris-Intertype (formerly Harris-Seybold) chairman George S. Dively and Pickands Mather chairman John Sherwin agreed to cochair the fundraising drive, while businessman George M. Steinbrenner III led a concurrent effort to raise another $1.25 million from the broader community.[23]

With full cooperation from the city's major television and radio stations, Silverman staged a dramatic introduction to *Cleveland: NOW!* on prime-time local television, followed by numerous short ads and radio spots. In the documentary, Stokes stood in Erieview Plaza to describe his vision for downtown renewal, ducked into a poolroom in the Central neighborhood to comment on job training, and shot baskets with kids in a Near West Side schoolyard to promote his recreation program. Tellingly, the latter scene included "boys and girls, white and Negro; Appalachian, central European, Puerto Rican, Mexi-

can."[24] Implicit was the notion that the mayor saw the future in that schoolyard: a diverse but unified Cleveland that stood in stark contrast to the
fragmented city that had erupted in riots fewer than two years earlier. As part
of the largest promotion of civic revitalization in the city's history up to its
time, Silverman also produced more than three hundred thousand pieces of
*Cleveland: NOW!* collateral material, ranging from buttons to bumper stickers. In the first two months following the campaign's launch, Dively and Sherwin raised $4 million in corporate support. Schoolchildren collected coins in
mason jars and developed small fundraising projects. A prominent couple in
suburban Bratenahl, moved by the documentary, gave $1 million to the com-
munity drive. As future Cleveland Foundation officer Timothy Armbruster
wrote that summer, *Cleveland: NOW!* possessed great psychological value:
"The city has a new outlook—a feeling exists that perhaps the city can be
saved after all."[25]

 *Cleveland: NOW!* was carefully crafted to remold Clevelanders' perception of the city from the grass roots to the business elite and to get them to
buy into the program, literally and figuratively. The morning after its unveiling, Stokes's program commanded the entire front page of the *Plain Dealer*,
including a large editorial cartoon titled "Pedestal for a City," in which Cleveland's downtown skyscrapers rose atop a Greek column representing *Cleveland: NOW!* The lion's share of the program's budget was earmarked for
building or rehabilitating housing and redeveloping downtown. More than a
bricks-and-mortar approach to revitalization, however, the program reflected
Stokes's understanding that construction alone could not fashion a total solution to community needs, so his plan also included significant allocations for
health and human services in neighborhoods and job training and provision
programs.[26]

 With Stokes's characteristic flair, *Cleveland: NOW!* also aimed to overcome a sense of civic stagnation. Since many of its goals would require
years—and massive federal funding—to fulfill, the administration learned
to use *Cleveland: NOW!* to brand even those initiatives that did not draw
directly from the program's funds, including some begun during the Locher
administration. In this respect, *Cleveland: NOW!* was as much package as
policy. Unlike in previous years, when city hall or the private sector launched
many varied projects, none of them capable of offering more than limited
answers to the city's problems, *Cleveland: NOW!* bundled otherwise unrelated undertakings, casting them as a total community drive that married
public and private interests. In fact, the mayor affixed the *Cleveland: NOW!*
imprint to a number of small-scale cosmetic or stopgap measures calculated
to produce a sense of excitement and progress.[27]

 Although the Glenville shootout surely deflated Stokes's popularity and
cast a shadow over *Cleveland: NOW!*, it was only one of several challenges
under which the administration labored. In the months that followed the

Glenville conflict, opposition to Stokes's initiatives hardened in the city council, which tightened its hold on the municipal purse and prevented many programs' enabling legislation from coming to the floor for a vote. The council even undercut his efforts to raise the income tax and eliminate rebates on taxes owed by suburbanites employed in the city. Meanwhile, Cleveland also suffered a series of blows to civic pride: In Playhouse Square, Sterling-Lindner closed two months after the Glenville shootout, depriving the city of its grandest Christmas tree, and a row of ornate movie palaces went dark in 1969, as the suburbs increasingly dominated shopping and entertainment. In the summer of 1969, the national media elevated an otherwise unremarkable fire on the polluted Cuyahoga River to a visceral marker of Cleveland's decline. Weeks later, Euclid Beach Park, a beloved lakefront amusement park, also closed—a victim of disinvestment, racial conflict, and white flight.[28] Along with the Glenville incident, this string of hits to the city's image reinforced the need for Stokes to rely on symbolic actions and an expansive approach to quantifying the accomplishments of his program. The remainder of this chapter explores the ways in which Stokes's *Cleveland: NOW!* civic revitalization effort, broadly defined, accentuated symbolic actions in an effort to manage the mood of citizens in a city beset by high inner-city unemployment, tens of thousands of substandard housing units, and a host of unmet basic human needs. As one *Washington Post* reporter suggested in 1969, even holding the line on the city's slide might be cause for hope.[29]

## "A Spectacular Little Chicago": Rebuilding the Downtown Experience

When Central National Bank announced in September 1966 that it would leave its scattered offices in the Midland and Rockefeller Buildings to erect a twenty-three-story headquarters on the southwest corner of Superior Avenue and East 9th Street, the news must have been a tremendous relief for Mayor Locher. The patchwork of desolate parking lots called Erieview and the burned-out, post-riot Hough neighborhood were symbols of Locher's urban renewal failures. Although Central National was building just outside Erieview's boundaries, it answered longtime complaints that local banks were not investing in the renewal of their own city, and it offered a needed diversion from city hall's quagmire on the East Side. By the time Central National broke ground a year later, the *Plain Dealer* was so fed up with the mayor that it did not bother to quote him at the ceremony. If the Central National tower was too little, too late to rehabilitate Locher's battered reputation, its completion, as David and Richard Stradling have argued, provided an opportunity for Stokes to bask in the glow of a renewed commitment to rebuilding downtown.[30]

Days after Mayor Stokes's election, the *Plain Dealer* editorialized that many hopeful locals "expect him to transform Cleveland into a spectacular little Chicago."[31] Indeed, Stokes became very adept with shovels and scissors, thanks to his many opportunities to break ground or cut ribbons during Cleveland's first sustained period of downtown construction in nearly forty years. By the summer of 1969, a spate of new downtown projects—including starts of a twenty-nine-story Cleveland Trust tower and the seventeen-story Investment Plaza; modernization of the turn-of-the-century, sixteen-story Schofield Building into Euclid-Ninth Tower; and active work to secure additional office towers in or near Erieview—emboldened the mayor to boast of his success. Although some projects, such as the Bond Court office and hotel complex and the thousand-unit Park Centre apartments, predated the Stokes era in their conception and postdated it in their long-delayed completion, the mayor could point to more than the many physical markers of Erieview's progress. He could also point to such successes as convincing Fortune 500 chemical giant Diamond Shamrock to commit to Erieview for its new twenty-three-story headquarters tower—the first downtown construction project undertaken by a black developer (Alonzo Wright).[32] On the day after the Apollo 11 lunar landing, Stokes suggested collecting rock samples in Erieview for analysis "to determine why life did not exist here to this extent under previous administrations." Looking back on Stokes's first year in office, the *Plain Dealer* commented, "If Cleveland's skyline does not look like New York's, at least ground has been broken and a significant start has been made toward a new downtown."[33]

Even as Stokes capitalized on HUD's restoration of funding to complete Erieview's first phase, his administration also sought to counter the longtime complaint that downtown was "drab and dreary," especially after the five o'clock rush of office workers to their suburban homes. On the heels of an 18 percent decline in downtown retail sales between 1954 and 1965, downtown lost its third department store and its four largest theaters in 1968 and 1969 and also faced growing safety concerns following the Glenville shootout and a spate of brazen downtown assaults and robberies.[34] Stokes understood the importance of not only pursuing millions of dollars of federal funding to respond to major problems, such as unemployment and abandoned housing, but also staying attentive to smaller actions that might generate a sense of movement in the city. In keeping with his reliance on personal charisma, Stokes extended his showmanship to low-cost, high-impact initiatives to combat the continuing erosion of the central business district. In fact, he made the downtown experience a key part of his public pitch for *Cleveland: NOW!* In his televised promotional documentary, Stokes spoke of a visiting writer from the French monthly magazine *Réalités*, who commented how deserted Cleveland's streets were in the early evening. The mayor talked of transforming the Mall into a "people place" and creating

Cleveland's answer to New Orleans's French Quarter along the Cuyahoga River on downtown's edge.[35]

Stokes's strategy reflected the imagination of his new properties director Edward J. (Ed) Baugh, who had left the Peace Corps to join the administration. Baugh, who was responsible for parks and other city-owned properties, believed that downtown needed to offer more leisure and recreation opportunities. His actions helped the Stokes administration emulate New York City mayor Lindsay's "Fun City" concerts and festivals in public parks, a trend that many cities would follow in the 1970s.[36] From the front steps of city hall, Baugh could glimpse a grassy corner of the Mall. Originally intended as the heart of a Daniel Burnham–designed "City Beautiful" assemblage of Beaux-Arts public buildings anchored by a large railroad station on its lake-facing side, the space had languished since Oris and Mantis Van Sweringen's massive redevelopment of the south side of Public Square into Cleveland Union Terminal in the 1920s. In the late 1950s, as detailed in Chapter 1, municipal officials had pushed unsuccessfully for convention-oriented developments that included amenities to excite not only tourists but also Clevelanders who had all but written off the Mall as, in the words of one civic booster, "a dark hole in the center of Cleveland, frequented by undesirable elements."[37]

The Leonard C. Hanna Jr. Fund had enabled the installation of ten large fountains on the Mall, which were ceremoniously activated by an electric signal relayed via satellite by President Lyndon B. Johnson from Atlantic City, New Jersey, following the 1964 Democratic National Convention.[38] Despite the Mall's augmented beauty, Baugh believed it remained too much of a place to see rather than do. Instead of relying on a large building to furnish a crowd, Baugh trusted the power of good public spaces. He imagined piping in music during the daytime; enlivening the fountains with multicolored floodlights at night; staging "funfests" featuring outdoor cafés, surrey rides, and band concerts; and even stocking trout in the fountain pool to delight children—in short, a little Tivoli on the Mall. First, however, his department set up a stand that sold sandwiches, salads, and soups next to the Hanna Fountains. On its first day in June 1968, the café served more than six hundred diners and, according to a newspaper editorial, was "another step in . . . changing the city's grim, all-business image."[39] The administration also took further steps to transform the Mall, sponsoring summertime events such as "Mall-A-Rama," which included games, crafts, sports, and model boat races in the reflecting pool, and "Fun Day on the Mall," a rock and R&B music festival that attracted a racially integrated audience (see Figure 4.1).[40]

Baugh's effort to make the Mall a fun place extended to the city's long-derelict riverfront. Even before the notorious ignition of an oil slick on the surface of the polluted Cuyahoga River cast Cleveland as an exemplar of the environmental aspect of the urban crisis, Stokes and Baugh recognized and

**Figure 4.1.** The third annual Fun Day on the Mall, sponsored by the Mayor's Council on Youth Opportunity on August 14, 1970, featured R&B acts headlined by Edwin Starr. (PG 429, Carl Stokes Photographs, The Western Reserve Historical Society, Cleveland, Ohio.)

supported early steps to reinvent the Flats, a rough-edged riverbank assemblage of docks, warehouses, and dive bars plied by sailors and steelworkers. Ex-vaudevillian Harry Fagan had taken a chance in the summer of 1964 when he opened the first new dining establishment in the Flats in decades. Located along the river on West 11th Street, Fagan's Beacon House featured a New Orleans–style jazz band and "New Year's Eve every weekend," which began to draw a younger clientele. When Fagan and other businessmen, including proprietors of new entertainment spots, including Diamond Jim's and Pickle Bill's, formed the Old Flats Association in the winter of 1968, Baugh assured them that the Stokes administration would help make the Flats "the total entertainment center for the city." That spring, the Cleveland Convention and Visitors Bureau (CCVB) ran its first advertisement for the Flats. CCVB compared the Flats to Chicago's Old Town, St. Louis's Gaslight Square, and "similar turn-of-the-century flash-back locales," adding that it was just down the hill from the nation's sixth-largest concentration of retail merchandise. True to its word, city hall added way-finding signage, installed nostalgic gas lamps along West 11th Street, and partnered with the Old Flats Association to host a "grand opening" of the Flats in June, at which Mayor Stokes ceremoniously rededicated the site of city founder Moses Cleaveland's

1796 landing.[41] At last, it seemed that Cleveland might become a "Fun City." *Plain Dealer* columnist George E. Condon, with his characteristic curmudgeonly humor, called the Flats a visible departure from a city in decline. According to Condon, many locals remarked that the Flats felt like another city, a sentiment he confirmed, adding that nowhere else was like "drab and dreary" downtown Cleveland, a place so depressing that it would "drive anybody to drink."[42]

In addition to its efforts to enliven downtown through amenities and events on the Mall and in the Flats, the Stokes administration hoped to cultivate a greater sense of nighttime security and excitement in the traditional downtown shopping district. In 1953, Cleveland, long a pioneer in electric illumination, had won recognition as the lighting center of the world. Since that time, the city had fallen behind advances in lighting technology. A national rise in urban crime rates in the 1960s put pressure on municipal leaders to respond with brighter streetlights. Mayor Locher had initiated such a program in late 1965 in Hough, but, after the rape and murder of a Cleveland Orchestra chorister near Wade Lagoon on an evening in November 1966, he redirected the project to University Circle to reassure rattled suburbanites. Mayor Stokes revived Locher's streetlight upgrade project in the spring of 1968. It became a focus for his utilities director, Ben S. Stefanski II. The son of a prominent banker in Cleveland's heavily Polish Ward 13, twenty-nine-year-old Stefanski left suburban Brecksville for an apartment at the Chesterfield, a move that facilitated his long workdays at city hall and served as a token of faith in downtown. Although he is remembered more for devising and carrying out a novel initiative to create chlorinated "swimming pools" in cordoned sections of polluted Lake Erie near popular beaches, Stefanski also secured cooperation between the city and CEI to change forty-five thousand streetlights citywide from incandescent to mercury-vapor bulbs and to install ultrabright Lucalox bulbs, developed at the GE Lamp Division's Nela Park laboratories, on key downtown streets.[43]

In contrast to Locher's unsuccessful streetlight plan, which had started in the service of token rehabilitation in an urban slum on the brink of exploding, Stokes's lighting campaign was a sweeping, successful, and relatively easily accomplished aspect of *Cleveland: NOW!* As Stefanski later reflected, "We determined that we wanted to change all these lights because this was something visual" to enable "taxpayers [to] see where their dollars were going." Stefanski pointed out that the Stokes administration, unlike its predecessor, undertook the initiative "prior to the big law-and-order cry" rather than in reaction to a crime. However, Stokes's lighting effort was similar to Locher's in a key respect: It showcased a part of the city seen as needing a boost.[44] Carried out before most of the city's neighborhoods got their new lights, this most symbolic part of Stokes's lighting campaign came in response to the closing of Playhouse Square's four largest theaters in quick succession in 1968–1969 but should also be viewed against the backdrop of growing concerns about downtown crime, the impact of two major riots, and the impending mayoral election.

By mid-October, the utilities department had activated some four hundred new Lucalox streetlamps along Euclid Avenue from Public Square to East 55th Street. Suggesting a persistent tension between decline and revitalization, Condon remarked that, while the new lights gave hope for renaissance, they also exposed the condition of downtown: "Now we see the dingy condition of the Square. . . . Sometimes it is painful to lift the shadows."[45] Those shadows did more than hide downtown decay; they also provided an imagined cover for rising crime. Although downtown remained statistically one of the safest parts of the city, it became a symbolic battleground for the larger issue of crime in the city. On October 30, 1969, the same day that Stokes was scheduled to dedicate the new downtown streetlights and just five days before the mayoral election, his Republican challenger, Ralph J. Perk, the son of Czech immigrants and a longtime city council representative of Ward 13 "cosmos," issued a campaign statement in which he decried downtown's lack of security. Pandering to racial fears among white ethnic Clevelanders, Perk urged voters to drive downtown with their car doors locked and observe the "iron grilles on the store windows." "This," he said, "is Cleveland: NOW! in 1969, after two years of Carl Stokes." Perk warned that, if unchecked, the crime problem that had originated in the East Side ghettos and spread into downtown would "leap across the Cuyahoga River to the West Side like a tidal wave."[46]

While Perk was conjuring a dark specter of hoodlums running unchecked through the city, Stokes officiated at a special evening "Turn-On Salute" ceremony at Euclid Avenue and East 13th Street that was staged by the recently formed 9-18 Corporation, a group of businessmen concerned about the closure of Playhouse Square's theaters. After accepting a miniature replica of the first Edison light bulb (three hundred of which reportedly equaled the lumens of a single Lucalox bulb), the mayor flipped a ceremonial switch to dedicate a relit downtown. The relighting bolstered public confidence, burnished Stokes's image, and provided bragging rights in a city that had had few new superlatives for a while. With the backing of GE, Stokes proclaimed that Cleveland had the brightest downtown in the United States, and he urged reinvestment in Playhouse Square.[47] Although the Lucalox upgrades did not extend to other downtown streets, their debut had served its symbolic purpose.

Soon after dedicating a brightened Euclid Avenue, the Stokes administration unveiled another *Cleveland: NOW!* downtown initiative calculated to create a sense of new energy. Since the 1930 opening of Cleveland Union Terminal, which had provided a single railroad and rail transit hub for the city, downtown backers and transit officials had tried repeatedly to offer loop bus service to distribute riders. In the mid-1950s, as retailing came under greater stress, Halle's had inaugurated free buses from Public Square to its Playhouse Square store during its long, ultimately futile wait for a downtown subway. Although Cleveland was reportedly the national model for downtown loop bus service, Cleveland Transit System (CTS) officials believed that the service was underutilized and therefore opted to double its fare to twenty cents in 1969.[48] Mayor Stokes saw in the loop bus an opportunity to bolster downtown revitalization while avoiding accusations from working-class neighborhoods that he was showing favoritism to downtown merchants, which had proven fatal for the subway plan a decade earlier.

That spring, the city of Cleveland, in cooperation with CTS, secured a $2.5-million federal grant to subsidize new bus loops in two phases: first to connect inner-city residents with industrial employment centers, and then to enhance downtown service, which Stokes called "a maze for the casual rider." The resulting Cleveland Transportation Action Program (CTAP), billed as part of *Cleveland: NOW!* and dubbed a national pilot, jettisoned its original idea of connecting the Near West Side with the industrialized suburb of Solon in favor of two routes that linked Glenville, Hough, Central, and Tremont with Jones and Laughlin (J&L) Steel's factory in the Flats and Metropolitan General Hospital in the Clark-Fulton neighborhood.[49] In time for the Christmas shopping season, CTAP also unveiled the "Santa Loop," a ten-cent loop bus service. With his characteristic flair, Mayor Stokes promoted his resuscitation of downtown by inaugurating the holiday shopping season from behind the steering wheel of a Santa Loop bus parked in front of Erieview Tower.[50] Inexplicably, the Santa Loop competed with CTS's preexisting twenty-cent loop buses and Halle's free bus; as a result, CTAP arrived at the unremarkable conclusion that downtown businesses should subsidize regular loop bus service to restore the ten-cent fare. Apart from the fact that the Santa Loop accomplished little of substance, its festive theme, complete with stops marked by large candles, represented a readily attained and visible piece of *Cleveland: NOW!* that had the potential to attract families with children to counter the city's image of danger.[51]

Continuing its efforts to appear actively involved in the renaissance of downtown, the Stokes administration parlayed the loop bus recommendations into a broader program for reenergizing downtown. Working with GCGA and representative downtown interests, the Stokes administration formed the Downtown Consortium in January 1970, billing it as the city's first public-private campaign to coordinate downtown revitalization. The move evoked earlier private-sector attempts in 1960 and 1966 to form a cohesive downtown organization in what remained a fragmented downtown establishment. In addition to improving loop bus service, the Downtown Consortium's key objectives included supporting the 9-18 Corporation's efforts to revive Playhouse Square and beautifying Superior Avenue by re-

planting its center median strip.[52] In September 1970, the Downtown
Consortium also sponsored a downtown festival. Such events had been held
regularly in the early 1960s before lapsing amid growing pessimism about
the state of downtown. Unlike earlier festivals that arose from merchant
interest, this one originated as part of Baugh's ongoing effort to "make
downtown people-oriented."[53]

The festival also provided an opportunity to study another old idea:
turning Euclid Avenue into a pedestrian mall. The 1959 downtown plan had
urged thinking of the street in terms of a shopping center anchored by department stores at Public Square and Playhouse Square and using a subway
and a covered sidewalk lined by continuous display windows to encourage
the circulation of shoppers between the anchors. Similarly, the 1965 downtown plan had recommended the use of landscaping, street furniture, and
coordinated awnings and false fronts on buildings to unify the street visu-
ally. The short-lived closure of Euclid Avenue to traffic during the 1970 festival did not produce a permanent reengineering of the city's main street, but
under Baugh's influence, Clevelanders caught another glimpse of a growing
national affinity for festive urban spaces, such as Victor Gruen's pedestrian
mall in downtown Kalamazoo, Michigan, and Lawrence Halprin's reimag-
ined Ghirardelli chocolate factory in San Francisco, as reactions to downtown decline.[54]

## "Band-Aids on the Wounds": Managing Deindustrialization

The compactness, central location, and symbolic value of downtown made
achieving visible improvement less daunting than the prospect of trying to
demonstrate progress against deindustrialization. While downtown occupied scarcely more than one square mile, contained the city's greatest concentration of offices and stores, and attracted more workers than any other
part of the metropolitan area, Cleveland's industrial landscape sprawled
along multiple corridors, including along the river, lake, and multiple railroads, and dotted neighborhoods throughout the city. Apart from its largest
steel mills and auto plants, Cleveland had few manufacturing facilities that
attained singular prominence. Moreover, actions taken to attract or retain
all but the largest factories seldom provided much psychological lift. With
little developable land and minimal latitude to offer competitive incentives,
the Stokes administration surely understood that fighting deindustrialization was likely to be among the more thankless tasks of *Cleveland: NOW!*
However, if the mayor and his staff did not clearly outperform previous public and private ventures in recruitment and retention, they did manage to
reframe the effort as one that might benefit from the resumption of urban

renewal and innovative workforce development as tools for serving industrial needs.

As seen in Chapter 3, private-sector efforts to promote manufacturing growth, such as those by GCGB, often conflicted with the municipal need to preserve jobs inside the city limits. Although those responsible for shaping urban renewal priorities in Cleveland never fully embraced aggressive measures to serve industry, they did allocate acreage for light industry in Gladstone (Area O), East Woodland (Area P), and University-Euclid and for research laboratories and offices in the latter project's Chester-Carnegie panhandle. Unfortunately, the total area set aside for industry amounted to fewer than three hundred acres, or about 5 percent of the overall land undergoing renewal planning—and fewer than many suburbs offered in single industrial parks. Few of those urban renewal acres saw industrial development. Through Locher's mayoralty, University-Euclid renewal never progressed significantly beyond University Circle, and public pressure on his successor redirected the city's energies toward pursuing a federal Model Cities grant to rebuild housing and support community services in western Hough and eastern Central. In addition, East Woodland residents, who had fixed up their homes based on promises by city hall only to be told later that their neighborhood would be redeveloped for industry, exerted mounting pressure to protect their investments. Stokes responded in 1968 by recommitting East Woodland to its original, pre-1964 purpose as a residential project and including it in his Model Cities proposal.[55]

With East Woodland off the books as an industrial park and University-Euclid efforts similarly redirected toward housing rehabilitation and rebuilding, it became clear that Stokes's delivery of industrial redevelopment was going to be as minimal as Locher's success with housing rehabilitation. *Cleveland: NOW!* simply could not offer something comparable to the large-scale reindustrialization opportunities undertaken by the Philadelphia Industrial Development Corporation (PIDC), the nation's first municipal land bank.[56] After a decade of planning and much inaction, the ninety-seven-acre Gladstone area attracted characterization as "a city dump" and "an ugly blot in the city's generally depressing renewal picture."[57] Under Stokes, Gladstone emerged as an industrial echo of the East 90th Street housing demonstration: Both were token symbols of the hope for a turnaround.

Community development director Green later commented that, in contrast with the Celebrezze and Locher administrations, which "never had enough faith to expend city funds and put in the kind of improvements that would even begin to get industry serious about coming in," Mayor Stokes had finally made Gladstone presentable. His administration cleaned up the industrial district and installed sewers, water mains, sidewalks, and streetlights, but it did so with more federal dollars and not until 1972.[58] Appearance certainly mattered, especially when Cleveland was competing against broad swaths of groomed land in suburban and rural communities, but attractiveness alone was insufficient to cement deals with prospective firms. HUD required that the city market the land in Gladstone for $45,000 an acre, almost double the amount the city had hoped to price it and much more than the going rate in outlying industrial parks.[59]

Under such unfavorable circumstances, the Stokes administration was forced to subsidize industry even after taking millions of federal dollars for a project that urban renewal director Lister had once called highly attractive to industry. As the original concept of light industry faltered, the newly formed GCGA, bending the Gladstone plan to fit the reality on the ground, recommended in June 1968 that the city focus on extending the existing combination of food processing and distribution and scrap metal and salvage operations in addition to courting light industry. Motivated by GCGA's recommended rebranding and prodded by complaints from Ward 13 residents of smoke from ongoing burning of hauled-in house debris in Gladstone, Stokes ordered the cessation of burning and proceeded to "stage" the renewal area "for sale and development."[60] Weeks later, at a press conference held on a recently acquired thirteen-acre Gladstone site, Stokes announced that a pair of companies planned to cooperate in constructing a Dinner Bell Meats processing plant. Although the deal ultimately required that Cuyahoga County issue $5 million in tax-free industrial development bonds to finance construction, Stokes, standing in front of a large sign that read, "Cleveland: NOW! is happening here," hailed the groundbreaking for Dinner Bell as a sign of the end of "a decade of delay" in the renewal area.[61] Joining Dinner Bell were American Poultry Company and American Wholesale Plumbing Supply Company, demonstrating just enough interest to enable Stokes to show progress but coming well short of completing Gladstone by the time he left office.[62]

While the Community Development Department under Stokes pursued the elusive industries needed to demonstrate progress in Gladstone, it supported University Circle leaders' effort to attract research-and-development enterprises to the city proper. As a major industrial center, Cleveland boasted many research laboratories, but most were in the suburbs. Since the late 1950s, CEI had advertised Greater Cleveland as a space-age research hub, but that status was more aspiration than reality. Then, in 1960, Cleveland renewal planners announced their intent to create a $100-million urban research park in a corner of the University-Euclid project on sixty-five acres bounded by East 100th Street, Carnegie Avenue, and the Nickel Plate Road. From their vantage point in 1960, they could see examples of this type of development sprouting nationwide, mostly in the suburbs of cities with research universities. Boston's Route 128, Stanford Research Park in the future "Silicon Valley," and North Carolina's Research Triangle Park all emerged in the 1950s. A more direct inspiration was Philadelphia's University City Science Center. Conceived in 1959, it was the nation's first urban research park and benefited from its proximity to the University of Pennsylvania. A similar park in Cleveland might attract lucrative federal science and technology grants to offset the effect of declining military contracts since the end of the Korean War and, in the process, reframe locals' impression of their town as a dirty smokestack city. As in Philadelphia, however, Cleveland's prospect of attracting industrial research divisions to an urban setting was anything but assured.[63]

Indeed, the UCRC plan languished for six years until university officials recommitted to the effort and managed to corral some local companies to locate in the park as a show of faith in Cleveland, much in the same fashion that local boosters had achieved the illusion of success by filling the Illuminating Building, the East Ohio Gas Building, and Erieview Tower with mostly local firms. After convincing Harris-Intertype chairman Dively to locate his corporation's electronics research lab in UCRC, the city broke ground in 1966. During construction, Cleveland-based Chase Brass and Copper committed to move its research-and-development division from Waterbury, Connecticut, to UCRC. After Stokes's election, Cleveland's Warner and Swasey also decided to relocate its headquarters from its machine-tool plant at East 55th and Carnegie to the new research park. Along with some smaller tenants, these three firms filled the first UCRC building, emboldening municipal and University Circle officials to break ground for a second building.[64] The project produced some friction between the Stokes administration and UCRC's president Willard W. Brown, who had campaigned unsuccessfully for mayor in 1962. Green scolded Brown following the latter's characterization of the project in the *Cleveland Press* as a private development, warning him not to omit mention of the importance of the public-private partnership as a key element in the city's revitalization.[65]

Ultimately, UCRC became a failure that neither Green nor Brown was eager to claim. Despite UCRC's intentional location next to what became the consolidated Case Western Reserve University in 1967 and the extension of an adjacent CTS line that created the nation's first airport-to-downtown rapid-rail connection, the research park struggled to overcome firms' preference for mostly suburban locations near larger concentrations of high-technology production. After Chase Brass and Copper consolidated its research division along the Route 128 corridor in Lexington, Massachusetts, in 1971, more than half of UCRC, including nearly all of its second building, stood empty. The park never employed more than several hundred of the expected seven thousand "brainworkers" but provided a decade's worth of image-making service for a city struggling to retool for an emerging new economy.[66]

With scant available space for new industry and a limited market for research labs in the city, Cleveland leaders also needed to sell the city to existing local manufacturers. GCGB had focused much of its energy on industrial retention in the early and mid-1960s. Although it had tried to mediate disagreements between manufacturing interests and city council members and to simplify the complexities of securing municipal permits that sometimes thwarted plant-expansion efforts, GCGB ultimately had little influence on council members or municipal procedures. Another fundamental problem was that GCGB represented a multicounty metropolitan area, so it viewed plant moves within that area as preferable to losses to other locales. The Growth Board managed to retain a number of mostly small plants in the city, but it was not enough to offset major losses, such as when National Screw and Manufacturing Company left its antiquated plant in East Woodland, taking 1,500 jobs to a modern facility in suburban Lake County.[67]

Like GCGB, the Stokes administration understood that there were clear limits to the city's ability to attract or even to retain industry. Neither the Growth Board's promotion and services nor the city's Gladstone project could produce much more than symbolic reindustrialization, particularly inside the city limits. In keeping with its *Cleveland: NOW!* campaign to create the image of a revitalizing city, the administration grasped the need to craft a better reputation as a municipal government that was friendly to business and to address the mismatch between manufacturers' workforce needs and the growing pool of unemployed inner-city residents. To that end, in January 1968, Stokes named former GCGB staffer John A. Keever to serve as a liaison to business and industry—essentially to do what Keever had done with GCGB, but from within rather than outside government.[68] Several months later, Stokes went further, creating a cabinet-level division called the Department of Human Resources and Economic Development (HRED), which was billed as the national model for combining manpower and economic programs in a single agency. Under the leadership of David G. Hill, whom Stokes recruited from an antipoverty position in Pittsburgh's government, HRED inherited from the former GCGB a role as a clearinghouse for industries seeking to cut through the red tape of municipal politics and procedures. As a service to industry, HRED shepherded requests for a range of permits and approvals through the maze of city hall. Unfortunately, HRED fell short of its goals, because it lacked adequate staff to meet with industrial leaders before rather than after they had decided to move from the city. This forced the department into the position of changing the minds of disgruntled clients. As Hill later recalled, insufficient funds relegated HRED to "putting band-aids on the wounds instead of really treating the wounds."[69]

In addition to cultivating a new pro-business reputation through direct assistance, HRED also tried to solve another vexing problem for industry: lack of skilled labor to meet industrial demand. Although it coordinated a number of manpower programs, HRED found particular symbolic resonance in one federally funded Cleveland Public Schools program. Several months before HRED's formation, the city school district accepted GE's donation of its closed industrial electric equipment service facility at 4966 Woodland Avenue and its promise to train and then hire students and drop- outs for jobs assembling lighting parts and machinery. GE's departure to Erieview in 1966 had helped Mayor Locher claim progress in downtown renewal but had left behind a hulking brick shell on the northern flank of Gladstone. The company's decision to unload its Woodland Avenue building offered something for everyone: Cleveland Public Schools obtained a new means for assisting youth, GE rid itself of a burden and gained potential workers, and *Cleveland: NOW!* gained a dynamic and ideally sited symbol to demonstrate Stokes's commitment to manpower needs. The resulting Wood- land Job Center opened in September 1968, with several firms joining GE in leasing space for training workers. GCGA facilitated industrial firms' com- mitments to hire workers trained at the new center. Although the program sprang from the collaboration of the school district, GCGA, GE, and other firms, benefiting from a $2-million grant, the Stokes administration counted the Woodland Job Center as a $50,000 in-kind expenditure by GE under *Cleveland: NOW!*—another indication of the mayor's expansive branding of not only his administration's programs but also those of other public and private entities.[70] As with HRED's industrial retention campaign, however, its antipoverty programs were insufficient to produce enough job placements for those they sought to assist. As plants moved to the suburbs, a lack of extensive rapid transit service hindered city residents from commuting to these new locations. Meanwhile, industrial employment eroded further in the city, which compounded the problems faced by antipoverty programs. Even the novel merger of industrial and employment policies proved unable to overcome the powerful attraction of suburban, southern, and overseas enticements to industry but were an integral part of Stokes's effort to trans- form Cleveland and create a symbol in the process.[71]

## "Green Grass and Affordable Housing in Five Years": Rehousing Cleveland

Although jumpstarting a sagging downtown and mitigating deindustrializa- tion were important in Stokes's campaign to restore Cleveland to greatness, neither objective was at its heart. Rather, Stokes viewed the provision of housing as the cornerstone of his mayoralty and made it the centerpiece of *Cleveland: NOW!* As Stradling and Stradling have observed, "Stokes's talent, of course, was seeing beyond downtown's skyscrapers and into the city's neighborhoods."[72] Following the virtual collapse of private-sector home con- struction in the city in the mid-1960s, Stokes hoped to expand public hous- ing and restore federal funding for housing construction and rehabilitation by private and nonprofit builders. He promised to add at least 4,600 new

units of housing in Cleveland.[73] Three of city hall's most ambitious and substantive projects reflected Stokes's understanding of the need to rebuild inner-city housing and push affordable housing into the city's periphery to
disperse poverty while waiting for growing nonprofit-sector commitments
to fair housing to take root.

First, in 1968, the Stokes administration submitted an application for
funds under President Johnson's Model Cities program to attack problems
of housing, jobs, and education in eastern Central and western Hough, areas
that had largely missed coverage under the city's urban renewal program.
Locher's administration had submitted an incomplete application the previous year, adding to the city's pariah status in Washington, D.C. Stokes's attempt, although successful in garnering funds, failed to devise an inclusive
planning process that satisfied neighborhood leaders. The Model Cities project still had not left the drawing board after his four years in office.[74]

Second, as it struggled to create a workable process in Cleveland's two
most distressed inner-city neighborhoods, the Community Development
Department also worked to disperse poverty by attempting to build a combination of federally subsidized, privately built houses and public housing in
the Lee-Seville area of southeastern Cleveland, not far from where vocal
middle-class white opposition had thwarted CMHA's similar effort in the
Lee-McCracken area fifteen years earlier. Like the earlier failure, Lee-Seville
prompted outcry from many middle-class residents. This time, however,
those residents were predominantly African Americans who had moved out
of the inner city and now hoped to close the door behind them to preserve
their hard-won attainment of middle-class status and homes that mimicked
those in the lily-white suburbs. They worked through their ward's council
members to secure opposition on the city council, similar to the efforts that
doomed the Lee-McCracken project.[75]

A third initiative aimed to obtain federal funds under Title VII of the
New Communities Housing Act of 1968 for a complete planned community
on 865 acres of city-owned land in suburban Warrensville Township, several
miles east of Lee-Seville. This "new town," christened Warren's Ridge, also
languished as a result of similar social fears. Warren's Ridge failed to obtain
needed approval by the mayors of surrounding suburban municipalities. The
leader of opposition to the project was Mayor Raymond J. Grabow of Warrensville Heights, who had worked in previous years to contain racial integration in his municipality by channeling black residents into a single
neighborhood in one corner of the town.[76]

These three initiatives were very important to Stokes's efforts to meet
*Cleveland: NOW!* program objectives. The Model Cities proposal promised
a programmatic response to urban renewal failures, disinvestment, arson,
vandalism, inadequate social services, and the Hough riots. Lee-Seville and
Warren's Ridge represented a test of whether long-standing social barriers to

solving the problem of housing could be overcome. As all three projects struggled and ultimately failed to win support among residents, city council members, and suburban mayors, respectively, Stokes looked to shorter-term initiatives that could produce visible progress while pressing for larger breakthroughs that were not as fully within grasp. Several city-sponsored projects in riot-torn Hough aimed to show the mayor's concern for the inner city, while a novel collaboration with Shaker Heights promised to add affordable housing in the outer-city black neighborhood of Mt. Pleasant.

In Hough, the Stokes administration went well beyond Locher's reliance on a token rehabilitation demonstration project. After defeating Locher in the 1967 Democratic primary, Stokes had predicted that Hough would be "green grass and affordable housing in five years" and would thereby "erase forever that image which has gone out across the land."[77] As before, new housing initiatives arose chiefly in the nonprofit housing sector, with support from religious organizations and federal loan guarantees as well as rent supplements under the 1965 Housing and Urban Development Act. The most ambitious was the Better Homes for Cleveland Foundation's five-hundred-unit apartment rehabilitation project. Dubbed "The Pride of Hough," Lexington Square encompassed fifty rehabilitated apartment buildings in a four-block area bounded by Hough and Lexington Avenues between East 73rd and 79th Streets. As with many private-sector initiatives, *Cleveland: NOW!* money was intertwined, in this case in the form of an on-site community center in a repurposed automotive repair garage.[78]

As the Stokes administration awaited a breakthrough in its Model Cities effort to improve a 1,600-acre swath of the East Side, it undertook symbolic actions to inspire a sense of comeback in Hough. The mayor worked with Baxter Hill's Cleveland Pride, a local grassroots black nationalist organization, to plant a forty-block section of western Hough with sod donated by landscape contractors in the summer of 1968. The action expanded and contrasted with the previous year's efforts spearheaded by a white suburbanite from Rocky River in partnership with the Hough's "slum priest."[79] In effect, the initiative bought time by creating an early, tangible marker of Stokes's vision of Hough as a neighborhood of "green grass."

Another symbolic action was Stokes's proclamation of July 20, 1968, as "Hough Memorial Day" to mark the anniversary of the Hough riots. In leading the second annual community parade from League Park to the city's Community Development field office in University-Euclid, Stokes inserted himself directly into an observance that had originated the previous summer on the anniversary of the riots.[80] Whether intentional or not, the route's direction and start and end points embodied the transformation of Hough in two respects. First, at least from city hall's perspective, over the course of two decades, the focal point for revitalization hopes had shifted from western to eastern Hough. Second, League Park may have been a reminder of the late-1940s, white-dominated Hough Area Council (HAC) vision for renewing Hough, while the city's field office provided a focus for a late-1960s partnership between the city's first black mayor and the black-led Hough Area Development Corporation (HADC) that was reenergizing the city's bellwether neighborhood renewal project. On another level, Stokes, who yearned to place himself close to his constituents, knew he could curry favor in a rapidly evolving scene of African American activism by presiding over an event that might stitch a common fabric from multiple threads: black and white municipal leaders, nonprofit housing advocates, civil rights activists, neighborhood clergy, and emergent black nationalist groups. Although it may have seemed a good idea to accentuate the distance the mayor's office had come since Locher's mayoralty, Stokes's appearance alongside black, red, and green flag-waving marchers proved ill-timed, coming just two days before the outbreak of gunfire between police and black nationalists in nearby Glenville—an event that greatly eroded Stokes's political capital.

In contrast to the growing distance between city hall and HAC during the Thomas A. Burke, Celebrezze, and Locher mayoral administrations, Stokes's *Cleveland: NOW!* program directed funding to HADC, which had emerged after the collapse of HAC but reflected the rise of black leadership that coincided with Hough's decay. Formed in 1967, HADC was among the nation's pioneering community development corporations (CDCs), along with Brooklyn's Bedford-Stuyvesant Restoration Corporation and the Harlem Commonwealth Council. Led by president Rev. DeForest Brown, a minister turned social worker whom some likened to a "modern day Moses in Cleveland," HADC enjoyed seed money from Harris-Intertype president Richard Tullis as well as a $1.6-million federal grant from the Office of Economic Opportunity and *Cleveland: NOW!* matching funds (see Figure 4.2).[81] The Stokes government supported several substantial housing developments in Hough by purchasing and clearing lots and making them available to HADC to redevelop. HADC's most innovative undertaking—one that mirrored the spirit that Stokes projected—was a combined shopping and apartment complex it planned to build on the southwest corner of Wade Park Avenue and Crawford Road in eastern Hough. For this effort, HADC raised funds—including approximately $62,000 from *Cleveland: NOW!*—to match federal money. Dubbed Martin Luther King Jr. (MLK) Plaza soon after the civil rights leader's assassination, the three-story precast concrete complex, with its two-level townhouses overlooking an open-air courtyard built atop a ground-level retail mall, was hailed in the local press as a national model, even though some detractors rightly noted that it created unnecessary density at a time when Hough was depopulating and had many abandoned homes in need of rehabilitation. Mayor Stokes characterized MLK Plaza as "a symbol of the turning of the corner of the American black man." Indeed, the project not only reflected African American leadership in planning but

**Figure 4.2.** DeForest Brown, the president of the Hough Area Development Corporation (HADC), is shown here outside the community development corporation's offices in 1968. HADC, also known as Hough Development, was a major catalyst for revitalization efforts during the Stokes mayoralty. (Photo by Glenn Zahn. Cleveland Press Collection, Cleveland State University.)

also retained a black-owned architecture firm (Madison, Madison and Madison) and a black-owned builder (Ozanne-Kinsdale Construction). Following the groundbreaking ceremony in 1969, however, MLK Plaza construction did not actually commence in earnest until 1971 as a result of a federal-grant stipulation that all tenants be signed before grant funds could be collected.[82] This unfortunate delay denied Stokes the opportunity to dedicate the complex before he left office.

In addition to its effort to step up the rehabilitation or rebuilding of housing in Hough by encouraging and sometimes assisting nonprofit housing developments, the Stokes administration initiated the Community Housing Corporation (CHC) to coordinate low- and moderate-income housing development in the city. CHC began in earnest in April 1969, when Stokes attracted Robert D. Knox, the former head of the Detroit Housing Commission, to serve as its executive director. Consequently, many people saw Knox as an "extension of City Hall." Although CHC was a separate organization, its initial $6-million budget was listed as a *Cleveland: NOW!* expense, giving the impression that it was a municipal program, an image furthered by the fact that its first board meeting took place in the Tapestry Room, the mayor's ceremonial chamber in city hall.[83]

Not even two months after CHC's inception, the Cleveland Development Foundation (CDF), which had recently merged executive committees with GCGA, announced that it would pull out of the housing field and divest itself of commitments in Garden Valley and on East 90th Street. As a result, CHC asserted itself as an umbrella organization for coordinating public-private partnerships to develop housing in the city.[84] With a year having passed since *Cleveland: NOW!* had promised 4,600 units of new housing, Knox's agency needed to speed the city's provision of housing. With time running short, Knox turned to some time-saving options, including investigating the introduction of "instant housing"—building modular homes on vacant lots in Hough and other neighborhoods and even moving suburban houses condemned for redevelopment or highway construction to sites in the city.[85]

The latter approach included Knox's attempt to relocate up to four hundred houses that stood on the Ohio Department of Transportation's right of way for Interstate 80 (later renamed I-480) from Garfield Heights to Hough and other neighborhoods. Although Knox succeeded in securing the Ohio legislature's approval for making homes in the path of planned highways available for free to nonprofit housing organizations to move at their own expense, he failed to persuade the Garfield Heights City Council to drop its ban on moving houses outside its boundaries. At the same time, Garfield Heights slashed its demolition bond by 75 percent, all but ensuring the demolition of the houses Knox sought for Cleveland.[86]

In the meantime, CHC made a token breakthrough in negotiations with the city of Shaker Heights. Named less than a decade earlier as the nation's wealthiest incorporated community, Shaker Heights had faced growing pressure from fair-housing activists to accept upwardly mobile African American homebuyers. Ludlow, which straddled the Cleveland–Shaker Heights line, had spent twelve years actively promoting controlled integration, an approach that the nearby Shaker neighborhood of Moreland (also known as Kinsman-Lee) also adopted as its largely Jewish population moved further eastward amid racial turnover in Moreland and the Cleveland neighborhood of Mt. Pleasant to its west. If Shaker officials and residents proved willing to welcome more-affluent black professionals as neighbors, they remained fearful of an influx of less-prosperous African Americans into the modest houses that stood along the suburb's southwestern border with Cleveland, especially in light of rapid racial turnover that had recently made the suburb of East Cleveland a residential revolving door. Since the early 1960s, the Shaker Heights government had invested, sometimes covertly, in confidence-building projects for reinforcing its boundary with Cleveland to discourage white-panic selling, even buying properties at sheriff's auctions to hold off the market.[87] In a prelude to the divisive installation of street barricades that dissuaded motorists from Cleveland's Mt. Pleasant and Lee-Harvard neighborhoods from venturing across the Shaker Heights city line, the suburb's residents approved a bond issue in 1968 to close several streets near the border in Moreland to build Shaker's new service center and a "park-townhouse" development called Sutton Place. The new developments would enable the exclusive suburb to not only cut off three Cleveland streets at the city limits but also begin to create a buffer to protect its pricier residential neighborhoods and rid itself of its most affordable houses.[88]

Shaker's desire to eliminate low-cost housing meshed well with the Stokes administration's need for better housing inside the central city, and the prospect of putting some of Cleveland's poorest residents in relocated Shaker Heights houses held rich symbolic value. Shaker's government worked out a deal whereby it would give twenty-eight houses to the city of Cleveland, which would pay to have them moved on flatbed trucks from Shaker Heights to vacant lots in the nearby Mt. Pleasant neighborhood. There the homes would be rehabilitated by CHC as a *Cleveland: NOW!* project and sold to families displaced by urban renewal projects in the inner city. By the end of 1969, the houses were in place, and the following June, Mayor Stokes presented the keys to the first of them, a small Dutch colonial frame house moved from Pennington Road to East 114th Street, to Helen Willis and her three children. Thanks to the mortgage supplement provision under Section 235 of the Housing Act of 1968 for families displaced by public action, Willis enjoyed an almost 50 percent savings in her monthly mortgage bill.[89]

Ultimately, Mayor Stokes made good on his promise of 4,600 new units of housing under *Cleveland: NOW!*, delivering more than that number by the time he left office in 1971, although close to half were public housing units already planned before Stokes took office. Regardless, even when coupled with the ongoing Operation Demolition, the construction of new housing fell far short of offsetting the city's more than fifty thousand units of substandard housing. The accomplishment also reflected assumptions made at a time when city officials believed that demand for affordable inner-city housing was still rising. However, suburban options were opening up to African Americans seeking better homes. In the 1960s, tens of thousands of blacks left Hough and other inner-city neighborhoods as the promise of affordable and open housing began to be fulfilled, notably in East Cleveland, Corlett, and Lee-Harvard.[90] In contrast to the city's assumption in the 1950s and 1960s that substandard housing needed to be rehabilitated or replaced to meet continuing demand, the large-scale departure of residents—with few incoming migrants to replace them—left more abandoned houses than the city could afford to demolish, even with federal subsidies. Nonetheless, the upbeat public face of Mayor Stokes, and the nonprofit housing initiatives his administration supported, created at least an image of renewed faith in the residential future of the central city.

Concerns about the city's image were inseparable from Stokes's commitment to housing provision itself. In the absence of progress in Lee-Seville,

CHC's work might help salvage the reputation of the mayor's housing effort. *Cleveland: NOW!* offered a useful way to brand a wide field of endeavors as being at least tethered to the mayor, but when these efforts fell short of public expectations, their *Cleveland: NOW!* brand implicated city hall in unwanted ways. CHC was under pressure to produce visible results, but too many factors hampered its ability. The Shaker house-moving project had seemed a useful expedient, but cost overruns in rehabilitating the houses ballooned its price tag to well over $700,000, which was nearly half of all money spent by CHC.[91]

Contemporaries found *Cleveland: NOW!* difficult to assess. As one newspaperman observed as early as 1969, the program was "a big bag of slippery marbles[,] hard to count and hard to weigh. But they must be sorted, counted and weighed to see what has been the fulfillment of the civic promise that blossomed in orange and black signs and lapel buttons almost a year ago." The campaign was from the start a nebulous assortment of large and small initiatives. The same reporter groused that the program "seems to exert a kind of fourth-dimensional magnetism. Things that started before Cleveland Now have been identified as Cleveland Now projects. So have others launched under the 'Now' banner but not mentioned in the original prospectus." *Cleveland: NOW!* succeeded or failed depending on the metric one applied in judging it. The program could be counted a success—if one measured the program, as Stokes did, against the inertia of past mayoral administrations; if one counted, as Stokes did, the total contributions of other entities; if one did not look too closely, as the mayor did not, at which actions actually developed under and were funded by the *Cleveland: NOW!* budget; and if one overlooked project delays that sometimes spanned well into the 1970s.[92]

Perhaps more of substance might have been accomplished had Fred "Ahmed" Evans not holed up with a gun in a Glenville home in July 1968. The revelation that Evans had received *Cleveland: NOW!* funds for a community center but redirected them to buy the weapons used in the shootout further hobbled a mayor reeling from his decision to remove white police from Glenville. The bitter recriminations lodged against Stokes thereafter, which arose among those who never showed much interest in city affairs until a black mayor took the helm, contrasted pointedly with the ease with which the mayor had seemed to smooth over ethnic, racial, and class tensions in the autumn of 1967.[93] His *Cleveland: NOW!* program, although an effective brand, was unsustainable, particularly because federal dollars became harder to obtain, city council opponents stood in the way, and the mayor proved unable to secure public approval to raise the city's income tax. Soon after Stokes announced that he would not seek reelection in 1971, one close follower of city hall's fortunes commented that, with its budget some $26 million in the red, "the city's on its knees."[94] The comment echoed a similar one by Celeste four years earlier and highlighted once again how much uncertainty pervaded attempts to locate a turning point in Cleveland's troubled path. Despite the rise of strident opposition, Stokes managed to retain some steadfast believers. As municipal finances withered, an anonymous couple gave $81,000 to enable the city to continue offering its "pools in the lake," while the Cleveland Federation of Musicians donated its services to preserve the "little bit of Paris" that Baugh's outdoor café had created on the Mall.[95]

As Growth Association chairman Grabner once commented, if *Cleveland: NOW!* was unlikely to reverse every downward trend, it was at least a morale builder, "something to help us sell Cleveland to ourselves."[96] At the Flats Fun Festival, a special event co-sponsored by city hall and the West 11th Street Flats Association in October 1970 as a follow-up to that year's successful downtown festival, Mayor Stokes, who had promised to "walk on water" as a demonstration of his faith in the budding entertainment district, donned yellow rubber fishermen's boots and clambered down a dock ladder behind Fagan's Beacon House. There, he sloshed through the murky Cuyahoga River water on a submerged platform as the crowd cheered.[97] The mayor's "walk on water" was emblematic of a messianic quality he brought to city hall. More than any Cleveland mayor before him, Stokes elevated public expectations of miraculous civic renewal in a downtrodden community. Almost a decade before the rise of so-called messiah mayors, who "preached a message of revival" in cities from Boston to St. Louis, Stokes ministered to a citizenry yearning for change or at least signs of change.[98] His talent, stretched nearly to its breaking point by the Glenville shootout, lay in his ability to create the semblance of progress even when he faced insurmountable obstacles to ending an urban crisis whose causes were metropolitan, national, and even global.

# 5

# "Color, Pizzazz, Magnetism, Lift"

*The Struggle to Enliven Downtown*
*Cleveland in the 1970s*

❝The 175th anniversary of Cleveland came at a very inopportune time," observed *Plain Dealer* columnist George E. Condon several days after the city's big birthday celebration in July 1971. "This is not a good year for celebrating anything in Cleveland, no matter how hard we try to persuade ourselves otherwise." Condon continued, drawing attention to two celebratory events held at symbolic sites in downtown Cleveland:

> Part of the grotesquery of the festival week just past was that one of the largest so-called gala affairs featured a guest list made up mainly of former Clevelanders who long ago had chosen to live elsewhere. The expatriates had the unique distinction of being honored by the city they have fled. Furthermore, the dinner in their honor was staged appropriately enough in the dusty old Palace Theater that has been shuttered for a long time[,] shut down by the decline of downtown, along with all the other theaters in the old Playhouse Square area. It was, to be sure, an ironic setting for a celebration. . . . The most ludicrous scene of the week . . . was the attempt to recreate the landing of Moses Cleaveland and his men on the east bank of the Cuyahoga River as it may have happened in 1796. . . . Moses was the only bright spot of the week's program because his tricorn hat kept falling down over his face everytime [*sic*] he made a big point and bobbed his head. There was a lot of speechmaking during the week, but nobody spoke a word that the city was hoping to hear. Nobody spoke with candor and greeted the dismal scene honestly. Everybody spoke progress and growth, despite the obvious fact that there has been little of either

since the city's last big birthday celebration, its sesquicentennial of 1946. . . . Perhaps all the celebrators should have been taken by slow-moving caravan out Superior Avenue, past E. 105th Street, to Euclid Avenue, past the burned-out apartments, the deserted business blocks, and the charred ruins of homes and factories that line that once-prosperous avenue in a scene reminiscent of bombed Berlin after World War II.[1]

Condon's stinging indictment of civic boosters reflected the gloom felt by many Clevelanders shaken by an emerging realization that their city was bearing the brunt of the deepening urban crisis. His recommendation of a funeral-like procession through the riot-scarred Hough and Glenville neighborhoods on the city's East Side instead of a downtown celebration not only channeled neighborhood discontent with the growth coalition's fixation on downtown but also suggested that any notion that Carl Stokes's election four years earlier had produced a Cleveland turnaround was premature.

Condon also pinpointed two sites that boosters were trying to harness in their attempt to refashion downtown as the showcase for an exciting city, a preoccupation shared by their counterparts in other downtowns across the nation. These sites—the Flats and Playhouse Square—represented the origin and destination, respectively, in downtown's eastward push from the Cuyahoga River along Euclid Avenue over the course of the late nineteenth and early twentieth centuries. In a downtown that was adding new office buildings but losing its luster as a shopping, dining, and entertainment center amid the headlong rush to the suburbs, these two sites had particular declension narratives to overwrite. Despite the hum generated by a few riverfront restaurants and taverns in the previous few years, the Flats—the arrival site of Cleveland's "founding father" and namesake—remained an incomplete answer to popular entertainment districts, such as Underground Atlanta or New Orleans's Bourbon Street.[2] Even so, despite the infamous 1969 Cuyahoga River fire, the Flats seemed ripe with potential. Likewise, after four of its large theaters closed in 1968 and 1969, Playhouse Square was to become a focus of efforts to stimulate downtown as a destination for suburbanites and tourists and, in the process, make downtown a touchstone for rehabilitating Cleveland's battered image.

Business and civic leaders continued their struggle to re-create downtown Cleveland after more than a decade of disappointing results from expensive, unheeded plans and large-scale projects, including the downtown subway and the Erieview urban renewal area. Their efforts in the 1970s extended and amplified strategies recommended in the 1965 downtown plan and undertaken in limited form in the late 1960s by the Stokes administration and a small cast of entrepreneurs. This chapter follows the struggle to "save" downtown into the 1970s, focusing on the tilt of attention away from a short-lived office-building boom along Superior Avenue and toward the rejuvenation of the city's wharf-and-warehouse district nestled between Public Square and the Cuyahoga River, its entertainment district at Playhouse Square, and the link between them: Euclid Avenue.

Specifically, this chapter spotlights Raymond K. (Ray) Shepardson and Herbert E. (Herb) Strawbridge, two men who separately spearheaded civic campaigns that epitomized the more varied approaches to downtown revitalization that followed the public backlash against urban renewal. Shepardson, a Seattle transplant and former schoolteacher, used the specter of two Playhouse Square theaters' demolitions for a parking lot to build civic backing to save them. Similarly, when a proposal to open a junkyard on the presumed site of Moses Cleaveland's landing in the Flats became known, Strawbridge, who had arrived from Chicago in 1955 to work under John P. Murphy at Higbee's and later rose to become president and then chairman of the department store, sprang into action. As historian Alison Isenberg has pointed out, following a time marked by "strenuously forward-looking modernization strategies, downtown investors began to mine the past for inspiration."[3] Although Shepardson and Strawbridge tapped the growing national prominence of historic preservation as a tool for urban revitalization, they did not think of themselves as preservationists. Rather, they imagined melding the old and the new to create exciting, historically evocative settings for downtown leisure and entertainment. Even if they had chosen to reach out to potential preservation advocates, perhaps neither could have counted on significant support from the city's nascent preservation movement. Cleveland was a relative latecomer, forming its Cleveland Landmark Commission and its Downtown Restoration Society (the precursor of today's Cleveland Restoration Society) in 1972. Its landmark ordinance, like those it emulated, applied only to building exteriors, which in the case of the theaters offered little help, given that the exquisite spaces were encased in rather unremarkable buildings. Nor was the city's budding preservation community focused on the Flats at a time when it was working to secure landmark status for the city's most outstanding architectural gems.[4]

Shepardson and Strawbridge also attempted to align their specific plans with the latest push by the growth coalition to create a blueprint for revitalizing the entire downtown—an effort that drew the Greater Cleveland Growth Association (GCGA), the Cleveland Foundation, and city hall into tight orbit. Boosters' interest in recasting downtown was inseparable from their need to manage often negative public perceptions of metropolitan change. Although not universally recognized or accepted, the role of downtowns everywhere was evolving, with offices taking precedence over traditional retail and entertainment focuses. Even as Cleveland, like other cities, added tens of thousands of people to its downtown workforce (which ballooned from 116,200 to 142,800 between 1950 and 1970), a corresponding increase in suburban retailing offset what might otherwise have been a boon to downtown stores.[5] As the focus of shopping, leisure, and recreation peeled away to the suburbs, new downtown complexes became self-contained, insular realms where office workers alighted from parking garages, lunched in food courts, and returned to their cars at the end of the day. This was central to critiques of Erieview, which had gradually replaced long-vacant parcels with glass-and-concrete towers, only to capture most of the downtown office expansion to the detriment of street-level retailers. Rather than serve as the catalyst for a Cleveland comeback, Erieview was, in the words of Philip W. Porter, "The Mistake That Ruined Downtown."[6] A pedestrian's-eye view on Euclid Avenue in the 1970s seemed to confirm his brother Albert Porter's prediction in the 1950s that downtown would become the service center for an impoverished inner-city population. With fewer suburban white shoppers trekking downtown, the city's famed retailing street now saw many longtime stores close in the 1960s, their spaces repurposed as savings and loans, airline ticket offices serving the jet-age travel needs of downtown businesses, or discount apparel stores catering to a captive clientele dependent on public transportation.[7] Likewise, such theaters as the Hippodrome and the Embassy peddled exploitation films, and the corner of Ontario Street South Roadway on Public Square in front of the May Company—still the highest-valued frontage in Cuyahoga County—was now crowded with peddlers, street preachers, panhandlers, and teenage loiterers, many of them African American.[8] The perceived transformation of downtown into a black space, coupled with growing media attention to downtown crime, only reinforced the belief, held most commonly by white suburbanites, that downtown was unmistakably going downhill. In this climate, finding a way to reignite urban excitement that might entice white suburbanites and tourists was a growing preoccupation for boosters as the 1970s dawned.

Against this backdrop, Shepardson's vision for Playhouse Square and Strawbridge's for the Flats became synonymous with the perceived need to burnish downtown's tarnished image. Their plans, as will become apparent, intersected with the commissioning of yet another downtown plan, this one more attentive than past plans to strengthening and showcasing existing resources in the cityscape, and more dependent on an expansion in the vision of Cleveland's philanthropic community. Ultimately, however, the 1970s presented economic, political, and social challenges that virtually guaranteed that the coalition's vision of a vibrant downtown would be a dream deferred. As a result of such obstacles, the campaign to remake downtown Cleveland took on the added burden of managing attitudes toward a place that, like other downtowns, continued to face insurmountable impediments to a true comeback.

## "Alive and Well": Ray Shepardson's Mission to Save Playhouse Square

In 1968, at the age of twenty-four, Shepardson left Seattle to take a position as the staff assistant to Cleveland Municipal School District superintendent Paul W. Briggs. Raised on a dairy farm in Washington State, Shepardson had never spent time in America's "legacy cities." Nothing he had seen in his limited travels prepared him for the sense of awe he felt when, one day in 1970, he happened upon the abandoned State Theater in Playhouse Square while scouting possible meeting places for teachers' events. He knew right away that he wanted to find a way to reopen not only the State but also three neighboring theaters. Shepardson soon quit his job and formed the Playhouse Square Association, selling $120 life memberships to anyone he could interest. His goal was to stage a variety of performances that would demonstrate the theaters' ability to entice suburbanites back to the city at night and thereby encourage significant support for restoring the theaters as part of an entertainment complex that would play a leading role in revitalizing downtown. Shepardson identified July 22, 1971—the city's 175th birthday—as a symbolic date for reopening the theaters. The grand but derelict Palace Theater was tidied up to play host to Cleveland entertainer Bob Hope and other luminaries as part of the city's "super-sesquicentennial" festivities, but the real work lay ahead.[9]

Playhouse Square had emerged five decades earlier as a major downtown entertainment district with the opening of the Allen, Hanna, Ohio, State, and Palace Theaters in 1921–1922. These theaters, containing a combined twelve thousand seats, soon supported several large restaurants and supper clubs and added to an already-vibrant retail concentration that included the ten-story Halle's department store. The theaters remained vital through the middle years of the century, but a combination of competing suburban theaters and drive-ins and the rise of television gradually whittled away business. In an attempt to wrest suburbanites from their living rooms, in 1956, the Palace Theater added Cinerama, a new widescreen projection process that utilized three projectors and a curved screen to create a new sense of excitement around movies. However, Cinerama proved incapable of rescuing the Palace, whose closure in July 1969 capped a fifteen-month spate of cinema closings that left only the Hanna, a legitimate stage theater, open.[10] These closings occurred alongside the decline of downtown retail businesses. Unlike Higbee's and the May Company, which continued to benefit from their location near the hub of Cleveland's transit system, Playhouse Square retailers suffered from their more peripheral location.[11] Soon after the Sterling-Lindner department store closed in 1968, Halle's purchased the Loew's State Building, which housed the State and Ohio Theaters, to hold them until it could find a redevelopment opportunity that might strengthen the district.[12] Then, in 1970, the Halle family sold its chain to Chicago-based Marshall Field's, which tried without success to reposition the upscale store to attract more middling customers. It endured slumping sales for another dozen years before closing. Similarly, the once fashionable women's apparel store Bonwit Teller closed in 1972 after a brief, unsuccessful reorganization as a discount clothing outlet, and the Cleveland-based Stouffer's chain shut down its six-hundred-seat Playhouse Square restaurant later that year.[13]

Although his effort was to become the most recognized and ambitious theater restoration campaign in the nation, Shepardson was not entirely without models. A handful of other cities had already begun reviving closed-down theaters, notably Pittsburgh's Penn Theater, which saw new life when it was restored and reopened in 1971 as Heinz Hall. Following close on the heels of the Pittsburgh Pirates' and Steelers' move from Forbes Field in the Oakland neighborhood to Three Rivers Stadium, the Pittsburgh Symphony Orchestra left its own longtime concert hall in Oakland to move downtown to Heinz Hall. These relocations reinforced an already impressive downtown Pittsburgh renewal more than two decades in the making and only added to the sense that Cleveland needed something to spark new faith in its downtown.[14]

Shepardson's campaign to prove Playhouse Square's potential began in earnest in the autumn of 1971, when the Playhouse Square Association contracted to lease the Allen Theater from the Millcap Corporation for three years. The same company, which formed in 1970 to purchase the Bulkley Building in which the Allen was located, had also acquired the adjacent Loew's State Building from Halle's.[15] With the support of another founding member of the Playhouse Square Association, Hungarian newspaper publisher and early Chesterfield apartment dweller Zoltan Gombos, Shepardson booked the Budapest Symphony Orchestra to perform the first in a series of varied shows in the Allen Theater over the coming year. Even the act of stripping layers of old paint, rewiring, and illuminating the long-darkened Allen marquee with 2,200 donated bulbs in preparation for the performance created a sense of community around downtown revitalization. Newly elected Mayor Ralph J. Perk, who had assisted volunteers in painting the marquee a few days before the concert, showed the audience his gold-paint-dabbled brush, which he told them symbolized a bright future for Playhouse Square (see Figure 5.1). Although the theater was cold and drafty, it was filled to capacity, leading one newspaper theater critic to exclaim that if Cleveland's dismissive establishment was right that Shepardson was just "an impractical kid," then perhaps what the city needed was "a couple dozen more impractical kids just like him."[16]

Following this success, Gombos warned that "Cleveland cannot be a part-time city. It must have a vital downtown cultural life that lives after the 5 P.M. rush hour."[17] But Shepardson and his disciples would need to replicate the crowd on a regular basis to banish the gloom of night and the sense of danger

**Figure 5.1.** Mayor Ralph J. Perk pauses for a photo as he helps Playhouse Square Association volunteers prepare the shuttered Allen Theater for the first of a number of shows calculated to draw suburbanites back downtown for evening entertainment. (Photo by Tim Culek. Cleveland Press Collection, Cleveland State University.)

it conjured. The Stokes administration's installation of brilliant Lucalox street lighting scarcely four months after the closing of the Palace had been an attempt to stimulate evening activity. However, the brightness of the Lucalox treatment called all the more attention to how dark it was just a block off Euclid. As Condon remarked in 1972, the radiance was oddly limited to Euclid Avenue and Public Square, along with "tiny islands of light," such as in front of the Central National Bank headquarters and the new Park Centre apartment tower, and along the block of East 14th Street where the Hanna remained Playhouse Square's lone surviving theater. Condon observed that "pedestrians walk into a pool of brightness for a block and then disappear in the darkness, sometimes never to be seen again."[18] He left to readers' imaginations whether these pedestrians simply chose never to risk coming downtown again after dark or, worse, they stumbled upon a killer lying in wait.

Indeed, Shepardson had to overcome the oft-expressed idea that downtown was dull by day, yet dull *and* dangerous by night. He also had to fight resignation and apathy among downtown leaders. For decades, downtown interests had seldom come together with a common sense of purpose. A Downtown Cleveland Council, formed in 1960, had included no representatives from the Playhouse Square area. When the 1965 downtown plan was released, among its most adamant prescriptions was for the formation of an organization to unite all downtown interests. From that recommendation emerged the Downtown Cleveland Corporation in 1966. Yet that organization and its successor, the Downtown Consortium (formed three years later), would be short-lived. The seeming inability to create an entity to promote downtown, let alone to reverse the progressive loss of downtown retail, left a lingering sense of hopelessness by the early 1970s. If traditional efforts to revive downtown proved ineffectual, downtown leaders also proved impervious to new approaches. Shepardson's fervent grassroots movement struck them as too naïve and fanciful to take seriously.

GCGA's downtown committee partnered with the Perk administration to scrape together $200,000 to match an equal amount in federal funding to create a block-long pedestrian mall on Huron Road in Playhouse Square, but Shepardson understood that it would take much more than trees, planters, and benches to reintroduce Clevelanders to the neglected Playhouse Square area.[19] Unable to convince local banking, foundation, and corporate leaders to invest in his vision, Shepardson turned to prominent women in the Junior League of Cleveland. More than merely the well-connected wives of prominent Cleveland businessmen, these women were deeply committed agents of civic change. The Cleveland chapter was well-recognized for having supported progressive but controversial projects, including the Maternal Health Association's mobile unit that took family-planning information into underserved neighborhoods.[20] Shepardson quickly learned where to apply himself to leverage action. He turned to Kay Halle, the daughter of one of the founders of the Halle Brothers department store, who hosted salonlike parties for other prominent women. With what one Junior Leaguer later recalled as "enlightened self-interest," Halle proved receptive to Shepardson's entreaties.[21]

By 1972, the Junior Leaguers were building the courage to support Shepardson's plan, despite its seeming impracticality. When the Millcap Corporation announced its intent to demolish the Loew's State Building and replace it with a parking lot, the matter of saving the State and Ohio Theaters became critical. Aware that Shepardson was trying to obtain funding to enable the Playhouse Square Association to lease the building with an option to purchase, architect Peter van Dijk, a member of the Cleveland Planning Commission, implored the Junior League to act. Van Dijk also moved quickly to buy time by working with fellow commissioners to reject the parking lot plan and require the owner to return with a revised design in two weeks. Soon after, the Junior League voted to give $25,000 to the Playhouse Square Association, averting the theaters' demolition. League member Elaine G. (Lainie) Hadden and her husband gave an additional $50,000, and other members contributed as well.[22]

The Junior League's leap of faith was a marked contrast from the reaction by Playhouse Square interests. Upon learning of the parking lot plan, for example, Halle Brothers president Chisholm Halle reportedly remarked, "I see the demolition and the future development as a positive move for everybody's benefit."[23] Junior League women also diverged from the growth coalition's longtime focus on encouraging the construction of office towers to attract new corporate headquarters as a means of revitalizing downtown. Moreover, their commitment helped steer the venerable Cleveland Foundation, which was beginning to elevate economic development to greater importance in its grant making, toward a civic effort that epitomized the growing national trend toward repurposing historic buildings as an approach to downtown renewal.[24] In the meantime, however, Shepardson, with the enthusiastic support of volunteers from the Junior League and others who believed in downtown's future, was the sole steward of Playhouse Square.

To save the State and Ohio Theaters, Shepardson had to divert his attention from booking the Allen Theater, where he had produced eighteen shows in as many months. Soon after Playhouse Square Associates, a newly formed operating syndicate that included Junior Leaguers Hadden and Gwill York, had secured a five-year lease of the Loew's State Building for the Playhouse Square Association in December 1972, Shepardson hit on the idea of staging a cabaret-style dinner and show in the State Theater lobby. The idea came to him after he attended a play directed by Cleveland State University (CSU) drama professor Joe Garry. The production, *Jacques Brel Is Alive and Well and Living in Paris*, so impressed Shepardson that he invited Garry to present it for a three-week run in the inner lobby of the State. Attendees paid between $7.75 and $11.75 for tickets for the show and a dinner prepared in the kitchen of a former restaurant next door and served buffet-style in the theater's outer lobby.[25] The popularity of *Jacques Brel* appeared boundless. Going to see the production became a demonstration of faith in downtown. By the time three weeks had turned into four months of nightly performances, one couple had attended fifteen times, while another fan had reportedly persuaded at least 150 friends to attend.[26]

If *Jacques Brel* did not produce the groundswell of commitment to the theater restoration from the city's growth coalition that might have ensured the theaters' success, it certainly created some foot traffic that emerging nearby projects, such as Park Centre and the Huron Road pedestrian mall, also promised but were yet to deliver. The lively scene built confidence in a number of entrepreneurs who were starting to invest in new restaurants and shops in Playhouse Square. Among the first to test the market was Hamilton F. Biggar III, the twenty-six-year-old son of the vice president of Ostendorf-Morris, one of Cleveland's largest real estate developers. In February 1973, two months after Playhouse Square Associates began leasing the Loew's State Building, Biggar, who already operated a nightspot in Underground Atlanta, opened a cinema-themed bar and restaurant called the Last Moving Picture Company (a play on the title of the 1971 film *The Last Picture Show*) in the space vacated by Stouffer's the previous year. In doing so, Biggar called attention to the idea that a new generation of Clevelanders was the key to downtown's renaissance: "All the over-50s in town told us Playhouse Square was dead. No amount of money could help."[27] Playhouse Square Associates attracted the California-based chain Rusty Scupper to open a restaurant in the Point Building at Euclid and Huron. The arrival of additional businesses in the Point Building—such as the Elegant Hog Saloon, Publix Bookstore, Long's Planthouse, and the Best Things (a gift shop opened by a group of suburban women whose name was inspired by the Growth Association's latest slogan, "The Best Things in Life Are Here")—was an encouraging sign for the few remaining nearby longtime businesses, including Cikra Furs, Cowell and Hubbard, Murray Bender Shoes, Travellers Shoppe, and Weiss Furs.[28] The transformation of the once-struggling Point Building into a "showcase" of downtown's potential seemed to validate a comment that Shepardson had made in 1974 when Woolworth's closed its longtime dime store on Playhouse Square. Shepardson said he was not concerned, because he believed that Playhouse Square's future was as a district that catered to "specialized tastes" rather than the "mass market."[29] His comment suggested that downtown's revitalization could not be judged by the standards that applied to an earlier time, when downtown was a place that by necessity gathered a broad cross section of Clevelanders seeking shopping and entertainment. Yet, as would become painfully clear, those with specialized tastes had to be continually reassured to pursue them amid the perceived danger that accompanied the socially diverse downtown streets.

## "The Process of Agreeing": Lawrence Halprin's Take Part Workshop

In the meantime, as Shepardson and his supporters were struggling on a shoestring budget to prove the merit of their idea for revitalizing downtown, the growth coalition was preparing to pay a princely sum for yet another downtown study, this time by Lawrence Halprin and Associates of San Francisco. Halprin, well known for his 1964 conversion of a San Francisco chocolate factory near Fishermen's Wharf into a shopping, dining, and entertainment complex called Ghirardelli Square, was in considerable demand as an urban landscape and environmental planner. Apart from his work in San Francisco (where he was also a planner for Embarcadero Plaza and Market Street in conjunction with freeway and subway projects), he had designed Lovejoy Plaza, a multiterraced public space in Portland, Oregon; and Nicollet Mall, a pedestrian mall in Minneapolis.[30] Halprin was no stranger to key figures in Cleveland's business establishment. He had met a number of them, including

Strawbridge and James A. (Dolph) Norton of the Cleveland Foundation, at seminars led by Greek planner Constantinos Doxiadis, whom Higbee's had cosponsored in 1970 to study how to "plan Cleveland's emergence from its listlessness" (an exercise whose resulting vision of a northern Ohio megalopolis offered little encouragement to downtown interests).[31] The fifty-six-year-old Halprin, who liked to wear a Greek fisherman's cap, mod-cut suits, Indian jewelry, and a bell on a brass-chain necklace, styled himself as an "urban physician" who made "house calls" to prescribe remedies for ailing cities.[32] The "doctor" and his assistant, Barry Wasserman, arrived in Cleveland on a frigid February evening. Politely refusing Strawbridge's offer to meet them at the airport, they instead rode the rapid to Cleveland Union Terminal to take a look around downtown. They tried in vain to find the river from Public Square, an experience that moved Halprin to pronounce his hosts "magicians," because they had managed to hide this body of water. The *Plain Dealer* quoted Wasserman as calling Cleveland "one of the darkest cities I've ever seen." After a whirlwind tour of downtown and meetings with a range of downtown stakeholders, Halprin offered little of substance, calling Cleveland a city with "physical and emotional holes" and adding that it would take more time, and presumably money, to arrive at a more specific diagnosis.[33]

A little more than three months later, Halprin and Wasserman returned on a $30,000 commission by the Cleveland Foundation to conduct a two-and-a-half-day "Take Part Workshop."[34] Halprin's trademark Take Part Process, which he employed in a number of cities, emerged as a response to strident public rebuke of the top-down approach that characterized urban renewal planning in the 1950s and 1960s. As Halprin's biographer Alison Bick Hirsch has argued, his motives were at once rooted in a principled "ethics of inclusion" and a pragmatic desire for "optimizing the potential for implementation."[35] Halprin's modus operandi meshed well with Cleveland leaders' perspective on why past plans had failed: Too many had been hatched behind closed doors and then failed to win public acceptance. Further, with the city's history of internecine feuding that hobbled any unified effort to renew downtown, it was important to present a more-inclusive planning process that might produce consensus and resolve. To that end, the Cleveland Foundation assembled thirty-six Clevelanders, including business, government, and civic leaders; journalists; urban planners; and a sprinkling of everyday people, including homemakers, blue-collar workers, a student, and a public housing resident.[36] Halprin and Wasserman sent participants roving about downtown to record their experiences and impressions before gathering them inside the "glass-walled social room atop the Chesterfield" to discuss the state of downtown and to brainstorm ideas for its future.[37]

As important as diversity supposedly was to the process, the ability to reach consensus seems to have been the overriding requisite. Drawing on interviews with participants and the Halprin document arising from the work-shop, contrarian journalist Roldo Bartimole, who had left the *Plain Dealer* in the late 1960s to publish his own, unabashedly antiestablishment newsletter, *Point of View*, believed that the entire exercise was one more example of the growth coalition's trying to engineer or, to borrow Hirsch's kinder term, "cho-reograph" an outcome favorable to its own narrow interests. Quoting the Hal-prin report, Bartimole called the Cleveland Foundation's claims—"a new forum whereon to establish fresh lines and modes of communication between people of varying interests and commitment" and the need for a "process of agreeing on input for downtown planning"—"pure, unadulterated bull." Bar-timole argued that the Halprin workshop was calculated to produce a sense that downtown growth was inevitable and that Clevelanders had an opportu-nity to ensure that the growth would incorporate "human amenities." Barti-mole also charged that the city's foundations "merely create the façade and publicity behind which the profit-makers operate." He added that even many of the participants drawn from outside the growth coalition were part of a "predictable mixture" possessing "one overwhelming quality: They belong to institutions which depend upon Foundations for help, particularly financial." In short, Bartimole believed, the Take Part Workshop was a "stacked deck" calculated to elevate to centrality the idea that downtown needed to be "saved," despite the fact that many of Cleveland's neighborhoods were crumbling.[38]

The object of Bartimole's critique was also the occasion for the *Plain Dealer*'s endorsement. An editorial celebrated the fact that "most" workshop participants were "opinion-makers" who "get around in the Cleveland busi-ness and social establishment." Whatever its backers' motivations or its participants' connections, the workshop led ineluctably to conclusions strik-ingly similar to those in the 1965 downtown plan. Participants, according to the report, agreed on the need for better public transit from all parts of the city to downtown, more downtown cultural and entertainment venues, more residential development, more retailers, improvements along the river and lake, and attractions aimed at tourists. They concluded, in echo of the growth coalition's oft-cited assertion, that downtown was "the 'glue' that binds Cleveland together," and that it should be "fun" and a "glittering magnet."[39] Halprin's good impression prepared the ground for a much larger commit-ment to applying the excitement of Ghirardelli Square on a grander scale in Cleveland, a city desperately in need of a new image.

## Herbert Strawbridge, Settlers' Landing, and Halprin's Concept for Cleveland

One Take Part participant who had a deep stake in making downtown more attractive to residents and tourists was Higbee's chairman Strawbridge. His flagship on Public Square—thanks to its policy of perpetual remodeling and its proximity to Cleveland Union Terminal that received tens of thousands of riders daily from the Shaker and CTS rapids and the Erie and Lacka-wanna commuter train from Youngstown—remained a bright spot in an increasingly cloudy downtown retailing climate. However, Strawbridge un-derstood well that his store's future, like those of other downtown retailers, required more than merely offering an incomparable selection of merchan-dise in an attractive setting and appealing to more than a captive audience of downtown office workers shopping on their lunch hour. If Higbee's were to survive in the long run, it would also need to attract tourists. This goal was a tall order: Most of the few downtown convention hotels had long since developed reputations as careworn, if not rundown, and Cleveland increasingly struggled to attract sizable conventions.[40] The convention prob-lem may have been beyond his power to resolve, but Strawbridge would play a leading role in trying to rebuild downtown's reputation around urban ex-citement.

Long before Halprin came to Cleveland, in 1966, Strawbridge had taken an unforgettable trip to San Francisco, where he and his wife discovered Ghi-rardelli Square. Strawbridge imagined the Flats as a fitting location for a simi-lar waterfront transformation. Then, in November 1972, the fifty-four-year-old department store chairman read a cryptic mention in a *Plain Dealer* column about a plan to turn the riverfront site of Moses Cleaveland's landing into a junkyard.[41] As Strawbridge later remarked, "Could Higbee's permit Cleve-land's 'Plymouth Rock' to become an auto junkyard? The answer was abso-lutely 'No,' at least not without a fight." But the broader impetus, as Strawbridge also identified, was his sense that Cleveland was in the "doldrums" and a "na-tional joke." Higbee's board approved the purchase of the historic site, saving it from an ignominious fate.[42] In contrast to Chisholm Halle, who at first saw little value in saving the shuttered theaters near his store, Strawbridge became determined to write a different script for the future of the decaying wharf district along the Cuyahoga River's east bank, and he saw Halprin playing a producing role.

At the time when the Cleveland Foundation was preparing to bring Hal-prin for a "house call," Strawbridge also reached out to Halprin to encourage him to examine the Flats' potential for a major development. Halprin's en-thusiasm for the riverfront during his February 1973 visit convinced the Hig-bee's board to approve the purchase of additional land around the initially acquired parcel. Working through an agent, Higbee's quietly assembled sev-eral acres of land, including the eight-story, Burnham and Root–designed Western Reserve Building at Superior Avenue and West 9th Street, once headquarters to Pickands Mather (an iron-ore shipping firm), as well as three nearby structures with brick or cast-iron facades. Indeed, when Halprin, during his June 1973 workshop, crafted a consensus among participants that riverfront redevelopment was desirable, he did so with full knowledge that Higbee's was "secretly underway" on a project there. Like the clandestine planning that undercut the 1959 downtown by birthing Erieview, Halprin's inside knowledge helped him craft a "plan" that encompassed another secretly hatched civic project. Scarcely a month later, Higbee's unveiled the $20-million Settlers' Landing plan, which Strawbridge compared to Ghirardelli Square and Underground Atlanta. It included a mixture of renovated and new buildings containing a hotel, apartments, theaters, and more than one hundred shops and restaurants arrayed around a small park dedicated to Moses Cleaveland and early settler Lorenzo Carter.[43]

Strawbridge faced extraordinary obstacles. Soon after the announcement of the Settlers' Landing plan, the United States plunged into a recession that produced rampant inflation, which in turn caused construction costs to soar and put a lid on most major downtown projects. Then, on February 11, 1974, an arson fire—one of many that wracked Cleveland in the 1970s—claimed the National Furniture Company warehouse and other nearby buildings, which were essential pieces of the Higbee's plan. The fire forced a dramatic scaling back of Settlers' Landing but did not crush Strawbridge's commitment to transforming the Flats. In 1975, Higbee's opened Cleaveland Crate and Truckin' Company, a restaurant and discotheque in a converted truck terminal, included an old truck cab from Cleveland-based White Motor as an interior feature, and added one more popular gathering place with a view of the river's restless choreography of freighters, tugboats, trains, and lift bridges (see Figure 5.2). The renovated Western Reserve Building languished nearly empty for months in 1976 and 1977, and Higbee's was forced to open its own sandwich shop to fill a key ground-floor space intended for a destination restaurant. Halprin's Bulgarian-born designer Angela Tzvetin created a new lobby inside the Western Reserve Building, but although the building eventually became a prime office location, the Settlers' Landing project offered Halprin no further opportunity to shape what only emerged (in piecemeal fashion) in the 1980s as a nationally known entertainment district.[44]

In the time that Halprin was waiting for the Settlers' Landing project to take shape, he devised a new downtown plan that proved similarly incapable of overcoming the inertia of a poor national economy. Bringing Halprin and Wasserman back to Cleveland after their initial fact-finding junket required boosters to dig deeper into their pockets than for any previous downtown plan. GCGA contributed $125,000, the Cleveland Foundation gave $100,000, and the municipal government approved allocating $50,000 plus another $40,000 in city hall staff time. Although a few council members—including future mayor Dennis J. Kucinich—questioned spending so much for a plan that privileged downtown at a time when many neighborhoods were struggling to reverse their declines, the city council ultimately approved the legislation to commit funds toward the $315,000 Halprin plan by a 29–3 vote.[45]

**Figure 5.2.** The site of Higbee's Settlers' Landing project remained a rough-and-tumble riverfront district of wharves, warehouses, and a few dive bars well into the 1970s. Higbee's acquired the Western Reserve Building (left of center, with scaffolding on top) and, soon after this photo was taken in 1975, converted the O.K. Truck Terminal (center foreground) into a popular restaurant, Cleaveland Crate and Truckin' Company. (Cleveland Press Collection, Cleveland State University.)

In a reprise of the 1973 Take Part Workshop, Halprin and Wasserman facilitated a series of four workshops in 1974 and 1975 in the Point Building on Playhouse Square in a vacant storefront that had previously housed a high-end women's shoe store. As much as the Halprin workshops were intended to inform a new plan for downtown, they were perhaps valued more for their potential to build a sense of unified purpose and faith in downtown's future as the city grappled with its own "rough road to renaissance," to borrow Jon Teaford's phrase. Unlike the initial workshop in 1973, these workshops were directed toward power players with direct stakes in downtown, with broader public engagement relegated to an open invitation to view displays in the workshop center's windows or to stop inside to share their input. The workshops were exercises meant to manage public attitudes about the state of downtown as well as to produce consensus that might make Halprin's recommendations actionable. Ironically, as the workshop participants were building their ideal downtown with "felt tip pens, paints, lettuce, and cereal boxes," they could look across the street and see the string of closed theaters that had yet to attract significant investment despite the overwhelming success of Shepardson's Playhouse Square Cabaret.[46] Although Halprin liked Playhouse Square, he was more interested in focusing on streetscapes and public spaces. To the extent that he involved himself in supporting bricks-and-mortar projects, he was partial to the Flats as a result of his separate commission to work on Settlers' Landing.

For all the flashiness of Halprin's "people-oriented" approach to planning an exciting downtown, his resulting *Concept for Cleveland* plan was unremarkable and highly derivative of past plans. His call for a pedestrian mall and trolley line on Euclid Avenue and a loop route to carry buses and automobiles around the periphery of downtown had been discussed periodically since the mid-1950s. Halprin's recommendation to extend the Burnham-designed Mall northward over the railroad tracks to provide public access to the lakefront recalled elements of the Outcalt "Civic Center" plan of 1957, and his renderings of a revamped Public Square—including closing Ontario Street, running Superior Avenue below grade, and creating a terraced park with a restaurant on the level of the lower concourse of Cleveland Union Terminal—were just an updated version of what architect Howard B. Cain had drafted in his "International Square" plan in 1958.[47] Condon, a rare dissenting voice among the typically boosterish pronouncements in the mainstream press, dismissed the Halprin plan as "very unoriginal." He wrote, "The curious thing about Cleveland is that the more plans are devised to make it more interesting, the more it stays the same. . . . No city in America has undergone such close scrutiny by so many planners for so many dollars for so few results." Despite these plans, Condon continued, in a clear jab at the old "Best Location in the Nation" slogan, "the city continues as it has been, plain and prosaic, the headquarters of the most phlegmatic establishment in the nation. . . . Turning colorless Cleveland into Fun City, U.S.A., couldn't possibly be done cheaply, no matter what plans are followed."[48]

In addition, as Halprin's biographer Hirsch points out, at a time when city planning director Norman Krumholz had just produced the *Cleveland Policy Planning Report*, with its emphasis on social equity planning, Halprin's plan "seemed to gloss over the social injustices of the time and place."[49] Indeed, as Edwin S. Weiss, a prominent local psychologist, warned, the city's leaders were "drowning out the voices of dissent and rebellion by building more Severance Halls or Park Centres or beer halls on the river" and placing faith in "some guy with a beard from San Francisco."[50] But the plan's lack of originality and avoidance of vexing social issues seemed largely irrelevant to Cleveland's growth coalition. Although events in the mid- to late 1960s had forced them to reckon with such concerns as race relations and unemployment, they continued to try to separate economic and image development from broader

community planning. By the 1970s, after twenty years that saw less downtown renewal than they had hoped, boosters were content to put a shiny new
wrapper on an old package. In fact, more than in the 1950s and 1960s, the
mere appearance of progress was something they were pleased to tout. Since
*Cleveland Press* editor Louis Seltzer had retired in 1966, there had been no
greater cheerleader for Cleveland than Thomas Vail, a patrician who lived in
posh suburban Hunting Valley and had become the publisher and editor of
the *Plain Dealer* in 1963. A concern for not only Cleveland's well-being but
also its image appeared frequently in Vail's editorials. One of these carried the
title "Halprin Plan Offers Hope." It called the plan a turning point for downtown and predicted that at least some of its recommendations would be realized, because Halprin had gotten civic leaders personally involved. Another
editorial, published one day after the plan's unveiling, exclaimed that Clevelanders "should be inspired by the beautiful new downtown plan," adding
that it "has color, pizzazz, magnetism, lift. It could make Cleveland one of the
most attractive cities of America." Furthermore, the editorial opined, the
Halprin plan delivered a sort of civic reveille that might "enlist every Clevelander in the push to make it happen, enriching life for all in a city that fills
them with pride." Still another editorial commented that "a certain depth of
despair has to be reached before communities are impelled to action to renovate and repopulate their deserted downtowns." It cited the faltering of
Erieview in the mid-1960s as the onset of downtown's nadir and listed several recent downtown projects as evidence that the time was ripe for Halprin's
plan.[51] Indeed, in a city where the act of performing comeback rituals was
well-rehearsed, the importance of generating "hope" for the city's future and
a sense that the city had turned a corner was almost more noteworthy than
any particular proposal contained in the plan itself.

Halprin understood the inertia that seemed to pervade Cleveland development, and he was careful while presenting his plan to disclaim responsibility for its inception and implementation. Halprin wisely shied away from
calling *Concept for Cleveland* a "plan," instead dubbing it a "road map for
Clevelanders." Contrary to one reporter's characterization of him as a "Lance-
lot come out of the West to save the city from itself," Halprin insisted that
"hundreds" of locals had supplied the ideas behind the plan and that Clevelanders would have to "do with it what they want."[52] The key to the plan's
implementation, leaders agreed, was an organization that included prominent
stakeholders who would be committed to shepherding its many components
to completion. A new Downtown Cleveland Corporation (DCC) was formed
in the summer of 1975 to oversee implementation of the Halprin plan. It
named the Euclid Avenue mall and traffic loop and the redevelopment of
Public Square and Playhouse Square as its priorities. May Company chairman
Francis A. Coy and Thomas A. Albert of the Cleveland Foundation agreed to

serve as the president and the vice president/executive director, respectively. The Cleveland Foundation, GCGA, and the city of Cleveland provided a combined $100,000 to underwrite DCC's first year of operation.[53]

Coy and Albert argued, like many others before them, that the health of downtown was a matter of critical importance for the entire metropolitan area. Coy called it "the home fire, the center core, the point of dynamic reaction for the total community." Albert pointed out that "the image of the city is the downtown," offering the example of Manhattan as the image-maker for New York.[54] However, the men also understood the cynicism with which many Clevelanders regarded development plans, because so many efforts had fallen short of expectations. Coy promised to have what a newspaper reporter characterized as "something visible" to show within twelve to eighteen months, but later he cautioned that progress would be gradual and insisted, "We want no high profile until there is high success." If Coy was already trying to manage a potential outcry should the Halprin recommendations prove slow to materialize, he got no help from the *Plain Dealer*, which editorialized that, this time, things would be different, because the people forming DCC "very definitely are not file-and-forget types."[55] Perhaps close observers also hoped that, with the departure of so many theaters and stores from Playhouse Square and the sale of Halle Brothers to Marshall Field's, the long and counterproductive rivalry between anchors on each end of downtown's Euclid Avenue axis might not hamstring DCC as it had some earlier attempts to create unity.

## The Cleveland Foundation's Gradual Embrace of Playhouse Square

The Halprin plan certainly appeared capable of creating a unified, appealing downtown. Perhaps because Halprin so skillfully wove together many varied projects with committed advocates and gave attention to the entire corridor between Public Square and Playhouse Square, his plan and the organization charged with carrying it out could take credit for individual successes while remaining aloof from initiatives that did not succeed. For example, the Garden Club of Cleveland, headed by the *Plain Dealer* publisher-editor's wife, Iris Vail, adopted the enhancement of Public Square as a cause. Piggybacking on the approaching U.S. bicentennial, the Garden Club held a patriotically themed benefit ball at the Arcade in 1975, netting $175,000 that seeded a less-ambitious plan than Halprin's for revamping Public Square.[56] Likewise, although the Playhouse Square revitalization campaign predated Halprin's arrival by a few years, its chief advocates, including members of the Junior League, were among the short list of leaders to whom Halprin was introduced in 1973, and he continued to cultivate them during the workshop process. The inclusion of Hadden as a cochair of DCC's Playhouse Square committee and of Shepardson and other dedicated backers of the theater district revival as committee members was an acknowledgment of the promise of that effort, a way of claiming a connection to it, and an attempt to pull what had started as a grassroots movement into the orbit of the growth coalition.[57]

As the Cleveland Foundation situated itself more openly and directly within the growth coalition through its sponsorship of Halprin's plan, its leaders also warmed to the idea of embracing Playhouse Square, but they did so on their own terms. Shepardson's Playhouse Square Cabaret shows—especially *Jacques Brel*, which closed in the summer of 1975 after a remarkable 522 performances that grossed more than $1.5 million from more than 135,000 attendees—had proven that suburbanites would spend an evening downtown if given something fun to do. Yet these shows did little to move the needle in terms of generating the necessary funding to undertake the kind of transformational redevelopment that an increasing number of observers expected and that a much-maligned city seemed to require for improving its image. Even after the commencement of Junior League backing, Shepardson remained accustomed to doing little better than breaking even. Sometimes the only profits his shows netted came from the sale of popcorn, liquor, and concessions. Cleveland Foundation executive director Homer Wadsworth later characterized Playhouse Square's backers somewhat dismissively as "a bit naïve" and their efforts as resembling "cocktail party planning."[58]

More than simply a concern about the lack of a solid business footing gave pause to the foundation. There was, Hadden noted, a desire to see something approximating Ghirardelli Square or Boston's soon-to-open Faneuil Hall Marketplace, which was garnering considerable national attention as a new model for downtown renewal. It is worth recalling that, as late as 1975, Strawbridge's Settlers' Landing project in the Flats, with its location near Higbee's and the planned Tower City Center, still looked more likely to anchor a strong shopping, dining, and entertainment concentration than Playhouse Square. As the Cleveland Foundation's historian Diana Tittle has pointed out, the foundation was weighing where to invest in downtown, and it considered these other projects alongside the theaters.[59] The Tower City Center concept had originated in a 1968 study by U.S. Realty Interests and Penn Central Railroad, the owners of Terminal Tower and Cleveland Union Terminal, respectively, to investigate converting the railroad station into a mixed-use complex, including a shopping mall and a downtown airline terminal, that might utilize the new Cleveland Transit System (CTS) rapid transit line to Cleveland Hopkins International Airport. The idea, which ballooned into an elaborate $350-million plan, languished as the city government and railroad companies failed to agree on who was responsible for repairs to five bridges traversing the subterranean station. With Tower City Center and Settlers' Landing facing uncertain futures, the once unlikely Playhouse Square revitalization emerged as a safer bet.[60]

After van Dijk had worked to stall the demolition of the Loew's State Building, he and some architecture students from Kent State University prepared a large model showing how Playhouse Square's theaters could be interconnected to form a unified performing arts complex akin to New York's Lincoln Center. The model showed how Dodge Court and other rear alleys might be turned into cobblestone walks lined by restaurants, clearly a nod to Ghirardelli Square. As a native of Eindhoven, Netherlands, home to the lighting giant Philips, van Dijk also felt inspired to include a lighting museum to show off Cleveland's own pioneering history in lighting (e.g., Charles Brush's arc lamp and General Electric's [GE's] Nela Park innovations). Van Dijk showed the model to anyone who expressed an interest for some time before he received a telephone call from Wadsworth, who had left his longtime position as the head of the Kansas City Association of Trusts and Foundations to become the director of the Cleveland Foundation in 1974. Unbeknownst to van Dijk, Wadsworth had recently been with a group of men who viewed the model and was very impressed. Wadsworth indicated to van Dijk that the Cleveland Foundation might provide support to work toward implementing such a plan.[61] The Cleveland Foundation, according to Tittle's account, was less than thrilled that the Playhouse Square operation was carrying a deficit of more than $1 million as a result of its reliance on free shows, and some in the foundation believed that Shepardson's vision, which included carving some of the theater spaces themselves into shops and restaurants, was too haphazard. By some accounts, van Dijk's model played a more direct role than Shepardson's popular shows in convincing the foundation to become actively involved.[62]

The Cleveland Foundation worked mostly behind the scenes, eschewing publicity of its aid to Playhouse Square. In January 1976, the foundation declined a request by Shepardson's group to fund $189,000 in operating costs and instead hired an outside evaluator, who agreed that something along the line of van Dijk's plan was a better means of preserving the theaters' function as performing arts spaces. The foundation ultimately awarded a much more modest sum in December of that year to hire Gordon E. Bell, a friend of Shepardson's, to serve as the executive director of a reorganized Playhouse Square Foundation (the successor to Playhouse Square Associates) to try to place the theaters' operation on a more businesslike footing. Within a year, Bell convinced the Cuyahoga County Board of Commissioners to purchase the Loew's State Building as a site for county offices, which guaranteed that the Ohio and State Theaters would avoid the wrecking ball.[63] With the Playhouse Square Foundation's additional acquisition of the Palace Theater placing most of the complex under its control, the Cleveland Foundation took the next step in its exploration of van Dijk's idea. In 1978, it hired the American City Corporation, headed by James W. Rouse of Baltimore, to study the feasibility of creating a unified multiuse complex of the sort that Strawbridge had tried in the Flats but centering instead around the theaters. Although Rouse headed a company that developed many conventional suburban shopping malls, he had become a national authority on downtown revitalization as a result of his transformation of Boston's Quincy Market into a "festival marketplace" in 1976. Within another five years, he would make the cover of *Time* magazine for a feature article titled "Cities Are Fun," which was precisely the result that Cleveland leaders were trying to produce. Although he echoed Halprin's praise for Playhouse Square's potential, Rouse stopped short of committing to a project there.[64] Thus, the Cleveland Foundation turned its attention to solidifying the district's core attraction by working to assemble as many performing arts organizations in Playhouse Square as possible. It also helped obtain a $1.75-million National Endowment for the Arts challenge grant, which the foundation matched with a $250,000 grant of its own, to fund six arts organizations. The Playhouse Square Foundation got the largest share, one-quarter of the $2-million funding package, a hint of what would become a growing commitment to elevate Playhouse Square to the level of University Circle's cultural fixtures.[65]

## "Grants and Charity": Political Fragmentation, Racial Fear, and the Limits of Subsidized Downtown Renewal

Apart from incremental steps forward in Settlers' Landing and Playhouse Square, in the late 1970s, downtown boosters lost much of the sense of momentum that had greeted the unveiling of the Halprin plan in 1975. Just as earlier promises of achieving a turnaround in downtown's fortunes had proved premature, DCC was similarly undermined by the ongoing centrifugal effects of suburban expansion and the all-too-familiar impacts of political and social fragmentation. Downtown stakeholders had more to fear than suburban competition. Despite Halprin's claim that his brand of inclusive, participatory planning would produce lasting consensus, his plan foundered, as some individual interests continued to place their own wishes first. The election of Kucinich as mayor in 1977 also ushered in a short but volatile period during which he clashed bitterly with business elites and city council members, producing a climate in which downtown development was subjected to the populist mayor's jaundiced view as well as to the gridlock borne of acrimony within city hall itself. In addition, as many white suburbanites came to regard downtown sidewalks and businesses as the preserve of African Americans (a concern inseparable from sensational media attention to downtown crime since the late 1960s), promoters faced growing difficulties in framing downtown as an enticing alternative to the comforting homogeneity of suburbia, leaving one observer of Playhouse Square to wonder whether the area could ever thrive without "grants and charity."[66]

With Settlers' Landing drastically scaled back, Tower City Center enmeshed in red tape, and Public Square's Halprin redesign having yielded to the Garden Club's simplified quadrant-by-quadrant overhaul, boosters were about to face other disappointments, as downtown interests clashed and a new mayor locked horns with the city council. These political feuds, exacerbated by the promise of a federal grant to build a novel but controversial light-rail loop, contributed to the failure to build Halprin's Euclid Avenue transit mall, seen by many as the linchpin in the fight to revive the city's historic downtown shopping street. Just as the Garden Club rejected Halprin's Public Square design, Mayor Perk, with DCC's assent, worked in 1976 to obtain a federal grant for an elevated "people mover," sidestepping questions about how or whether it would fit Halprin's call for a pedestrian mall and trolley line on Euclid Avenue.[67] While cautioning that the system might create "visual pollution" and "places for muggers to play hide-and-seek with pedestrians," one *Plain Dealer* contributing writer could not resist the notion of "brightly colored, rubber-tired trains . . . quietly zipping around an elevated guideway taking those economic miracle workers—free-spending conventioneers—from a meeting in the ballroom of a revived Sheraton-Cleveland Hotel, to a visit with the mayor at City Hall, then to drinks, dinner and a show at Playhouse Square." He added that an infusion of federal dollars for a people mover to "pull together disconnected parts of the central city"—literally packaging downtown—might be exactly the spark needed to realize Halprin's Euclid Avenue mall, help Erieview "out of its funk," and jump-start Playhouse Square's "lagging redevelopment."[68]

Cleveland got an early Christmas present with the December 22, 1976, announcement that it had been designated one of four "demonstration cities" for a people mover. Promoters of the downtown subway plan of the 1950s had come to see rail transit less as a way to preserve downtown and more as a tool for reversing downtown's decline. Right from the start, however, backers of the people-mover concept positioned it as an opportunity to resuscitate downtown and the overall image of the city. With praise matching that for the 1959 Euclid Avenue subway plan, the *Plain Dealer* editorialized that the people mover "could be the single greatest catalyst in bringing about downtown restoration." Soon after the plan won federal funding, Mayor Perk told the Exchange Club, "This one project can do more to change the image of the City of Cleveland than any within our power to provide."[69]

However, if tens of millions of dollars in federal subsidies for the people mover seemed to the Perk administration to be too good to pass up, the people mover drew fire from a range of sources, reflecting a familiar pattern in other cities in which ambitious urban rail transit plans were either scaled back (e.g., Buffalo's reduction of a 65-mile rapid transit system to a single 7.5-mile subway) or canceled (e.g., Pittsburgh's failure to build a $228-million rubber-tired tram connecting its suburbs to the Golden Triangle).[70] City planning director Krumholz decried the people mover's unfair and potentially unsustainable privileging of downtown, and he feared that the system offered little benefit for the vast majority of local transit riders. Many suburban city councils passed anti–people mover resolutions in the winter of 1977 that cited concerns about cost overruns or the need to focus instead on improving area-wide transit.[71] In an op-ed piece, CSU urban studies professor Thomas Bier expressed a very different concern. He called Euclid Avenue a place of singular importance for "furthering the social stability of our city," because it still attracted "rich, poor, black, white, young, old." Bier also pointed out that in recent years, Euclid Avenue between Public Square and East 9th Street had become a racial boundary, with more whites on its north side and more blacks on its south side. He feared that a people mover built atop the sidewalk along the south side of the street, unlike the Halprin-designed pedestrian mall, might remove whites from street level, thereby promoting racial separation and undercutting the efforts of boosters to revitalize downtown, a critique often leveled at Detroit's Renaissance Center, Atlantic City's casinos, and the skywalk systems in many cities.[72]

Even before Kucinich became the mayor in November 1977, he promised that, if elected, he would pull the plug on the people mover. Just weeks into his tenure, Kucinich asked the Urban Mass Transit Administration (UMTA) to revoke its $41-million grant to the city, and in January 1978, UMTA obliged, despite a city council resolution opposing the mayor's action.[73] The demise of the people-mover plan did not kill the Euclid Avenue mall plan, but Kucinich was not finished. Indeed, Kucinich, who had been critical of the entire Halprin plan as a councilman, had not changed his opinion. Although little of that plan seemed likely to be realized any time soon, DCC remained committed to the pedestrian mall idea. However, a pedestrian mall required a bus and auto loop to handle the traffic removed from Euclid, and key Playhouse Square interests broke rank with DCC over the issue of extending East 17th Street two blocks southward from its Euclid Avenue terminus as part of the loop. The Playhouse Square Association and Hanna Building owner Donald T. Grogan (whose father Timothy Grogan had been a major proponent of the downtown subway plan) now argued that extending the street to turn it and East 18th into a pair of one-way, north–south arteries would act as a barrier dividing CSU from Playhouse Square. Unlike his father, who had feared that closing East 13th Street might cut off Playhouse Square from any new bustle in Erieview, Grogan complained that the extension of East 17th would also connect Playhouse Square's image with that of "unwholesome bar, lounge and pornographic night traffic" along Prospect Avenue, one block south of Euclid.[74] Kucinich, siding with the Playhouse Square interests, said he would seek to remove the extension from consideration for federal matching funds. Although he appeared to shift course a few days later by promising to study the plan, the mayor never ceased his obstruction of DCC's effort.[75] His hostility toward the growth coalition, mixed with Playhouse Square interests' apparent belief that a connection to seedy Prospect Avenue canceled whatever advantages might accrue from beautifying Euclid Avenue, produced another case of the civic inertia that Clevelanders were well-conditioned to expect.

The challenges facing downtown revitalization went beyond fragmentation among municipal and business interests. As in many other American cities, the legacy of the urban crisis and heightened racial tensions and concerns over law and order also constrained efforts to renew downtown Cleveland. Bier's aforementioned perception of Euclid Avenue as a color line or racial boundary in downtown only hinted at mind-sets that governed the degree to which Clevelanders believed their downtown had a bright future. After only three years in operation, in 1976, the Last Moving Picture Company closed its restaurant and became solely a discotheque. Ironically, its last night of serving food was in support of a Playhouse Square Association–sponsored progressive dinner aimed at attracting suburbanites.[76] The following year, the business's secretary-treasurer complained to a *Plain Dealer* reporter that poor security and lack of parking in Playhouse Square had driven away the Last Moving Picture Company's target clientele—"white single people in the 21 to 30 age group." He added that those who replaced them "don't spend as much as the more affluent suburbanites. We're not particularly happy with the situation. We're contemplating a move, if conditions don't improve." If the reference to African Americans was too veiled, the reporter laid bare its meaning: "In their [white suburbanites'] place have come Cleveland residents, largely blacks, to dance and drink."[77]

African Americans' presence was not only an irritant to the business operators, who closed the Last Moving Picture Company a few months later, but also one more cue to write off downtown, as GCGA downtown development director Robert J. Zion commented in 1978 when he observed that white suburbanites "think of downtown as a black area and fear blacks."[78] On some level, this issue—a combination of the departure of more-affluent, mostly white Clevelanders to the suburbs and their perception of the central city as being dominated by the poorer, mostly black residents they left behind—was inseparable from the growth coalition's continuing push to preserve the image of downtown as a place hospitable to whites. Similar references to remaking increasingly black downtowns for white suburbanites and visitors accompanied other cities' projects, including Chicago's planned State Street Mall.[79] Wadsworth summed up this mind-set well when he characterized Playhouse Square revitalization as "worth doing unless you want to be another Newark. The alternative you have to keep in front of you justifies the risks. You are heavily black in the city and have virtually no in-city middle class population and if you're not very careful and don't do something about it you can close the town down at six P.M. daily. This is the situation in Newark."[80] Indeed, the Cleveland Foundation in the 1970s shared the same fears about the central city that had motivated the Cleveland Development Foundation (CDF), GCGA, and the University Circle Development Foundation (UCDF) to reinvigorate key parts of Cleveland in the 1950s and 1960s.

In his memoir, Strawbridge recalled that downtown had "entered its darkest period" in 1973. Even then, however, Shepardson's phenomenal success with *Jacques Brel* cast a bright spotlight on at least one corner of downtown.[81] Six years later, a similar paradox continued to confront downtown boosters: Downtown was simultaneously declining and revitalizing, and its overall trajectory was anything but clear. Although the public had no idea that Halle's was just three years from the end of its ninety-one-year run, by 1979, a department store that once catered to the "carriage trade" was reshuffling its departments and contemplating eliminating some of its selling space on upper floors in a last-ditch effort to get out of the red.[82] Believing in Cleveland was not easy. The *Plain Dealer* entertainment writer Emerson Batdorff observed that "many brave merchandisers have surged in, only to leave empty stores and whitewashed plate-glass windows behind them." He lamented that only the confluence of a large number of shows ending at about the same time could produce, for a few fleeting moments, the feel of Times Square as thousands of people rushed to their cars.[83] Some observers suggested that downtown's future might be a story of perpetual "bootstrapping" in which Clevelanders bore the unceasing burden of trying to rekindle a fire that would not burn on its own. Batdorff, for instance, wrote that whenever he attended a show in Playhouse Square, he believed that he was "performing a civic duty, like not littering, . . . digging away the snow that hides fireplugs during blizzards or participating on [sic] the WCLV Cleveland Orchestra Marathon."[84] The paper's theater critic Bill Doll described a similar feeling of burden by likening Clevelanders' response to the closing of old theaters to the way they might respond to the news of "the impending death of an aunt to whom we once were close but haven't seen for years." Doll believed he detected "something cold and artificial as well as sadly sentimental about the resuscitation efforts" in Playhouse Square.[85]

Perhaps a fierce loyalty to downtown revitalization efforts—tinged with the nagging fear that the entire exercise of renewal was flawed and possibly futile—was a symptom of a condition that gripped those who cared deeply about the future of America's downtowns. Burdened with the memory of downtown as it functioned in the early to mid-twentieth century, they struggled to come to terms with what it meant to support a post-urban-crisis downtown, especially when they could never be certain that a turnaround was actually at hand. Expressing a sentiment that would hardly have been foreign to Shepardson, Strawbridge, or any downtown booster, *Plain Dealer* reporter William F. Miller wrote that "in nearly ten years of covering Playhouse Square, I have found that all victories there must be won an inch at a time."[86]

# 6

## The "Ohio City Renaissance"

*The Contested Comeback on Cleveland's Near West Side*

On September 12, 1971, in the year of Cleveland's "Super Sesqui" celebration of the 175th anniversary of its founding, more than five hundred people showed up to tour nine restored nineteenth-century homes in the vicinity of West 30th Street and Bridge Avenue on the city's Near West Side. Billed as "A Super Sesquicentennial Salute to Ohio City," the event also included a flea market and kiddie rides. Proceeds from the event were to be directed to the Cleveland Society for Crippled Children and the Urban Community School, a three-year-old institution combining the former St. Patrick and St. Malachi parochial schools with the aim of educating an increasingly diverse neighborhood population that included growing numbers of Puerto Rican children. However, the event also showcased "Ohio City," a neighborhood concept upheld by its promoter, the Ohio City Community Development Association (OCCDA), as a new hope for rebuilding Cleveland by encouraging a back-to-the-city movement of white suburbanites that might succeed where urban renewal planners had failed. After the tour, visitors and VIPs boarded a London-style double-decker bus and Ford Model A's that rumbled through narrow streets to the old Superior Viaduct, a cobblestone-paved remnant of a sandstone bridge off Detroit Avenue and West 25th Street that once traversed the Cuyahoga River. There, "amid the sounds and smells of the Cuyahoga," the infamous polluted river that had burned just two years before, a local Hungarian gypsy violinist played as the party dined by flickering candlelight on chicken paprikash and stuffed cabbage.[1]

The choice of the Superior Viaduct as the location to end the day's festivities surely drove home a key message. By situating a crowd that included many East Side suburbanites in view of downtown Cleveland, OCCDA implicitly presented the opportunity to create a new lifestyle built around an imagined past and urban excitement. The sales pitch was hardly unique, of course; in fact, OCCDA drew direct inspiration from Georgetown in Washington, D.C.; College Hill in Providence, Rhode Island; and especially German Village in Columbus, Ohio. Historic preservation—pioneered in the years after World War I in a handful of cities, including Charleston, South Carolina, and New Orleans, and stimulated by the popularity of the Depression-era reconstruction of Colonial Williamsburg—counted many successes in cities across America. Where local grassroots initiatives, such as the Curtiss-Olive demonstration, and large-scale, government-funded housing rehabilitation projects, such as University-Euclid, had failed to triumph over blight, energetic preservation efforts—emboldened by the passage of the National Historic Preservation Act of 1966—seemingly offered a path toward urban revitalization.[2] The do-it-yourself ethos of the Ohio City restorers, coupled with their memory of recent urban riots and a burning river, stoked their belief that they were active instruments of change and, in this festive moment of civic commemoration, agents in the vanguard of Cleveland's rebirth.

This chapter briefly recounts the dissolution of the original Ohio City into Cleveland's Near West Side (a convenient but vague shorthand for a checkerboard of streets fanning westward from the Cuyahoga River along Detroit and Lorain Avenues. It also examines the narrative of Near West Side decline, the birth of the Ohio City renaissance as a means of rescuing Cleveland from urban crisis, and the ways in which "Ohio City" and "Near West Side" came to embody competing perspectives of the state of the city and its proper direction. Summoning—and simplifying—its history, architecture, and social diversity, Ohio City's champions made it the bellwether neighborhood in their efforts to reframe the image of post-riot Cleveland. As in similar gentrifying inner-city neighborhoods across America, the Ohio City renaissance also offered a template for carrying the battle against neighborhood decay into the era of "comeback cities." While East Side neighborhoods were hollowed by the ebbing urban crisis and fair-housing advocates and black pioneers were training their eyes on opening once-exclusive suburbs, Ohio City not only was spared the bulldozer but also became a beneficiary of longtime residents' obstruction of integration.

## The Rise and Fall of the Near West Side

Carved from Brooklyn Township on a bluff overlooking the west bank of the meandering Cuyahoga River, the "City of Ohio," or Ohio City, was incorporated as a municipality three days before Cleveland in 1836. At the time, with its original population of "Connecticut Yankees" swelled by Welsh, German, and Irish immigrants, Ohio City was about one-third the size of Cleveland, its rival across the river. Both enjoyed a major boost from the Ohio and Erie Canal (completed four years earlier), which connected Lake Erie at Cleveland to the Ohio River at Portsmouth, Ohio. River and lake trade spurred industrialization on both sides of the Cuyahoga, but when real estate speculators erected the first permanent bridge over the "Crooked River," Columbus Street Bridge, in 1835 to serve their Cleveland Centre development on Ox Bow Bend in the Flats, its diversion of wagon traffic away from Ohio City sparked violent mob action that came to be known as the Columbus Bridge War. Militiamen, a court injunction, and plans for additional bridges quelled the unrest, but Ohio City never recovered its pre-bridge advantage of controlling trade on the west bank. On June 5, 1854, four years after Cleveland annexed lands eastward to Willson Avenue (present-day East 55th Street), the city absorbed most of the area from the Cuyahoga River westward to Waverly Avenue (now West 58th Street) between Lake Erie and Walworth Run, a tributary of the Cuyahoga.[3] Although Ohio City lost ground to its rival across the river during its eighteen years as a separate municipality and few buildings from that era survived into the twentieth century, it bequeathed a later generation of Clevelanders an imagined past that could be romanticized and potentially used to reframe their city's image.

If the 1830s to 1850s provided the most compelling historic narrative for the future, with few exceptions, the 1850s to 1910s furnished the historic cityscape. Scions of old Connecticut settlers, along with German and Irish immigrants, amassed wealth in commerce and industry, with the wealthiest able to erect fine mansions that made Franklin Boulevard second only to Euclid Avenue among Cleveland's illustrious addresses. Houses designed in a range of architectural styles lined most of the other streets, providing an essential ingredient for future "quaintness." In addition, key institutional landmarks augmented a skyline dominated by older church spires. In 1888, St. Ignatius Preparatory College built a new Second Empire–style main building capped by a 159-foot tower. Then, in 1912, the municipal government erected the cavernous, neoclassical- and Byzantine-style West Side Market at the corner of Lorain and West 25th, whose 137-foot-tall clock tower became perhaps the most recognizable landmark on the Near West Side.

Between the mid-nineteenth and early twentieth centuries, the former Ohio City, now simply part of the expanding West Side, reached the peak of its influence before beginning what some came to view as its long descent. Even as the former Ohio City reached its apex, however, many of its more affluent businessmen and industrialists were already starting to disperse into newer outlying neighborhoods. The Near West Side filled rapidly with new immigrants from central and eastern Europe, notably Czechs, Hungarians, and Poles, many of whom worked in nearby breweries, bottle works, and foundries and in steel mills in the Flats. Detroit and Lorain Avenues and Pearl Street (West 25th Street) continued to be thriving commercial corridors, while many of the mansions lining Franklin Boulevard became boarding-houses. Owners converted modest houses on narrow lots into two-family dwellings, and, increasingly, crowded tenements lined the streets and back alleys in between.[4]

After World War II, the white middle class resumed its outward flow to the suburbs, now joined by growing numbers of ethnic working-class Cleve-landers. However, the Near West Side's population loss during and soon after the war was offset to great extent by an influx of migrants, mostly from the South and Puerto Rico. Migrants crowded into rooming houses and apart-ment buildings even as many single-family homes fell vacant. Two prewar public housing projects on the fringes of the Near West Side—Lakeview Ter-race and Valleyview Homes—fell far short of meeting the growing demand for decent, inexpensive housing. With federal enforcement of fair-housing provisions still beyond the horizon, southern black migrants landed prepon-derantly in the spreading East Side slums, where they found less resistance to their arrival. Their relative absence from the Near West Side lessened the pressure of overcrowding on a housing stock that otherwise was not greatly dissimilar from that in Hough. Although these migrants arrived in greatest numbers at a time when the Near West Side was widely viewed as declining, all except blacks would be added to the "melting pot" in narratives that sought to recast an uneasy ethnic patchwork as an essential part of a "color-ful" Ohio City.

As in Hough, the 1940s and 1950s brought growing concerns about neighborhood decay on the Near West Side. While planners directed more attention to the East Side, which suffered the most acute housing problem in the city, the Near West Side did not entirely miss renewal efforts. The Cleve-land City Planning Commission first recognized the need for rehabilitation on the Near West Side in 1944, at which time it singled out the eastern por-tion of the area as needing more drastic redevelopment.[5] However, it took more than a decade for neighborhood conservation to commence there. In 1957, the planning commission directed a $46,000 federal grant and $23,000 in city matching funds to support a small-scale, two-year demonstration project by the West Side Civic Council (WSCC) and the Cleveland Welfare Federation in the Monroe Area, a ninety-three-acre community named for the Monroe Street Cemetery and bounded by Lorain Avenue, Fulton Road, West 25th Street, and the New York Central Railroad.[6]

Soon after the Monroe Area project got underway, a newly formed group of West 25th Street area businesses and institutions called Ohio City Plan-ning Sponsors committed $12,000 to commission a plan by two local archi-tects affiliated with the same firm that was planning the future of University Circle. Their approach contrasted with the Monroe Area project and heark-ened to the City Planning Commission's earlier call for redevelopment. The group hoped to foster business expansion, improve traffic flow and parking facilities, and remediate blight along the West 25th corridor. Called *Ohio City—Central Park West*, the plan was the first appropriation of the name "Ohio City" in the service of urban revitalization. Commission chairman Ernest J. Bohn applauded the effort and observed that the area was "going down but can be the best location in the nation. With its own business section and office buildings, it is a wonderful location for walk-to-work apartments."[7]

The *Ohio City—Central Park West* report recommended, among other actions, clearing blighted properties to provide expansion room for Lutheran Hospital, providing off-street parking for businesses and converting West 25th Street between Bridge and Chatham Avenues to a pedestrian mall to create a "shopping center" around the West Side Market, rerouting north–south traffic onto a new loop road, establishing a large parking lot and loop bus service to assist downtown commuters, and redeveloping the Fulton Road area with new apartments arrayed around a large park.[8] The report drew fire from both WSCC and the City Planning Commission. The former denounced the Ohio City Planning Sponsors' plan as a land grab to force out low-rent housing to benefit businesses, institutions, and developers. In a prescient moment that anticipated later outcry against gentrification, WSCC's director insisted on "guarantees . . . to protect the people who live here now." Likewise, the planning commission, which had called for studying a broader area extending as far as West 65th Street in Ward 3, rejected most of the plan's proposals and emphasized the need to rehabilitate existing structures rather than clear and redevelop the area.[9]

Urban renewal, whether focused on redevelopment or rehabilitation, went nowhere on the West Side in the 1960s. It was in part a casualty of growth coalition leaders' preoccupation with rehousing blacks to contain integration on the East Side. Despite the deterioration of the Near West Side, renewal leaders saw the area as a low priority in comparison to the East Side, where rapidly changing neighborhoods on the eastern flank of Hough and Central seemed unlikely to stall the march of integrationist pressures toward their suburban communities in the Heights. With racial transition pushing eastward, West Side city council members and their heavily white ethnic constituents urged rehabilitation-based urban renewal for the Near West Side while decrying its East Side application and guarding against Bohn's efforts to build public housing west of the river. In 1961, some West Side council members fought unsuccessfully to stop the rezoning of property that the Cleveland Metropolitan Housing Authority (CMHA) had acquired and cleared to build a high-rise public housing project, fearing it would allow the Near West Side, at the time only 0.3 percent black, to be "infiltrated by Negroes." In contrast, no amount of lobbying on their part seemed capable of activating urban renewal. Ward 3 councilman Michael Zone tried without success to lobby Ohio congressional leaders to push for a more liberal application of Section 112—originally used to enable cities to count university construction expenses toward their contribution to urban renewal projects—to cover expenditures by secondary schools, including St. Ignatius and Lourdes Academy, two institutions debating whether to remain in the city.[10]

Although the City Planning Commission issued a new plan for rehabilitation and redevelopment of one thousand acres on the Near West Side in 1963, it gained little traction. As noted in Chapter 1, by the 1960s, James Lister's urban renewal office at city hall and the Cleveland Development Foundation (CDF) largely ignored the planning commission and set their own renewal priorities. The failures they experienced on the East Side owed to the challenges of implementing a flawed federal program and trying to privilege downtown renewal while tackling more neighborhood renewal plans than they could manage. By 1963, two years after the approval of the bond issue that had launched Erieview, voters responded to warnings that Issue 8, the latest urban renewal bond issue, would waste taxpayers' money on so-called slum clearance by lavishing money on Erieview even as it proposed the demolition of some 1,300 homes and properties on the Near West Side. The issue garnered only 49 percent of the vote, well short of the 55 percent required for passage. Although opposition was reportedly strongest in "cosmopolitan wards," the bond issue's unpopularity on the West Side and on the East Side demonstrated a growing disapproval of urban renewal that cut across racial lines.[11]

As Cleveland's urban renewal difficulties mounted, the Near West Side joined a backlog of stagnant projects, including Erieview, University-Euclid, and Gladstone. With its hands full on the East Side, CDF directed smaller sums of grant funding to revive renewal planning in such areas as the Near West Side that had been set back by the bond issue defeat. In April 1964, CDF released $25,000 from the Leonard C. Hanna Jr. Fund to the recently formed Near West Side Development Association, an organization headed by one of the members of the group that sponsored the failed 1958 plan.[12] After the U.S. Department of Housing and Urban Development (HUD) froze renewal funds in Cleveland in January 1967, concerned citizens began to speak out against the Near West Side plan's catering to the expansion wishes of St. Ignatius, Lourdes, and Lutheran Hospital, arguing that residents had been allowed no input in a plan they charged was skewed to the benefit of "those who drive in or are bussed in from the suburbs." Their opposition forced Community Development director Barton R. Clausen to recast the consultants' study as merely a "preliminary proposal."[13]

Even after Mayor Carl Stokes took office in November 1967 and HUD resumed federal support for renewal, the Near West Side continued to languish. Although on casual examination the area's housing was "not as shocking to the eye" as in some East Side areas, observed *Plain Dealer* reporters Roldo Bartimole and Donald Sabath, "tucked away in back alleys and on dirt paths are buildings reminiscent of an old western main street." One such multiunit building, accessible only from an alley between two houses, was known to neighbors as "Dodge City."[14] Nevertheless, having escaped the ravages of urban renewal and rapid racial transition, the Near West Side, with its catalog of mid- and late Victorian houses situated close to downtown, offered an intactness, stability, and atmosphere that would appeal to the first wave of young "urban pioneers" who hoped to do their part to bring Cleveland back. The Near West Side's potential as a model for revitalizing Cleveland neighborhoods benefited from the fact that the area had no dominant, entrenched nationality group weighing whether to stay and defend its insularity or flee to the suburbs, nor did it lie in the path of rapid racial transition.[15]

The best example in Cleveland for illustrating why these factors mattered was Buckeye, a mostly Hungarian neighborhood along Buckeye Road on Cleveland's far East Side (adjacent to the Ludlow section of Shaker Heights). Desperate to maintain the neighborhood's "continental atmosphere," a goal inseparable from fighting racial integration, the Buckeye Neighborhood Nationalities Civic Association (BNNCA) contemplated trying to secede from Cleveland to join Shaker Heights in 1967. Understanding that city council approval of secession would be difficult to secure, BNNCA instead began studying Columbus's German Village in 1968 at almost exactly the time that Ohio City promoters were doing the same thing. However, BNNCA's hope to turn a section of Buckeye into "Hungarian Village" faltered because of white flight, and despite the subsequent formation of an integrationist organization called the Buckeye-Woodland Community Congress, the neighborhood never became a strong model for neighborhood revitalization, in stark contrast to Ohio City.[16]

## Ohio City as the Cradle of Cleveland's Rebirth

Bruce W. Hedderson, a CMHA public relations officer who had moved to Cleveland Heights from Toronto in the early 1960s, liked to spend his lunch breaks and weekends exploring the historic architecture of the Near West Side. One day, he discovered the Monroe Street Cemetery and began reading the inscriptions on its old tombstones. Soon he was researching the early history of Ohio City; by 1967, he saw the Near West Side as a neighborhood that should be preserved to lend a focal point for turning around a beleaguered city. Hedderson observed that the area's historical significance and location near downtown made it similar to Georgetown and German Village. He added that, unlike "a Hough or a Harlem, where the bulldozer would be a better answer," the Near West Side was largely intact.[17] As with Brooklyn, New York's so-called brownstoners, whom urban historian Suleiman Osman has described as a new, postindustrial, young, professional-managerial class, Hedderson and his fellow Ohio City proponents found an antidote to suburban boredom in urban neighborhoods like Cleveland's Near West Side. However, Ohio City's newest "pioneers" did not fit so neatly into Osman's description of young men and women locked in "an existential battle against a new machine—the New Deal pro-growth coalition . . . who since World War II spearheaded a program of urban redevelopment in cities around the country." To be certain, Hedderson and his associates decried urban renewal and suburbanization. Indeed, Hedderson once likened modern homes to mass-produced "gum drops—all looking the same but for their different hues." However, the Ohio City movement, while idealistic, also reflected pragmatism in tailoring its strategy to fit the growth coalition's civic agenda. Similarly, renewal leaders had never unified behind a singular vision of redevelopment; in fact, as early as 1963, Cleveland urban renewal director Lister had publicly expressed his hope that the Near West Side's "local color" might be preserved. Lister's comment demonstrated renewal boosters' ability to modulate approaches, a capacity rooted in their bias against black neighborhoods.[18]

Hedderson's vision appealed to CDF, which had been trying without success for four years to stimulate renewal on the Near West Side. In 1966, CDF had appointed Near West Side Development Association executive director Thomas J. Miller as CDF's executive vice president in an attempt to make a more concerted effort there. In the winter of 1968, Hedderson pitched a project he dubbed "Ohio City Restoration" to Miller, requesting almost $172,000 from CDF for what he called "a significant step forward in attracting the middle class back to our inner city." Although CDF was not prepared to offer that level of funding, it did provide other forms of assistance. CDF set up a meeting in which Upshur Evans introduced Hedderson and his CMHA colleague William B. Hammer to the top brass of Cuyahoga Savings Association, enabling them to pitch the idea of offering favorable lending terms to a core group of would-be home restorers and renovators. When Cuyahoga Savings president Clarence Bryan suggested approaching savings and loans on the West Side, CDF promised to assist in that effort too.[19]

Evans and Miller also aided Ohio City Restoration in other ways. While Hedderson and Hammer urged a German Village–like restart of Ohio City as an alternative to clearance in correspondence with Very Rev. Fr. James W. Kirby, the president-rector of St. Ignatius High School, Evans approached Rt. Rev. John H. Burt, the bishop of the Episcopal Diocese of Ohio, and Rev. Alan J. Eichenberger, the rector of St. John's Episcopal Church, whose stone building on the northern end of old Ohio City was once a station along the Underground Railroad. Evans urged preservation of the church's historic rectory, which Eichenberger wanted to replace with a modern building better suited to the needs of his parish's many outreach programs for impoverished neighborhood residents. Evans overstepped when he suggested that, prior to CDF's encouragement of Erieview and the formation of Cleveland

State University, "anyone could have fired a cannon down the nave of Trinity Cathedral only to hit the empty altar." Before the bishop could reply, a perturbed Eichenberger shot back that if one were to fire a cannon into St. John's, "nine out of ten of those potentially injured would be local residents of this area. They come in assorted shapes, sizes, colors, languages, and backgrounds." He added that the church struggled to meet community needs while maintaining antiquated facilities and that it seemed that those who cried the loudest for preservation of St. John's were "even more distressed" when asked to contribute to maintaining it "in all of its historical purity."[20]

Because their direct appeals to neighborhood stakeholders did not always yield the responses for which they hoped, the Ohio City promoters also explored other avenues. Hedderson, Evans, and Miller worked closely in the spring of 1968 to assemble historical materials about old Ohio City. They also consulted with Frank Fetch, the president of the German Village Society in Columbus, and University Circle Development Foundation (UCDF) planning director Allen Fonoroff on developing a "land protective code" for Ohio City. Following a CDF-brokered meeting in which Fonoroff recommended that Hedderson and Hammer seek a historic area ordinance, Evans authorized Fonoroff to use CDF funding to work with Ohio City Restoration to research and develop such a code. Because it would be important to establish clear talking points to sell such an ordinance, Hedderson also got CDF to underwrite a concise history of Ohio City and turned to Richard N. Campen, an architectural historian from Chagrin Falls who had written a number of photo essays on historic landmarks for the *Plain Dealer* in recent years. Campen worked feverishly to produce a full draft of *The Story of Ohio City* in fewer than six weeks so that Hedderson might have it in time for an expected meeting with the director of the National Trust for Historic Preservation (a Washington, D.C.–based nonprofit organization for national preservation advocacy chartered by Congress in 1949) to discuss the neighborhood's merit as a historic district. Meanwhile, Fetch told Hedderson that the German Village architectural control ordinance was based on similar codes written for Society Hill in Philadelphia and other places. Fetch added that to secure city council support, "our Society provided a receptive atmosphere by inviting the councilmen under very pleasant social conditions so that any objections would be ironed out before the ordinance was actually presented to the City Council."[21]

CDF's and Ohio City Restoration's hope of creating an ordinance-controlled historic district that would compel a high standard in neighborhood improvements drew a mixed response. Councilwoman Margaret McCaffery, who had moved to the Near West Side to represent Ward 8 after redistricting abolished her Ward 22 post in 1965, had had her own personal experiences with displacement as a result of rent increases associated with racial transition in Hough. But perhaps her experience in Hough had also taught her the value of not gainsaying plans that promised to reverse decline. Whatever her reason, McCaffery said she would be willing to sponsor legislation to change zoning to support the restoration of Ohio City. In contrast, St. John's rector Eichenberger feared that "poor people would be forced out" and could not brook granting concessions "to a group of people that don't live here." Although he denied any intent to force out existing residents, even Hedderson admitted that "you can't expect a landlord to completely renovate a place and still charge only $45-a-month rent."[22] Likely hoping to avoid further confrontations over the neighborhood's future direction, the young Ohio City promoters abandoned discussion of a zoning ordinance covering a large swath of the Near West Side and set out instead to carve out a small demonstration area that might gradually accomplish their goals.

Accordingly, Hedderson began giving slide lectures about Ohio City, where he met others who shared his dream of an "Ohio City renaissance." One was Bruce Wade, a local architect, whom he tapped to identify available houses to renovate. Wade acquired a dilapidated frame house on a narrow lot at 2910 Bridge Avenue, which he began to renovate in a contemporary style, adding space by opening up living space under the eaves. Wade carefully documented his costs and turned his investment into more than just his home. He and his partner David Brown, a musician, made it a "demonstration house" to prove to young professionals that Ohio City was "a fun place" and give longtime residents new hope for the neighborhood's future.[23] Eugene and Marilyn Marx, introduced to Hedderson by Miller, their neighbor in University Heights, became enchanted with the Ohio City vision and agreed to commit themselves to purchasing and restoring a house there. Assisted by Wade, the Marxes found, bought, and restored a careworn century-old home at 3803 Bridge Avenue. Marilyn Marx explained their decision as one of believing in the city: "To us this was the opportunity to do something in the city, not just sit in the living room and gripe about Cleveland going downhill."[24]

When CDF offered seed money and West Side Federal Savings and Loan Association (WSFS) promised mortgage financing, Hedderson and his new friends founded OCCDA in late December 1968.[25] Within a month, OCCDA was formally incorporated, and CDF and WSFS were represented on the organization's board of trustees. At a time when most banks actively avoided giving loans for home renovations in inner-city neighborhoods, the linchpin in the venture was WSFS president Carl C. Heintel's and vice president Edward J. Wagner's decision to support Ohio City. Founded as Cleveland West Seite Bauverein Company by German immigrants in 1886, WSFS remained in the vicinity of Lorain Avenue and West 25th Street for the next sixty-six years before moving its main offices eight miles westward on Lorain to Fairview Park in 1952 to reposition itself closer to suburban depositors. Now, just two decades later, WSFS, which still maintained a branch office on West

25th, was recommitting itself to the inner city, including revitalization projects in Hough and Ohio City. As Wagner later observed, "How many more Houghs could Cleveland afford?" The company formed the WSFS Development Corporation in 1970 to buy homes and sell them under attractive terms on the condition that they be restored within three years.[26] For the next several years, WSFS, which became Cardinal Federal in 1974, almost singlehandedly financed the Ohio City renaissance. WSFS's incentives and boosterism appeared to be enjoying some help from national trends: An energy crisis and rising interest rates that made suburban living more expensive lent new promise to a "back-to-the-city" movement that had been predicted for more than a decade.

WSFS became involved in more than just approving mortgages in a redlined neighborhood. In the summer of 1971, for example, WSFS partnered with the May Company, the city's largest downtown department store, to showcase OCCDA's work. They sponsored a five-day "Save A House" home restoration seminar that addressed all aspects of finding, financing, restoring, decorating, and landscaping a historic property, placing the focus on Ohio City. One of the sessions, titled "Here's How to Help the City," explicitly connected the Ohio City restoration effort to the broader revitalization of Cleveland. In 1973, WSFS advertised its role in Ohio City, averring that "we wanted to do something extra for Cleveland." Accordingly, WSFS customers could open an "ABC" savings account, whose deposits would be invested in "ABC—A Better Cleveland."[27] Later that year, WSFS also purchased a Bridge Avenue home believed to be the birthplace of John W. Heisman, a pioneering football coach for whom the Heisman Trophy is named, and worked with *Plain Dealer* sports editor Hal Lebovitz to establish a foundation to try to turn the house into a museum. Although the museum never came to fruition and Heisman's actual birthplace was later discovered to lie nearly one mile to the west, the football icon's fame nonetheless provided an impetus for one more restoration in the heart of Ohio City (see Figure 6.1).[28]

The Ohio City renaissance won the attention of civic boosters for its seeming ability to go beyond simply rehabilitating inner-city housing for primarily lower-income residents. Here was an endeavor that also seemed capable of doing more than superficial "clean-up, fix-up, paint-up" drives and nonprofit-financed minimal rehabilitation of a block of houses, which at best persuaded people to stay in the city, or federally funded urban renewal projects, which often did more to drive away residents than to retain them. In contrast, the Ohio City renaissance was newsworthy, mainly because it contributed more clearly to the prospect of repopulating the depleted city with the kind of people whose educational attainment and employment gave them the luxury of choice in housing. These were people for whom concerns about urban image mattered. However, the restoration movement also breathed new life into tired or vacant storefronts, adding to Ohio City pro

**Figure 6.1.**
This house at 2820
Bridge Avenue
underwent restoration
in the early 1970s.
Bridge Avenue
between West 28th
Street and Fulton
Road was at the
heart of the first wave
of the "Ohio City
renaissance." (The
Western Reserve
Historical Society,
Cleveland, Ohio.)

moters' dream of a complete in-town community and giving new hope to merchants despite the gradual erosion of business caused by population flight and the destruction of thousands of homes to build I-90, which sliced east and west through the neighborhood anywhere from one-fifth to four-fifths of a mile south of the Lorain Avenue business corridor.

The businesses that opened in Ohio City in the early to mid-1970s, like those in gentrifying neighborhoods in other American cities, moved decisively beyond filling needs. Rather, they supported the cultivated lifestyles of young professionals who sought to package consumption in a wrapper of urban authenticity. The originator of the Ohio City restoration movement, Hedderson, also opened the neighborhood's first art gallery with two other co-owners on Fulton Road in 1973.[29] He was hardly alone. After returning home from the College of William and Mary, John T. Saile rented an apartment in Shaker Heights and joined his family's Euclid-based beer distribution business. He soon tired of the "sterile streets" of the Heights and, with "visions of colonial Williamsburg" still in his head, in 1969, the twenty-six-year-old bought and began restoring an "elegant ruin" of a large red-brick home at Jay Avenue and West 28th Street. For Saile, who within a decade would become known to many as the unofficial "Mayor of Ohio City," a self-professed determination to do his part "to attract members of the middle class back into the inner city" purportedly led him to start a series of businesses. Teaming with his sister and a master weaver in 1972, Saile opened Twelvetree and Company, an antique and fine crafts shop named for a nineteenth-century Ohio City firm. The shop was part of an early-1970s upsurge in antiques stores along a three-mile stretch of Lorain Avenue, a development that mirrored a national trend connected to the rise of gentrification and historic preservation.[30] Two years later, Saile opened two more businesses, Ohio City Haberdashery and Heck's Café, in a restored former corner grocery at Bridge Avenue and West 30th Street. Heck's became instantly known for its long menu of gourmet sandwiches, including signature half-pound burgers topped with caviar, sour cream, and Bermuda onion. Saile reached back several decades to appropriate the name "Heckmann," the family who ran a small corner grocery that also served cheap sandwiches that were popular with St. Ignatius students.[31] In doing so, Saile erased associations with Ray's Corner Lunch, Heck's Café's predecessor, which reflected the Near West Side's postwar history as a destination for Hungarian immigrants and for Appalachian, Puerto Rican, and American Indian migrants, many of whom labored in steel mills in the Flats and refreshed themselves in neighborhood dive bars, hot dog stands, and luncheonettes like Ray's.

Saile was not the first to recognize the potential for a destination restaurant in Ohio City. Paul Martoccia, a South High School teacher who also operated a burger restaurant in the East Side neighborhood of Buckeye, became fascinated with Ohio City, where he had salvaged several tons of stained-glass windows prior to the demolition of St. Mary's Church to make way for a St. Ignatius school expansion in 1968. Martoccia acquired and restored a century-old Bridge Avenue building that had long housed Joe's Bar, a Hungarian-owned saloon, in which to open the upscale Ohio City Tavern, from whose ceiling he hung the stained-glass windows, in 1973. In explaining his decision to open a restaurant, Martoccia cited his hope to attract downtown workers at lunchtime and suburbanites in the evening, adding that he had believed in Cleveland before it became "fashionable to start boosting the city." The restaurant even became a tool for attracting newcomers to St. John's Episcopal Church. St. John's rector Rev. Wilbur R. Ellis, who in contrast to his anti-gentrification-minded predecessor hoped to attract suburbanites and newly arrived Ohio City homeowners, experimented with selling $15 tickets for a package that included a special Saturday evening service and champagne "happy hour" at St. John's followed by dinner at Martoccia's Ohio City Tavern.[32]

In appealing to a seemingly insatiable appetite for "authentic" urban experiences, Saile and Martoccia, like Hedderson and fellow OCCDA "pioneers," charted what surely appeared to the growth coalition to be a simpler and more self-reliant approach to revitalizing Cleveland and its tarnished image than they found in Hough. Indeed, it is hardly an accident that CDF embraced the minimal financial needs of the architects of the Ohio City renaissance even as it withdrew from the housing field on the troubled East Side. In contrast to Hough, where no amount of federal or charitable subsidy appeared capable of reversing private-sector disinvestment and the combination of blacks' desire to leave and whites' reluctance to return, Ohio City seemed ready to point the way to a Cleveland renaissance dependent on middle-class white "urban pioneers" who, if not self-sufficient, needed little more than willing lenders and insurers.

## "Did They See the Problems of the 20th Century?": Ohio City versus Near West Side

Although it had its own declension narrative to overcome, Ohio City had avoided the unfortunate fate of Hough and Glenville in the 1960s. Unlike an East Side marred by urban renewal demolitions, Ohio City had the advantage of a relatively intact Victorian cityscape with some outstanding early- and mid-nineteenth-century landmarks that provided at least the illusion of a refuge from the urban crisis. Ohio City also escaped the heavy burden of race by being situated away from the path of racial succession in one of the nation's most segregated metropolitan areas. Its location on the city's overwhelmingly white West Side, whose three thousand blacks (scarcely 1 percent of the city's total black population) were almost completely contained in three public housing projects near the river, seemed to provide fertile ground for seeding Cleveland's first attempt to sidestep the urban crisis.[33] As it turned out, its promoters' efforts to craft an image of harmonious diversity could not easily overcome the social rifts into which they inserted themselves as new pioneers. Indeed, the specter of decline would linger in the midst of the triumphalism of urban rebirth.

The effort to cast the Ohio City renaissance as a celebration of Cleveland's ethnic profusion followed a well-worn path. Like many other cities, Cleveland had a long history of shaping its image of social diversity. In contrast with early-twentieth-century amusement parks' ethnic depictions, the "Streets of the World" exhibition at the 1936–1937 Great Lakes Exposition, and promotions of Cleveland's international connections at the time of the St. Lawrence Seaway's opening in 1959, which packaged foreign exoticism as an object of curiosity, the city's actual ethnic roots shaped Cleveland's identity throughout the twentieth century.[34] For example, the Cleveland Cultural Gardens, begun in the 1910s in the Olmsted Brothers–designed Rockefeller Park, expanded into a string of nationality-based sculpture gardens that enabled different ethnic groups to tell their own stories through public art.[35] And, by the 1970s, Cleveland, like Milwaukee, Baltimore, Detroit, and other deindustrializing cities, tried to highlight its ethnic diversity as part of an effort to smooth over tense race relations and pivot toward a consumption-based economy by appealing to tourists and suburbanites, including white ethnics who had once occupied the city's older neighborhoods.[36] Hewing to this trend, Cleveland's city government tried to showcase the melting pot in the central, neutral space of downtown when it launched the All-Nations Festival in 1971, drawing tens of thousands of people annually to the Hanna Fountains on the Mall. In a similar vein, a U.S. bicentennial project produced a short-lived Greater Cleveland Ethnographic Museum inside downtown's Arcade several years later to celebrate the contributions of Cleveland's many European nationality groups.[37] However, a number of Cleveland's neighborhoods continued to be strongholds of various nationalities, with ethnic culture on daily display. The challenge was how to bind them to a broader civic function.

In the post-riot years, Clevelanders continued to tell themselves and others a familiar story of their city. Founded by sturdy Connecticut Yankees who followed Moses Cleaveland to the Western Reserve, Cleveland grew into a great industrial powerhouse through the ingenuity of its visionary men and the hard work of the sons and daughters of dozens of European lands. However, as the city began to lose ground to competitors after World War II and drifted toward Rust Belt status, its story morphed to emphasize the legacies of these contributions—fine museums, generous philanthropic and charitable foundations, a blue-chip corporate community, and strong ethnic villages with colorful festivals and culinary and handicraft traditions. Ohio City promoters latched onto this rhetoric but struggled, because they were mostly newcomers lacking prior connections to the neighborhood, not to mention that Ohio City had lost most of what once made it a recognizably Irish- and German-dominated community as it absorbed a wide range of immigrants and migrants whose presence complicated social relations and efforts to brand the area.[38]

A *Plain Dealer* feature story in 1974 suggests how the narrative of Ohio City's comeback sometimes tried to resolve its complicated history by skirting much of it. The article told a greatly simplified and highly selective story in which early Ohio City residents traded their "simple frame dwellings" for more substantial "mini-mansions before moving on to the palaces of Euclid Avenue. Ohio City was a very fashionable address then." The twentieth century, the narrative continued, saw the children of Millionaires' Row residents move "to the mansions of the Heights," leaving urban decay in their wake. In a clever but dubious leap, the article argued that "the great-great-great grandchildren of the sturdy settlers of Ohio City" were rebuilding a neighborhood that, implicitly, had no history worth telling between the close of the Victorian era and the advent of the Ohio City renaissance. Of course, such a gloss of the city's history left out the African American and white ethnic industrial working classes.[39]

To the extent that they could, Ohio City boosters and the dominant local press smoothed over the tensions that each wave of newcomers had brought to the neighborhood and the city. "Local color" provided an effective veil that enabled boosters to reorient public attention away from the problems associated with race, class, and ethnic conflict. Articles about the Ohio City renaissance often pointed to what George Condon called its "cosmopolitan mixture" of ethnicities.[40] One could still see Hungarian gypsies with "their colorful Old World costumes" and a "strong core of established residents of Middle European descent who spoke with fascinating accents and bargained over the meat and produce counters of the West Side Market."[41] With an implicit gesture that any reader familiar with such bohemian haunts as New York's Greenwich Village or New Orleans's French Quarter would have recognized, one writer, in a flight of fancy, likened Ohio City to "a village in the midst of the city," a product of its "many ethnic groups" and "the rural atmosphere of the tree-lined streets." In his estimate, the "well-tailored tweedy feeling of the immigrants from the suburbs" blended effortlessly into the colorful ethnic assemblage.[42] When discussing Ohio City, newspapers safely contained the presence of Appalachians, Puerto Ricans, Native Americans, and African Americans within references to culture-specific cuisines or simply the "melting pot."[43]

Notwithstanding efforts to portray Ohio City gentrifiers as agents reprising an old story of urban growth and prosperity by vanquishing a chapter of urban decline, the so-called urban pioneers were but one of many fragmented groups in a Near West Side that was simultaneously declining and revitalizing in the 1970s, its condition in the eye of the beholder. The city's daily newspapers, especially the *Plain Dealer*, effectively cordoned off "Ohio City" from the "Near West Side" in the public imagination. To obscure the tension between decline and revitalization, they generally reserved the former name for romanticizing the area's past or promoting its gentrification, relegating the latter to stories about alcoholism, arson, crime, decay, drug abuse, juvenile delinquency, low educational attainment, poverty, prostitution, racism, and xenophobia. As already seen, Ohio City was a place in which social diversity offered a colorful vitality to which everyone—longtime residents, recent immigrants and migrants, and middle-class ex-suburbanites—contributed. The Near West Side, by contrast, was one in which diversity created a battleground of mutual distrust and social discord.

The challenges faced by large but marginalized populations of Appalachian and Puerto Rican migrants, most of whom had settled either in Hough or on the Near West Side in the 1950s and 1960s, largely escaped comment in the mainstream press. Only in the mid-1960s did the *Plain Dealer* finally mention the Near West Side as a focal point for an influx of impoverished migrants who had been flocking to Cleveland to work in factories, mills, and greenhouses since at least the Korean War. It focused on how high rents and poor-quality housing exacerbated transiency, which, as one resident observed, made it difficult for people to become rooted in place and develop a sense of neighborliness and a capacity to organize. Almost six years later, the paper printed the next significant examination of Near West Side Puerto Ricans, at which time it acknowledged that their long struggle for recognition by the broader community had been "frustrating," adding the prediction that "it will continue to be." By that time, an estimated ten thousand Puerto Ricans lived on the Near West Side, many in "windowless bedroom[s]" of the sort that middle-class white reformers since Jacob Riis had bemoaned for decades. The image of back alleys littered with "the brown paper bags used by glue sniffers and . . . discarded needles of the heroin addict" was one that the newspaper affixed to what it carefully labeled the Near West Side, making no mention of the fact that this was the same geography as the one it called Ohio City when trumpeting urban revitalization.[44]

If newspapers tried to separate Ohio City from the problems of the Near West Side in the public imagination, the tension between neighborhood names was more than merely a matter of semantics. People of widely varying backgrounds understood that the effort to make the neighborhood part of Cleveland's revitalization would produce winners and losers. As early as 1969, a group of concerned Near West Siders leafleted their neighborhood to urge residents to attend a meeting at the West Side Community House to discuss unwanted impacts that they believed "Ohio City" portended. The flyers charged that OCCDA's actions were attuned to making the entire Near West Side "reflect the Ohio City era. . . . The Ohio City group is not concerned with your housing needs, they only want you out of the area. What are you going to do about it?"[45] Early misgivings toward the Ohio City renaissance grew into more insistent demands by the early 1970s. When OCCDA held its daylong "Salute to Ohio City" on September 12, 1971, a contingent of demonstrators, including Volunteers in Service to America (VISTA) members, social workers, and neighborhood residents, styling themselves the Near West Side People's Preservation Society, carried placards and distributed leaflets to tour-goers. They urged OCCDA to support scattered-site public housing, have its members sign noneviction pledges, collaborate with the Near West Side–Tremont Housing Coalition, and add representatives of the poor to its board of directors.[46] Their critiques and demands echoed those that had appeared months earlier in the *Plain Press*, a Near West Side community paper that provided a voice for underrepresented populations, such as Appalachians and Puerto Ricans. Observing that "Bridge Avenue was blocked off so the women in old fashioned dresses and antique cars could travel from house to house," a *Plain Press* writer wondered, "Did they see the problems of the 20th century?"[47] These critiques shattered any illusion that Ohio City was an unchallenged model for remaking Cleveland and brought a repeated recasting of community organizations as alliances shifted.

The Ohio City renaissance continued to struggle against the notion that it was little more than the latest attempt by suburbanites to remake the city as a place that appealed to suburban tastes. The fact that OCCDA limited its membership to property owners shut out the majority of Near West Siders, coupled with the gradual diminishing of need for its promotional activity, suggested the appropriateness of some other organization that represented diverse neighborhood interests.[48] With OCCDA receding in influence, the Near West Side People's Preservation Society also disappeared. Two new organizations emerged to fill the void. In 1975, the Ohio City Redevelopment Association (OCRA) formed with startup funding from the Cleveland Foundation and the recently created federal Community Development Block Grant (CDBG) program. Chaired by Wagner of Cardinal Federal Savings and Loan, a longtime cheerleader of Ohio City's role in revitalizing Cleveland, OCRA was a business-oriented community development organization that supported large institutions, including St. Ignatius and Lutheran Hospital, as they invested millions of dollars in expansions in the late 1970s. OCRA also promoted the same kinds of West 25th–Lorain business district improvements that the Ohio City Planning Sponsors had done twenty years earlier but did so at a time when the surrounding neighborhood was, paradoxically, further decayed and further revitalized.[49]

A second new organization, the Ohio City Block Club Association (OCBCA), emerged from neighborhood opposition to expansion plans by St. Ignatius in 1976. When a large Puerto Rican family was evicted from their Carroll Avenue home, their neighbor, Thomas Wagner, a St. Ignatius alumnus (and no relation to Edward J. Wagner), discovered that the eviction was part of the school's secretive purchase of several properties on its perimeter on Carroll and Lorain Avenues. Wagner and others in the neighborhood confronted St. Ignatius leaders, who agreed to involve residents in future planning. The following year, neighbors formed OCBCA, whose purpose was to coordinate the activities of residential street clubs. OCBCA worked to be an inclusive organization that might avoid the interloper status that had plagued OCCDA.[50]

Both organizations felt themselves becoming estranged from city hall following the election of Dennis Kucinich as mayor. The son of a Croatian truck driver and an Irish American homemaker, Kucinich had served from 1969 to 1977 as a city councilman for Ward 7, the ward just south of Ohio City that contained the Clark-Fulton and Tremont neighborhoods. At age thirty-one, Kucinich became the youngest mayor of a major American city, a fact that earned him the nickname "Boy Mayor." The outspoken young mayor entered office determined to challenge the power of the city's growth coalition. In this way, Kucinich was essentially a forceful, sometimes reckless champion of the concept of equity planning that city planning director Krumholz had been trying to inject into policy for several years under two previous mayors. Like Krumholz, Kucinich wanted to look beyond the growth coalition's usual tendency toward large-scale development projects, which had a long history of channeling their benefits to the powerful at the expense of worsening conditions for an increasingly marginalized, impoverished municipal citizenry.[51] And, also like Krumholz, Kucinich had little use for projects aimed at improving the city's image, which he viewed as frivolous in light of persistent systemic problems that had failed to find resolution under preceding mayors. Better known for his refusal to sell the city-owned Municipal Light Plant to the Cleveland Electric Illuminating Company (CEI; detailed in Chapter 7), Mayor Kucinich also resisted pressure from OCRA and OCBCA to give special attention to matters they believed were essential for revitalizing the Near West Side, viewing them as mouthpieces for privileged Clevelanders.

Under Kucinich's predecessor, Mayor Ralph J. Perk, the city council had begun considering whether to allocate CDBG funds to improve the area around the West Side Market by installing brick sidewalks, planters and other landscaping, street furniture, and a small park on the northwest corner of West 25th and Lorain, known as Market Square, because it was once the site of the Pearl Street Market that preceded the West Side Market.[52] However, when Kucinich took office, he quickly served notice that he did not intend to continue supporting what he characterized as community development corporations' (CDCs') "cosmetic and experimental cures which may have no lasting effects." He was also determined to rein in the use of CDBG funds, which he believed had been misdirected toward such "cures" in downtown and a few key neighborhoods under his predecessor, an issue that transcended Cleveland and prompted greater federal oversight in expenditures. One dismayed Cleveland CDC leader lamented Mayor Kucinich's action: "We try to focus on the affirmative, to create a positive attitude in the area. We use the public money we have to show the private sector that there is interest, to generate excitement." Indeed, CDCs like OCRA understood their role in managing public perceptions of neighborhoods struggling against a city's decline. In contrast, Kucinich hoped to redirect federal grant money from visible, symbolic, neighborhood-level movements toward city-wide sewer replacement and repair.[53]

OCRA's dream of a Market Square park as a centerpiece for the revitalization of the Ohio City business district benefited from the growing difficulties that Mayor Kucinich faced. In 1978, a mayoral recall movement got underway. Among the movement's spark plugs was Ward 8 councilman William T. Sullivan, who incidentally was also exploring the feasibility of calls from some of his constituents for Ohio City to secede from Cleveland.[54] With the recall election looming, Kucinich reversed his decision to withhold funds from the Ohio City improvements. Although some "City Hall observers" claimed the mayor did so to defuse anger in Ward 8 over the standoff between Kucinich and Sullivan that they believed had estranged the mayor from Cleveland's bellwether neighborhood, the action likely owed more to city council's threats to block approval of all CDBG funds until Kucinich accepted the long-delayed Market Square plan.[55]

Not only did business leaders in the Ohio City renaissance join the broader growth coalition in going against a mayor that they believed was derailing Cleveland's comeback; they also found themselves making common cause with many renovating homeowners who bolted OCBCA when a "dissident majority" (renters) took over the organization in March 1979 and renamed it Near West Neighbors in Action (NWNIA).[56] As OCRA worked to refurbish West 25th Street storefront façades and coordinated walking tours and special events to attract suburbanites and tourists, NWNIA took a markedly different approach. It waged court battles against slumlords, pressed city hall for better municipal services and police protection, pushed banks to make more loans in the neighborhood, and set up a task force to combat a rash of arson incidents that threatened the area's stability. As one reporter noted, NWNIA was "a model of participatory democracy."[57] NWNIA, along with similar organizations in some other Cleveland neighborhoods, challenged CDCs that effectively decentralized but continued to pursue the larger goals of the growth coalition.

Ohio City and the Near West Side, like Cleveland itself, stood in tension in the 1970s—revitalizing and declining at the same time. Clevelanders who identified with each neighborhood name also continued to coexist uneasily. Both names persisted in the public imagination and in community organizations serving the area. Despite its much-touted "renaissance," Ohio City lost 34 percent of its population in the 1970s, a rate of loss greater than that of the city as a whole and steeper than the decline of the neighborhood in the previous three decades combined. Some of Ohio City's population loss reflected conversions of multifamily dwellings into one- or two-family houses, but hundreds of units were lost to arson or to demolition for surface parking or institutional expansion. In addition, for the time being, the back-to-the-city movement could not offset the continuing pull of the suburbs and, increasingly, other regions. Indeed, Cuyahoga County's population peaked in 1970 at 1,721,300 before falling to 1,498,400 ten years later, an indication that the metropolitan area was beginning to mirror the continuing decentralization of Cleveland, whose population loss was even steeper.[58]

Born with CDF's blessing in the hope that it might inspire a larger civic rebirth, the 1970s reincarnation of Ohio City neither prevented continuing deterioration on the Near West Side nor stemmed the tide of population loss in Cleveland, which accelerated as a result of worsening deindustrialization and court-ordered busing to redress segregation in the city's public schools in the late 1970s. Nevertheless, Ohio City, along with downtown, took its place alongside Shaker Heights, Lakewood, Rocky River, and Chagrin Falls as a focal point among metropolitan Cleveland's attractive housing options in booster literature. With its "exciting urban living experience," Ohio City exemplified the image of the livable city that urban boosters across the country sought to highlight in the 1970s. In most such publications aimed at corporate executives and middle- to upper-middle-class professionals, Ohio City was the only inner-city neighborhood to be featured. Its status as "Cleveland's oldest neighborhood" now earned the gentrifying Ohio City mention in conjunction with "magnificent period homes" of the Heights and "white clapboard mansions" of the Chagrin Valley's cultivated countryside. Likewise, the "urban pioneer" who made "regular runs to lumber yards and paint stores" now took his place alongside the "gentleman farmer" in what remained a heavily suburban residential ideal shaped by a growth coalition whose members were themselves largely suburban.[59]

As in bellwether neighborhoods in other cities, Ohio City seemed to offer a template for other Cleveland neighborhoods. Any place that escaped the bulldozers and wrecking balls of urban renewal and survived the panic-peddling solicitations of the blockbusting real estate broker could potentially craft urban excitement from tree-shaded side streets, historic churches, and ethnic restaurants. While African American neighborhoods like Hough continued to struggle against a negative image, a handful of white ethnic enclaves enjoyed a degree of revitalization. The old Warszawa neighborhood in Ward 13 got Polish "Hylander" façade treatments on its Fleet Avenue storefronts and was rebranded in 1977 as "Slavic Village."[60] Similarly, the old central and eastern European neighborhood of Tremont in Ward 7 showed early signs of building a future around its villagelike isolation (a by-product of interstate highway construction on its southern and western flanks) and magnificent churches, including the iconic onion-domed St. Theodosius Russian Orthodox Cathedral, where part of the movie *The Deer Hunter* was filmed in 1978.[61] And the onetime Romanian and Italian section of the Near West Side to the west of Ohio City made a critical turn in 1978, when the five-year-old Detroit Shoreway Community Development Organization rallied to save its historic but crumbling Gordon Square Arcade as a centerpiece for a decades-long revitalization effort that was just getting underway.[62] In contrast, the old Hungarian Buckeye neighborhood continued to serve as an alter ego to Ohio City in Cleveland's nascent neighborhood revitalization efforts. As a 1975 study warned, Buckeye merchants would "have to adopt more liberal racial attitudes and modern marketing techniques" if they hoped to have a neighborhood renaissance of their own.[63] Clearly, this movement reflected a continued failure to come to terms with the deeply in-grained racism of a divided city.

Like advocates of Slavic Village, Tremont, and Detroit Shoreway, who hoped to catalyze their own versions of the Ohio City renaissance, Ohio City boosters battled not only the pull of the suburbs but also arson, crime, poverty, redlining, and other ills. A pair of *Plain Dealer* articles from 1983 suggests the persistent tension between decline and renewal that such communities endured. One article argued that Ohio City shared more in common with Cincinnati's Over-the-Rhine neighborhood than with Columbus's German Village. Unlike German Village, which an earlier observer had called a "Teutonic Williamsburg" as a result of its tidy, narrow streets lined with brick cottages, Ohio City and Over-the-Rhine suffered "image problems, stemming from their still mean streets." The article lamented that Ohio City's plethora of subsidized housing and "ramshackle houses," lack of a unifying architectural style, growing crime problem, and loss of interest by the financial community were stunting its renewal.[64] Meanwhile, a second article pointed out that, while it was not a sign of impending secession, Ohio City now had its own flag, a red, white, and blue flag adapted from the original seal of the City of Ohio, with stars denoting Ohio and the twenty-five states of the Union when the town was incorporated. The star-studded flag was a sure sign that Ohio City, in spite of its ongoing challenges, now occupied an assured place in the firmament of Cleveland's comeback efforts. However, at a pricy $35 each, the flags, available from OCRA, were also clearly one more marker to distinguish the "pioneers."[65] Just as they had stood out at the opening salvo of the Ohio City renaissance campaign fifteen years before, those on the front lines of Cleveland's back-to-the-city movement certainly understood that theirs would continue to be an uphill battle.

# 7

## The Best Things in Life Are Here

*Rebranding "The Best Location in the Nation"*

A man, with a bucket hat over his eyes and an English setter at his side, lounges on a grassy knoll beneath a tree overlooking a serene brook. Enveloped by a verdant forest, he seems a world away from a city whose river burned. This tranquil photo was the centerpiece of a 1974 advertisement developed by the Greater Cleveland Growth Association (GCGA). "Man should not live on concrete alone," its headline intoned. The ad highlighted an eighteen-thousand-acre metropolitan park system, most of which stretched in a broad arc more or less fifteen miles from downtown Cleveland. The ad's tagline, "Cleveland: The Best Things in Life Are Here," represented an effort to update a thirty-year-old tradition of proclaiming Cleveland to be "The Best Location in the Nation."[1] (See Figure 7.1.) Accordingly, the Growth Association's new slogan reflected city boosters' sharpening sense that Cleveland's outdated reliance on its traditional strength in heavy industry was losing potency after the transformation of the United States into a "consumers' republic."[2] Manufacturers' pursuit of modernized plants and cost savings made them favor suburbs over central cities and, increasingly, the Sunbelt over the Midwest and the Northeast. As many firms sought to augment or replace older product lines with new ones, such as electronics, older cities no longer could rely on onetime advantages, such as proximity to a navigable river, railroads, or well-developed concentrations in primary industries, to generate further industrial development.

By the 1970s, then, there was little point in arguing that Cleveland's location was a true advantage. Rather, it became important to smooth the city's transition to a service and managerial economic base. GCGA did not forsake boosters' long-standing attention to attracting and retaining industry

**Man should not live on concrete alone.**

Look, we're not complaining. Cities wouldn't be cities without it. But then, without a little relief from all the concrete, they wouldn't be terribly livable either.

That's why we also believe in parks. To break the monotony of the cold, hard stuff. To raise the spirits, awaken the soul.

Which, of course, is why we've surrounded ourselves with all this, literally and figuratively.

Huntington Reservation: 103 acres
Bradley Woods Reservation: 767 acres
Rocky River Reservation: 5,612 acres
Big Creek Reservation: 367 acres
Hinckley Reservation: 1,924 acres
Royalton-Brecksville Parkway: 283 acres

Brecksville Reservation: 2,768 acres
Bedford Reservation: 1,334 acres
Bedford-South Chagrin Parkway: 690 acres
South Chagrin Reservation: 614 acres
Chagrin Valley Parkway: 513 acres
North Chagrin Reservation: 1,719 acres
Euclid Creek Reservation: 343 acres
Brecksville-Bedford Parkway: 547 acres

And 40 more places both mammoth and modest, in or near every neighborhood all over town.

As you can see, we're not just talking about a few patches of green somewhere.

All those acres — all 18,000 of them — offer this city a commodity that's in exceedingly short supply around most

others, our size or not.

Sanctuaries for people and other living things. Complete with one swell zoo and six Metropolitan Park golf courses and seventeen sled runs and forty-nine ballfields and eighty-eight miles of bridle paths and ninety different picnic spots and infinitely more.

All in all, they're one of the very concrete reasons we can say the grass is really greener here.

**CLEVELAND**
The best things in life are here.

**Figure 7.1.** In 1974, the Greater Cleveland Growth Association placed nine advertisements, including this one, in the *New York Times Magazine*. The ads were part of a new slogan campaign, "The Best Things in Life Are Here." (Greater Cleveland Partnership.)

through a variety of means. Rather, the Growth Association supplemented these efforts by trying to build on Cleveland's nationally third-ranking concentration of major corporate headquarters (defined as the number of Fortune 1000 firms in the metropolitan area), a task that required appealing to the executives who made locational decisions for their companies. The new slogan, however, responded to more than just the economic transition that forced many cities' leaders to retool their approaches to economic development. Cleveland's boosters worried that their city's image had reached an all-time low after years of suffering at the hands of national comedians whose jokes recalled the polluted Cuyahoga. A positive message might rehabilitate Cleveland in the eyes of the nation and, critically, dispel the civic melancholy that had settled on too many Clevelanders.

This chapter reveals why concerns about Cleveland's image became acute, and it delineates those rooted in problems common among American cities versus maladies peculiar to Cleveland. Clevelanders, both leaders and the general public, often believed their city was facing particular challenges and failing to measure up to other cities. However myopic and parochial their sense of Cleveland's condition was in reality, this civic inferiority complex—already forming before the river burned—was a powerful shaper of the city's collective identity as a place where too much was wrong. Although local media sometimes drew comparisons between Cleveland's plight and the urban crisis that afflicted so many other cities, too often they also pandered to the notion that woebegone Clevelanders brooded under their own cloud. The 1970s provided more than enough fodder to nurture the belief that Cleveland was a singularly unfortunate city. Certainly some of the evidence was trivial in nature: a mayor who accidentally set fire to his own hair and whose wife declined a meeting with President Richard Nixon because it was her bowling night, a ten-cent beer night gone awry at the stadium, a school board president arrested for mooning from a car window, and perennial letdowns by the city's professional sports teams. But some of it was substantive: At various points in the 1970s, Cleveland endured the nation's highest black unemployment rate, one of the country's worst disparities between central city and suburban income, a city hall at war with itself, a mayor who barely escaped removal from office, and the dubious status as the first major U.S. city to suffer municipal default since the Great Depression. (New York City came perilously close to the same fate.) Accordingly, this chapter considers the real and imagined state of Cleveland in the years immediately following Mayor Carl Stokes's exit from office and across the mayoralties of Ralph J. Perk and Dennis J. Kucinich in the 1970s.

This chapter also explores efforts to reframe how outsiders and locals saw Cleveland and how they fared as the ongoing tension between decline and revitalization proceeded. It examines key themes that emerged in two consecutive booster campaigns and how they worked to offset particular liabilities, real or perceived, in an effort to cast Greater Cleveland as a place that might attract new businesses and residents. The image campaigns of the 1970s attempted to not only manage public perceptions but also disrupt the widespread notion of a declension narrative still in the making. Although there was some disagreement over whether area residents or outsiders were more inclined to respond positively toward the city, boosters also believed it was important to "sell" Cleveland to Clevelanders. By accentuating the positive, boosters hoped their campaigns might restore Cleveland's lost stature or at least modulate opinions as the city weathered tough times.

## "The Mistake on the Lake"

Cleveland entered the 1970s facing challenges similar to those in many other cities in the Northeast and Midwest. Over the previous ten years, the city proper had lost about 14 percent of its population, a figure not far from that in Detroit, St. Louis, Pittsburgh, Buffalo, Cincinnati, and Minneapolis, all of which lost between 9.5 and 17 percent.[3] Although the population of Cuyahoga County and the Cleveland metropolitan area grew during the same period, eventually it became apparent that 1970 marked these areas' peak census-measured population and that Greater Cleveland was declining—something the central city had been doing for two decades. Cleveland's losses in manufacturing employment also reflected regional trends. From 1958 to 1973, the city itself shed nearly fifty thousand manufacturing jobs (more than one quarter of its total), most of them after 1967. The census recorded similar rates of decline in Detroit, Baltimore, St. Louis, Buffalo, and some other cities.[4] Likewise, Cleveland's racial climate remained tense into the 1970s. Some blacks had moved to the suburbs, but the vast majority remained inside the central city (itself almost entirely segregated), increasingly distant from industries that were moving to the periphery. The inner city, like that in many cities, was the repository for the metropolitan area's worst socioeconomic hardships.

Yet Cleveland's declension narrative drew preponderantly on a single event that set it apart. Many of the leading heavy manufacturing firms in the city, including growth coalition standouts Republic Steel and Standard Oil of Ohio (Sohio), had compromised air and water quality for decades even as they had anchored "The Best Location in the Nation." When an oil slick ignited on the filmy surface of the Cuyahoga River on June 22, 1969, it drew scant attention from Clevelanders. As on many urban waterways, fires had occasionally plagued the industrialized Cuyahoga for a century, and the few that had earned notice were larger ones, such as a 1952 fire that damaged riverside property. The 1969 fire was no such incident. Only when *Time* magazine featured Cleveland in an article on the problem of urban water pollution, using a more dramatic 1952 photo showing flames atop the water and billowing plumes of black smoke (because the recent fire went out too quickly to photograph), did the burning river capture attention.[5] Beginning that autumn, Cleveland seemed to overtake perennial laughingstocks Brooklyn and Philadelphia as the city most likely to inspire ridicule. On a regular basis, Cleveland became the butt of jokes on national television, most infamously when Dan Rowan and Dick Martin bestowed one of their weekly "Flying Fickle Finger of Fate" awards on Cleveland for its burning river during an episode of the hit television program *Rowan and Martin's Laugh-In*. The unwelcome national attention to Cleveland's difficulties—a recurring feature on the *Tonight Show Starring Johnny Carson*, thanks in part to the contributions of writers from Cleveland, such as Jack Hanrahan and Pat McCormick—played a real, if incalculable, role in exacerbating a local penchant for taking a jaundiced view of the city.[6]

In the course of the 1970s, more and more commentators adopted and thereby spread a derisive nickname that some Clevelanders had used for years: "The Mistake on the Lake." Ironically, however, a name that for outsiders surely conjured images of a river billowing smoke or a dying lake—as Lake Erie was widely said to be in the early 1970s—actually grew out of very different concerns. The large, poorly proportioned, underutilized, and aging Cleveland Municipal Stadium, built in the 1930s on fill next to the city's harbor, sometimes earned the nickname "The Mistake on the Lake." As the city itself also aged, some of its more vulnerable citizens began to appropriate the nickname to counter the "Best Location in the Nation" slogan coined by the Cleveland Electric Illuminating Company (CEI). Although its exact origin in this context is murky, the nickname first appeared in print in 1964, as Cleveland's onetime reputation as a leader in race relations had greatly eroded.[7] That year, a Glenville woman used the "Mistake" nickname in a letter to the *Call and Post* in which she registered her disgust with a city whose boosters could crow about its being the "best location" while ignoring a racial order that had led to the death of Rev. Bruce Klunder. The white minister, while protesting the construction of a public school in Glenville seen as part of an effort to avoid integrating nearby largely white schools that had space for additional students, was accidentally crushed by a bulldozer working on the project. Soon after, the term appeared in the *Plain Dealer* for the first time when NAACP Cleveland chapter president Clarence Holmes remarked that some called Cleveland "the best location in the nation," but it was named "more accurately by others as the 'mistake on the lake,'" because it "suffer[ed] from the crisis of conscience, and a sick soul." Another example was a resident of Wade Park, a largely African American neighborhood between Glenville and University Circle, who argued in 1965 that if urban renewal funds had been directed more toward rehabilitation than land acquisition in Hough, "Cleveland would still be 'The Best Location in the Nation' instead of . . . 'The Mistake on the Lake.'"[8]

Prior to the 1969 river fire, to call Cleveland "The Mistake on the Lake" was to express resistance to the growth coalition's combination of ebullient boosterism and apparent aloofness from the city's worsening problems, such as those that fueled the Hough riots. "The Mistake on the Lake" was, quite simply, a catchy subversion of "The Best Location in the Nation," a slogan that became increasingly aggravating in the 1950s and 1960s, especially to African

Americans.[9] Well before boosters came to acknowledge the need to devise a new civic slogan rather than simply step quietly back from the existing one, in 1967, *Plain Dealer* columnist George E. Condon published a book whose title, *Cleveland: The Best Kept Secret*, implied a need for an alternative to what he called a form of "braggadocio" that "places a city at a terrible disadvantage." Condon argued that the slogan not only squandered an opportunity to make visitors to the city "shiny-eyed" with anticipation of seeing it but also rankled cynical locals. The affront of the slogan was compounded by the fact that Cleveland's fortunes were not moving in the direction Condon claimed to expect. Although he acknowledged the social and economic challenges the city faced, Condon suggested that Cleveland was a "convalescent city" from 1930 to 1955 but was now more than a decade into a period of revival.[10] Blinded by hope in the face of so many signs that the city was actually moving in the other direction, Condon would ultimately succumb to the same creeping gloom that settled over the city during the next few years. In the years after the river fire, "The Mistake on the Lake" nickname found wider usage. Having appeared in the *Plain Dealer* only eight times from 1964 to 1969, the moniker found its way into the paper thirty-nine times over the next ten years.[11]

## "The Best Things in Life Are Here": A Salve for Wounded Civic Pride

In January 1974, GCGA unveiled a new ad campaign designed to counter years of jokes about Cleveland and negativity toward the city. With the sanguine tagline "The Best Things in Life Are Here," the campaign implicitly recognized that CEI's "The Best Location in the Nation" rhetoric no longer matched the reality of population loss and industrial flight. The Growth Association's decision to focus on a metropolitan lifestyle reflected a realization that economic development could no longer be induced by touting the strength of transportation, utility networks, and other pragmatic considerations alone. Moreover, boosters still hoped to cast Cleveland alongside other places, such as southern California, Silicon Valley, Boston, and Raleigh-Durham, that had developed reputations for the research and development of space-age electronics, instruments, and materials; they also wanted to bolster the city's reputation as a major corporate headquarters hub. Strong schools, universities, and cultural and recreational amenities were important selling points. GCGA's campaign, of course, built on and repeated the kinds of assertions that the Greater Cleveland Growth Board (GCGB) had foregrounded in its mid-1960s advertising, described in Chapter 3. Such ads, part of a broader trend in older industrial cities in the 1960s and 1970s, prefigured the "Best Things" ad drive.[12]

If the Growth Board's ads offered a template, GCGA's "Best Things" campaign sprang from a different milieu and aimed to accomplish different ends. In the 1960s, boosters still believed it was possible to preserve Cleveland's heavy industrial economy while diversifying into high-technology production and research. Although some Cleveland-based corporations turned in this new direction, their decisions unfortunately often led them to expand facilities in other parts of the country at the expense of local plants whose operations they phased out. The Growth Board and its successor, the Growth Association, also failed to stem the loss of manufacturing jobs in the city's dominant metals and machinery sectors, which were frequent victims of foreign competition and labor-saving efforts. By the mid-1970s, any booster campaign had to take stock of a very different economic climate.

GCGA updated, expanded, and repurposed quality-of-life arguments that had been tested more than a decade earlier. However, it was not the first organization to do so. Indeed, at the annual meeting at which they unveiled the "Best Things" campaign, GCGA leaders passed out copies of a new color brochure developed by the Cleveland Convention and Visitors Bureau (CCVB). Titled *15 Minutes*, the brochure had little to do with promoting conventions or tourism, at least not as an end in itself. Many cities, notably Boston and Baltimore, made tourism an important building block, if not the cornerstone, in their renaissance efforts in the 1970s. Boston and Baltimore epitomized cities' big investments in creating tourist bubbles around marketplaces or harbors. Likewise, New York City, long a prime tourist city, redoubled its branding efforts to offset the "Fear City" reputation it had acquired.[13] In contrast to such concerted efforts, Cleveland's tourist trade was neglected because of the city's failure to cultivate or to create and promote iconic attractions as well as its dearth of accommodations. With only a handful of large, aging downtown convention hotels until the much-delayed opening of Bond Court Hotel in 1975 (a situation so dire that Mayor Perk even proposed docking cruise ships in the harbor to provide accommodations), CCVB was essentially powerless to fill the convention center to anywhere near its capacity, let alone mount an effective tourism promotion campaign. Accordingly, rather than promote Cleveland as a good place to visit, *15 Minutes* asked its readers to take just fifteen minutes to learn why it was a good place to live.[14]

Presaging the "Best Things" ads, *15 Minutes* elaborated on Cleveland's quality of life. A whole section was devoted to choices of where to buy a home. With the exception of brief mentions of downtown apartments and Ohio City historic homes (along with a surprising nod to new housing in Hough), virtually all the featured communities were in the suburbs or outlying rural areas. The brochure compared Shaker Heights to Grosse Pointe, Michigan; Darien, Connecticut; and Wellesley Hills, Massachusetts. At a time when many parts of Greater Cleveland continued to harbor resentments toward the arrival of black home-seekers, *15 Minutes* also emphasized that Cleveland was a place that gave one a remarkable degree of choice among fine, affordable residential areas—provided, of course, that one was arriving with an executive's salary. One could opt for "a stately English Tudor" overlooking the Shaker Lakes, "become a gentleman farmer on a multi-acre spread in [the] Chagrin [Valley]," or "play country squire on a rolling estate" in Pepper Pike, "where acre-plus lots are the law"—a "law" that, as historian Andrew Wiese has shown, made zoning "an invisible rampart" that enabled a handful of prestigious suburban villages in the easternmost reaches of Cuyahoga County to shut out African Americans while appearing to be colorblind. Even the brochure's suggestion that suburbia "'donuts' Greater Cleveland" seemed to celebrate the very suburban chauvinism that exacerbated the central city's plight as the hole in the so-called donut.[15]

Through the mid-1970s, even CCVB was selling Cleveland primarily to business executives in the hope that the relative few who attended conventions there might be persuaded to return and invest. Rather than showing them a good time, as visitor bureaus in such cities as Las Vegas or New Orleans were adept at doing, CCVB hoped to convince them that Cleveland would be an ideal place to expand their businesses and enjoy life with their families. In addition, *15 Minutes* gave attention to Cleveland's number-three national ranking as a headquarters city, number-six position among research and development centers nationally, manageable commute times, excellent schools and universities, nationally prominent Cleveland Clinic, and prestigious cultural institutions and museums. It also tried to turn environmental and climatic liabilities into assets. The brochure championed the fact that the city whose river had caught fire just five years before had emerged as a trailblazer in fighting water pollution and now counted forty species of fish in its harbor. At the water's edge, one could enjoy yacht clubs and nighttime excitement in the Flats. Acknowledging Cleveland's reputation as a rainy and snowy city, *15 Minutes* quickly pointed out that the rain also accounted for why "Cleveland's suburbs are among the most lush [*sic*] anywhere," and it quipped that the heavy snowfalls ensured that "Saint Nicholas never misses his rounds." It added, "The beautiful change of season[al] pageantry would make a New Englander jealous."[16]

In a similar manner, GCGA crafted the "Best Things" campaign around its hope to expand Greater Cleveland's corporate headquarters concentration by appealing to executives. However, the campaign also aimed to rekindle pride among Greater Clevelanders, or at least to coax them to modulate their responses to destabilizing metropolitan changes that produced winners and losers. Both goals required attention to reframing Cleveland's longtime image as a gritty, dirty, dull industrial city, a place of snow, smokestacks, a dead lake—and a river that burned. Nine "Best Things" ads appeared over several months of 1974 in the *New York Times Magazine*, which, according to GCGA president Campbell W. Elliott, offered "exactly the kind of influential, elite readership we were after." At the time, GCGA's ad campaign was said to be the largest single-city promotion in the magazine's history. One of the ads reprised CEI's longtime assertions about geographical advantages by pointing to Cleveland's situation within a day's drive or an hour's flight of more than half the nation's population. But the other eight focused, respectively, on Cleveland's headquarters concentration, comfortable commuting times, cultural institutions, schools and universities, recreational opportunities, natural environment, excellent medical care, and colorful ethnic array (see Figure 7.1). Just as the man relaxing by the babbling brook connoted a superb quality of life calculated to dispel images of befouled waterways and smoke-filled skies, other ads' depictions—a young businessman hugging his daughter in the open doorway of a presumably suburban colonial-style home, a grandson and a grandfather admiring art in a museum, and colorfully costumed servers bearing trays of ethnic specialties—were designed to counter readers' beliefs that Cleveland was little more than a case study in the impacts of the urban crisis. At a time when many thousands of Clevelanders endured job insecurity, poor schools, inadequate health care, and struggling neighborhoods, the "Best Things" campaign attempted to rebuild Cleveland's image around the best the metropolitan region had to offer for those fortunate enough to have a choice of where to make their home.[17]

Although the "Best Things" campaign's major themes were intended to shape perceptions of Cleveland by outsiders and locals, its bias toward the presumed interests of more affluent audiences meant that the campaign did not resonate with the majority of locals. Most of the Cleveland metropolitan park system's eighteen thousand acres, touted in the ad described at the opening of this chapter and shown in Figure 7.1, lay out of reach of residents in Cleveland itself, including those who depended on public transportation. Another ad's mention of a polo field surely spoke more to a select few who might afford the luxury of a country estate along the Chagrin River in Hunting Valley than to hundreds of thousands of apartment dwellers in the central city or inner-ring suburbs. Likewise, yacht clubs and ski resorts mattered little to the vast majority of residents. The ads' elite focus reflected the fact that they were conceived from an affluent suburban perspective. Appealing to those who shared that perspective required carefully defining what "Cleveland" meant. Significantly, while GCGA used many of the same photos, titles, and even copy in its ads regardless of their placement, it tailored local ads by changing their tagline from "Cleveland: The Best Things in Life Are Here" to "Greater Cleveland: The Best Things in Life Are Here." Doing so acknowledged the schism between the central city and its suburbs and recognized that it might be easier to get suburbanites to see themselves as part of a "Greater Cleveland" than to get them to identify with a place that many of them had consciously abandoned in their pursuit of a better life-style.

The "Best Things" campaign's focus on accentuating the positive also risked appearing insensitive to problems that ran far deeper than image. GCGA's leaders understood this potential from the start and sought to manage public responses. Elliott promised that the campaign was not an effort to hide urban problems.[18] One full-page local newspaper ad directly confronted an anticipated outcry. Its copy began, "Hold everything, Cleveland. Nobody's suggesting that we deny our problems. Or sweep them under our municipal doormat." The ad suggested that Cleveland's problems were like those in many cities and that it was natural for cities to have problems. Rather than claiming that the campaign had any answers for Cleveland's difficulties, it presented an escapist fantasy that came close to implying that, maybe, if enough people would simply think positively, some of the problems might seem less daunting. The ad implored its audience to "stop thinking only about what's wrong with Cleveland. Consider what's right."[19]

The campaign also made it almost a civic duty for locals to play a role in accentuating the positive by urging them to assert their voice in the service of managing decline. To that end, the aforementioned ad concluded by attempting to enlist Greater Clevelanders' help in changing minds, stating, "When you stop to think about it, you're going to want to help us set the record straight."[20] A few months later, GCGA went a step further by hiring an ad agency to produce a one-minute television commercial in which several groups of Clevelanders sang the campaign's theme song in different locations around downtown. The struggling Halle's department store got on board too, offering "Best Things"–themed merchandise ranging from jewelry to commemorative plates and even umbrellas. When some Cleveland Indians fans (having consumed too many ten-cent beers thanks to Cleveland Municipal Stadium's "Beer Night" promotion) disrupted play at a game in June 1974 by hurling projectiles and rushing the field, prompting an embarrassing forfeit to the Texas Rangers, GCGA deployed its "Best Things" campaign to try to offset the latest damage inflicted on the city's image. The slogan was chosen as the theme for a festive "Rally Around, Cleveland" event planned to "help Cleveland fans redeem themselves" when the Rangers returned to town for another series.[21]

The "Best Things" slogan provided an upbeat message for a city sorely in need of one, but its superlative tone, like that of "The Best Location in the Nation," did not escape critique, despite GCGA's dubious assurance that it was not meant to deflect attention from the city's problems. One suggestion, however anecdotal, that the campaign could be more irritant than balm was in the form of letters to the editor of the *Plain Dealer*. A Collinwood man wondered why, if "the best things in life are here," the new Great Lakes cruise ship running between Chicago and Montreal was not making Cleveland a port of call. He then answered his own question with the quip that the cruise line probably did not care for Beer Night at Cleveland Municipal Stadium or downtown's "seamy movie houses and junky merchandise outlets," but perhaps its passengers would delight in seeing the city's "squirrel-cage City Council," a reference to the notorious schism between the mayor and the city council that had grown more strident during Perk's administration.[22]

Other letter writers challenged the campaign's notion that Cleveland's natural environment was worth touting. An Ohio City woman, recently relocated from Washington, D.C., complained that too much money was being wasted on puffery and too little on solving actual problems. She took particular issue with the "Best Things" ad titled "Man should not live on concrete alone." She agreed that the metropolitan park system was "indeed wonderful—but only if you have the time to drive 10 miles to use it (not to mention the car you'll need to get there). If you're stuck with your neighborhood park—in my case, Edgewater—you'd better have a pretty strong stomach to withstand the mountains of garbage that make that park, and most others, a disgrace."[23] A Shaker Heights resident wrote acerbically, "Anyone dumb enough to believe that 'the best things in life are right here in Cleveland' deserves to breathe Cleveland's air and live in Cleveland's filth. Cleveland is a rotting corpse clothed in a hazy, blue-gray shroud. Cute songs and slogans won't fix it. You fix a trash-heap like Cleveland by cleaning it up. You start with the air and work your way down. Period."[24]

Setting aside the rather limited record of open criticism of the campaign, by mid-decade, it still was not entirely clear whether Cleveland boosters had succeeded in steering their city toward a more positive image. Although the river fire was a tired joke, Cleveland also had not enjoyed an incontrovertible comeback to jar skeptics out of their dim view of a city whose fundamental problems remained essentially unchanged. As ever, the state of the city depended on one's perspective. On occasion, an outside reporter would blow into town and return home to write a kind article, as did Edmund Morris of the *New York Times* in early 1976. The *Plain Dealer* proudly reprinted Morris's article, in which he recounted the "guffaws" of fellow New Yorkers upon hearing of his travel plans. However, Morris also assigned Clevelanders a share of the blame for the city's negative image. He claimed that "many Clevelanders" had unfairly dismissed their city as "Nowheresville, U.S.A.," a view he rejected. Morris's review of Cleveland could just as easily have been cribbed from GCGA's ads in the *New York Times Magazine*. He wrote of Cleveland's "fairy-tale tower" (Terminal Tower), "Emerald Necklace" (Cleveland Metropolitan Parks), University Circle, Playhouse Square, Ohio City, a Cuyahoga River that "runs cleaner than it has in 20 years," and a "yacht-spiked" lakefront.[25]

Notwithstanding scant evidence that the outside world viewed Cleveland in a positive light, many observers echoed Morris's contention that Clevelanders might be their own worst enemy. One year after the "Best Things" unveiling, it was clear that a catchy jingle and upbeat ads could not fix Cleveland's image problem. Over the previous two years, a national recession had stalled downtown development, and metropolitan-area manufacturing employment had declined. GCGA president Elliott tried to put the best face on the city's situation, insisting that "one of the major problems of Greater Cleveland is a failure on the part of a large percentage of our citizens to think positively."[26] Similarly, on his first visit to Cleveland in sixteen years, *San Jose Mercury News* columnist Murry Frymer reported that despite many changes in the city's appearance, its citizens' mentality seemed much the same. The "Best Things" jingle reminded him of the "Best Location in the Nation" slogan, leading him to comment that, although Cleveland's problems were hardly unique, "Clevelanders are forever seeking assurances that they are not the laughing stock [*sic*] of the nation."[27]

Blaming Clevelanders' negativity alone was clearly a simplistic and thinly reasoned explanation for the metropolitan area's tribulations. In addition to the fact that Cleveland's problems resembled those of many older cities, public perceptions of those problems reflected the influences of metropolitan social, economic, and political fragmentation. Mayor Perk evinced some understanding of these divisions, but he was too quick to credit the cause for disagreement over the state of the city to whether one was a native or a relative newcomer. Speaking to the Cleveland Rotary Club, Perk lamented that "a growing paralysis, a festering cancer" was hobbling "our great city." The mayor posited that this "gigantic inferiority complex" curiously seemed to stem from provincial native Clevelanders, who saw the worst in their city with little regard for how it compared nationally. "Yet, talk to some of our transplants," he added. "People who have come here from some of the more so-called glamorous spots—men like Charlie Hugel, Brock Weir, Frank Coy, Claude Blair—talk to them and hear what they have to say about our home town, their adopted city. Suddenly you'll get a whole new perspective about our city." Perk's examples were top-level executives, all of them residents of Shaker Heights. Whatever might be said about judging a place from a perspective shaped by having lived elsewhere, it was much easier to hold a rosy view of Cleveland when seeing it from the leafy preserve of its suburbs.[28] Cleveland psychologist Edwin Weiss offered a more nuanced, if somewhat presumptive, explanation for why boosters faced such difficulty in reframing the local mood. He argued that the growth coalition, in gearing its booster messages primarily toward the suburban affluent, failed to convince the majority of locals and, worse, marginalized their concerns. Weiss believed that promoting the Cleveland Orchestra, the Cleveland Museum of Art, or the Cleveland Metroparks appealed to "the classes" but not so much "the masses," whom he suggested tended to identify more with the Cleveland Indians or Browns.[29]

Public expressions of confidence in Cleveland's future contrasted sharply with less-sanguine admissions out of the public eye. In his final year in office, Mayor Perk continued to complain that many Clevelanders seemed to possess "an almost desperate urge to tear our city down." Ironically, even as he lamented the figurative destruction of the city, Perk was presiding over a municipal program of demolition of blighted houses and buildings that he claimed had tripled the rate seen under Stokes. Perk claimed that his administration's actions had delivered the city from even greater distress and that locals' negativity was beginning to recede in the face of civic progress.[30] Perk's seeming optimism mirrored that in a GCGA ad in *Forbes* magazine in June 1977. "Defining an American city can be a word association game," it suggested. "Think of autos. Of steel. Of railroads. Of film. Of stage theater. Of insurance. Of oil. Of electronics. Of aircraft. Specific cities come to mind." Cleveland, on the other hand, had no singular symbol. Placing a positive spin on what it claimed was a substantial issue, the ad argued that "though this blank is Cleveland's identity problem, it is, more importantly, its greatest asset." Cleveland was purportedly blessed with so many superlatives (headquarters hub; home of one of the world's top orchestras; "rock-and-roll capital of America"; world leader in medicine; nation's largest producer of machinery, tools and dies, auto parts, and paint; and the list went on) that no one could "extract a single metropolitan image."[31] Conversely, however, city planning director Norman Krumholz, who had come to Cleveland in 1969 to work under Mayor Stokes and had continued under Perk, confided to the head of the Northeast Ohio Areawide Coordinating Agency (NOACA) in November 1977 that he saw a darker future than either a boastful mayor or private-sector boosters wished to admit. Krumholz cited U.S. Census estimates that showed a population loss for the seven-county region served by NOACA from 1970 to 1975. He warned that if the recent trend continued, the metropolitan area might not experience any population growth in the next twenty years. But even he expressed a hint of optimism, arguing that the census projection of a central city population of 515,000 for the year 2000 "may be unduly pessimistic" based on the planning commission's contention that the city had at least 665,000 residents in 1975, more than 25,000 above the census estimate.[32] Krumholz's prediction, rooted in population statistics, would almost seem beside the point just a year later, when the city's downward slide became a given and attention pivoted toward a string of demoralizing events that tarnished Cleveland's image far more than measures of decline could have done on their own.

## "Power to the People!": Political Spectacle as Civic Decline

Thirty-one-year-old former Ward 7 councilman and municipal clerk of courts Kucinich announced his intention to seek the mayoralty in 1977. In the primary election, he and another candidate, Cuyahoga County commissioner Edward F. Feighan, faced the incumbent Perk. Kucinich and Feighan garnered broad public support for their hostility toward Perk's plan to sell the Municipal Light Company (Muny Light) electric power plant to CEI to help reduce the city government's debt. They managed to edge out Perk to face each other in the general election. Kucinich, who styled himself as a fiery progressive populist in the tradition of Cleveland's early-twentieth-century mayor Tom L. Johnson, narrowly beat Feighan. Ten years earlier, Stokes had promised to restore public faith in Cleveland, but intractable problems compromised the effectiveness of the nation's first big-city black mayor. The youthful Kucinich also wanted to rehabilitate Cleveland by inviting new ideas and, quite literally, a new generation of young leaders to city hall.[33]

The "Boy Mayor" took office at a time when Cleveland's fortunes were clearly diverging from the rosy rhetoric of its boosters. The growth coalition, whom Kucinich vowed to confront, labored to muster optimism as most indications anticipated what the next decennial census would confirm: The city of Cleveland lost 23.6 percent of its population in the 1970s (the worst ten-year decline in its history); Cuyahoga County, despite a continuing outflow of people from city to suburbs, shed 12.9 percent of its population (the first decline in its history); and even the five-county metropolitan area lost 6.3 percent of its people (also the first decline in the area's history). No one knew at the time that a modest recovery of manufacturing in the middle years of the decade was about to meet a sharp reversal that would cost the metropolitan area some seventy thousand industrial jobs over the next six years as scores of employers moved operations to the Sunbelt. Although the losses were more than offset by nonmanufacturing gains, many workers were unable to transition to other jobs that provided comparable income.[34]

In addition to the loss of population and industry, Cleveland faced other problems as Kucinich entered office. Among them, racial segregation in housing and schools remained worrisome. For all the national fixation on the Cuyahoga River as a sink for the city's industrial polluters, the "Crooked River" also remained a symbolic boundary that almost completely divided the races. Despite nationally acclaimed successes in crafting integrated communities in Shaker Heights and Cleveland Heights, fair-housing advocacy and federal laws were slow to break a decades-long pattern of incremental outflow of African American residency along well-worn eastward paths from the city, and most West Side suburbs' populations were less than 1 percent black. So serious was the problem in the city's public school system that a federal court order was finally issued to compel desegregation through a busing plan. Although Cleveland would manage to avoid the level of vitriolic white backlash against "forced busing" that occurred in Boston, the inception of busing in Cleveland in 1978 also accelerated white (and black) flight to the suburbs.[35]

Another problem, years in the making, also leaned toward crisis. Cleveland's municipal government, like that of numerous deindustrializing cities, struggled to provide fundamental public services. As people and businesses left, central cities lost large portions of their tax bases. Even in those few Rust Belt cities, such as Detroit and Pittsburgh, where valuations increased in the 1970s, tax revenues failed to keep pace with inflation. Cleveland was even less fortunate. As Jon Teaford has shown, Mayor Perk had taken some actions to try to rectify the problem, such as securing city council approval to sell Muny Light (which Kucinich deftly made the third rail of the 1977 election), shedding its responsibility for such properties as transit and sewers to new metropolitan authorities, and cutting back on the number of municipal employees. But the Perk administration had also dealt with the fiscal problem by borrowing more money from leading Cleveland banks and secretly redirecting bond receipts from capital improvements to cover operating costs.[36] Meanwhile, city services eroded, a problem that became especially evident when the city's depleted snow-removal truck fleets magnified the impact of the epic 1978 blizzard.[37]

To a degree, boosters had become adept at deflecting attention from these problems by concentrating on Greater Cleveland's residual strengths. Indeed, the area remained one of the nation's leading population centers and most productive industrial powerhouses. Also, exceptional success stories—Cleveland Public Schools' well-regarded magnet school program and Shaker Heights schools' ability to absorb thousands of black children and youth amicably while maintaining national recognition for academic excellence—made it easier to ignore the worsening overall situation in the Cleveland city system. More broadly, promoting *Greater Cleveland* [emphasis mine] allowed boosters to shirk discussion of such mundane matters as a declining tax base and fiscal crisis. Just as GCGB, like CEI, had extolled industrial expansion in the "Greater Cleveland Growthland" in the early and mid-1960s despite the plight of central-city employment, the private-sector wing of the growth coalition continued to shape Cleveland's image from the suburbs—and in accord with suburban tastes—into the late 1970s. A 1977 promotional book published by CEI was telling. CEI, which had quietly dropped its "Best Location in the Nation" slogan in the late 1960s, essentially piggybacked on GCGA's "Best Things" campaign. The book's cover was a cutaway in the shape of a leaf, which framed a frontispiece photo of a (white) family surrounded by autumnal nature. The book defined Cleveland as 1,800 square miles on the southeast shore of Lake Erie, a place with "pleasant suburbs," an "internationally acclaimed" orchestra, tens of thousands of acres of parklands, and the nation's third-largest concentration of corporate headquarters.[38]

However, Kucinich's election made it abundantly clear to big business leaders that they could not assume they had a pliable partner in the mayor's office. From practically the moment he took office, Kucinich clashed with the city council, especially council president and Ward 27 (Glenville) councilman George L. Forbes, and executives in the city's major banks and corporations. In Kucinich's mind, one of the business establishment's worst injustices was its support of tax abatements, such as the ones that Perk had secured in 1977 for National City Bank and Sohio to build new headquarters towers, and the new mayor vowed to fight future abatements.[39] Kucinich not only snubbed genial relations with the city's business elite; he also governed using a confrontational style that sometimes demonstrated all too clearly in the eyes of boosters his willingness to sacrifice economic development or opportunities to stave off municipal fiscal crisis if they conflicted with his interpretation of the people's best interests. One mayoral action after another incensed business leaders and tarnished the city's image beyond what might have happened without this unwelcome spectacle of political dysfunction. The city careened toward a crisis of leadership that contributed to what many saw as a new nadir for Cleveland—worse than that of the late-1950s inertia of urban renewal, the Hough and Glenville uprisings, or certainly the 1969 river fire. Despite the fact that the "burning river" gradually became mythologized locally and nationally as the pivotal event in the city's fall from grace, 1978 actually provided the "rock bottom" from which to climb, at least in the estimate of another "new generation"—not Kucinich's youthful cabinet but a cohort of civic boosters, most of whom rose to the helm of the city's powerful establishment in the 1960s and 1970s. Their rejection of Kucinich's vision of Cleveland's future inspired a new hook for a comeback narrative whose key themes were already many years in the making.

On March 24, 1978, after only four months in office, Mayor Kucinich reached the conclusion that he and Cleveland police chief Richard Hongisto, whom he had hired three months earlier, had irreconcilable differences in their views of how Hongisto should run the police department.[40] Kucinich fired Hongisto on live local television. His action, one of many internal clashes that had beset city hall since the mayor's term began, led to a community-wide effort to oust him from office. Less than a week later, the Recall Committee to Save Cleveland launched a petition drive to hold a recall election. Heading this committee, whose very name suggested a city teetering on the brink of disaster, were Cleveland State University history professor and unsuccessful 1977 mayoral candidate Thomas F. Campbell, city councilman and Kucinich rival William T. Sullivan, and former city councilman Albert A. Ballew, who had lost his office to a Kucinich ally in 1977. Throughout the recall campaign, additional problems plagued the city. In a single week in July 1978, Moody's Investors Service downgraded Cleveland's municipal bond rating for the second time in just over a month, Standard and Poor's suspended the city's bond rating, a police strike resulted from the mayor's firing of thirteen officers for refusing to patrol alone in the city's public housing projects, and Kucinich and his cabinet members stormed out of a council meeting with a vow to boycott future meetings after Forbes refused to renounce his support of a port-authority proposal to build an ore dock for the Cleveland-based Republic Steel Corporation.[41] Cleverly invoking the public's recognition of the city's longtime booster slogan, Campbell charged in a *Plain Dealer* op-ed that Kucinich was to blame for making Cleveland the "crisis center of the nation."[42] Following a successful petition drive, a recall election (the city's first) was set for August. Although efforts had been made to recall Ralph Locher in 1966 and Stokes in 1970, neither had succeeded in accumulating enough signatures to force an election.[43]

Kucinich narrowly survived the recall, amassing 60,250 votes—just 236 votes more than the total favoring his removal from office (see Figure 7.2).[44] Although the petition drive had collected most of its signatures on the West Side, Kucinich enjoyed a substantially higher level of support from the city's whites than from African Americans, who often saw the mayor as yet another product of the notoriously integration-averse "cosmopolitan wards" and deplored the racial fear tactics that some of his supporters deployed. The mayor's staunchest support came from heavily ethnic white wards on the West Side, especially the Clark-Fulton and Old Brooklyn neighborhoods, and from similar pockets abutting racial boundaries on the East Side, notably Slavic Village, St. Clair–Superior, and Collinwood. In such places, the mayor won by two-to-one or even three-to-one margins. In contrast, largely black neighborhoods on the East Side, such as Glenville, Mt. Pleasant, and Lee-Harvard, favored the recall by similarly wide margins. If the city's ethnic whites carried the day for Kucinich, the majority of the funding for the recall campaign originated not inside the city but in the affluent suburbs, the preserve of the area's business establishment leaders.[45]

Notwithstanding a notable (and exceptional) success in which the Kucinich administration cooperated with GCGA and the Woodland East Community Organization (WECO) to assemble incentives that persuaded Orlando Baking to choose a new plant site in the former East Woodland renewal area rather than in Solon, Kucinich became a lightning rod for mounting concerns about the city's dysfunctional leadership and Greater Cleveland's worsening economy and image.[46] Although the city's new bond ratings were of serious concern to the business establishment, the private wing of the growth coalition was beside itself after Kucinich appeared ready to sacrifice the Republic Steel ore dock. Republic Steel, although not as large an employer locally as the Big Three automakers, was unquestionably the leading Cleveland-based industrial corporation and a powerful symbol of the area's dominant metals sector. Republic had expanded its footprint over the years in the Flats along the Cuyahoga River, but it faced growing problems—the high cost of equipment to mitigate air pollution, growing competition from American and foreign steelmakers, and now the prospect of being unable to maneuver one-thousand-foot, next-generation ore freighters

**Figure 7.2.** Members of the Recall Committee to Save Cleveland celebrate prematurely, wrongly assuming that their 1978 bid to unseat Mayor Dennis J. Kucinich has prevailed at the polls. (Photo by Bernie Noble. Cleveland Press Collection, Cleveland State University.)

up the serpentine Cuyahoga to its upriver mills. When Republic first proposed that the city lease land at the mouth of the river for construction of a new ore dock, the mayor and the city council were supportive, but Kucinich soured on the idea once he discovered that Republic wanted a preferential cargo loading/unloading rate in return for floating bonds to fast-track the project without need for public approval. Such was the clash that led to a standoff between Kucinich and Forbes during the height of the mayor's recall struggle.[47]

With Republic insinuating that building the ore dock would help ensure the corporation's future expansion in Cleveland, the Cleveland district of the United Steelworkers (USW) and business leaders feared another hit to a city whose manufacturing economy was already increasingly fragile. Union leaders, and surely the workers they represented, saw in Cleveland the potential for a repeat of the recent blow to nearby Youngstown, Ohio, where the closure of Youngstown Sheet and Tube left more than four thousand workers jobless.[48] Additionally, Cleveland boosters viewed the mayor's vow to veto council legislation allowing the ore dock as more than a threat to the prospect for local expansion of the city's largest locally based industrial firm. Just as unionists viewed the controversy through the lens of Youngstown mill closures, boosters surely regarded it in the context of the first cracks in

Cleveland's once ironclad reputation as a city hospitable to large industrial corporations. Before detailing the fate of the ore dock, it is worth considering how Cleveland's corporate-seat reputation began to fray at the very time that it became a selling point in booster campaigns.

For most of the 1970s, Greater Cleveland's number of major headquarters had ranked third, behind Greater New York and Chicagoland. Importantly, the status referred to Fortune 1000 headquarters located throughout northeastern Ohio rather than Fortune 500s inside the corporate limits; archrival Pittsburgh actually topped Cleveland in the latter category. Earlier in the decade, GCGA had been so bold as to declare Greater Cleveland "Headquarters City U.S.A." and to comment on the central city's unusual resilience as a headquarters hub. From 1956 to 1974, the city of Chicago lost about 30 percent of its Fortune 500 headquarters, Philadelphia lost about 43 percent, and Detroit dropped fully half of its blue-chip headquarters in the same period. Even the nation's top Fortune 500 city, New York, had lost almost 29 percent of its headquarters in the seven years after 1967. As Teaford has observed, "Corporate executives were coming to the same conclusion as the middle-class resident, the shopper, and the retailer. Fun City was no fun; it was not a desirable place to live or work, and it was getting worse rather than better." Nevertheless, in this context, Cleveland boosters had been right to seize on the city's large corporate community as an outstanding asset in the "Best Things" campaign in 1974. In contrast to the aforementioned cities and Pittsburgh, which had lost fully one-third of its twenty-two corporate headquarters since 1956, Cleveland retained seven-eighths (fourteen of sixteen) of its Fortune 500 headquarters.[49]

However, the Republic ore-dock controversy unfolded at a time when two more Fortune industrials had just pulled up stakes. The first, Harris Corporation (formerly Harris-Intertype), announced plans in August 1977 to move its 100-employee headquarters from the Illuminating Building to Melbourne, Florida. Harris, an early pioneer in the production of offset printing presses, had delivered its first blow to Cleveland in 1966, when it closed its 1,200-worker East 71st Street plant and moved to Fort Worth, Texas, following the union's refusal to accept labor-saving machine tools and adjustments to the seniority system.[50] Harris had also gravitated toward producing electronics for the space industry—the epitome of what nearly two decades of Cleveland booster campaigns had viewed as the city's future salvation—but had done so by acquiring Melbourne-based Radiation Incorporated in 1967 and then concentrating the lion's share of new production near Cape Canaveral. By 1977, with more than 6,500 of its 15,000 workers concentrated in the Melbourne area and only about 400 in the Cleveland area, Harris unsurprisingly moved its headquarters closer to the new center of production. Chairman Richard Tullis, a longtime luminary among civic boosters, was quick to forestall handwringing about Cleveland's loss, insisting that the decision had been a wrenching one made for purely internal reasons and that Harris would maintain its ties to Cleveland banks and law firms "to the maximum extent possible."[51] Still, it was hard to conclude anything except that Cleveland was being left with the crumbs under the table, as a *Cleveland Magazine* editorial suggested when it observed that, despite continuing losses from the city and its suburbs, "local media and business community promoters persist in the argument that the economy of Cleveland and northeast Ohio has bottomed out, that the flow of jobs to the Sun Belt has been stanched; that what happened to Harris Corporation is an isolated case; that, you might say, we are on the brink of a Modern Renaissance."[52]

The second headquarters loss was revealed in November 1977, when Addressograph-Multigraph, an office-machine manufacturer founded in Cleveland in 1932, announced its intent to move from the Tower East office building in Shaker Heights to southern California. The company was just emerging from a twenty-week machinists' union strike at its Collinwood plant, which had prompted the company to shift production to other plants in Ohio and Illinois. Chairman Roy Ash and his wife maintained a small apartment in Shaker Heights but spent almost every weekend in their ten-thousand-square-foot, tile-roofed villa in Beverly Hills. Although it is tempting to conclude that Ash simply wanted to move his company's headquarters closer to his home or to evade the grip of unionized labor, Addressograph-Multigraph, like Harris, was also embracing an electronics industry rooted along the East and West Coasts. When Ash became the chairman in 1976, he moved quickly to expand into high-tech office products, releasing AMtext 425, the company's first word processor—a slightly belated answer to market-leading Xerox's and I.B.M.'s product lines. As with Harris, Addressograph-Multigraph's departure to Los Angeles left Cleveland with only 850 residual workers at the firm's Euclid fabricating plant.[53] In the wake of the city's second corporate-departure decision, a suburban Clevelander, in his letter to the editor of the *Plain Dealer*, resurrected a long-simmering complaint. Referencing GCGA president and Glidden vice president John Lathe Jr.'s lament about Addressograph-Multigraph's announcement, the writer pointed out that Glidden had shifted most of its production away from Cleveland in recent years, just as an earlier GCGB president and Sohio chief had moved a refinery to Toledo in the 1960s. The writer concluded cynically that it was "commendable for Cleveland businessmen to donate some of their time to the promoting of Cleveland, but one wonders if the main reason and motive behind it all is just another way of promoting the image of their own companies and not all that much for the Best Location in the Nation." However, Larry J. B. Robinson, the head of the downtown-based J. B. Robinson Jewelers chain and often called "the Diamond Man," warned that Clevelanders should stop bemoaning the fact that Cleveland had no First Family like

Pittsburgh's Mellons (owners of Mellon Bank and Gulf Oil), Minneapolis's Daytons (owners of Dayton's department stores and Target discount stores), or Kansas City's Halls (owners of Hallmark Cards and Halls department stores) to "'save' Cleveland." In a seeming oblique reference to the Kucinich administration and the growth coalition, he urged that Clevelanders should elect better leaders and "clear the dead wood out of community groups."[54]

Against the backdrop of corporate divestment, the Republic ore-dock matter appeared hopelessly deadlocked as bitter recriminations between Kucinich and Forbes seemed to crush any hope of compromise. Republic Steel attempted to break the impasse in August by offering to pay 33 percent more per ton to use the proposed dock and to give a portion of the payment up front to assist the cash-starved city government. Forbes claimed that the steel company's officials told him that if the mayor failed to relent on his refusal to approve leasing land for the dock by Labor Day, Republic would build instead in Lorain, a steel-mill town located thirty miles west of Cleveland. Soon after, the mayor and the council president came to an agreement to accept the company's offer when Forbes secured city council's consent to allow the sale of more city-owned properties to cover growing debts.[55] What followed was a long, unsettling wait for Republic Steel's final decision. In late December 1978, the steelmaking giant announced that it would build the dock in Lorain. But, in the manner of one whose tentacles were tightly interwoven with those of the growth coalition, Republic Steel's news release carefully softened the blow by packaging the dock relocation with an otherwise unrelated decision to build a new slab caster that would employ fifty to one hundred workers in Cleveland. However, its construction was said to be contingent on Republic's future earnings. Despite taking more than three additional months to respond to the city's approval, the corporation also used its news release to point out that Cleveland's delay—and fears of further hassles with additional necessary municipal approvals—had forced the company's decision.[56] It would not be the last time that a Cleveland-based Fortune 500 firm used a major business decision as an opportunity to vent its disdain for the Kucinich administration.

However, big business leaders kept themselves out of the news on the ore-dock issue. Just as they preferred to allow the mayoral recall issue to unfold as an apparent grassroots campaign of ordinary citizens, boosters also allowed union leaders and city council members to serve as their attack dogs in the ore-dock battle. Indeed, with USW district director Frank J. Valenta keeping up a barrage against Kucinich, business leaders felt little need to insert themselves publicly into the process. As a culmination of months of leading the charge against the mayor's refusal to approve the ore dock, in a letter to the editor of the *Plain Dealer* soon after Republic's announcement, Valenta even co-opted an argument that big business leaders might have espoused: "Whatever happened to 'The Best Location in the Nation,' and 'The Best

Things in Life Are Here?'" he inquired. Buying into the dominant booster argument that now replaced the alleged problem of negativity with that of misgovernment and ignoring larger patterns of capital migration that were upending other cities' economies, he continued, "The truth of the matter is Cleveland still contains all of the necessary elements to once again make it a thriving community. That is, except for the present administration in City Hall."[57] His letter appeared in print on December 29, 1978, exactly two weeks after another, even more devastating blow for the city's economy and image, one that growth coalition leaders saw as not only a new low for Cleveland but also an opportunity—a turning point.

Cleveland's fiscal crisis—like those of many older cities, a product of decades of decentralization—became entangled with the politicization of Muny Light, which CEI had tried to buy in 1975 as a way to eliminate its competitor while appearing to do a good deed for a struggling city government.[58] Yet Mayor Kucinich, unlike Mayor Perk, seized on the Muny Light plant not as a commodity to be sold to pay off mounting debts held by the city's banks but instead as a popular symbol. Vowing "Power to the People," Kucinich made safeguarding Muny Light as a publicly held asset the cornerstone of his effort to advance a different model for what it meant to have a successful city.[59] Although CEI had for more than thirty years played a leading role in branding and marketing Cleveland to the nation, it had been unable to gain complete control over electric provision because of Muny Light. By rejecting CEI's offer—over the vociferous objections of his city council foes—Kucinich was implicitly linking himself with Mayor Johnson, who had made the public electric utility a centerpiece of his own progressivism. More importantly, the Boy Mayor was asserting a very different interpretation of where power lay in the metropolitan area.[60]

In 1978, CEI moved to force the city to pay $18 million in debts owed to it as a result of the deterioration of the Muny Light plant in the 1970s and the consequent need to purchase power from CEI. With little money available once the city was effectively shut out of the bond market, Kucinich stubbornly drew on the city's operating funds to pay CEI.[61] The matter came to a head in December, when Cleveland Trust, the city's leading bank and the largest holder of an additional $14 million in municipal debt notes coming due in the near term, issued an ultimatum to Kucinich to pay back $5 million in loans.[62] On December 15, when the city could not repay its short-term debts, Cleveland Trust officials in a closed-door meeting with Kucinich refused the mayor's offer to guarantee payment, thus forcing the city into default, an unfortunate distinction it would endure for almost the next two years.[63] Although he managed to save Muny Light, Kucinich did so at great cost to his mayoralty. Triumphant over the failed recall effort just months earlier, the mayor would not survive the next election.

## "A New Generation": Plotting the New Cleveland Campaign

The default virtually ensured that Kucinich would be a one-term mayor, and it capped a decade of mounting frustration for the business establishment. It also galvanized new resolve by offering a seeming conclusion to the city's chapter of decline, one that might at last permit boosters to draft a new chapter with a convincing comeback narrative. Boosters did not wait to plan this new narrative, which incidentally updated themes developed over the previous two decades. Indeed, they were crafting the city's latest booster chapter well before the default. Just as Kucinich, like Stokes, had attempted to advance the idea that a new generation of forward-thinking leaders was the answer to Cleveland's malaise, big business leaders envisioned and worked to cultivate a different sort of new generation.

The effort to engineer a comeback, or at least the image of one, had appeared repeatedly over the three decades since CEI had christened Cleveland "The Best Location in the Nation." Hopes of a turnaround had also marked the downtown subway plan, Erieview, University-Euclid and University Circle, Gladstone and the Greater Cleveland Growthland, Stokes's *Cleveland: NOW!* Program, Ray Shepardson's and Herb Strawbridge's visions for downtown, the Ohio City renaissance, and "The Best Things in Life Here" campaign. Concerns about downtown decline, neighborhood decay, and deindustrialization, although still significant, had become increasingly intertwined with a growing concern about the city's image itself apart from the combination of fact and fiction that had forged the image. By the late 1970s, booster efforts reflected the culmination of a long-standing concern that now seemed to be a crisis: dysfunctional leadership that boosters feared was stunting Cleveland's long-awaited turnaround.

To whatever degree the Growth Association's "Best Things" campaign had been accepted locally, by the time Kucinich entered office in 1977, it had faded almost entirely from the scene. Like CEI's "Best Location," the "Best Things" reflected efforts to cling to the memory of Cleveland as one of the nation's foremost cities. But Cleveland had long since lost its popular "Sixth City" rank, and decades of difficulties had produced considerable cynicism toward booster claims that Cleveland still enjoyed the "best" of anything. Rather than holding on to past glory, boosters increasingly understood the need to accentuate Cleveland's residual strengths while reframing public responses, especially by locals, to the dislocations wrought by metropolitan change. It was in this context that the Growth Association rolled out a revamped slogan, "Cleveland. A New Generation," in January 1978. Developed for GCGA by Cleveland-based public relations firm Edward Howard, the new $140,000 print, television, and radio campaign was inspired by the city's changing economy and a desire to move away from a slogan that the firm's president characterized as "a kind of mass self-hypnosis." The campaign, he claimed, "does not hide the facts that Cleveland is losing manufacturing jobs and has tough winters" but rather focused on the positives.[64]

The first item produced under the "New Generation" campaign was a forty-page color booklet that highlighted the city's corporate, legal, medical, financial, and research strengths. It also offered upbeat Cleveland trivia: Cleveland, for instance, had more major corporate headquarters than Atlanta, Boston, and Philadelphia combined, as well as more summer sunshine on average than Tampa, Houston, or San Diego. Notwithstanding its creator's claim to the contrary, the booklet dodged the city's problems, reflecting a determination to deflect attention from them by changing the subject. Importantly, although the booklet was certainly intended for wide circulation, it needed to reeducate Clevelanders about their city. To that end, it featured vignettes of twelve Clevelanders who expressed their faith in the city's future. One in particular, a management consultant and Cleveland transplant, epitomized the "new generation." He volunteered that his wife "didn't want to move to Cleveland," adding, "but now that she's here, you couldn't get her to leave." His comment echoed the oft-stated booster claim that newcomers became the strongest champions of Cleveland once their own experience proved at odds with their impressions of the city prior to moving there. Tellingly, a brochure made to announce the booklet's availability to locals stated, "Here, finally, is the reason why despite all the jokes about our city, Clevelanders have the last laugh. You'll want copies at home and at work, and to send to friends in other cities."[65]

No matter how compelling the message, the latest image campaign's budget was insufficient to create a large-scale, sustained effort. At this point, *Plain Dealer* publisher and editor Thomas Vail became directly involved. Vail, who had overseen his paper's eclipse of the *Cleveland Press*, believed that one of Cleveland's major problems was that it lacked a dominant, wealthy leader willing to invest significant resources to catalyze a civic renaissance. Cleveland not only possessed no counterpart to Detroit's Henry Ford II or Pittsburgh's Richard King Mellon; it suffered, Vail thought, from the self-satisfied indifference of Cleveland's blueblood families toward active civic engagement. Vail saw in his own family a parallel to the city and "thought they were both living in the past." They had made their industrial fortunes between the 1860s and 1920s, and their descendants, Vail thought, had become content "enjoying themselves on their ancestors' money" and turning toward cultural endeavors, such as supporting United Way, the Cleveland Foundation, and the Cleveland Museum of Art, rather than running the companies their forebears had founded. Elite Clevelanders, he argued, had coasted through World War II thanks to the brief heavy industry boom that it brought, only to be unprepared for the postwar turn toward high technology and consumerism. The problem was exacerbated by the fact that the city's chamber of commerce (later the Growth Association) had continued to be dominated by "big steel, iron ore, [and] heavy industry."[66] Vail's dismay at old-line Clevelanders' conservatism as a drag on development was hardly new. The now-suburbanized descendants of founding New England WASPs and the city's large central and eastern European population had been the targets of such charges for decades. Nor was Vail's critique peculiar to Cleveland. Such concerns also found voice in other Great Lakes cities, such as Milwaukee and Buffalo.[67]

Just as Vail had brought a new generation of younger journalists into his newspaper in the 1960s, he wanted to pump new life into civic promotion. He drew inspiration from a trip he had taken to Kansas City in 1976 to cover the Republican National Convention (RNC). While there, Vail was impressed by the city's three-year, million-dollar "Kansas City Prime Time" image campaign, spearheaded in 1973 by Hallmark Cards chairman Donald J. Hall and Midwest Research Institute president Charles N. Kimball, to rebrand a city long dominated by agribusiness—and burdened by jokes that it was a "cowtown"—as the "Prime Time" city. The campaign, whose message centered far more on economic development than Cleveland's concurrent "Best Things" campaign, was widely credited with helping Kansas City land the RNC. GCGA's abandonment of the "Best Things" slogan in favor of "A New Generation," coupled with Cleveland's worsening condition by 1978, convinced Vail to try to expand on GCGA's lead.[68]

Vail became a cochairman of the resulting New Cleveland Campaign, which his newspaper announced in April 1978, one month after the mayoral recall effort swung into action. Vail tapped Art Modell to serve as his cochairman. Modell, a native of Brooklyn, New York, had become the owner of the Cleveland Browns football franchise in 1961 and had assumed responsibility for operating Cleveland Municipal Stadium in 1973 under a long-term leasing arrangement that removed a large financial burden from the cash-strapped city government. More recently, he had bankrolled the operation of the badly neglected Sheraton-Cleveland as its court-appointed receiver in 1976 and 1977 until Stouffer's, Thompson Ramo Wooldridge (TRW), Higbee's, and other investors purchased and restored it as a show of their commitment to the revitalization of downtown. Under Vail and Modell, the New Cleveland Campaign set out to raise $4.3 million for an initial three-year campaign modeled on the one in Kansas City. The Growth Association quickly pledged $250,000 per year, while Cuyahoga County commissioners offered $100,000 for the first year and promised to push for state legislation to permit the county to levy its own hotel-bed tax to generate an equal amount in the next two years. Vail hoped to raise additional funds from the new generation of non-native business leaders who he said were beginning to remake the city.[69]

The New Cleveland Campaign was easily the city's largest, best financed, and most concentrated image-improvement initiative up to its time. Unsurprisingly, given its leadership by a newspaperman, the drive included setting up special news bureaus in Cleveland and in New York. In addition to an ad campaign, it planned to issue visitors' guides, newsletters, and position papers on key topics relating to Greater Cleveland's strengths. It also opened information centers in downtown and at Cleveland Hopkins International Airport and assisted CCVB, whose budget then ranked an abysmal forty-fourth nationally among visitor bureaus, with creating new materials. With Modell sharing leadership, it was similarly unsurprising that boosters' longtime tactic of mailing Cleveland Orchestra records to influential executives in other cities was now expanded to include autographed Browns footballs.[70]

Despite the initial fanfare, however, Vail, Modell, and their associates shrewdly delayed a major national push to market Cleveland. Each time they considered rolling out the campaign, more damaging developments reinforced the city's beleaguered image. The ongoing clashes within city hall and between the mayor and business leaders extended to who was responsible for Cleveland's poor image. Kucinich's economic development commissioner, Jack Nicholl, defended his boss's record as a welcome departure from a big business–dictated development agenda. He also credited the administration with "rejecting crackpot promotional schemes" and, mocking the New Cleveland Campaign, warned that the business elite needed to be shaken up by "a 'new generation' of business leaders who respect the people of Cleveland."[71]

Notwithstanding Nicholl's argument, Cleveland's image problem grew so dire that it seemed to float free as an independent concern. Business and professional leaders lamented their growing inability to overcome the drag of Cleveland's bad image when they tried to recruit top graduates—a "new generation" in the truest sense—for otherwise attractive positions in locally based corporations and law or accounting firms. It might be easy to feel mild irritation when a Tampa radio station awarded contest "losers" an all-expenses-paid weekend in Cleveland (where they reportedly had a fine time), but, in spite of anecdotes about newcomers finding Cleveland a surprisingly pleasant place, it was difficult to put a favorable spin on a nationally prominent Cleveland law firm recruiter's story of failing to attract a single top prospect from the Harvard Law class of 1979.

When Diamond Shamrock, a longtime Cleveland-based Fortune 500 chemical, oil, and gas firm, decided in May 1979 to move its headquarters to Dallas, its chief executive William Bricker not only cited the company's growing presence in the South and the Southwest but also blamed the Kucinich administration's allegedly deleterious effect on his company's ability to attract top candidates for management positions.[72] The Diamond Shamrock move, which came as a surprise to the growth coalition, further elevated worries about the city's image. It colored how Cleveland leaders responded to bad news that followed, such as the loss of the Securities and Exchange Commission's Cleveland office, White Motor's headquarters' move to Detroit, and Cleveland Trust's decision to change its name to AmeriTrust. Along with White Motor's departure, Diamond Shamrock's move also cost Cleveland boosters one of their most cherished talking points, for the Cleveland metropolitan area dropped from third to fifth in the number of Fortune 1000 headquarters between 1978 and 1979, yielding to Dallas and Los Angeles.[73] Above all, it added another reason to withhold the New Cleveland Campaign a little longer, especially with the next mayoral election coming in only six months.

The mayoral election in November 1979, along with the onset of the city's default eleven months earlier, became the de facto starting point for Cleveland's emergence as the "Comeback City" in the 1980s. For a generation thereafter, Cleveland's big wheels crafted an entire mythology around the idea that the city, having sunk so low in the 1970s, was almost fated to rise again. As Richard Pogue, a managing partner of Jones, Day, Reavis and Pogue, the nation's second-largest law firm, told Myron Magnet of *Fortune* magazine in 1989, "In a sense, Kucinich was the best thing that ever happened because he became a unifying element." Indeed, E. Mandell (Del) de Windt, the chief executive of another Cleveland-based Fortune 500, the Eaton Corporation, rallied a cadre of top-level executives and persuaded them to reassess the nature of their involvement in civic affairs, essentially getting them to see that, in Magnet's words, "they had to get their hands dirty if they wanted to keep viable the Cleveland life they liked so much." De Windt spearheaded the effort to persuade Ohio lieutenant governor George V. Voinovich, a Republican of Slovenian background who had grown up in the Collinwood neighborhood, to return to run against Kucinich for mayor.[74] Voinovich's subsequent win finally freed Vail and Modell to activate the dormant New Cleveland Campaign, which played no small role in shaping the mythology of the comeback. At least for a time, Cleveland seemed to burst into full bloom after its long winter of despair.

The 1970s represented the culmination of a three-decade period that saw concerns about Cleveland's image become increasingly significant in guiding leaders' actions. In previous decades, implications for the city's image had entered public discussion as one of several facets of civic development. As Cleveland lost more and more traditional signs of being a first-order city, concerns about its image surfaced with increasing frequency. After the city, like others, had experienced the full brunt of the national urban crisis, it was primed to take part in a growing national trend: pursuing a "comeback." But, at the same time, Cleveland's sorrows were its own, and the fact that national observers and locals became fixated on such events as the burning river and the default also helped shape the mythology that Cleveland, having hit rock bottom, was thereby finally freed to reinvent itself. However, as this chapter demonstrates, the 1970s were a decade in which image itself became a preoccupation that, while still tenuously tied to substantive urban issues, took on a life of its own. The decade was also a time in which boosters and the broader public searched relentlessly for that pivotal rock bottom. Alongside the unsettling tension between boosters' rosy "Best Things in Life Are Here" image and the gloomy specter of the "Mistake on the Lake" that shaped so many Clevelanders' perception of the city stood the reality of a Rust Belt city coming to terms with the vexing problems that accompanied social, economic, and political transformation in postwar America.

# Epilogue

*Believeland*

James Semsak could never bring himself to believe that "The Best Things in Life" were in his hometown. Like many Clevelanders, the advertising agency co-owner wished for a civic image that more people could embrace, one that was a simple statement of fact rather than a debatable claim. One day in 1978, while peering out his office window overlooking Lake Erie, he was struck with the simple realization that a foreign country—Canada— lay directly across the lake from Cleveland. Semsak believed that Cleveland, like cities along the Atlantic, Pacific, or Gulf coasts, could claim a bona fide coast—a "North Coast." Although he did not know it at the time, he had resurrected an idea that had appeared in a 1963 Growth Board ad that touted the city's proximity to Europe via the St. Lawrence Seaway. Unlike that ad, however, Semsak's "Cleveland . . . on the North Coast" tagline aimed not at developing Cleveland's international trade connections but at reframing its negative image. His firm worked up a graphic of the city's harbor lighthouse above the word "Cleveland" in letters styled to evoke lapping waves. When Semsak wore a royal blue "North Coast" T-shirt to a 10K race in suburban Mayfield Village, so many people wanted to know where they could get their own that he made more to sell and shared the concept with the Greater Cleveland Growth Association (GCGA) and the Cleveland Convention and Visitors Bureau (CCVB). With support from the New Cleveland Campaign, the latter adopted the North Coast idea and soon rolled out a large-scale tourism promotion campaign that included images of colorful sailboats plying the lake with the downtown skyline as a backdrop or pleasure seekers lounging along the river in the Flats.[1]

North Coast imagery, prevalent through the 1980s, cleverly countered lingering national perceptions of a dying lake and a river that burned. It was a powerful symbol that connected Cleveland to a growing trend toward waterfront leisure and supported the city's nascent reputation as America's "Comeback City." This reputation emerged almost from the moment of Mayor George Voinovich's election in November 1979 and found outlet in a host of promotional initiatives, of which the North Coast campaign was only one. Civic boosters had been hard at work for almost two years on the New Cleveland Campaign. When Dennis Kucinich's mayoralty ended, the growth coalition stood poised to roll out a new Cleveland narrative to a national audience. Unlike the "Best Things" campaign and earlier boosterism more broadly, the New Cleveland Campaign was careful to do more than simply paint a rosy picture. Image maintenance had assumed signal importance, but it could not be handled carelessly. While the campaign trumpeted the city's expanding medical sector, it also admitted manufacturing losses and acknowledged the Sunbelt boom, noting simply that Cleveland "quietly and steadily grows." But, with less caution, the campaign placed ads in the *Wall Street Journal* and the *New York Times* in which it paired images of Mayor Voinovich and city council president George Forbes to make them appear to be standing together—connoting political cooperation and racial healing.[2]

The New Cleveland Campaign sought to counter a national media that seemed unwilling to let go of the image of the 1969 river fire, but its cochairman Thomas Vail also wanted to coax Clevelanders toward a more positive relationship with their city. After placing a poster in New York's LaGuardia Airport that proclaimed, "New York's the Big Apple, but Cleveland's a Plum," Vail seized on the idea of deploying the tagline closer to home. At an Indians-Yankees baseball game in May 1981, Mayor Voinovich launched the effort by throwing the ceremonial first pitch with a plum. Soon after, more than 480,000 copies of the *Plain Dealer* included purple "Cleveland's a Plum" bumper stickers for subscribers. Within two weeks, seemingly moved by the new slogan and possibly by some guilt for having moved its headquarters, the now Dallas-based Diamond Shamrock announced a $350,000 gift to the ongoing Playhouse Square restoration in a newspaper ad under the headline "We believe in Cleveland."[3]

Whether in Texas or in the Chagrin Valley, how easy it became to "believe in Cleveland" from afar! Under the two-decade leadership of Voinovich and then Michael White, an African American politician from Glenville who beat his protégé Forbes for the mayoralty in 1989, Cleveland put its best face forward and made measurable progress on a number of fronts. Notwithstanding its detractors and its impact on hastening population flight, busing enabled Cleveland's schools to achieve a degree of racial integration previously unknown in their history, albeit short-lived. Although Cleveland's municipal coffers continued to reflect the strain of Ronald Reagan–era rollbacks in fed-

eral assistance to cities (a subject that often set Voinovich at odds with national Republicans), the city avoided a repeat of the crisis of 1978 thanks to
Voinovich's deployment of a blue-ribbon panel of accountants and business
executives to stabilize its ledgers and to the cordial public-private partnership
that assured no *quid pro quo* like that presented to the embattled Kucinich.[4]

Cleveland boosters also believed they had a story to tell about the city's
economy, its neighborhoods, and its downtown. Despite continuing disappointments in manufacturing, the Cleveland area made notable gains in the
medical sector, which already comprised almost 8 percent of the local economy in 1983, thanks in part to major strides by Cleveland Clinic, which was
building on its reputation as a facility where Middle Eastern royalty sought
cardiac care. The city also seemed to be slowing the exodus from its neighborhoods. In the first half of 1983, the city proper actually registered an increase in home values that outstripped that in the Cuyahoga County suburbs
by a remarkable 450 percent, even as the city's median home price remained
under half that of suburbia.[5] Although the city's population continued to
slip, the revitalization that had made Ohio City the city's bellwether neighborhood in the 1970s was starting to spread to a handful of other neighborhoods. By the 1990s, thanks to an array of public subsidies, even Hough
could point to a small but notable return of more-affluent blacks who styled
eight acres near the epicenter of the 1966 riots as Renaissance Village, adding
to the previous decade's construction of more than two hundred, mostly
market-rate townhouses in Lexington Village.[6] Finally, under Voinovich and
White, downtown enjoyed a construction boom that led the *New York Times*
to compare Cleveland, albeit with qualification, to Dallas.[7] From 1980 to
1992, mirroring a national trend, downtown saw a building boom rivaling
that of the 1920s, including new headquarters towers for Society National
Bank, Standard Oil of Ohio (Sohio), National City Bank, and Medical Mutual, which together added 168 stories of new office space.[8] In addition, Playhouse Square's revitalization was largely completed, as was the Public Square
redesign that had originated in the previous decade. The Voinovich and White
administrations also oversaw the long-delayed fruition of Tower City Center,
Cleveland's landing of the Rock and Roll Hall of Fame, and new homes for the
Indians and Cavaliers teams that secured the former's tenure in Cleveland and
brought back the latter after its two-decade stay in the Richfield Coliseum, an
exurban venue located more than halfway to Akron near the confluence of
Interstates 77, 80, and 271.[9]

As in a host of other Rust Belt cities in the 1980s and 1990s, boosters' job
of "selling" Cleveland to the nation and to locals was now far less onerous
than in the 1970s, but the new comeback narrative they crafted all too easily
made it seem as though the urban crisis could be consigned to a tragic second act in a three-part drama, one that undid the accomplishments of the
first act—that long period of progress since the city's founding that often

tends to be glossed as a result of romantic, myopic chauvinism. Cleveland's opening act began with Moses Cleaveland's river landing in 1796. Although it may have begun to drag in the Great Depression, it actually lasted until sometime in the mid-twentieth century. To some degree, the Indians' 1948 World Series victory continues to represent a moment of glory that many Clevelanders associate with the city's peak. This book argues that the public's concern about Cleveland's decline, real or perceived, unfolded gradually but became palpable by the end of the 1950s. In the years that followed, well-publicized responses by growth-minded Cleveland leaders contributed to repeated bursts of hope that perhaps downward trends might be ephemeral, that Cleveland was still a great city. There seemed to be just enough success stories to support this sort of faith: Euclid Avenue's lingering, if fragile, reign as the nation's sixth-largest shopping street, the Big Three automakers' massive investments in northeastern Ohio that blunted the onset of deindustrialization in the 1950s, or—for those clinging to optimism for a particularly long time—the Browns' last NFL championship in 1964.

Just as no one could agree on when the city's first act yielded to its second, it was impossible to discern when the third act began—or whether, in fact, it had. The national media's fixation on the 1969 Cuyahoga River fire formed the most common marker between the second and third acts, at least from the perspective of those in the 1970s. However, as this book shows, civic leaders and everyday people had also assigned pivotal stature to the advent of urban renewal, especially Erieview, and, later, Carl Stokes's 1967 win following the seeming low point of the prior year's Hough uprising. And, after the 1970s brought a comeback-stunting national recession, a departure of leading corporate headquarters to the Sunbelt, the "political vaudeville" of the Kucinich years, and municipal default, it seemed as though the early-1980s' ascendancy of Cleveland Tomorrow—a top-drawer, CEO-headed organization patterned after the Cleveland Development Foundation (CDF) but with a broader, updated growth agenda and an eagerness to work closely with back-to-back "messiah mayors"—might enact the very script that the New Cleveland Campaign had penned in the darkest days of the 1970s.[10]

From the vantage point of 2016, when the Cleveland Cavaliers won the city's first pro sports championship in more than fifty years and the Republican National Convention (RNC) quickened the pace of an already impressive surge of investment in the central city from Detroit Shoreway to University Circle, it was again possible to see Cleveland as a comeback city. But in a time when decentered media and the shared experience of decades of prior disappointments muted the consensus-building power of booster voices of previous decades, an equivocal tone marked most discussions of the state of the city. Even the idea of the 1978 default as the city's nadir exerted little power thanks to what happened as the red-hot optimism of the

1980s through the mid-1990s cooled in the years that followed, leaving an uninformed or at least unimaginative national media to elevate the 1969 river fire to new mythic heights. Indeed, the smoldering oil slick on the Cuyahoga was irrepressible in the dominant media narrative and to some degree became imprinted in the minds of many Clevelanders.

After Cleveland celebrated its bicentennial in 1996 (or perhaps after the Indians lost a seventh-game lead in the World Series in Miami Gardens the following year), the city's alleged "comeback" seemed to lose momentum. Bad news again overshadowed good. Like St. Louis's Gaslight Square in the late 1960s and Underground Atlanta in the late 1970s, the Flats rapidly devolved around the turn of the millennium into a place known for disorder and then desolation.[11] The 2002 closing of the old Higbee's store—by then operated by Dillard's, based in Little Rock, Arkansas—capped a precipitous departure of virtually all of Tower City Center's upmarket national retailers in only a decade, leading many suburbanites (who had never mixed well with inner-city residents) to label Tower City a failure.[12] The downtown retail sector's demise was virtually complete by the early twenty-first century. Similarly, the much-touted comeback in Cleveland's neighborhoods all but evaporated. The ominous signs of the national foreclosure crisis of the late 2000s were already visible by the turn of the millennium in such neighborhoods as Slavic Village, whose Ohio City–like renaissance never fully crystallized.[13] After enduring a population loss of more than ninety-five thousand in the "comeback" of the 1980s and 1990s, Cleveland lost more than eighty-one thousand residents in the first ten years of the new millennium. Only downtown and University Circle experienced notable gains.

Additionally, the five-county Cleveland metropolitan area experienced steep declines in manufacturing jobs. Between 1983 and 2005, the metro area hemorrhaged more than 42 percent of its industrial jobs. Although the region continued to make impressive gains in health care, no employment sector except educational services topped the national average in growth, and the rate of overall job creation stood at less than one-quarter of the national rate. Cleveland Tomorrow's fortunes paralleled those of the area's corporate headquarters. Greater Cleveland's Fortune 500 seats fell from twelve to only seven in the two decades ending in 2005, depleting Cleveland Tomorrow's CEO-only membership. Nor could universities, hospitals, and private foundations—the new founts of economic development in many cities—overcome the massive impact of the continued downward spiral of manufacturing.[14] The *Plain Dealer* tried, to be sure, including upbeat testimonials by the heads of the Cleveland Clinic and Case Western Reserve University in its "Believe in Cleveland" slogan campaign in 2005. Despite image boosters' efforts to recast Cleveland as a hub for advanced manufacturing, high technology, and medicine, northeastern Ohio's economy had remained remarkably similar across two decades. Although the Cleveland area's proportion of manufacturing jobs in its overall workforce fell from about 26 percent to just under 14 percent, when viewed in relation to the nationwide labor force (which also saw manufacturing declines), Cleveland, with 138 percent of the national average in manufacturing in 1983, still had 135 percent of that average twenty-two years later. Boosters found it difficult to sell a comeback when the transformative changes cited as its building blocks simply were not transformative.[15]

For nearly a half century, the national media has persisted in using the 1969 Cuyahoga River fire as a point of departure for interpreting each new wave of optimism in Cleveland's resurgence. In contrast, despite some acceptance of the burning river as a yardstick for measuring progress, locals became so accustomed to disappointment that they greeted positive developments and upbeat image campaigns with considerable skepticism. Like generations of Clevelanders before them, locals managed their city's real or perceived decline by being at once deeply pessimistic about Cleveland and sharply intolerant of outsiders' seeming disrespect for the city. The same city that showed the capacity to laugh at itself when a pair of humorous YouTube videos titled "Hastily Made Cleveland Tourism Video" attracted millions of viewers saw an outpouring of indignation when *Forbes* magazine ranked Cleveland first among "America's Most Miserable Cities."[16] It is no accident that the city's convention and visitors' bureau, first renamed Positively Cleveland and then Destination Cleveland, adopted the simplistic slogan "This is Cleveland" and aimed recent advertising toward capturing a wider range of "authentic" activities enjoyed by Clevelanders—and not just well-heeled Clevelanders.[17]

When Akron native and NBA star LeBron James crushed northeastern Ohioans with "The Decision" in 2010 that he would leave the Cavaliers to play for the Miami Heat, America's Most Miserable City became a little more miserable. His move reopened a wound inflicted by Art Modell fifteen years earlier when he moved the Browns to Baltimore. Despite getting an NFL expansion team in 1999 that carried the Browns' name and colors, the city found it difficult to "believe" in the new Cleveland Browns, whose new stadium one wag dubbed the "Factory of Sadness."[18] Perhaps no other city can match Cleveland's accumulation of sports misfortunes, so great that they bear such names as "The Drive," "The Fumble," "The Shot," and "The Move." Although the tribulations of the Cleveland sports fan are not a direct focus of this volume, there can be little doubt that the capricious fortunes of professional sports teams shape the civic mood wherever such franchises are based, particularly in the Rust Belt, where games offer a brief escape from the harsh reality of an uncontrollable loss of factory jobs.[19] In any case, after just four years in Miami, James returned and delivered his hometown an NBA championship in 2016 following back-to-back finals appearances. He helped smash a long-standing mythology of a city whose sports teams were purportedly cursed. The Cavaliers' come-from-behind rally to beat the heavily favored Golden State Warriors prompted ESPN, which had released a *30 for 30* documentary called *Believeland* only one month before, to redo the ending of a film whose focus was on how Cleveland sports fans continued to "believe" despite having the nation's most unsuccessful franchises over the previous half century.[20] In decades past, Clevelanders periodically bemoaned the city's lack of a civic titan like Pittsburgh's Richard King Mellon who might boost the city's profile. Now the self-styled "King James" built a groundswell of affinity for Cleveland's emerging "Believeland" image.

The Cavaliers' championship did more than simply release the city from its sports stigma; it also diverted locals' gaze from the difficulties that had plagued Cleveland through the several decades that its teams languished. Such a historic victory would surely have been a catharsis regardless of how Clevelanders and the rest of the nation perceived the state of the city. Here was a city, to be sure, with countless boarded-up houses and some of the highest rates of poverty and racial segregation in the nation. However, viewed in context, the championship became part of a new comeback narrative, already several years in the making. Once more, as in many earlier moments chronicled in this book, boosters worked to shape a hopeful vision of a city on the rebound. Among the evidence for that claim was some $5 billion of investment in revitalizing a four-mile transit corridor between downtown and University Circle. Downtown enjoyed a new hotel boom, headlined by a thirty-two-story Hilton situated across the Mall from the site that Cleveland voters had rejected for a Hilton more than a half century earlier. An expanded convention center, a refresh of Public Square by the designer of New York's acclaimed High Line, and growing national attention to its food scene helped Cleveland regain lost momentum as a tourist city. The city celebrated an influx of millennials into downtown, whose surging population of more than fourteen thousand brought about the conversion of many underperforming office buildings into apartments. Cleveland saw a robust health care expansion led by its top two employers, Cleveland Clinic and University Hospitals, which together accounted for more than sixty thousand jobs in the metropolitan area—mostly in or near University Circle. In a departure from decades past, institutional investments began to radiate beyond the Circle itself, notably through the Evergreen Cooperative's businesses that employed hundreds of residents in impoverished neighborhoods, including Hough.[21]

As in illusory comebacks of the past, however, Cleveland—like many Rust Belt cities—struggles to make progress outside the limited area of heaviest investments.[22] Comeback rhetoric associated with image campaigns in Rust Belt cities has limited potential to produce meaningful growth. These campaigns are often hampered by their myopic or highly selective focus, not to mention that they are subject to regional, national, and global forces beyond their control. Moreover, image campaigns can do little more than modulate how people respond to Rust Belt metropolitan change, which resembles nothing so much as a tug of war between decline and revitalization. Nonetheless, image cultivation is an important and often overlooked mechanism for managing expectations in a region that many analysts argue will see little growth over the next generation.[23] The problem, of course, is that too often boosters try to sustain an appearance of unbroken progress that leads to incredulousness in times when metropolitan problems can be neither easily resolved nor fully deflected. Unless civic leaders and the broader public work together to find ways to smooth the peaks and valleys that epitomize urban development, "believing in Cleveland" may remain a challenge.

# Acknowledgments

This book project began in earnest in 2010, when Cleveland State University granted me a semester's post-tenure sabbatical that jump-started my research. In the seven years that followed, I accumulated many professional and personal debts. I thank the staffs of the libraries where I spent countless hours: Bill Barrow, Lynn Bycko, and Vern Morrison at the Michael Schwartz Library at Cleveland State University guided me to sources, listened as I struggled to define my research goals, and assisted with obtaining digital copies of visual materials. Judith Cetina at the Cuyahoga County Archives was similarly helpful, as was the staff at the Cleveland Public Library's Public Administration Library. Margaret Burzynski-Bays, Vicki Catozza, George F. Cooper III, and Ann K. Sindelar at Western Reserve Historical Society facilitated my use of numerous manuscript collections. I am grateful to Edward Miggins, who pointed me to the rich potential of the Maurice Klain Research Papers at Western Reserve Historical Society. John J. Grabowski of Western Reserve showed great interest in my project and worked closely with me to identify and consult with descendants of Klain's interviewees and to devise a system that enabled me to use restricted interviews while protecting confidentiality. Shana F. Marbury of Greater Cleveland Partnership lifted restrictions on certain archival collections at Western Reserve. Christopher Eck and David Winston at FirstEnergy Corp. facilitated my use of historical materials produced by the Cleveland Electric Illuminating Company.

Former graduate students Jim Dubelko and John Horan wrote excellent papers on Cleveland neighborhoods that helped shape my thinking and guided me to sources. I benefited immeasurably from discussions with commentators, panelists, and audiences at American Historical Association, Society of American City and Regional Planning History, and Urban History Association conferences. They include Robin Bachin, Michael Carriere, Aaron Cowan, Nicholas Dagen Bloom, Allen Dieterich-Ward, Howard Gillette, Guian McKee, Charlene Mires, Mark Rose, and LaDale Winling. I owe a particular debt to Roger Biles and Todd Michney, who read and commented on the complete manuscript. Lifelong Clevelanders on the staff of the Center for Public History + Digital Humanities Jim Dubelko, Jim Lanese, and especially Chris Roy also offered editorial and substantive critiques that strengthened the manuscript. Cartographer Nat Case expertly created the two maps in this book, and I am grateful to the Cleveland State University Office of Research, whose Graduate Faculty Research Support Program funded the maps' creation. I am also grateful for Susan Thomas's indexing of the book.

I cannot overstate the role played by Temple University Press (TUP) series editor David Stradling. In 2012, David attended my Urban History Association (UHA) conference panel in New York, and afterward we had the first of numerous discussions about my project and our mutual interest in Cleveland. David's encouragement led me to meet with TUP editor Aaron Javsicas at the next UHA conference in Philadelphia in 2014, at which time I decided to prepare my proposal for the press. David proved to be everything one could hope for in a series editor. Most importantly, he gave my work the close, incisive reading it needed, as did TUP's external peer reviewers. Other TUP staff members to whom I am indebted include Ann-Marie Anderson, Irene Imperio-Kull, Gary Kramer, Nikki Miller, Kate Nichols, and Joan Vidal, all of whom were quick to answer my many questions between manuscript submission and publication. In addition, TUP selected a fantastic copyeditor, Heather Wilcox. With so many helpful eyes on my work, any flaws that remain are my own.

Finally, words cannot express my appreciation to my family for enduring the demands of this project. My wife, Stacey, made many sacrifices to enable me to find time for research and writing, even while building her own successful academic career. She also read drafts of portions of the book, listened patiently as I struggled to make each breakthrough in the project, and offered encouragement and love. When I began my research in earnest, our daughter, Keely, was only twenty-one months old. She may never know the challenges her parents faced in balancing two academic careers as we raised her, but I take great comfort in seeing what a kind, thoughtful, and inquisitive person she is becoming—and much pride in her own developing sense of history.

# Notes

INTRODUCTION

1. Roger Mezger, "Cleveland's Booster Club; Local Media to Launch Campaign Touting What's Good About City," *Cleveland Plain Dealer*, September 3, 2005, p. C1.

2. Aaron Cowan, *A Nice Place to Visit: Tourism and Urban Revitalization in the Postwar Rustbelt* (Philadelphia: Temple University Press, 2016), chap. 5; Alison Isenberg, *Downtown America: A History of the Place and the People Who Made It* (Chicago: University of Chicago Press, 2004), chap. 7; C. Fraser Smith, *William Donald Schaefer: A Political Biography* (Baltimore: Johns Hopkins University Press, 1999), especially Part II.

3. I am indebted to Alison Isenberg, who wisely cautions that, "as an interpretive framework, decline obscures as much as it reveals." In her study of the history of downtowns, Isenberg eschews a narrative of decline followed by renewal, observing that "Main Street . . . has been constantly remade." See Isenberg, *Downtown America*, 8.

4. Many scholars have noted the influence of growth coalitions, entities first described (as part of "growth machines") in John R. Logan and Harvey L. Molotch, *Urban Fortunes: The Political Economy of Place* (Berkeley: University of California Press, 1987), chap. 3.

5. Howard Gillette Jr., *Camden after the Fall: Decline and Renewal in a Post-industrial City* (Philadelphia: University of Pennsylvania Press, 2006).

6. Carl Abbott, *The New Urban America: Growth and Politics in Sunbelt Cities* (Chapel Hill: University of North Carolina Press, 1981); Richard M. Bernard and Bradley R. Rice, eds., *Sunbelt Cities: Politics and Growth since World War II* (Austin: University of Texas Press, 1983); Larry Sawers and William K. Tabb, eds., *Sunbelt/Snowbelt: Urban Development and Restructuring* (New York: Oxford University Press, 1984).

7. Thomas J. Sugrue, *The Origins of the Urban Crisis: Race and Inequality in Postwar Detroit* (Princeton, NJ: Princeton University Press, 1996); Ronald H. Bayor, *Race and the Shaping of Twentieth-Century Atlanta* (Chapel Hill: University of North Carolina Press, 1996); Robert O. Self, *American Babylon: Race and the Struggle for Postwar Oakland* (Princeton, NJ: Princeton University Press, 2003); Kevin M. Kruse, *White Flight: Atlan-*

*ta and the Making of Modern Conservatism* (Princeton, NJ: Princeton University Press, 2005).

8. Jon C. Teaford, *The Rough Road to Renaissance: Urban Revitalization in America, 1940–1985* (Baltimore: Johns Hopkins University Press, 1990); Colin Gordon, *Mapping Decline: St. Louis and the Fate of the American City* (Philadelphia: University of Pennsylvania Press, 2008); Gillette, *Camden after the Fall*; Amanda I. Seligman, *Block by Block: Neighborhoods and Public Policy on Chicago's West Side* (Chicago: University of Chicago Press, 2005); Judy Mattivi Morley, *Historic Preservation and the Imagined West* (Lawrence: University Press of Kansas, 2006); Margaret Pugh O'Mara, *Cities of Knowledge: Cold War Science and the Search for the Next Silicon Valley* (Princeton, NJ: Princeton University Press, 2005).

9. A notable exception is Teaford's *Rough Road to Renaissance*, but it focuses extensively on how civic leaders responded to urban decline rather than probing the use of rhetoric and imagery in shaping perceptions of urban change. Another notable exception is Robert A. Beauregard, *Voices of Decline: The Postwar Fate of U.S. Cities*, 2nd ed. (London: Routledge, 2002), but it dwells on how the rhetoric of decline produced a sense of inevitability about that decline, leading to the notion of cities' being fated to failure.

10. On the problems posed by "ruin porn," see especially Dora Apel, *Beautiful Terrible Ruins: Detroit and the Anxiety of Decline* (New Brunswick, NJ: Rutgers University Press, 2015). On concerns about urban image as they related to using tourism as economic development, see, for example, J. Mark Souther, *New Orleans on Parade: Tourism and the Transformation of the Crescent City* (Baton Rouge: Louisiana State University Press, 2006); Alicia Barber, *Reno's Big Gamble: Image and Reputation in the Biggest Little City* (Lawrence: University Press of Kansas, 2008); Miriam Greenberg, *Branding New York: How a City in Crisis Was Sold to the World* (New York: Routledge, 2008); Cowan, *A Nice Place to Visit*.

11. Apart from very specialized treatments of narrow aspects of its recent history, Cleveland has drawn less scholarly attention than might be expected for a place that spent most of the twentieth century ranging between the fifth- and eighth-largest American city. Notable recent contributions are beginning to redress this paucity of scholarship. See especially Todd M. Michney, *Surrogate Suburbs: Black Upward Mobility and Neighborhood Change in Cleveland, 1900–1980* (Chapel Hill: University of North Carolina Press, 2017); David Stradling and Richard Stradling, *Where the River Burned: Carl Stokes and the Struggle to Save Cleveland* (Ithaca, NY: Cornell University Press, 2015); Daniel R. Kerr, *Derelict Paradise: Homelessness and Urban Development in Cleveland, Ohio* (Amherst: University of Massachusetts Press, 2011).

12. A partial list of scholarly studies of postwar Detroit's history after Sugrue's *Origins of the Urban Crisis* includes Lila Corwin Berman, *Metropolitan Jews: Politics, Race, and Religion in Postwar Detroit* (Chicago: University of Chicago Press, 2015); Colleen Doody, *Detroit's Cold War: The Origins of Postwar Conservatism* (Urbana: University of Illinois Press, 2013); June Manning Thomas, *Redevelopment and Race: Planning a Finer City in Postwar Detroit* (Detroit: Wayne State University Press, 2013); Joe T. Darden and Richard Walter, *Detroit: Race Riots, Racial Conflicts, and Efforts to Bridge the Racial Divide* (East Lansing: Michigan State University Press, 2013); George Galster, *Driving Detroit: The Quest for Respect in the Motor City* (Philadelphia: University of Pennsylvania Press, 2012); Joyce A. Baugh, *The Detroit School Busing Case: Milliken v. Bradley and the Controversy over Desegregation* (Lawrence: University Press of Kansas, 2011); John Gallagher, *Reimagining Detroit: Opportunities for Redefining an American City* (Detroit: Wayne State University Press, 2010); Amy Maria Kenyon, *Dreaming Suburbia: Detroit*

*and the Production of Postwar Space and Culture* (Detroit: Wayne State University Press, 2004); Heather Ann Thompson, *Whose Detroit? Politics, Labor, and Race in a Modern American City* (Ithaca, NY: Cornell University Press, 2001); John Hartigan Jr., *Racial Situations: Class Predicaments of Whiteness in Detroit* (Princeton, NJ: Princeton University Press, 1999).

13. Cowan, *A Nice Place to Visit*, chap. 4; Allen Dieterich-Ward, *Beyond Rust: Metropolitan Pittsburgh and the Fate of Industrial America* (Philadelphia: University of Pennsylvania Press, 2016); Patrick Vitale, "The Atomic Capital of the World: Suburbanization, Technoscience, and the Remaking of Pittsburgh during the Cold War" (Ph.D. diss., University of Toronto, 2013). Cowan also argues the role of the newly built Three Rivers Stadium and resurgent Pittsburgh Steelers football team in buoying Pittsburgh's image in the 1970s. In contrast, the struggling Cleveland Browns continued to play in an aging stadium that dated to the early years of the Great Depression; see Cowan, *A Nice Place to Visit*, chap. 4.

## CHAPTER 1

1. Transcript of Theodore W. Berenson, "Rewinding Cleveland's Mainspring," 38th Annual Meeting of the Euclid Avenue Association, Statler-Hilton Hotel, Tuesday, December 9, 1958, Cleveland Development Foundation Records (hereafter CDF), container 30, folder 9, Western Reserve Historical Society, Cleveland, OH (hereafter WRHS).

2. Classic accounts of urban renewal include Martin Anderson, *The Federal Bulldozer: A Critical Analysis of Urban Renewal, 1949–1962* (Cambridge: Massachusetts Institute of Technology Press, 1964); James Q. Wilson, ed., *Urban Renewal: The Record and the Controversy* (Cambridge: Massachusetts Institute of Technology Press, 1966). Among the best analyses from the 1980s and 1990s are Bernard J. Frieden and Lynne B. Sagalyn, *Downtown Inc.: How America Rebuilds Cities* (Cambridge: Massachusetts Institute of Technology Press, 1989); Jon C. Teaford, *The Rough Road to Renaissance: Urban Revitalization in America, 1940–1985* (Baltimore: Johns Hopkins University Press, 1990); Thomas H. O'Connor, *Building a New Boston: Politics and Urban Renewal, 1950–1970* (Boston: Northeastern University Press, 1993). More recent interpretations have placed urban renewal in gender, Cold War, and global perspectives. See Alison Isenberg, *Downtown America: A History of the Place and the People Who Made It* (Chicago: University of Chicago Press, 2004); Samuel Zipp, *Manhattan Projects: The Rise and Fall of Urban Renewal in Cold War New York* (New York: Oxford University Press, 2010); Christopher Klemek, *The Transatlantic Collapse of Urban Renewal: Postwar Urbanism from New York to Berlin* (Chicago: University of Chicago Press, 2011).

3. Jon Teaford's account of Cleveland's downtown revitalization, understandably constrained by its situation alongside analyses of eleven other cities, makes no mention of the downtown subway and, in its treatment of Erieview, includes a single sentence about opposition by some downtown property interests; Teaford, *Rough Road to Renaissance*, 160.

4. The only historical study on the downtown subway plan is J. Mark Souther, "A $35 Million 'Hole in the Ground': Metropolitan Fragmentation and Cleveland's Unbuilt Downtown Subway," *Journal of Planning History* 14, no. 3 (2015): 179–203. Few sustained historical accounts of Erieview exist. Kenneth Kolson, *Big Plans: The Allure and Folly of Urban Design* (Baltimore: Johns Hopkins University Press, 2001), 75–85, takes the form of a design critique; David Stradling and Richard Stradling, *Where the River Burned: Carl Stokes and the Struggle to Save Cleveland* (Ithaca, NY: Cornell University Press,

2015), 79–110, offers the best account to date, but much of its focus is on the project during the Stokes administration in the late 1960s.

5. "Maps Study of Subway Proposal; C.T.S. Board Will Discuss $35,000,000 Transit Plan," *Plain Dealer*, September 3, 1943, p. 1; Julian Griffin, "Subway Loop Included in New Transit Plan," *Cleveland Press*, November 20, 1944, Cleveland Press Collection Clipping File (hereafter CPC), folder "Subways—Cleveland," Cleveland State University Library Special Collections.

6. Alvin Silverman, "Transit Amendment Wins by 13,837," *Plain Dealer*, October 5, 1949, p. 1.

7. "A Matter of Timing Only" (editorial), *Plain Dealer*, July 14, 1953, p. 10.

8. "McDermott Favors Subway as Token of Faith in City," *Plain Dealer*, August 28, 1953, p. 12.

9. Harry Christiansen, "Subway Here Would Clear Choked Streets," *Cleveland News*, October 6, 1953, CPC, folder "Subways—Cleveland—2." The notion of metropolitan growth as being inseparable from the fortunes of downtown interests appeared repeatedly as Election Day neared. See, for example, "Let's 'Sell' the Subway" (editorial), *Plain Dealer*, August 27, 1953, p. 8; "Raps Downtown Freeway Funnel; Hyde Tells Rotarians He Favors Subway," *Plain Dealer*, September 25, 1953, p. 28.

10. Halle Brothers Company advertisement, *Plain Dealer*, November 2, 1953, p. 2.

11. "Subway, Slum Clearing to Get Speedy Action," *Cleveland Press*, November 4, 1953, CPC, folder "Subways—Cleveland"; "Rapid Transit's Future" (editorial), *Plain Dealer*, August 16, 1955, p. 12.

12. *Cleveland Subway: Operating and Engineering Feasibility* (Cleveland: Board of County Commissioners, Cuyahoga County, 1955), 58, Cleveland Public Library, Cleveland, OH (hereafter CPL).

13. On the allure of downtowns in the 1950s, see especially Michael Johns, *Moment of Grace: The American City in the 1950s* (Berkeley: University of California Press, 2002), chap. 2.

14. The report echoed similar assertions in the press. See, for example, "For the Subway Loop" (editorial), *Plain Dealer*, August 24, 1953, p. 14. See also Citizens Committee for 5 Vital Issues advertisement, *Plain Dealer*, October 28, 1953, p. 8.

15. Albert Porter, quoted in Cleveland Transit System, *The Future of Metropolitan Cleveland Depends on the Subway: Report to the Cleveland Transit Board Covering Pertinent Facts Relating to the Downtown Distribution Subway, April 1957* (Cleveland: Cleveland Transit System, 1957), 39, CPL.

16. "Porter Gets Huzzahs of Young GOP; Says Joe Citizen Only One on His Side," *Plain Dealer*, April 3, 1957, p. 27.

17. Interviews #443 and #344, Maurice Klain Research Papers, MS. 4219 (hereafter MKRP), WRHS; George Gund to John F. Curry, Joseph F. Gorman, Henry W. Speeth, April 5, 1957, Board of Cuyahoga County Commissioners, Proposed Subway System for Downtown Cleveland, 1953–1960 (hereafter BCCC), box 1, folder "Correspondence," Cuyahoga County Archives, Cleveland, OH (hereafter CCA). Klain conducted confidential interviews between 1957 and 1965. To protect confidentiality, WRHS assigned random numbers to these interviews. Where interviewees or their descendants later released an interview, I cite the exact page(s) in the transcription.

18. "Halle's Expansion of Store on Euclid to Cost Million," *Plain Dealer*, January 4, 1955, p. 17; "Halle Officer Makes Plea for Subway; Reports 750,000 Carried by Free Bus," *Plain Dealer*, March 27, 1957, p. 7.

19. Wilson Hirschfeld, "Subway's Backers Unmoved; Porter's Veto No Surprise, Hyde Comments," *Plain Dealer*, March 25, 1957, p. 1; "Harris Corp.," *Encyclopedia of Cleveland History*, https://case.edu/ech/articles/h/harris-corp/.

20. "Wait for Metro Report on Transit, Civic Groups Ask," *Plain Dealer*, June 14, 1957, p. 11.

21. Interviews #57 and #439, MKRP; Eugene Segal, "Master Plan Revives Subway; Would Use 35 Million Voted in '53," *Plain Dealer*, May 19, 1959, p. 1.

22. *Downtown Cleveland 1975* (Cleveland: Cleveland City Planning Commission, 1959), CPL; Eugene Segal, "Core of the City; Downtown Subway Was Answer in '59," *Plain Dealer*, August 20, 1963, p. 1.

23. J. Mark Souther, *New Orleans on Parade: Tourism and the Transformation of the Crescent City* (Baton Rouge: Louisiana State University Press, 2006), 28–29; Aaron Cowan, *A Nice Place to Visit: Tourism and Urban Revitalization in the Postwar Rustbelt* (Philadelphia: Temple University Press, 2016), 56–57.

24. Timothy W. Grogan, comments at "Public Hearing on the Downtown Subway before the County Commissioners," November 30, 1959, transcript pp. 62, 68–71, BCCC, box 1.

25. Charles M. Schloss to William F. Day, Frank H. Gorman, Henry Speeth, December 9, 1959, Larry Murtaugh Papers, box 12, folder "Downtown Subway: 1953–1959," CCA.

26. "Don't Be Misled—The Subway Isn't Just an 'Isolated Tunnel,'" *Cleveland Press*, November 27, 1959, CPC, folder "Subways—Cleveland."

27. Henry DuLaurence, comments at "Public Hearing on the Downtown Subway before the County Commissioners," December 1, 1959, transcript pp. 115–116, BCCC, box 1.

28. Philip W. Porter, "Porter on 'Subway'; Writer Calls Proposed Tube a Loading Zone for Rapid Subsidized by Taxpayers," *Plain Dealer*, November 28, 1959, p. 11.

29. Kenneth J. Sims, comments at "Public Hearing on the Downtown Subway before the County Commissioners," December 8, 1959, transcript pp. 802–804, BCCC, box 2.

30. "Perk to Try to Spike Plan for Subway," *Plain Dealer*, November 30, 1959, p. 38; Norbert G. Dennerll Jr. and Leonard P. Franks, comments at "Public Hearing on the Downtown Subway before the County Commissioners," December 8, 1959, pp. 759–761, 765, 768, 789–790, BCCC, box 2; "Pecyk Likens Subway Idea to Quiz Show," *Plain Dealer*, November 23, 1959, p. 5.

31. Cowan, *A Nice Place to Visit*, 46. The quote comes from the title of Kenneth T. Jackson, *Crabgrass Frontier: The Suburbanization of the United States* (New York: Oxford University Press, 1985).

32. "Proposal for Development of a New Downtown Center," *Clevelander* 32, no. 4 (1957): 5–7, 16; Cowan, *A Nice Place to Visit*, 79; Eugene Segal, "Gigantic Mall Center Development Unveiled," *Plain Dealer*, July 19, 1957, p. 1.

33. Murray Seeger, "Plan Is Presented to Rebuild Square; Architect Offers Council Leaders New Look for Center of City," *Plain Dealer*, April 15, 1958, p. 1-A.

34. Eugene Segal, "City to Sign Pact for Mall Center; Zeckendorf Links His Part to Bond Issue," *Plain Dealer*, August 15, 1957, p. 1.

35. "Don't Muff This Chance" (editorial), *Cleveland Press*, December 24, 1958; Interview #519, MKRP; "Not on the Mall" (editorial), *Plain Dealer*, December 25, 1958, p. 12-C.

36. "Perk Wants Public Vote on Mall Issue," *Plain Dealer*, February 17, 1959, p. 1.

37. Philip W. Porter, "Porter on Mall Plan," *Plain Dealer*, February 19, 1959, p. 17; Interviews #489 and #6, MKRP.

38. "Council and the Mall" (editorial), *Plain Dealer*, May 17, 1959, p. 4-B; Philip W. Porter, "Porter on Mall Hotel," *Plain Dealer*, May 23, 1959, p. 13.

39. Eugene Segal, "Grubb Opposes Mall for Hotel at Hearing," *Plain Dealer*, June 3, 1959, p. 19; "Mall Issue Wins Spot on Ballot; Ireland's Petitions Found to Be Valid," *Plain Dealer*, July 12, 1959, p. 1-A.

40. Eugene Segal, "New Mall Hotel Bond Sellers Wait and See," *Plain Dealer*, February 20, 1959, p. 1.

41. Board of Trustees, Citizens League of Greater Cleveland, "The Mall Hotel Issue" (position paper), September 30, 1959, CDF, container 21, folder "Committee for Civic Progress (Mall Hotel), 1959."

42. Eugene Segal, "Big Issue on Ballot—Mall Hotel Proposal Is to Rent City-Owned Land to Private Firm," *Plain Dealer*, October 25, 1959, p. 1-B.

43. Sanford Watzman, "Mall Hotel Foe Ireland Sees Vindication in Sheraton Plan," *Plain Dealer*, October 28, 1959, p. 24.

44. Ray Dorsey, "Recount Bids Flood Board of Elections," *Plain Dealer*, November 17, 1959, p. 9.

45. Peter B. Greenough, "Digging for Gold—Pittsburgh-Hilton Is Rich Paydirt," *Plain Dealer*, December 4, 1959, p. 38.

46. Upshur Evans to H. Horton Hampton, December 17, 1959, Cleveland Development Foundation Records, MS. 3514 (hereafter CDF), container 35, folder "Hampton, H. Horton," WRHS.

47. Interviews #62 and #342, MKRP.

48. Interviews #382 and #388, MKRP. On Pittsburgh's downtown renewal strategy, see Edward K. Muller, "Downtown Pittsburgh: Renaissance and Renewal," in *Pittsburgh and the Appalachians: Cultural and Natural Resources in a Postindustrial Age*, ed. Joseph L. Scarpaci with Kevin J. Patrick (Pittsburgh: University of Pittsburgh Press, 2006), 7–12.

49. Interviews #382 and #519, MKRP; Upshur Evans to Thomas F. Patton and Curtis Lee Smith, June 15, 1959, CDF, container 51, folder "Patton, Thomas F."

50. Interview #174, MKRP.

51. Upshur Evans to Thomas F. Patton, October 15, 1959, CDF, container 51, folder "Patton, Thomas F"; Thomas F. Patton to Carrol M. Shanks, October 20, 1959; Patton to Evans, October 26, 1959, CDF, container 51, folder "Patton, Thomas F."

52. Interview #519, MKRP; Allen Fonoroff, interview by Maurice Klain, Cleveland, OH, July 28, 1960, transcript p. 76, MKRP, container 5, folder 201.

53. Interviews #129 and #382, MKRP; Warren L. Morris, interview by Maurice Klain, Cleveland, OH, January 4, 1961, transcript p. 59, MKRP, container 9, folder 459.

54. Eugene Segal, "Gradual Development in the '60s Is Seen for Downtown Cleveland," *Plain Dealer*, January 4, 1960, p. 36; Donald Sabath and Roldo Bartimole, "Planners Last to Hear of Plans," *Plain Dealer*, February 28, 1966, p. 1.

55. On the low-income residential population of downtown that the growth coalition sought to displace, see Daniel R. Kerr, *Derelict Paradise: Homelessness and Urban Development in Cleveland, Ohio* (Amherst: University of Massachusetts Press, 2011), 137–138.

56. "History of Gateway Center," Records of Gateway Center, MSS#130, Historical Society of Western Pennsylvania, Senator John Heinz Pittsburgh Regional History Center, Pittsburgh, PA; Frieden and Sagalyn, *Downtown Inc.*, 27.

57. Curtis Lee Smith, interview by Maurice Klain, Cleveland, OH, August 8, 1961, transcript p. 97, MKRP, container 12, folder 603.

58. Interview #62, MKRP.

59. John Kovacic, interview by Maurice Klain, Cleveland, OH, n.d. [ca. 1960], transcript pp. 120–122, MKRP, container 7, folder 365.

60. Jeannette J. [Mrs. John B.] Dempsey to Anthony J. Celebrezze, November 13, 1960, Anthony J. Celebrezze Papers, Series II, MS. 4046 (hereafter AJC II), container 4, folder 67, WRHS.

61. Thomas F. Patton to Anthony J. Celebrezze, November 9, 1960, AJC II, container 4, folder 67.

62. Anthony J. Celebrezze, "Do We Have the Will?," speech to Chamber of Commerce, April 25, 1961, AJC II, container 9, folder 177.

63. Todd Simon, interview by Maurice Klain, Cleveland, OH, n.d. [ca. 1960], transcript p. 253, MKRP, container 11, folder 592.

64. Saul F. Keeti, letter to the editor, *Plain Dealer*, February 25, 1962, p. 3-AA.

65. John E. Bryan, "Closing Downtown—Bailey's to Expand in Suburbs Soon," *Plain Dealer*, February 15, 1962, pp. 1, 4.

66. This confusion over whether downtown change constituted "decline" is discussed in Isenberg, *Downtown America*, 169, 174–175. Isenberg points out that the notion of decline was inseparable from the mounting downtown retail crisis in the 1950s.

67. Philip W. Porter, "The Mistake That Ruined Downtown," *Cleveland Magazine*, November 1976, p. 100; Upshur Evans to H. Horton Hampton, October 4, 1961, CDF, container 35, folder "Hampton, H. Horton."

68. Marcus Gleisser, "Tenants Start Big Move to Erieview," *Plain Dealer*, August 16, 1964, Erieview Supplement, pp. 3, 5; Ohio Bell Telephone Company advertisement, *Plain Dealer*, August 16, 1964, Erieview Supplement, p. 4.

69. Jack Cleary, "Clearing House—Midtown Stouffer's to Get French Look," *Plain Dealer*, August 20, 1960, p. 18.

70. William G. Miller, "Bailey Co. Plans Full, Permanent Store Downtown," *Cleveland Press*, October 29, 1962; "Bailey Store Returns to Downtown Scene," *Cleveland Press*, November 1, 1962; "Bailey's Puts $50,000 in Downtown," *Cleveland Press*, May 30, 1963, CPC, folder "Bailey Co.—General—3."

71. Donald Sabath, "Feud over Erieview; Locher Lashes 'Gloom and Doom Boys,'" *Plain Dealer*, October 18, 1963, p. 9; Herbert E. Strawbridge, speech presented to Public Relations Society, n.d. [February 1963], Greater Cleveland Growth Association Records, MS. 3471, container 111, folder 2, WRHS.

72. John E. Bryan, "Higbee's Profits Rise by 41% for First Half of '64," *Plain Dealer*, August 30, 1964, p. 1-B; "May's Parkade Opens Tomorrow," *Plain Dealer*, November 22, 1964, p. 1-F; Sterling-Lindner advertisement, *Plain Dealer*, August 16, 1964, Erieview supplement, p. 5; "Halle Bros. Spending $1 Million on 2 Stores," *Plain Dealer*, August 13, 1965, p. 28.

73. For an overview of Cleveland's initial foray into neighborhood renewal in the 1950s, see William D. Jenkins, "Before Downtown: Cleveland, Ohio, an Urban Renewal, 1949–1958," *Journal of Urban History* 27, no. 4 (2001): 471–496. More critical assessments of 1950s urban renewal in Cleveland appear in Kerr, *Derelict Paradise*, 128–135, and Todd M. Michney, "White Civic Visions versus Black Suburban Aspirations: Cleveland's Garden Valley Urban Renewal Project," *Journal of Planning History* 10 (November 2011): 282–309.

74. "Erieview Plan Includes 5,500 Apartments," *Plain Dealer*, May 20, 1961, Better Living section, p. 7; Igor Marjanovic and Katerina Rüedi Ray, *Marina City: Bertrand Goldberg's Urban Vision* (New York: Princeton Architectural Press, 2010), 94.

75. Interviews #534, #66, and #519, MKRP.

76. Smith interview, transcript p. 37, MKRP, container 12, folder 602.

77. Interviews #6 and #153, MKRP.

78. To be sure, following the U.S. Supreme Court's *Shelley v. Kraemer* ruling in 1948 that proscribed enforcement of racially restrictive covenants, housing activists had applied great pressure to the FHA to embrace nondiscrimination, but the momentum of the late 1940s and early 1950s had slowed by the mid-1950s; see Arnold R. Hirsch, "Choosing Segregation: Federal Housing Policy between *Shelley* and *Brown*," in *From Tenements to the Taylor Homes: In Search of an Urban Housing Policy in Twentieth-Century America*, ed. John F. Bauman, Roger Biles, and Kristin M. Szylvian (University Park: Pennsylvania State University Press, 2000), 206–225. On Stuyvesant Town, see Thomas J. Sugrue, *Sweet Land of Liberty: The Forgotten Struggle for Civil Rights in the North* (New York: Random House, 2008), 210.

79. "Air Pollution Control Unit Meets Today," *Plain Dealer*, April 28, 1960, p. 20.

80. "New Furnaces to Help J&L Cut Air Pollution," *Plain Dealer*, December 4, 1960, p. 19-B.

81. Sanford Watzman, "City Issues Permits for Republic Job," *Plain Dealer*, January 6, 1961, pp. 1–2.

82. Interview #528, MKRP.

83. Louis S. Bing, interview by Maurice Klain, Cleveland, OH, June 26, 1961, MKRP, transcript p. 8, container 1, folder 36. Bing was one among many who shared this concern: See Interviews #144, #263, #272, #355, #364, and #468, MKRP.

84. Eugene Segal, "Downtown's Forgotten Master Plan Put Emphasis on Euclid," *Plain Dealer*, August 19, 1963, p. 1.

85. Interview #75, MKRP.

86. N. R. Howard, "Downtown 'Monopoly' Game," *Plain Dealer*, November 19, 1962, p. 41.

87. "Commission OK's Erieview 5 to 0," *Plain Dealer*, November 26, 1960, p. 5.

88. Interview #468, MKRP.

89. Albert A. Levin to Elmer L. Lindseth, October 11, 1963, CDF, container 43, folder "Lindseth, Elmer L. (I)"; Elmer L. Lindseth to Upshur Evans, October 29, 1963, CDF, container 43, folder "Lindseth, Elmer L. (I)."

90. Howard, "Downtown 'Monopoly' Game." On moves from older buildings to the Cleveland Union Terminal group, see especially "In New Quarters," *Plain Dealer*, January 28, 1928, p. 16; James G. Monnett Jr., "Builders Move to Terminal Group," *Plain Dealer*, November 11, 1928, p. 1; "Midland to Build in Terminal Area," *Plain Dealer*, March 31, 1929, p. 5; "Record Is Made on Medical Arts Job," *Plain Dealer*, June 29, 1929, p. 3; "Sohio in New Offices," *Plain Dealer*, October 8, 1930, p. 9.

91. "Commission OK's Erieview 5 to 0."

92. Interview #75, MKRP.

93. Quote from Interview #355, MKRP. Similar expressions are found in Interviews #12, #62, #123, #129, #534, and Thomas F. Coakley, interview by Maurice Klain, Cleveland, OH, October 24, 1962, transcript p. 48, MKRP, container 3, folder 95.

94. Interview #137, MKRP.

95. Quote from Interview #475, MKRP. Similar sentiments are expressed in Interviews #336 and #364.

96. Leo A. Jackson, interview by Maurice Klain, Cleveland, OH, n.d. [ca. 1961], transcript pp. 943–944, MKRP, container 6, folder 318.

97. Paul Lilley, "Foundation Aids Downtown Plans," *Cleveland Press*, June 3, 1963, p. A1, CDF, container 25, folder "Downtown Master Plan"; Ralph S. Locher to Upshur Evans, June 25, 1963, CDF, container 26, folder "Downtown Plan Re-Study 1963–1964 No. 1."

98. Eugene Segal, "Erieview Dead Ends Opposed," *Plain Dealer*, August 6, 1963, p. 1.

99. Eugene Segal, "E. 14 Doom Is Urged for Atmosphere's Sake," *Plain Dealer*, September 7, 1963, p. 1.

100. Eugene Segal, "Closing of E. 14th Hit by Bulkley," *Plain Dealer*, August 31, 1963, p. 1; Segal, "E. 14 Doom Is Urged for Atmosphere's Sake"; Todd Simon, "Erieview Brief Rings 'No Sale,'" *Plain Dealer*, September 7, 1963, p. 1.

101. "City to Keep E. 13th as Far as Superior," *Cleveland Press*, September 8, 1963, Ralph J. Perk Papers, MS. 4456, container 15, folder 215, WRHS.

102. Eugene Segal, "Core of the City; New Plan Sought for Downtown," *Plain Dealer*, August 18, 1963, p. 1-A. The series, which began with this article, continued with front-page articles on four consecutive days thereafter.

103. Board of Trustees, Cleveland Development Foundation, Confidential Progress Report on the Downtown Study, January 20, 1965, CDF, container 26, folder "Downtown Plan, 2 of 2."

104. Sydney N. Galvin to Barton R. Clausen, May 12, 1966, CDF, container 30, folder 9. Galvin copied his letter to Mayor Locher, Upshur Evans, Curtis Lee Smith, and City Planning Director Howard B. Klein.

105. "Wolf Pack Hunt on Downtown," *Plain Dealer*, March 4, 1966, p. 19; Donald L. Bean and E. J. Kissell, "Fear Forces Downtown to Take Protective Measures," March 7, 1966, p. 1; "Downtown Must Be Made Safe" (editorial), *Plain Dealer*, March 8, 1966, p. 12; Terence Sheridan, "Some Suburbanites View City as a Perilous Place," *Plain Dealer*, April 27, 1966, p. 54; "More Foot Patrolmen Join Fight on Downtown Crime," *Plain Dealer*, August 31, 1966, p. 41.

106. Halle's advertisement, *Plain Dealer*, August 20, 1966, p. 39.

107. William C. Barnard, "HUD Axes City Renewal Funds; Lack of Progress Imperils Entire Program Here," *Plain Dealer*, January 19, 1967, p. 1.


CHAPTER 2

1. "Foundation Film Tells City's Story," *Plain Dealer*, June 26, 1962, p. 23; "2,500 See Premiere of Film on Cleveland," *Plain Dealer*, August 4, 1962, p. 15.

2. Ray Dorsey, "350 on Annual Cruise for Fun and Knowledge," *Plain Dealer*, June 12, 1962, p. 18.

3. *Cleveland: City on Schedule* (Cleveland: General Pictures Corporation; Cleveland Development Foundation, 1962), http://flash.ulib.csuohio.edu/cmp/general/cmp-cleve landcityonschedule.html, accessed September 22, 2015. In addition to Virden, the committee that planned CDF included Charles M. White, the president of Republic Steel Corp.; Frederick C. Crawford, the chairman of Thompson Products; John K. Thompson, the president of Union Bank of Commerce; Walter F. Munford, the president of American Steel and Wire Company; John A. Greene, the president of Ohio Bell Telephone Company; and Elmer L. Lindseth, the president of Cleveland Electric Illuminating Company; see Eugene Segal, "Top Executives Form Group to Push City Redevelopment Plan," *Plain Dealer*, May 16, 1953, p. 1. On Garden Valley as an intended container for African American mobility, see Todd M. Michney, "White Civic Visions versus Black Suburban

Aspirations: Cleveland's Garden Valley Urban Renewal Project," *Journal of Planning History* 10, no. 4 (2011): 292–293.

4. "The Heights" is a generalized term that refers principally to Shaker Heights, Cleveland Heights, and University Heights, although occasionally it is conflated with an even broader swath of eastside suburbs. Although all cities experienced some degree of outward movement by their elite, Cleveland seems to have done so particularly early. See James Borchert and Susan Borchert, "Downtown, Uptown, Out of Town: Diverging Patterns of Upper-Class Residential Landscapes in Buffalo, Pittsburgh, and Cleveland, 1885–1935," *Social Science History* 26, no. 2 (2002): 311–346.

5. The definitive account of League Park is Ken Krsolovic and Bryan Fritz, *League Park: Historic Home of Cleveland Baseball, 1891–1946* (Jefferson, NC: McFarland, 2013).

6. On the Second Great Migration, see especially Nicholas Lemann, *The Promised Land: The Great Black Migration and How It Changed America* (New York: Knopf, 1992); and James N. Gregory, *The Southern Diaspora: How the Great Migrations of Black and White Southerners Transformed America* (Chapel Hill: University of North Carolina Press, 2005).

7. "Praises Hough Folks, Slaps 'Speculators,'" *Cleveland Call and Post*, May 30, 1953, p. 8-A.

8. Al Andrews, "Many Lured by Jobs Find City Life Tough," *Plain Dealer*, March 11, 1956, p. 1-B; Eugene Segal, "Family Life Is Hard Hit by Lag in Urban Renewal," *Plain Dealer*, April 20, 1957, p. 6.

9. Robert C. Stafford, "Hough Area Gets Support for Bond Issue," *Cleveland Press*, April 30, 1946, Cleveland Press Collection Clipping File (hereafter CPC), folder "Hough Area Council," Michael Schwartz Library, Cleveland State University, Cleveland, OH; "Leaders Map Plan to 'Save' Hough," *Cleveland Press*, June 8, 1959, CPC, folder "Hough—General."

10. "Housing for Negroes Drops since 1940," *Cleveland Press*, June 7, 1956.

11. "More Public Housing for Cleveland?," *Cleveland Press*, August 10, 1954; Interview #390, Maurice Klain Research Papers, MS. 4219 (hereafter MKRP), Western Reserve Historical Society, Cleveland, OH (hereafter WRHS); Thomas A. Burke, interview by Maurice Klain, n.d. [ca. February 1960], transcript p. 279, MKRP, container 2, folder 67.

12. Marty Richardson, "Race-Hate Suburbs Surround Cleveland," *Call and Post*, July 10, 1954, p. 1A.

13. Marian Morton, "Improved Retail Areas and Schools Are Scheduled for Hough Area," *Cleveland Press*, November 11, 1960, CPC, folder "Hough—General."

14. Marjorie Buckholz, *Twenty-Three Years of Work to Improve the Hough Area* (Cleveland: n.p., 1966), 1, 4–5, WRHS; Stafford, "Hough Area Gets Support for Bond Issue."

15. Buckholz, *Twenty-Three Years*, 9; *Plain Dealer*, "Slums and Rent Control" (editorial), September 22, 1952, p. 18.

16. Cleveland City Planning Commission, *Cleveland Today . . . Tomorrow: The General Plan of Cleveland* (Cleveland: Cleveland City Planning Commission, 1950), Cleveland Public Library, Cleveland, OH; Christopher Wye, "At the Leading Edge: The Movement for Black Civil Rights in Cleveland, 1830–1969," in *Cleveland: A Tradition of Reform*, ed. David D. Van Tassel and John J. Grabowski (Kent, OH: Kent State University Press, 1986), 132.

17. Jacob Rosenheim, interview by Patrick Miller, December 6, 2005, Cleveland Regional Oral History Collection, Interview 400019, http://engagedscholarship.csuohio

.edu/crohc000/44/. For context on the problem of blockbusting, see especially Amanda I. Seligman, *Block by Block: Neighborhoods and Public Policy on Chicago's West Side* (Chicago: University of Chicago Press, 2005), chap. 6.

18. Marc D. Gleisser, "Hough Council President Hits Property Neglect," *Plain Dealer*, June 4, 1955, p. 14; Hough Area Council, *Council Action* 7, no. 2 (1954), WRHS; "June Festival Set for Hough Families," *Plain Dealer*, June 5, 1955, p. 10-D; "300 at Hough Frolic; E. 86th Street Children Honored at Area Council's Party," *Plain Dealer*, June 27, 1955, p. 37.

19. Buckholz, *Twenty-Three Years*, 10–11; "Council Steps Up Its Interracial Program," *Call and Post*, September 8, 1951, p. 4-A; "What Good Neighbors Can Do" (editorial), *Cleveland Press*, September 20, 1951, CPC, folder "Hough—General"; Hough Area Council, *Council Action* 5, no. 2 (1952), WRHS.

20. Hough Area Council, *Council Action* 5, no. 4 (1952) and 5, no. 8 (1952), WRHS; "Growing Old Isn't Fun, Welfare Meeting Is Told," *Plain Dealer*, March 5, 1952, p. 6.

21. Eugene Segal, "Hough Area Face-Lift Drive to Demonstrate How to Halt City Blight," *Plain Dealer*, July 30, 1952, p. 1; Eugene Segal, "Residents Hope Behind 'Save Hough Area' Idea," *Plain Dealer*, July 31, 1952, p. 1.

22. "Curtis[s]-Olive Neighborhood Improvement Idea Spreads," *Plain Dealer*, October 15, 1953, p. 10; Richard Murway, "Hough Area Cites Year's Cleanup, Plots Future," *Cleveland Press*, September 16, 1952, CPC, folder "Hough Area Council"; Eugene Segal, "Hough Area Rehabilitation Project Will Be Expanded," *Plain Dealer*, October 1, 1952, p. 25.

23. L.B.S. [Louis B. Seltzer], "Putting This City Back Where It Belongs," *Cleveland Press*, n.d. [ca. September 11, 1952], CPC, folder "Hough—General."

24. "Elephant House Riles Hough Area; Mayor Hit on Enforcing of Building Code," *Plain Dealer*, October 15, 1954, p. 7; "Says City Pampers Monkeys, Ignores Humans; Hough Area Residents Hit Office Negligence," *Call and Post*, October 23, 1954, p. 3-A.

25. Cleveland's experience of rapid racial turnover was hardly unique, as many scholars of other northern cities in the postwar years have demonstrated. See especially Thomas J. Sugrue, *The Origins of the Urban Crisis: Race and Inequality in Postwar Detroit* (Princeton, NJ: Princeton University Press, 1996); Matthew J. Countryman, *Up South: Civil Rights and Black Power in Philadelphia* (Philadelphia: University of Pennsylvania Press, 2006), 68–69; June Manning Thomas, *Redevelopment and Race: Planning a Finer City in Detroit* (Detroit: Wayne State University Press, 1997), 87–89.

26. Norman Krumholz, "The Kerner Commission Twenty Years Later," in *The Metropolis in Black and White: Place, Power, and Polarization*, ed. George C. Galster and Edward W. Hill (New Brunswick, NJ: Rutgers University Center for Urban Policy Research, 1992), 25. It is important to note that outlying neighborhoods, such as Lee-Harvard, afforded some opportunities for blacks to acquire suburban-type homes; see Todd M. Michney, *Surrogate Suburbs: Black Upward Mobility and Neighborhood Change in Cleveland, 1900–1980* (Chapel Hill: University of North Carolina Press, 2017).

27. W. Dennis Keating, *The Suburban Racial Dilemma: Housing and Neighborhoods* (Philadelphia: Temple University Press, 1994), 98–99.

28. "Hough Leaders Open War on 'Panic Selling,'" *Cleveland Press*, June [illegible], 1954, CPC, folder "Hough—General."

29. "Says Race-Hate Used to Bring High Rents," *Call and Post*, July 2, 1955, p. 1-A; "Councilwoman Knocks Out 'White Only' Sign," *Call and Post*, April 13, 1957, p. 3-A; Charles L. Sanders, "No Negroes Wanted!," *Call and Post*, April 18, 1959, p. 1-A; Charles L. Sanders, "'Colored Rent' Routs Councilman; Negroes Move In, McCaffery Moves Out," *Call and Post*, June 18, 1960, p. 1-A.

30. Hough Area Council, *Council Action* 9, no. 1 (1955), WRHS; "Hough Area Council to Discuss U.S. Program," *Plain Dealer*, April 17, 1956, p. 15.

31. K. C. Parsons, *A Report on the Preliminary Plan for the Hough Community* (Cleveland: City Planning Commission, 1957), CPL; Eugene Segal, "View Plan to Remake Hough Site; Commissioners See Result of Long Study," *Plain Dealer*, January 26, 1957, p. 1.

32. Eugene Segal, "Seek Rehabilitation for Dunham Section," *Plain Dealer*, February 5, 1958, p. 20; Eugene Segal, "33 Million Is Cost of Hough Project," *Plain Dealer*, February 15, 1958, p. 7.

33. "Bruere Sees Possibility of Ghetto Here," *Plain Dealer*, February 26, 1959, p. 42. See also "Biggest Housing Need Is for Middle-Income Negroes," *Cleveland Press*, February 13, 1958.

34. "Bohn Ties Urban Program to Housing for Negroes," *Plain Dealer*, June 25, 1953, p. 16; Ernest J. Bohn, "How Industrial and City Officials Teamed Up for Urban Renewal" (speech), September 27, 1956, Ernest J. Bohn Papers (hereafter EJB), General Files, container 1, folder 5, Special Collections, Kelvin Smith Library, Case Western Reserve University, Cleveland, OH; Bohn, "Cleveland's Future in Housing the Poorly Housed" (speech outline), January 11, 1958, EJB, General Files, container 10, folder 1; Bohn to Anthony J. Celebrezze, July 31, 1959, EJB, Cleveland Metropolitan Housing Authority, container 2, folder 1.

35. For a fuller exploration of the role of University Circle institutions in shaping urban renewal in Cleveland, see J. Mark Souther, "Acropolis of the Middle-West: Decay, Renewal, and Boosterism in Cleveland's University Circle," *Journal of Planning History* 10, no. 1 (2011): 30–58.

36. Michael Carriere, "Fighting the War against Blight: Columbia University, Morningside Heights, Inc., and Counterinsurgent Urban Renewal," *Journal of Planning History* 10, no. 1 (2011): 5–29; Arnold R. Hirsch, *Making the Second Ghetto: Race and Housing in Chicago, 1940–1960* (Chicago: University of Chicago Press, 1983), chap. 5; John L. Puckett and Mark Frazier Lloyd, *Becoming Penn: The Pragmatic American University, 1950–2000* (Philadelphia: University of Pennsylvania Press, 2015), 60–65.

37. Rabbi Daniel J. Silver, interview by Maurice Klain, May 1, 1962, transcript pp. 13–14, MKRP, container 11, folder 588. Silver's father, Rabbi Abba Hillel Silver, headed the synagogue at the time of the decision to stay in eastern Hough.

38. John S. Millis to Harold T. Clark, January 2, 1952, University Circle, Inc., Records, MS. 3900 (hereafter UCI), container 50, folder 81, WRHS; John S. Millis, minutes of first meeting of University Circle Conference Committee, September 20, 1952, UCI, container 50, folder 80; Interview #222, MKRP.

39. Interview #72, MKRP; *University Circle: A Plan for Its Development* (Cambridge, MA: Adams, Howard and Greeley, 1957), 3–5.

40. *University Circle: A Plan for Its Development*, 16–18, 59–60.

41. Agenda, University Circle Development Foundation Advisory Board, July 30, 1958, UCI, container 50, folder 92. The Cleveland Development Foundation shared the goal of creating a corridor to link the city's downtown and eds-meds-cultural district. See Minutes of Sixth Annual Meeting of Members of Cleveland Development Foundation, January 14, 1960, Cleveland Development Foundation Records, MS. 3514 (hereafter CDF), container 1, folder "Cleveland Development Foundation Minutes—Annual Meeting, 1954–1969," WRHS.

42. Grant Anderson, "University Circle Looks to the Future," *Case Alumnus*, December 1957, 11, UCI, container 50, folder 79.

43. Bill Tanner, "Jobs for Tomorrow; Research Park Held Vital Need," *Cleveland Press*, October 26, 1961.

44. Neil J. Carothers to Donald M. Lynn, June 19, 1958, UCI, container 15, folder 444.

45. "University Circle's Future," *Plain Dealer*, April 19, 1959, PD pictorial magazine, p. 2.

46. *The First Two Years: A Progress Report on the University Circle Development Foundation (October 15, 1957 to October 15, 1959)* (Cleveland: University Circle Development Foundation, 1959), 7–8, UCI, container 2, folder 180; Neil J. Carothers to Harold T. Clark, March 10, 1960, UCI, container 20, folder 640; Paul Lilley, "Tudor Arms Sought as Dormitory," *Cleveland Press*, July 28, 1960, p. A1.

47. Neil J. Carothers to Albert Rains, January 21, 1960, UCI, container 20, folder 640.

48. Neil J. Carothers to Paul Ylvisaker, November 15, 1960, UCI, container 20, folder 640.

49. "Climate for Culture," n.d. [ca. 1960], UCI, container 15, folder 444.

50. Allen Fonoroff, interview by Maurice Klain, July 28, 1960, transcript p. 89, MKRP, container 5, folder 201; Interview #15, MKRP.

51. Eugene Segal, "Hearing Set on U-Circle Plan Dec. 30," *Plain Dealer*, December 18, 1960, p. 6-B; Eugene Segal, "City Renewal Ball Tossed to Council," *Plain Dealer*, January 15, 1960, p. 1.

52. "Charge Urban Renewal Ignores Slum Dweller," *Cleveland Press*, May 3, 1961; "At Last a City's Dreams Are Coming True," *Cleveland Press*, February 1, 1961.

53. Faith Corrigan, "Hough Area 'New Look' Previewed," *Plain Dealer*, June 15, 1962, p. 2.

54. "University Circle—A Project for Mankind," typescript, n.d. [ca. 1960], UCI, container 15, folder 444.

55. "Review of University Circle Public Relations and Outline for Program for 1962–3," May 1962, pp. 1–2, 6, UCI, container 15, folder 444.

56. Notes from Neighborhood Relations Project Interview with Rabbi Daniel J. Silver, May 11, 1962, UCI, container 15, folder 454.

57. Michael Copperman, "University Circle, Public Relations, and the Surrounding Neighborhood," January 30, 1964, pp. 2–6, 13, UCI, container 5, folder 89.

58. Upshur Evans to Oliver Brooks, April 19, 1962, CDF, container 58, folder "University Circle Development Foundation—Correspondence."

59. Len Watkins, "An X-Ray of Hough: Surveys Accomplish What?" *Call and Post*, August 18, 1962, p. 3A.

60. Neil J. Carothers to Anthony J. Celebrezze, September 14, 1960, UCI, container 20, folder 640; "University-Hough Plan Faces Hearing Delay," *Plain Dealer*, December 1, 1960, p. 30.

61. Sanford Watzman, "Brown Raps City on Lake Filth," *Plain Dealer*, November 2, 1962, p. 42.

62. "Hough Area 'Boondoggle,'" *Call and Post*, May 25, 1963, p. 2C.

63. Philip W. Porter, "What's Urban Renewal?" *Plain Dealer*, October 26, 1963, p. 11.

64. Donald Sabath, "University-Euclid Job Is Renewal at Its Worst," *Plain Dealer*, February 14, 1965, p. 1-A; Donald Sabath, "Rehabilitation Begins in University-Euclid," *Plain Dealer*, May 23, 1965, p. 8-B.

65. Eugene Segal, "Slowdown Is Noted in Housing Renewal," *Plain Dealer*, January 26, 1964, p. 1; Donald Sabath, "University-Euclid Renewal Is Slow; Staff Is Lacking," *Plain Dealer*, February 15, 1965, p. 1.

66. Faith Corrigan, "Vandalism Perils Renewal, East Side Landlord Says," *Plain Dealer*, August 22, 1964, p. 1.

67. Donald Sabath, "Garden Finance Plan Suggested; for University Renewal," *Plain Dealer*, January 8, 1965, p. 12.

68. Donald Sabath, "Hough Rehabilitation Snarled in Red Tape; Aide Complains," *Plain Dealer*, March 12, 1966, p. 1.

69. Doris O'Donnell, "Housing Code Unenforced, Probers Told," *Plain Dealer*, April 5, 1966, p. 1.

70. Thomas, *Redevelopment and Race*, 89–98.

71. Seymour Raiz, "1961 Is Called Decision Year for Hough," *Cleveland Press*, January 6, 1961.

72. Pat Royse, "Hough Population Drops but Poverty Homes Gain," *Cleveland Press*, February 14, 1966; Paul Lilley, "Coming Year Will Tell Whether Hough Dies," *Cleveland Press*, January 7, 1966, p. B1, CPC, folder "Hough—General."

73. "Cleveland Area Exceeding Pace; 20-Year Development May Be Complete in 11 Years," *New York Times*, March 22, 1963, p. R10.

74. "Talbot Area Upgraded by Trees, Lawns," *Plain Dealer*, September 27, 1963, p. 22.

75. Faith Corrigan, "Hough Area Notes Pretty Spots; Distortions Resented," *Plain Dealer*, November 26, 1963, p. 18.

76. "Setting an Example" (editorial), *Plain Dealer*, May 24, 1964, p. 6-AA.

77. "Hough Repair Start Nearing Completion," *Plain Dealer*, December 17, 1963, p. 13; *Plain Dealer*, "Demands City Speed Renewal," December 18, 1963, p. 14.

78. Donald Sabath, "Renewal Job Challenge to Neal Bellos," *Plain Dealer*, December 13, 1964, p. 8-AA.

79. Walker and Murray Associates Inc., "Interim Report: University-Euclid Urban Renewal Area No. 1," February 1965, CDF, container 59, folder "University-Euclid Urban Renewal Project III."

80. Neil J. Carothers, memo to [UCDF] Board of Trustees, May 19, 1965, UCI, container 2, folder 160.

81. "Renewal Job Hard Here, Weaver Says," *Plain Dealer*, May 22, 1965, p. 19; Donald Sabath, "Rehabilitation Begins in University-Euclid," *Plain Dealer*, May 23, 1965, p. 8-B.

82. Ralph S. Locher, Press Releases, October 6 and 21, 1965, Ralph Sidney Locher Papers, MS. 3337, container 8, folder 5.

83. "Jackson Opposes Old Home Fix-Up," *Plain Dealer*, July 9, 1965, p. 37; "$18,000 Tag for Fix-Up Is Questioned," *Plain Dealer*, July 13, 1965, p. 5.

84. "Bids Are Sought for Hough Fix-Up; 2 Homes to Be Models," *Plain Dealer*, September 22, 1965, p. 1; "Seawright and Associates Begin Federal Renewal Project in Hough Area," *Call and Post*, March 19, 1966, p. 1A; "A New Start" (editorial), *Plain Dealer*, September 23, 1965, p. 18.

85. Donald Sabath, "Lister Quits as City Renewal Boss," *Plain Dealer*, January 14, 1966, p. 1; "Shakeup in Renewal Is Ordered by Locher," *Cleveland Press*, April 29, 1966; Donald Sabath, "Nonprofit Unit Plans Hough Apartments," *Plain Dealer*, April 9, 1966, p. 1.

86. Michney, "White Civic Visions versus Black Suburban Aspirations," 302–303.

87. "Nonprofit Groups Aid Home Renewal," *Plain Dealer*, April 2, 1966, p. 39.

88. Daisy Craggett, "Cleveland's Disgrace: Public Housing at It's Worse [sic]," *Call and Post*, July 2, 1966, p. 12A; Mrs. Mitsuko E. Marsh to T. Keith Glennan, May 12, 1966, and accompanying untitled document dated April 4, 1966, UCI, container 11, folder 318.

89. "Rehabilitate Old Housing Is Plea," *Plain Dealer*, June 20, 1965, p. 11-AA; Donald Sabath and Roldo Bartimole, "Renew Old or Build New? Dispute Holds Key to Hough," *Plain Dealer*, August 8, 1965, p. 1-A.

90. "Private Group Starts Project in Hough Area," *Plain Dealer*, August 1, 1965, p.

22-A; "Nonprofit Groups May Aid Hough; Low Interest Loans Possible," *Plain Dealer*, October 5, 1965, p. 42.

91. J. F. Saunders, "City Owes Much to a Stranger," *Plain Dealer*, January 8, 1967, p. 6-AA; Thomas J. Monahan, "Priest Needs $8,000 to Make a Home," *Plain Dealer*, June 26, 1966, p. 1-A.

92. Burk Uzzle, "A Bitter and Insistent Plague," *Life*, December 24, 1965, pp. 106–117.

93. Oliver Brooks to John S. Millis, March 25, 1966, UCI, container 4, folder 40.

94. Leonard N. Moore, *Carl B. Stokes and the Rise of Black Political Power* (Urbana: University of Illinois Press, 2002), 47–49.

95. "Hough Speaks, Let's Hear Them," *Call and Post*, August 13, 1966, p. 8B.

96. "Demonstration Apartments Continue Open House," *University-Euclid News* [City of Cleveland, Division of Urban Renewal], October 1966, CDF, container 21, folder "Cleveland Urban Renewal Agency Correspondence, January 1957-."

97. "Contractor Calls Hough's 1st Project Inadequate; Bill May Run $20,000 Over," *Plain Dealer*, October 1, 1966, p. 16; Bob Williams, "Seawright, Glad, Sad Too, Rebuilds E. 90th St. Flat," *Call and Post*, October 8, 1966, p. 2A.

98. Robert G. McGruder and Roldo Bartimole, "A Signpost to Hope in Hough," *Plain Dealer*, October 25, 1966, p. 62.

99. Donald Sabath, "Foundation Launched $1-Million Hough Plan; 106 Apartments to Be Renovated," *Plain Dealer*, September 21, 1966, p. 1; "Hough Unit Seeking Lease of Apartment," *Plain Dealer*, December 14, 1966, p. 38.

100. Roldo Bartimole, "Hough Uplift Financed by Warner and Swasey," *Plain Dealer*, October 20, 1966, p. 1.

101. Margaret Taylor, "No Backsliding on Crawford Road," *Plain Dealer*, April 20, 1969, Sunday PD magazine, p. 42.

102. "Hough Plans 'Demands' in Poverty War," *Plain Dealer*, March 5, 1965, p. 47; Bob Williams, "Hough Council 'Disgusted' with Rev. Bruere on CAY," *Call and Post*, October 30, 1965, p. 4C.

103. Bartimole, "Hough Uplift Financed by Warner and Swasey."

104. "Foundation Scored on Renewal Failures," *Plain Dealer*, December 21, 1966, p. 6.

105. "Cleveland 1st City to Get Demolition Funds," *Call and Post*, November 22, 1969; Donald Sabath, "Developers to Bid on 3 Hough Sites for Low-Income Housing," *Plain Dealer*, July 28, 1966, p. 10; Daniel Kerr, "Who Burned Cleveland, Ohio? The Forgotten Fires of the 1970s," in *Flammable Cities: Urban Conflagration and the Making of the Modern World*, ed. Greg Bankoff, Uwe Lübken, and Jordan Sand (Madison: University of Wisconsin Press, 2012), 343.

106. Roy W. Adams, "Protestants Map Multimillion-Dollar Hough Homes Plan," *Plain Dealer*, July 30, 1966, p. 4.

107. Fred McGunagle, "Plans Shown to Make Hough $2,000,000 Brighter," *Cleveland Press*, March 29, 1967; Roldo Bartimole, "HOPE's Rehabilitation Effort Held Imperiled by Landlords," *Plain Dealer*, April 11, 1967, CPC, folder "Hough—General." Neither major newspaper reported the cancellation of the plan, but the project's failure to materialize spoke for itself.

108. Russ Musarra, "Suburban Greenery Brightens Hough," *Cleveland Press*, May 5, 1967; "Donated Greenery, Volunteers Work to Brighten Hough Area," *Plain Dealer*, May 7, 1967, CPC, folder "Hough—General."

109. Fred McGunagle, "Vacant Homes Show Hough Area Decay," *Cleveland Press*, May 25, 1967; Paul Lilley, "[missing word] and Decay Still Grip Hough," *Cleveland Press*, January 11, 1967, A1, CPC, folder "Hough—General."

110. "It's Still Yesterday in Cleveland," *Montage* (WKYC-TV 3, Cleveland, Ohio), February 3, 1967, http://flash.ulib.csuohio.edu/library/montage/still-yesterday.html, accessed October 5, 2015; Thomas Brazaitis, "Celeste Is Man with a Mission: Save Cleveland," *Scoop* [Collinwood, Cleveland, OH], September 14, 1967, Ralph J. Perk Papers, MS. 4456, container 17, folder 251, WRHS.

## CHAPTER 3

1. *Complex Patterns of a Vigorous City* (Cleveland: Greater Cleveland Growth Board, [ca. 1963]), Greater Cleveland Growth Association Records, MS. 3471 (hereafter GCGA), container 132, folder 3, Western Reserve Historical Society, Cleveland, OH (hereafter WRHS).

2. On the social and environmental consequences of deindustrialization, see especially Tracy Neumann, *Remaking the Rust Belt: The Postindustrial Transformation of North America* (Philadelphia: University of Pennsylvania Press, 2016); Steven C. High and David W. Lewis, *Corporate Wasteland: The Landscape and Memory of Deindustrialization* (Ithaca, NY: ILR Press, 2007); Jefferson Cowie and Joseph Heathcott, eds., *Beyond the Ruins: The Meanings of Deindustrialization* (Ithaca, NY: ILR Press, 2003); Steven C. High, *Industrial Sunset: The Making of North America's Rust Belt, 1969–1984* (Toronto: University of Toronto Press, 2003); Sherry Lee Linkon and John Russo, *Steeltown U.S.A.: Work and Memory in Youngstown* (Lawrence: University Press of Kansas, 2002); Thomas J. Sugrue, *The Origins of the Urban Crisis: Race and Inequality in Postwar Detroit* (Princeton, NJ: Princeton University Press, 1996); Kathryn Marie Dudley, *The End of the Line: Lost Jobs, New Lives in Postindustrial America* (Chicago: University of Chicago Press, 1994).

3. *Headlines from Cleveland*, August 6, 1945, pp. 2–3, Cleveland Mayoral Papers, MS. 4276, container 3, folder 67, WRHS.

4. Michael Kelly, "Area Sold on Slogan," *Plain Dealer*, November 22, 1964, p. 1-AA.

5. Advertisement reprinted in *Clevelander*, April 1944, p. 3.

6. Jon C. Teaford, *The Rough Road to Renaissance: Urban Revitalization in America, 1940–1985* (Baltimore: Johns Hopkins University Press, 1990), 23–25, 135. See also Howard Gillette Jr., *Camden after the Fall: Decline and Renewal in a Post-industrial City* (Philadelphia: University of Pennsylvania Press, 2005), 50–51.

7. *Directory of Cleveland Manufacturers Employing 100 or More Persons* (Cleveland: Cleveland Chamber of Commerce, 1959), GCGA, container 150, folder 6. The directory also included additional factories in Akron and its suburbs, Elyria, and Lorain, which I have omitted in these figures, because they stood outside the Cleveland Metropolitan Statistical Area and CEI's service area. In contrast to Cuyahoga and Lake Counties, which had a considerable diversity of industries, Akron's well-known tire and rubber industry accounted for nearly all of its handful of factories among those employing more than one thousand. In fact, its top five tire factories alone employed about 49,400 workers.

8. Michael Kelly, "Job Crisis in Cleveland," *Plain Dealer*, April 18, 1965, p. 1-AA.

9. Adin C. Rider, "Sixty Trust Is Buyer in 3-Way Deal," *Plain Dealer*, December 5, 1951, p. 1.

10. "A Challenge to Cleveland," *Clevelander*, May 1956, p. 5; emphasis original.

11. "Chemists Told of 300 Million Put in Industry Here," *Plain Dealer*, November 16, 1955, p. 11; Kelly, "Area Sold on Slogan."

12. Cleveland Electric Illuminating Company, Annual Report, 1953, p. 6, Cleveland Public Library, Cleveland, OH (hereafter CPL).

13. Ralph M. Besse to Employees, July 11, 1957, Centerior Energy Corporation Records, MS. 4791 (hereafter CEC), container 5, folder 113, WRHS.

14. *Question: Does the Location Offer Prime Building Land and Facilities in Communities Eager to Cooperate with New Industry and Business? The Answer for Cleveland–Northeast Ohio* (Cleveland: CEI, n.d. [ca. 1962]), GCGA, container 131, folder 10; *More Land for Industry: A Basic Planning Survey for the Best Location in the Nation* (Cleveland: CEI, 1960), CPL.

15. Raymond Curtis Miller, *The Force of Energy: A Business History of the Detroit Edison Company* (East Lansing: Michigan State University Press, 1971), 144; *Public Utilities Fortnightly* 61 (1958): 161–163; Niagara Mohawk Power Corporation, Annual Report, 1949.

16. "Welcome Aboard" (editorial), *Plain Dealer*, November 18, 1955, p. 14; Interview #272, Maurice Klain Research Papers, MS. 4217 (hereafter MKRP), WRHS.

17. "SAE to Tour Plant," *Plain Dealer*, May 11, 1958, p. 10-G.

18. "GM Closing Clinton Unit, Shifting 400," *Plain Dealer*, November 7, 1961, p. 39.

19. Kelly, "Job Crisis in Cleveland"; "Draft: Technical Appendix," p. 2, attached to Frank Maris, memo to R. DeChant and J. Sheehan, May 20, 1977, Daniel J. Marschall Papers, MS. 4561 (hereafter DJM), container 1 folder 19, WRHS.

20. Cleveland Electric Illuminating Company, Annual Reports, 1954, 1956–1959, CPL.

21. Peter B. Greenough, "Murray Ohio Gets Shell Contract; $8,000,000 Army Award Goes to Toy Company," *Plain Dealer*, March 3, 1951, p. 7; Phil G. Goulding, "Low-Tariff Foes Cite Ohio Losses," *Plain Dealer*, February 3, 1955, p. 12; "Murray Ohio, Union Agree in Transfer; Will Pay Severance, Pension Rights," *Plain Dealer*, February 22, 1957; Ted Princiotto, "Where to Now? Ask 450 Workers Who Lose Plant; Dixie-Bound Company Leaves Its Employe[e]s Sad and Confused," *Plain Dealer*, February 23, 1957.

22. Princiotto, "Where to Now?" Howard Gillette Jr. describes a similar obliviousness toward industrial decline in Camden, New Jersey, into the early 1960s; see Gillette, *Camden after the Fall*, 49–50.

23. Interview #517 and #6, MKRP; Robert H. Herrick, "Ford Launches Work on Walton Hills Plant," *Plain Dealer*, October 15, 1953, p. 1.

24. N. R. Howard, "Lest We Forget: Our Industry Makes City," *Plain Dealer*, April 25, 1960, p. 19.

25. Elmer L. Lindseth, Report to Employees, August 16, 1961, CEC, container 5, folder 113.

26. Curtis Lee Smith, interview by Maurice Klain, Cleveland, OH, May 17, 1962, transcript p. 475, MKRP, container 12, folder 605.

27. Minutes of GCGB Executive Committee meeting, January 31, 1962, GCGA, container 131, folder 2; list of donations to GCGB in 1962, dated January 10, 1963, GCGA, container 132, folder 1.

28. Budget and Plan of Action for the Greater Cleveland Growth Board, Calendar Year 1962, GCGA, container 131, folder 2.

29. Report of Brainstorming Session held March 13, 1962, Greater Cleveland Growth Board Executive Committee Meeting, March 29, 1962, GCGA, container 131, folder 5.

30. Repr.: "World Port," GCGB advertisement, *Wall Street Journal*, April 10, 1963, GCGA, container 132, folder 4; Greater Cleveland Growthland Advertising Coordinator, n.d. [1962], GCGA, container 131, folder 7.

31. Repr.: "Shift of 3 Propulsion Projects Gives Cleveland Key Space Role," GCGB advertisement, *Wall Street Journal*, February 27, 1963, GCGA, container 132, folder 3.

32. Repr.: "New Big Shot," GCGB advertisement, *Wall Street Journal*, May 8, 1963, GCGA, container 132, folder 5.

33. Repr.: "What Your Wife Knows about Finding a Plant Site," GCGB advertisement, *Wall Street Journal*, April 8, 1964, GCGA, container 133, folder 2.

34. Murray Seeger, "Port Missing Out on Full Potential of Seaway Trade," *Plain Dealer*, May 27, 1962, p. 1.

35. Interview #429, MKRP.

36. Peter B. Greenough, interview by Maurice Klain, Cleveland, OH, September 29, [1960?], transcript pp. 3, 97, 101–102, MKRP, container 5, folder 252; Thompson-Ramo-Wooldridge advertisement, *Plain Dealer*, August 13, 1959, p. 32; Interview #463, MKRP. On a similar situation in Pittsburgh, see Patrick Vitale, "Decline Is Renewal," *Journal of Urban History* 41, no. 1 (2015): 36. On Boston's Route 128 technology corridor, see David Koistinen, *Confronting Decline: The Political Economy of Deindustrialization in Twentieth-Century New England* (Gainesville: University Press of Florida, 2013), 160–220. On the emergence of Silicon Valley, see Margaret Pugh O'Mara, *Cities of Knowledge: Cold War Science and the Search for the Next Silicon Valley* (Princeton, NJ: Princeton University Press, 2005), 97–141.

37. *Executives Talk about Business Climate in the Cleveland Area* (Cleveland: Special Surveys, 1963), CPL; John E. Bryan, "Worsted Mills to Be Dissolved, Says Head of Strike-bound Firm," *Plain Dealer*, December 31, 1955, p. 1.

38. Curtis Lee Smith, interview by Maurice Klain, Cleveland, OH, August 8, 1961, transcript p. 272, MKRP, container 12, folder 604.

39. A Strictly Confidential 1962 Annual Report, First Year Activities and Progress, Greater Cleveland Growth Board, February 11, 1963, GCGA, container 132, folder 2; "Growth Board Efforts Keep Plant in City," *Cleveland Press*, July 9, 1963, GCGA, container 132, folder 6.

40. "Pecyk Raps Locher for Job Losses," *Plain Dealer*, September 22, 1963; GCGB Confidential Activity Report, August 28–September 26, 1963, GCGA, container 132, folder 7.

41. John J. Cleary, "Sohio Refinery Here and 430 Jobs Lost," *Plain Dealer*, July 10, 1964, p. 1; Al Ostrow, "Why Cleveland's Going Downhill," *Lake County News-Herald* (Willoughby, Ohio), September 19, 1966, vertical file, Public Administration Library, CPL.

42. Kelly, "Job Crisis in Cleveland"; "Draft: Technical Appendix," p. 2, attached to Maris memo, DJM.

43. Leonard N. Moore, *Carl Stokes and the Rise of Black Political Power* (Urbana: University of Illinois Press, 2002), 20.

44. Harold Joseph Austin, letter to the editor, *Cleveland Call and Post*, March 14, 1959, p. 3C.

45. Daniel R. Kerr, *Derelict Paradise: Homelessness and Urban Development in Cleveland, Ohio* (Amherst: University of Massachusetts Press, 2011), 145.

46. "The Best Location in the Nation?" (editorial), *Call and Post*, March 24, 1962, p. 2C. The "spatial mismatch" phenomenon, in which job expansion occurs most often far from concentrations of poverty, is widely cited in scholarship. See, for example, William Julius Wilson, *The Truly Disadvantaged: The Inner City, the Underclass, and Public Policy* (Chicago: University of Chicago Press, 1987).

47. Interview #283, MKRP; Smith interview, transcript p. 477. This attitude toward the problems of the inner city echoed that of urban renewal leaders, but in contrast, the latter described Garden Valley housing as industrialists' gift to "their" workers; see Todd

M. Michney, "White Civic Visions versus Black Suburban Aspirations: Cleveland's Garden Valley Urban Renewal Project," *Journal of Planning History* 10, no. 4 (2011): 290–291.

48. "Urges More Public Housing; Railroad Head Backs Redevelopment Plan," *Call and Post*, January 31, 1953, p. 2A.

49. Eugene Segal, "Lister Is Ready to Get Ball Rolling in Area O," *Plain Dealer*, November 12, 1955, p. 9; "Slum Label Given Area O; Cleanup Eyed," *Plain Dealer*, April 14, 1956, p. 24; Ted Princiotto, "NKP's Loss City's Gain in Urban Job; H. Horton Hampton, 70, to Retire Friday," *Plain Dealer*, February 27, 1957, p. 5.

50. Eugene Segal, "Mayor Stalls Slum Agency Plan," *Plain Dealer*, June 5, 1957, p. 2; "Lister Promises Orderly Relocation for Area O," *Plain Dealer*, September 17, 1957, p. 16.

51. Eugene Segal, "City Skips Any Federal Aid in 'Area O' Redevelopment Project," *Plain Dealer*, September 25, 1957, p. 26.

52. Teaford, *Rough Road to Renaissance*, 149–150; Colin Gordon, *Mapping Decline: St. Louis and the Fate of the American City* (Philadelphia: University of Pennsylvania Press, 2008), 205.

53. Robert J. Drake, "Bleeding Hearts in Belt's Path," *Plain Dealer*, February 1, 1958, p. 14.

54. Eugene Segal, "Outlook Bad for Area O Renewal Job," *Plain Dealer*, May 3, 1960, p. 1; Robert Burke Jones, memo on Gladstone, Cleveland Development Foundation Records, MS. 3514 (hereafter CDF), container 35, folder "Hampton, H. Horton," WRHS; Eugene Segal, "Federal Aid for Gladstone Area Sought," *Plain Dealer*, May 24, 1960, p. 32.

55. Al Sweeney, "Mayor Finally Gets Moving on 'Area O,'" *Call and Post*, June 9, 1962, p. 1A; Len Watkins, "Call Post Series of Exposes Led the Way to Action on Blighted Area," *Call and Post*, April 13, 1963, p. 5A.

56. Bill Brown, "Cleveland Employment—Stability or Stagnation?," Supplement A: The Gladstone Fiasco, n.d. [1962], GCGA, container 112, folder 1.

57. "N.J. Congressman Hints Erieview Is Cover-up for Woodland Flop," *Plain Dealer*, March 31, 1964, p. 5; "Housing Project Opens Tomorrow," *Plain Dealer*, June 29, 1956, p. 14; Eugene Segal, "Slum Chasers Set Sights on E. 79th Site; New Project Planned for 45-Acre Plot," *Plain Dealer*, June 30, 1956, p. 1.

58. Eugene Segal, "E. Woodland Urban Cost under Fire," *Plain Dealer*, May 13, 1958, p. 1; John J. Cleary, "Empire Varnish Buys Olo Paint," *Plain Dealer*, April 17, 1963, p. 18.

59. Eugene Segal, "Woodland Renewal Change Pondered," *Plain Dealer*, February 15, 1964, p. 10; Donald Sabath, "Industry for E. Woodland OK'd on Lister's Pledge," *Plain Dealer*, January 9, 1965, p. 8.

60. J. Mark Souther, "Acropolis of the Middle-West: Decay, Renewal, and Boosterism in Cleveland's University Circle," *Journal of Planning History* 10, no. 1 (2011): 39, 42.

61. "Cleanup Under Way in University-Euclid, Locher Says," *Plain Dealer*, March 4, 1965, p. 57; Donald Sabath, "Gladstone Serves as City Dump; Blight Spawns Hazards, Rats," *Plain Dealer*, May 3, 1965, p. 22; Roldo Bartimole, "Tenants Ousted by Renewal May Get Relocation Funds," *Plain Dealer*, October 27, 1966, p. 12.

62. "2d Firm Eyes Gladstone Renewal Area," *Plain Dealer*, May 24, 1965, p. 37.

63. "Growth Corp. Studies 3 Projects," *Plain Dealer*, May 29, 1965, p. 18; Minutes of meeting of trustees, Greater Cleveland Growth Corporation, May 28, 1965, GCGA, container 134, folder 2.

64. "Gladstone Eyed by Poultry Firm," *Plain Dealer*, August 25, 1965, p. 19.

65. "Gladstone Renewal Site Sought by Express Agency for Terminal," *Plain Dealer*, August 19, 1965, p. 35; "City of Apartment Again Delayed," *Plain Dealer*, March 29, 1966, p. 30; "REA May Give Up on City," *Plain Dealer*, August 26, 1966, p. 9; Donald Sabath,

"Brave New Gladstone World a Junk Heap; Project Sinking Beneath Refuse," *Plain Dealer*, January 7, 1967.

66. Donald Sabath, "More Renewal Purchases Called Likely," *Plain Dealer*, October 5, 1966, p. 42; Sabath, "Brave New Gladstone World a Junk Heap."

67. "Crayton's Plans Major Expansion; Shot in Arm for Renewal Area," *Plain Dealer*, December 24, 1966, p. 4.

68. "Woodland Landmark Business to Close," *Plain Dealer*, July 23, 1966, p. 5.

69. Patrick J. Ziska, "Renewal-Marooned Store Sues City; Asks $1 Million," *Plain Dealer*, February 28, 1967, p. 5.

70. Sabath, "Brave New Gladstone World a Junk Heap."

71. Minutes of GCGB Executive Committee meeting, March 12, 1963, GCGA, container 132, folder 3.

72. Minutes of meeting of the Industrial Development Committee, May 17, 1960, CDF, container 35, folder "Cleveland Chamber of Commerce Industrial Development Committee"; The Industrial Development Potential of the Gladstone Urban Renewal Project, A Report to the Cleveland Development Foundation by Dorothy A. Muncy, A.I.P., A.I.D.C., Industrial Planning Consultant, May 1965, Arlington, Virginia, CDF, container 33, folder "Gladstone—Area O, 1964–1966."

73. On Sunbelt industrial inducements, see, for example, Elizabeth Tandy Shermer, "Sunbelt Boosterism: Industrial Recruitment, Economic Development, and Growth Politics in the Developing Sunbelt," in *Sunbelt Rising: The Politics of Space, Place, and Region*, ed. Michelle Nickerson and Darren Dochuk (Philadelphia: University of Pennsylvania Press, 2011), 31–57.

74. John Emmeus Davis, *Contested Ground: Collective Action and the Urban Neighborhood* (Ithaca, NY: Cornell University Press, 1991), 137–138, 144; Teaford, *Rough Road to Renaissance*, 150; Colin Gordon, *Mapping Decline: St. Louis and the Fate of the American City* (Philadelphia: University of Pennsylvania Press, 2008), 209; Guian McKee, "Urban Deindustrialization and Local Public Policy: Industrial Renewal in Philadelphia, 1953–1976," *Journal of Policy History* 16, no. 1 (2004): 83.

75. Marcus Gleisser, "Stouffer Began as Lunch Counter," *Plain Dealer*, July 24, 1990, p. 10-A.

76. Peter Phipps, "How the City Withers Away," [unknown periodical], ca. 1970s, p. 53, DJM, container 1, folder 21.

77. "Frozen Food Plant Set for Solon by Stouffer," *Plain Dealer*, August 12, 1966, p. 45; Kenneth E. Banks Jr., "Solon's Rapid Industrial Growth No Accident," *Plain Dealer*, March 22, 1967, p. 28.

78. Edward J. Walsh, "The Suburb That Moved Over for Industry," *Cleveland Magazine*, July 1978, p. 92, DJM, container 1, folder 20; Kerr, *Derelict Paradise*, 145; Watkins, "Call Post Series of Exposes Led the Way."

## CHAPTER 4

1. "Sealed Area Is Quiet; Glenville, Hough Keep Own Peace," *Plain Dealer*, July 25, 1968, p. 1; Carl B. Stokes, *Promises of Power: A Political Autobiography* (New York: Simon and Schuster, 1973), 216–217.

2. Jon C. Teaford, *The Rough Road to Renaissance: Urban Revitalization in America, 1940–1985* (Baltimore: Johns Hopkins University Press, 1990), 255.

3. John P. Coyne, "City's Critics Get an Answer," *Plain Dealer*, June 13, 1967, p. 30;

John Skow, "The Question in the Ghetto: Can Cleveland Escape Burning?" *Saturday Evening Post*, July 29, 1967, Cleveland Development Foundation Records, MS. 3514 (hereafter CDF), container 13, folder "Various Articles, Cleveland, City of," Western Reserve Historical Society, Cleveland, OH (hereafter WRHS).

4. Skow, "The Question in the Ghetto."

5. H. L. Florian to Editor, September 13, 1967, Ralph S. Locher Papers, MS. 3337 (hereafter RSL), container 14, folder 7, WRHS; Mayor Ralph S. Locher, Remarks at Cleveland City Club, September 22, 1967, RSL, container 15, folder 9.

6. "Isn't It about Time We Had a *Successful* Mayor? Frank P. Celeste" (advertisement), *Plain Dealer*, September 24, 1967; emphasis original.

7. "Two More Locher Years? No!" (editorial), *Plain Dealer*, September 29, 1967, p. 24.

8. Leonard N. Moore, *Carl B. Stokes and the Rise of Black Political Power* (Urbana: University of Illinois Press, 2002), 20; "White Voters Urged to 'Save Cleveland,'" *Plain Dealer*, September 21, 1967, p. 10.

9. Locher, Remarks at Cleveland City Club.

10. Repr. of James M. Naughton, "Cleveland: 'I Must Prove Their Fears Are Groundless'—Stokes," *New York Times Magazine*, November 5, 1967, CDF, container 13, folder "Various Articles, Cleveland, City of"; Moore, *Carl B. Stokes*, 91.

11. Stokes for Mayor Committee advertisement, *Plain Dealer*, July 28, 1967; emphasis original.

12. James M. Naughton, "Stokes Defeats Locher by 18,000 in Record Vote," *Plain Dealer*, October 4, 1967, p. 1; James M. Naughton, "Stokes Is Elected Mayor; Victory Margin Is Less Than 2,500 Votes," *Plain Dealer*, November 8, 1967, p. 1.

13. Teaford, *Rough Road to Renaissance*, 168–176.

14. Interview of Arnold Pinkney, Cleveland, OH, July 1971, transcript p. 24, Carl B. Stokes Papers, MS. 4370 (hereafter CBS), container 7, folder 104, WRHS.

15. Roy J. Ferrette to Carl B. Stokes, January 9, 1968; "Brag a Little" Campaign list of expenses; Mark J. D'Arcangelo to Carl B. Stokes, March 15, 1968; Roberta Dike to Carl B. Stokes, March 4, 1968, CBS, container 36, folder 659.

16. Interview of Henry J. Matt, Cleveland, OH, July 1971, transcript p. 20, CBS, container 7, folder 103.

17. Stokes, *Promises of Power*, 108–109; repr. of James M. Naughton, "Mayor Stokes: The First Hundred Days," *New York Times Magazine*, February 25, 1968, CDF, container 13, folder "Various Articles, Cleveland, City of."

18. "Stokes Is Proud of His 'Able' Team," *Plain Dealer*, February 21, 1968, p. 40; Donald Sabath, "Stokes Wins Renewal Grant; U. Circle to Get Apartments," *Plain Dealer*, March 5, 1968, p. 1. Weaver's decision still required direct persuasion by Stokes and Vice President Hubert Humphrey; see Moore, *Carl B. Stokes*, 69–70.

19. Roldo Bartimole, "Cleveland Now: Another Gimmick," *Point of View* 1, no. 1 [1968], Cleveland State University Library Special Collections, Cleveland, OH; Sabath, "Stokes Wins Renewal Grant."

20. Stokes, *Promises of Power*, 129; Peter B. Levy, "The Dream Deferred: The Assassination of Martin Luther King, Jr., and the Holy Week Uprisings of 1968," in *Baltimore '68: Riots and Rebirth in an American City*, ed. Jessica I. Elfenbein, Thomas L. Hollowak, and Elizabeth M. Nix (Philadelphia: Temple University Press, 2011), 5–6.

21. Stokes, *Promises of Power*, 129.

22. John P. Coyne, "PR Firm Takes On Big Job of Improving City Image," *Plain Dealer*, April 15, 1968, p. 19.

23. "A Death, Rare Cooperation Moved Plan," *Plain Dealer*, May 2, 1968, p. 2-A.

24. Interview of Richard Murway, Cleveland, OH, July 1971, transcript pp. 19–20, CBS, container 7, folder 104; "Special Gets 'Rush' Action," *Plain Dealer*, May 2, 1968, p. 1.

25. Timothy D. Armbruster, "Crisis in Cleveland: Rx: Instant Public Relations for an Ailing City," *Public Relations Journal*, August 1968, 10–12, CBS, container 13, folder 226; Carl B. Stokes, "The Quality of Our Environment," undated [ca. 1970] speech given in St. Petersburg, FL, CBS, container 51, folder 951.

26. "Federal Grants Will Cover Lion's Share of $177 Million," *Plain Dealer*, May 2, 1968, p. 1.

27. Stokes, *Promises of Power*, 130.

28. Victoria W. Wolcott, *Race, Riots, and Roller Coasters: The Struggle over Segregated Recreation* (Philadelphia: University of Pennsylvania Press, 2012), 221.

29. Bernard D. Nossiter, "Business Helps Showman Mayor," *Washington Post*, March 23, 1969, p. C1, CBS, container 28, folder 497.

30. Donald Sabath, "Bank to Build Skyscraper; Central National Tower to Rise at E. 9th, Superior," *Plain Dealer*, September 9, 1966, p. 1; "Bank Building Ground Is Broken," *Plain Dealer*, September 19, 1967, p. 17; David Stradling and Richard Stradling, *Where the River Burned: Carl Stokes and the Struggle to Save Cleveland* (Ithaca, NY: Cornell University Press, 2015), 79.

31. "Big Moment in City's History" (editorial), *Plain Dealer*, November 14, 1967, p. 16.

32. R. F. Evans to All Cleveland Employees of Diamond Shamrock Corporation, November 25, 1969; Jack Keever to Carl B. Stokes, January 12, 1970, CBS, Container 76, folder 1453; "Ground Broken for Wright's Diamond Shamrock Building; Dream-Come-True," *Cleveland Call and Post*, March 20, 1971, p. 16A.

33. Remarks by Mayor Carl B. Stokes, Groundbreaking for Public Utilities Building, East 12th and Lakeside Ave., 9:30 A.M., Tuesday, July 22, 1969, CBS, container 51, folder 964; "Carl Stokes' First Year as Mayor" (editorial), *Plain Dealer*, November 17, 1968, p. 1-AA.

34. *Development Program, Downtown Cleveland: Guidelines for Action* (Cleveland: Ernst and Ernst, 1965), 70, Cleveland Public Library, Cleveland, OH (hereafter CPL).

35. Cleveland: NOW! Downtown and Port Authority Segment, Location: Erieview Plaza [April 30, 1968], CBS, container 12, folder 208.

36. Teaford, *Rough Road to Renaissance*, 170. On the shift toward leisure in cities, see especially Alison Isenberg, *Downtown America: A History of the Place and the People Who Made It* (Princeton, NJ: Princeton University Press, 2004), chap. 7.

37. James C. Blainey to Upshur Evans, James M. Lister, and Curtis Lee Smith, January 2, 1959, CDF, container 36, folder "Hilton Hotels Corp. Correspondence, Jan. '58–June 30, 1959."

38. J. A. Wadovick, "Big Day for Cleveland and Its Giant New Hall," *Plain Dealer*, August 29, 1964, p. 1.

39. William C. Barnard, "Mall Envisioned as 'Fun Place'; Transformation Planned," *Plain Dealer*, March 21, 1968, p. 4; "Mall Diner Opening May Draw Stokes," *Plain Dealer*, June 3, 1968, p. 18; "Dining on Mall Gets Off to Brisk Start," *Plain Dealer*, June 4, 1968, p. 25; "Downtown Boost" (editorial), *Plain Dealer*, June 5, 1968, p. 16.

40. "Mall Fete Draws Scads of Children," *Plain Dealer*, August 8, 1969, p. 1-B; "Music, Laughter at Mall Fun Day," *Plain Dealer*, August 16, 1969, p. 2-B; "'Woodstock' Downtown—Fun Day," *Call and Post*, August 22, 1970, p. 2A.

41. George E. Condon, "The Mayor of the Flats," *Plain Dealer*, February 26, 1967, p. 6-AA; Kenneth D. Huszar and Dennis B. Doris Jr., "Our Jumping Flats," *Plain Dealer*,

March 10, 1967, PD Action Tab section, pp. 2–3; "Flats Bar Renaissance Plans Hailed," *Plain Dealer*, March 2, 1968, p. 16; "Old Flats," CVB Tourism Dept. advertisement, *Plain Dealer*, May 30, 1968, p. 2-C; "Fete Set to Inaugurate Flats as Recreation Area," *Plain Dealer*, May 17, 1968, p. 30; "'Old Flats' Dances into Fun Spot Role," *Plain Dealer*, June 20, 1968, p. 15.

42. George E. Condon, "A City Goes Down the Hill," *Plain Dealer*, April 10, 1969, p. 7-D.

43. Ralph S. Locher, press release, October 6, 1965, RSL, container 8, folder 5; Neil J. Carothers, memo to Board of Trustees, November 4, 1966, University Circle, Inc., Records, MS. 3900, container 2, folder 159; "Vapor Lights Ordered for University Circle," *Cleveland Press*, November 9, 1966, p. A1; William C. Barnard, "Stokes' Cabinet Is Knit by Cause; Camaraderie, Youth Mark New Mayor's Executives," *Plain Dealer*, June 9, 1968, p. 1-AA; Stradling and Stradling, *Where the River Burned*, 113–114.

44. Interview of Ben S. Stefanski II, Cleveland, OH, July 1971, transcript pp. 9–11, CBS, container 7, folder 106.

45. "Great Bright Way" (editorial), *Plain Dealer*, October 18, 1969, p. 10-A; George E. Condon, "Out of the Darkness at Last," *Plain Dealer*, October 16, 1969, p. 11-A.

46. Ralph J. Perk, untitled statement, October 30, 1969, Ralph J. Perk Papers, MS. 4456, container 6, folder 96, WRHS.

47. "City Proclaims Its New Lights Downtown Are Brightest of All," *Plain Dealer*, October 31, 1969, p. 7-G.

48. Douglas Bloomfield, "Loop Bus Improvement Would Cost $130,000," *Plain Dealer*, January 30, 1969, p. 4; Douglas Bloomfield, "CTS Fare Hike Is in Effect; Hearing on Legal Action Due," *Plain Dealer*, March 30, 1969, p. 30.

49. "Stokes Sees Volpe on Transit Revamp," *Plain Dealer*, April 3, 1969, p. 13-A; Douglas Bloomfield, "$2.5-Million Transit Project Given Go-Ahead," *Plain Dealer*, May 27, 1969, p. 12-E; "Inner City, Hospital Trip Eased," *Plain Dealer*, September 16, 1969, p. 8-A; "Stokes Unveils New Bus Runs to J&L," *Plain Dealer*, September 18, 1969, p. 5-C.

50. "'Santa Loop' Is Shoppers' Bus Service," *Plain Dealer*, November 23, 1969, p. 14; Michael Kelly, "Invasion of Shoppers Opens Buying Season," *Plain Dealer*, November 29, 1969, p. 13-A.

51. John Clark, "10-Cent Shopper Loop Bus Urged," *Plain Dealer*, February 20, 1970, p. 1-A; "Special Bus Routes Set to Aid Inner City," *Plain Dealer*, December 13, 1969, p. 9-A.

52. Francis A. Coy to Carl B. Stokes, January 21, 1970, CBS, container 31, folder 568; "Consortium Maps Downtown Improvement Projects," *Plain Dealer*, February 24, 1970, p. 5-A.

53. "Downtown Has a Future—If" (editorial), *Plain Dealer*, September 15, 1970, p. 14-A; "Festival Turns On Downtown," *Plain Dealer*, September 12, 1970, p. 10-A.

54. "Euclid Avenue to Close for Fest; Conversion to Mall Studied," *Plain Dealer*, August 26, 1970, p. 3-A; *Downtown Cleveland 1975* (Cleveland: Cleveland City Planning Commission, 1959), 63–65, CPL; *Development Program, Downtown Cleveland*, 147. On Kalamazoo Mall, see M. Jeffrey Hardwick, *Mall Maker: Victor Gruen, Architect of an American Dream* (Philadelphia: University of Pennsylvania Press, 2004), 193–197. On Ghirardelli Square, see Isenberg, *Downtown America*, 283–292.

55. "Grant for Model City Planning in 4 Months Vowed by Stokes," *Plain Dealer*, April 3, 1968, p. 9; Donald Sabath and Roldo Bartimole, "Homeowners Lose in Renewal Change," *Plain Dealer*, March 1, 1966, p. 1; Donald Sabath, "Renewal Foes Lose Lawsuit, but Stokes Grants Their Wish," *Plain Dealer*, June 25, 1968, p. 1.

56. Guian McKee, "Urban Deindustrialization and Local Public Policy: Industrial Renewal in Philadelphia, 1953–1976," *Journal of Policy History* 16, no. 1 (2004): 66–98.

57. Donald Sabath, "Industrial Outlook Bright for Gladstone Renewal," *Plain Dealer*, February 3, 1968, p. 4; "Life in Gladstone" (editorial), *Plain Dealer*, June 19, 1968, p. 12.

58. Interview of Richard Green, Cleveland, OH, July 1971, transcript p. 11, CBS, container 6, folder 99; "$7.5-Million Request OK'd for Gladstone Renewal," *Plain Dealer*, May 31, 1972, p. 8-C.

59. George P. Rasanen, "Perk to Seek Cut in Price of Gladstone Land," *Plain Dealer*, October 31, 1972, p. 1-C.

60. Richard R. Green to Evelyn Schebek, June 13, 1968, CBS, container 36, folder 665; Donald Sabath, "Three Separate Uses Suggested for Gladstone," *Plain Dealer*, June 8, 1968, p. 26; Statement by Mayor Carl B. Stokes, June 17, 1968, CBS, container 51, folder 957.

61. "Ghetto Plant Bond Approved," *Plain Dealer*, September 23, 1969, p. 9-A; Statement by Mayor Carl B. Stokes, Sept. 29, 1969, CBS, container 51, folder 965.

62. "Gladstone Industrial Renewal Is under Way after 6 Years," *Plain Dealer*, April 23, 1969, p. 7-B; Jack Keever to Carl B. Stokes, March 3, 1970, CBS, container 31, folder 568.

63. Margaret Pugh O'Mara, *Cities of Knowledge: Cold War Science and the Search for the Next Silicon Valley* (Princeton, NJ: Princeton University Press, 2005), 71–73, 110–126, 158–165; William M. Rohe, *The Research Triangle: From Tobacco Road to Global Prominence* (Philadelphia: University of Pennsylvania Press, 2012), 61–92; John L. Puckett and Mark Frazier Lloyd, *Becoming Penn: The Pragmatic American University, 1950–2000* (Philadelphia: University of Pennsylvania Press, 2015), 97–103; J. Mark Souther, "Acropolis of the Middle-West: Decay, Renewal, and Boosterism in Cleveland's University Circle," *Journal of Planning History* 10, no. 1 (2011): 41.

64. Donald Sabath, "The Changing Mood of Technical Research," *Plain Dealer*, May 26, 1968, Sunday PD magazine, p. 30; Gene I. Maeroff, "Chase to Move Research to Circle; In U. Circle Center," *Plain Dealer*, March 1, 1967, p. 1; "Warner and Swasey Plans to Move; To Research Center," *Plain Dealer*, January 18, 1968, p. 5; "U. Circle Project's Start Set," *Plain Dealer*, April 23, 1968, p. 19.

65. Richard R. Green to Willard W. Brown, April 22, 1968, CBS, container 69, folder 1319.

66. "University Circle Research Center Attracts Industry," *Plain Dealer*, December 10, 1969, Ohio Industrial Land Development supplement, p. 12; "Chase Brass Axing 35 Jobs at U. Circle," *Plain Dealer*, July 27, 1971, p. 3-A; Allen Wiggins, "Circle Research Mecca Is Still 'Idle' Dream," *Plain Dealer*, June 7, 1972, p. 1.

67. George Rasanen, "City Faces Reconstruction; Losing Productive Plants, People," *Plain Dealer*, June 16, 1970, p. 1-A.

68. "Mayor Picks Keever to Bolster City's Industry," *Plain Dealer*, January 30, 1968, p. 2.

69. "Hill Sworn In as Manpower Head; Helped Create Resources-Economic Unit," *Plain Dealer*, September 26, 1968, p. 60; Interview of David Hill, Cleveland, OH, July 1971, transcript p. 8, CBS, container 6, folder 100.

70. Donald Sabath, "Center for Jobless Gets Pledge of Jobs," *Plain Dealer*, September 8, 1968, p. 5-AA; Donald Sabath, "Greater Cleveland Growth Association Is Completing a Year of Work: A Review," *Plain Dealer*, November 28, 1968, p. 1-AA; "$4 Million Sought from Business; NOW! Campaign," *Plain Dealer*, February 27, 1969, p. 5-A.

71. David G. Hill to Carl B. Stokes, June 15, 1971, CBS, container 6, folder 100;

Annual Report, Department of Human Resources and Economic Development, City of Cleveland, June 16, 1969—June 15, 1970, CBS, container 6, folder 101. On the problems posed by the failure to merge industrial and employment programs, see Guian A. McKee, *The Problem of Jobs: Liberalism, Race, and Deindustrialization in Philadelphia* (Chicago: University of Chicago Press, 2008).

72. Stradling and Stradling, *Where the River Burned*, 101.

73. Robert G. McGruder, "Riot-Panel Report Sparked the Idea," *Plain Dealer*, May 2, 1968, p. 9.

74. Donald C. Sabath, "Big Change in Renewal Seen Here," *Plain Dealer*, October 5, 1967, p. 19; Donald Sabath, "Hough Project Wins Model Cities Grant," *Plain Dealer*, September 7, 1968, p. 4; "Lawsuit Threatens Model Plan," *Plain Dealer*, January 9, 1969, p. 15.

75. Moore, *Carl B. Stokes*, chap. 5.

76. Leslie Kay, "Suit on 'New Town' Threatened; Warrensville Heights Mayor Acts," *Plain Dealer*, March 25, 1971, p. 4-C. On the Title VII program, see especially Nicholas Dagen Bloom, "The Federal Icarus: The Public Rejection of 1970s National Suburban Planning," *Journal of Urban History* 28, no. 1 (2001): 55–71.

77. "Stokes, Celeste Team at Ground-Breaking," *Plain Dealer*, October 6, 1967, p. 7.

78. "Mayor Stokes Breaks Ground in Hough Rehabilitation Project," *Plain Dealer*, December 16, 1967, p. 26; Brochure: "Lexington Square: 'The Pride of Hough,'" n.d.; untitled Lexington Square typescript, n.d., CBS, container 56, folder 1054.

79. "Sod-Planting Set for Hough," *Plain Dealer*, June 23, 1968, p. 23; "Rain Helps Greening of Hough," *Plain Dealer*, June 26, 1968, p. 2.

80. "Parade Marks Riots in Hough," *Plain Dealer*, July 21, 1968, p. 3-AA.

81. Hough Area Development Corporation Historical Sketch, n.d.; Cleveland Black Economics Seminar, November 1, 1968, CBS, container 56, folder 1049; Nishani Frazier, "A McDonald's That Reflects the Soul of a People: Hough Area Development Corporation and Community Development in Cleveland," in *The Business of Black Power: Community Development, Capitalism, and Corporate Responsibility in Postwar America*, ed. Laura Warren Hill and Julia Rabig (Rochester: University of Rochester Press, 2012), 71–72. On the HADC's New York counterparts, see Brian Goldstein, "Abyssinian Development Corporation," in *Affordable Housing in New York: The People, Places, and Policies That Transformed a City*, ed. Nicholas Dagen Bloom and Matthew Gordon Lasner (Princeton, NJ: Princeton University Press, 2016), 269.

82. "Project Announced under NOW! Drive," *Plain Dealer*, June 15, 1968, p. 52; "$1.6-Million Grant to Aid Hough Area," *Plain Dealer*, July 3, 1968, p. 4; "King Plaza in Hough Is Started," *Plain Dealer*, November 1, 1969, p. 3-A; Donald L. Bartlett, "HADC Produces Reports, Promises," *Plain Dealer*, April 13, 1970, p. 1; "King Shopping Plaza to Rise in Hough Area," *Call and Post*, January 9, 1971, p. 3A.

83. Frank T. DeStefano, *Evaluation of the Community Housing Corporation: Report to the PATH Association Task Force*, February 1971, p. 42, CBS, container 30, folder 544; "How City Will Spend," clipping from unknown newspaper, May 2, 1968, CBS, container 13, folder 224; Carl B. Stokes to Worth Loomis, January 30, 1969; Community Housing Corporation, First Board Meeting Agenda, February 7, 1969, CBS, container 65, folder 1223.

84. Statement of Objectives and Policies of the Community Housing Corporation, CBS, container 30, folder 544; "Detroit Man to Lead Community Housing," *Plain Dealer*, April 19, 1969, p. 14-A; Donald Sabath, "15-Year-Old Foundation Quitting Housing Field," *Plain Dealer*, July 2, 1969, p. 6-A.

85. Speech by Carl B. Stokes, n.d., CBS, container 12, folder 205.

86. Donald Sabath, "Ban Block Relocation of Homes from Path of I-80," *Plain Dealer*, July 24, 1969, p. 24-D; Richard D. Peters memo to Directors Baugh, Davis, Green and James, March 30, 1970, CBS, container 30, folder 544; "Garfield Hts. Reduces I-80 Demolition Bond," *Plain Dealer*, September 15, 1970, p. 17-A.

87. Cynthia Mills Richter, "Integrating the Suburban Dream: Shaker Heights, Ohio," Ph.D. diss., University of Minnesota, 1999, 135–142, 154–155; Interviews #9, #48, #127, #543, and Kenneth S. Nash, interview by Maurice Klain, July 28, [1961], transcript p. 221, Maurice Klain Research Papers, MS. 4219, container 9, folder 474, WRHS.

88. Richter, "Integrating the Suburban Dream," 165–168.

89. "Relocation of Shaker Homes Set," *Plain Dealer*, July 8, 1969, p. 6-A; "Mayor Gives Key to Owner of Cleveland Now! Home," *Call and Post*, June 20, 1970, p. 18A; "Relocated Shaker Houses Now Being Purchased," *Community Housing Corporation Report*, July 1970, CBS, container 30, folder 544.

90. "Hough Rapidly Becoming Ghost Area," *Plain Dealer*, May 11, 1968, p. 11-B. On East Cleveland, see Andrew Wiese, *Places of Their Own: African American Suburbanization in the Twentieth Century* (Chicago: University of Chicago Press, 2004), 249–251. On Corlett and Lee-Harvard, see Todd M. Michney, *Surrogate Suburbs: Black Upward Mobility and Neighborhood Change in Cleveland, 1900–1980* (Chapel Hill: University of North Carolina Press, 2017), 165–176.

91. DeStefano, *Evaluation of the Community Housing Corporation*, pp. 16–18, 20.

92. Robert T. Stock, "Cleveland: NOW! One Year Later," *Plain Dealer*, April 6, 1969, p. 1-AA; DeStefano, *Evaluation of the Community Housing Corporation*, 26, 31.

93. Moore, *Carl B. Stokes*, 90–91; Thomas S. Andrzejewski, "Ugly Hate for Mayor Stokes," *Plain Dealer*, February 20, 1971, p. 9-A.

94. Francis Ward, "Stokes Leaves Cleveland Uncertain Fate," *Long Island Press* [Jamaica, NY], May 7, 1971, CBS, container 28, folder 497.

95. John P. Coyne, "Gift of $81,000 to Put Clevelanders in Swim," *Plain Dealer*, June 8, 1971, p. 1-A; William F. Miller, "Mall Is Touch of Paris with Music, Flowers, Parade of Pretty Girls," *Plain Dealer*, June 15, 1971, p. 10-A.

96. Repr. of "Business Now Backs Cleveland," *Business Week*, September 21, 1968, CBS, container 28, folder 499.

97. Michael Ward, "West 11th St. Jumps Tonight as Flats Festival Opens," *Plain Dealer*, October 9, 1970, PD Action Tab, p. 10; Kenneth E. Banks, "Flats Fun Festival Finds Equatic [*sic*] Stokes," *Plain Dealer*, October 11, 1970, p. 11-A.

98. Teaford, *Rough Road to Renaissance*, 255.


**CHAPTER 5**

1. George E. Condon, "An Anniversary to Be Forgotten," *Plain Dealer*, July 29, 1971, p. 13-A.

2. Harvey K. Newman, "Race and the Tourist Bubble in Downtown Atlanta," *Urban Affairs Review* 37, no. 3 (2002): 308–309; J. Mark Souther, *New Orleans on Parade: Tourism and the Transformation of the Crescent City* (Baton Rouge: Louisiana State University Press, 2006), 46–52, 165; Richard Campanella, *Bourbon Street: A History* (Baton Rouge: Louisiana State University Press, 2014), 201–221.

3. Alison Isenberg, *Downtown America: A History of the Place and the People Who Made It* (Chicago: University of Chicago Press, 2004), 255.

4. George P. Rasanen, "Citizens Group to Help City Landmark Commission Designate Buildings Worth Saving," *Plain Dealer*, December 10, 1972, p. 29-A.

5. "Downtown Cleveland—A Magnet for People," *Plain Dealer*, December 1, 1971, Downtown section, p. 2.

6. Philip W. Porter, "The Mistake That Ruined Downtown," *Cleveland*, November 1976, pp. 68–70, 98–104.

7. Cleveland city directories, 1960–1970, Cleveland Public Library, Cleveland, OH (hereafter CPL).

8. "Cleveland Is," *Plain Dealer*, April 14, 1974, p. 3-AA. For national context, see Jon C. Teaford, *The Rough Road to Renaissance: Urban Revitalization in America, 1940–1985* (Baltimore: Johns Hopkins University Press, 1990), 209–210.

9. "Reopening Theaters; Challenge Issued on Playhouse Sq.," *Plain Dealer*, August 21, 1970, p. 8-A; Tim Joyce, "Playhouse Square; Talking It Over with Ray Shepardson," *Plain Dealer*, December 7, 1975, Sunday PD magazine, p. 5.

10. "Playhouse Square," *Encyclopedia of Cleveland History*, https://case.edu/ech/articles/p/playhouse-square/; "Cinerama for Cleveland," *Clevelander* 31, no. 7 (1956): 26.

11. J. Mark Souther, "A $35 Million 'Hole in the Ground': Metropolitan Fragmentation and Cleveland's Unbuilt Downtown Subway," *Journal of Planning History* 14, no. 3 (2015): 190.

12. William F. Miller, "Loew's Ohio and State Theaters to Be Razed," *Plain Dealer*, May 25, 1972, p. 1-A.

13. "Halle Brothers Co.," *Encyclopedia of Cleveland History*, https://case.edu/ech/articles/h/halle-brothers-co/; William F. Miller, "Bonwit Teller to Turn into Discount Store," *Plain Dealer*, April 19, 1972, p. 1-A; "Million-Dollar Dropout?" *Plain Dealer*, May 28, 1972, p. 1-B; Karl Burkhardt, "Stouffer Restaurant Will Close on Playhouse Square July 31," *Plain Dealer*, April 29, 1972, p. 1-A.

14. John Hemsath, interview by Andreana Somich and J. Mark Souther, May 10, 2006, Cleveland Regional Oral History Collection (hereafter CROHC), interview 319003, http://engagedscholarship.csuohio.edu/crohc000/16; "Pittsburgh Switches On and Cleveland Plugs In," *Plain Dealer*, April 5, 1973, p. 14-A; Aaron Cowan, *A Nice Place to Visit: Tourism and Urban Revitalization in the Postwar Rustbelt* (Philadelphia: Temple University Press, 2016), 101–104.

15. "Allen Theater Sign Not Easy to Relight," *Plain Dealer*, November 7, 1971, p. 23-A; Cappadora Miller Buildings advertisement, *Plain Dealer*, November 8, 1970, p. 8-B.

16. William F. Miller, "Effort to Revive Theaters Slated; Budapest Orchestra Due at Allen," *Plain Dealer*, October 17, 1971, p. 47-D; "Allen Theater Sign Not Easy to Relight"; Judy Sammon, "Allen Theater Sellout Is Downtown Victory," *Plain Dealer*, November 22, 1971, p. 3-A; Robert Finn, "Theater Concerts Rates Bravos," *Plain Dealer*, November 28, 1971, p. 13-F.

17. "Playhouse Square Lights on Again," *Plain Dealer*, December 1, 1971, Downtown section, p. 8.

18. George E. Condon, "Brightening the Fearful Gloom," *Plain Dealer*, November 12, 1972, p. 4-AA.

19. Donald Sabath, "Grant Approved for Huron Mall to Uplift Square," *Plain Dealer*, May 31, 1972, p. 18-A.

20. Mary Strassmeyer, "Junior Leaguers Area Putting Their Money Where Their Hearts Are," *Plain Dealer*, October 15, 1972, p. 12-E.

21. Mrs. John A. Hadden Jr., interview by Jeannette Tuve, January 26, 1985, transcript, pp. 28–29, Cleveland Families Oral History Project, MS. 4345 (hereafter CFOHP), container 1, folder 5, Western Reserve Historical Society, Cleveland, OH (hereafter WRHS).

22. Peter van Dijk, interview by Nina Gibans, August 31, 2006, CROHC, interview 951011, http://engagedscholarship.csuohio.edu/crohc000/224; William F. Miller, "Junior League Pledges Cash to Save Theaters," *Plain Dealer*, June 3, 1972, p. 1-A; Hadden interview, pp. 29–31.

23. George E. Condon, "The Contrast Is Positively Sad," *Plain Dealer*, May 28, 1972, p. 4-AA.

24. Diana Tittle, *Rebuilding Cleveland: The Cleveland Foundation and Its Evolving Urban Strategy* (Columbus: Ohio State University Press, 1992).

25. Hemsath interview; "Group Leases Two Theaters; Demolition Averted," *Plain Dealer*, December 23, 1972, p. 6-C; Kathlin Fisher, "Downtown: The Table Is Set; Cabaret Adds Glitter to City Scene," *Plain Dealer*, April 19, 1973, p. 3-B.

26. Mary Jean Powers, "It's Only August, but They're Banking on a Christmas Tree," *Plain Dealer*, August 5, 1973, p. 7-F.

27. "Restaurant-Club Set Downtown," *Plain Dealer*, January 6, 1973, p. 6-A; Mary Strassmeyer, "Downtown Isn't Dead Anymore; The Line Forms on Euclid," *Plain Dealer*, June 17, 1973, p. 1-E. Hamilton F. Biggar III was also the nephew of former Stouffer's executive James M. Biggar, mentioned in Chapter 3.

28. Donald Sabath, "Downtown Is Verging on New Glory," *Plain Dealer*, January 14, 1974, p. 22-C; Marcus Gleisser, "Downtown Showing New Growth and Life," *Plain Dealer*, July 7, 1974, p. 23-D; William F. Miller, "Playhouse Square Corners New Entertainment Spots," *Plain Dealer*, January 12, 1976, p. 1-C; Christine J. Jindra, "Bouncing Back; Playhouse Square Pulse Beats Faster," *Plain Dealer*, June 19, 1977, sec. 1, p. 1; William F. Miller, "Vision, Sweat Transform the Point Building into Showcase," *Plain Dealer*, September 10, 1977, p. 18-A.

29. Miller, "Vision, Sweat Transform Point Building"; Andrea Naversen, "Playhouse Store Closing," *Plain Dealer*, January 13, 1974, p. 25-A.

30. Alison Bick Hirsch, *City Choreographer: Lawrence Halprin in Urban Renewal America* (Minneapolis: University of Minnesota Press, 2014), 7, 72–99, 124–138.

31. Herb Strawbridge, *Remembering Higbee's* (Cleveland: Western Reserve Historical Society, 2004), 226–227; Tittle, *Rebuilding Cleveland*, 203.

32. "Famed Planner to Scan Downtown Entertainment," *Plain Dealer*, February 11, 1973, p. 1-A.

33. "Halprin Begins Two-Day Study; Urban 'Doctor' Examines Cleveland," *Plain Dealer*, February 13, 1973, p. 10-A; Strawbridge, *Remembering Higbee's*, 227; "Perk to Halprin: Give Us Ideas for Downtown," *Plain Dealer*, February 14, 1973, p. 10-A.

34. Robert H. Holden, "36 'John Q's' Take Fling at Remaking Downtown," *Plain Dealer*, June 3, 1973, p. 1-A.

35. Hirsch, *City Choreographer*, 185–187.

36. Holden, "36 'John Q's' Take Fling at Remaking Downtown"; Lawrence Halprin and Associates, *Cleveland Take Part Workshop: Objectives for Downtown; Report and Recommendations, May 31, June 1, 2, 1973, Cleveland, Ohio* (Cleveland: Greater Cleveland Growth Association and the City of Cleveland, 1973), Cleveland State University Library Special Collections, Cleveland, OH (hereafter CSU).

37. Halprin, *Cleveland Take Part Workshop*; quote, 14.

38. Roldo Bartimole, "Downtown—The Means to an End," *Point of View* [Cleveland,

OH] 6, no. 4 (September 8, 1973), CSU. Hirsch acknowledges the manipulative tendency of Halprin's process but tempers the assessment by noting that the planner nonetheless sought to engage, educate, and persuade participants to rethink their opinions within a broader context in which he had spent his career; see Hirsch, *City Choreographer*, 262–265.

39. "Look Around Downtown" (editorial), *Plain Dealer*, July 1, 1973, p. 4-AA; Halprin, *Cleveland Take Part Workshop*, 27–28; "Turn Downtown into Funtown, Planners Urge," *Plain Dealer*, June 30, 1973, p. 1-A.

40. Upshur Evans to Robert Burke Jones, October 26, 1959, Cleveland Development Foundation Records, MS. 3514 (hereafter CDF), container 57, folder "Town and Country Magazine," WRHS; Allen Wiggins and Harry Stainer, "The Hotel Squeeze; Room Shortage Slows Down Convention Trade Here," *Plain Dealer*, June 18, 1972, p. 1-A.

41. Strawbridge, *Remembering Higbee's*, 223; Michael Kelly, "Higbee Plans to Give Riverfront New Life," *Plain Dealer*, July 3, 1973, p. 1-A.

42. Strawbridge, *Remembering Higbee's*, 224–225.

43. Kelly, "Higbee Plans to Give Riverfront New Life"; Strawbridge, *Remembering Higbee's*, 227–228.

44. William F. Miller, "Construction Activity Downtown Headed for a Lull After 10 Years," *Plain Dealer*, January 27, 1975, p. 1-A; Strawbridge, *Remembering Higbee's*, 230–235; William F. Miller, "Renovated Offices Lack Occupants," *Plain Dealer*, September 12, 1976, sec. 2, p. 1.

45. William F. Miller, "Planning Commission OK's City's Share of Downtown Study," *Plain Dealer*, June 22, 1974, p. 9-C; William F. Miller, "Council OK's $90,000 Share of Halprin's Downtown Study," *Plain Dealer*, June 25, 1974, p. 1-A.

46. Hirsch, *City Choreographer*, 260; William F. Miller, "Civic Leaders Try to Find New Ideas for Downtown," *Plain Dealer*, January 16, 1975, p. 3-B.

47. Lawrence Halprin and Associates, *Concept for Cleveland: A Strategy for Downtown* (Cleveland: Greater Cleveland Growth Association; City of Cleveland, 1974–1975), CPL. On earlier plans for Euclid Avenue and the Mall, refer to Chapter 1. On Cain's International Square idea, see items in CDF, container 11, folder "Cain, Howard B.," WRHS.

48. George E. Condon, "Derailed by City Hall; 'Transit Thriller' Ignored," *Plain Dealer*, March 17, 1976, p. 13-A.

49. Hirsch, *City Choreographer*, 261.

50. George Barmann, "On the Couch: Jokes about Cleveland," *Plain Dealer*, September 14, 1975, Sunday PD magazine, p. 6.

51. "Halprin Plan Offers Hope" (editorial), *Plain Dealer*, May 31, 1975, p. 4-B; "A City on the Move" (editorial), *Plain Dealer*, August 13, 1975, p. 1-A; "Right Time for Plan" (editorial), *Plain Dealer*, September 15, 1975, p. 20-A.

52. William F. Miller, "Downtown Plan Start Seen in 12–18 Months," *Plain Dealer*, August 13, 1975, p. 1-A; Helen Cullinan, "Halprin's Plan: Give People Shops, Restaurants, Trees[,] Arcades and *Joie de Vivre*," *Plain Dealer*, September 14, 1975, sec. 5, p. 1.

53. Miller, "Downtown Plan Start Seen."

54. William F. Miller, "Downtown Revitalization Plans Shaping Up," *Plain Dealer*, January 1, 1976, p. 25-A.

55. Miller, "Downtown Plan Start Seen in 12–18 Months"; "Downtown Plan Gains" (editorial), *Plain Dealer*, December 11, 1975, p. 44-A.

56. "Garden Club to Spruce Up Public Square; Will Join Halprin in Bicentennial Project," *Plain Dealer*, June 26, 1974, p. 1-A; Mary Strassmeyer, "Public Square Dinner Does City Proud, Raises $170,000," *Plain Dealer*, October 5, 1975, sec. 1, p. 1; "Square

Gets $2.6 Million; NE Sector, Superior to Be Beautified First," *Plain Dealer*, August 25, 1977, p. 1-A.

57. "Downtown Revitalization Priorities Are Established," *Plain Dealer*, December 11, 1975, p. 1-A.

58. Peter Bellamy, "'Jacques Brel' Closes After 522 Performances," *Plain Dealer*, June 30, 1975, p. 1-A; Tim Joyce, "Playhouse Square: Talking It Over with Ray Shepardson," *Plain Dealer*, December 7, 1975, Sunday PD magazine, p. 5; Michael Ward, "'Impossible' Gets Easier; Playhouse Square Thrives on Free Admission," *Plain Dealer*, October 24, 1976, sec. 5, p. 1; Homer C. Wadsworth, interview by Jeannette Tuve, April 10, 1985, transcript, p. 25, CFOHP, container 2, folder 12.

59. Hadden interview, p. 33; Tittle, *Rebuilding Cleveland*, 242.

60. Douglas Bloomfield, "Tower Study Under Way; Airline Terminal Eyed," *Plain Dealer*, July 20, 1968, p. 28; "Colossal Project Unveiled," *Plain Dealer*, June 15, 1972, p. 2-A; William F. Miller, "City, Union Terminals Reach Tentative Accord on Tower City," *Plain Dealer*, May 31, 1975, p. 8-A.

61. Van Dijk interview; "Wadsworth, Homer C.," *Encyclopedia of Cleveland History*, https://case.edu/ech/articles/w/wadsworth-homer-c/; Tittle, *Rebuilding Cleveland*, 243.

62. Tittle, *Rebuilding Cleveland*, 244; Van Dijk interview; Wadsworth interview, p. 28; Hemsath interview.

63. Tittle, *Rebuilding Cleveland*, 244–245.

64. *Time*, August 24, 1981; William F. Miller, "Mall Developer Studies Playhouse Square as Area for Retail Stores," *Plain Dealer*, November 11, 1978, p. 5-A; William F. Miller, "Study Maps Revamp of Playhouse Square," *Plain Dealer*, July 3, 1979, p. 8-B. On the Quincy Market transformation, see especially Nicholas Dagen Bloom, *Merchant of Illusion: James Rouse: America's Salesman of the Businessman's Utopia* (Columbus: Ohio State University Press, 2004).

65. Wadsworth interview, p. 29; "6 Arts Groups Share Grants of $2 Million," *Plain Dealer*, October 30, 1979, p. 20-A.

66. Emerson Batdorff, "Lights On!" *Plain Dealer*, April 22, 1979, sec. 7, p. 1.

67. Andrew Juniewicz, "U.S. Funds Sought for People Mover Here," *Plain Dealer*, May 5, 1976, p. 12-A; Andrew Juniewicz, "'People Mover' for City Gains Support," *Plain Dealer*, May 13, 1976, p. 26-A.

68. James M. Wood, "People-Mover Could Pull Together Disconnected Parts," *Plain Dealer*, December 12, 1976, sec. 5, p. 2.

69. "A Boost for Downtown" (editorial), *Plain Dealer*, December 23, 1976, p. 16-A; Ralph J. Perk, Address to Exchange Club, January 5, 1977, Ralph J. Perk Papers, MS. 4456 (hereafter RJP), container 31, folder 429, WRHS.

70. Teaford, *Rough Road to Renaissance*, 237–239.

71. Norman Krumholz and John Forester, *Making Equity Planning Work: Leadership in the Public Sector* (Philadelphia: Temple University Press, 1990), 143–144; resolutions found in Seth Taft Papers, box 7, folder "People Mover Project 1976–1978," Cuyahoga County Archives, Cleveland, OH.

72. Thomas E. Bier, "Social Implications of the People Mover," *Plain Dealer*, February 2, 1977, p. 15-A; Joe T. Darden et al., *Detroit: Race and Uneven Development* (Philadelphia: Temple University Press, 2010), 49–51; Bryant Simon, *Boardwalk of Dreams: Atlantic City and the Fate of Urban America* (New York: Oxford University Press, 2004), 194–216; Trevor Boddy, "Underground and Overhead: Building the Analogous City," in *Variations on a Theme Park: The New American City and the End of Public Space*, ed. Michael Sorkin (New York: Hill and Wang, 1992), 123–153.

73. Kucinich for Mayor, press release, October 14, 1977, Daniel J. Marschall Papers, MS. 4561, container 2, folder 62, WRHS; William Carlson, "Kucinich Flags People Mover; Battle Is Due," *Plain Dealer*, December 1, 1977, p. 1-D; Thomas J. Brazaitis, "U.S. Suspends People Mover Aid," *Plain Dealer*, January 10, 1978, p. 3-A.

74. William F. Miller, "City Puts Up Barrier to 17th St. Extension South of Euclid Ave.," *Plain Dealer*, February 10, 1978, p. 7-A.

75. "Federal Funding Out for Extension of E. 17th," *Plain Dealer*, February 17, 1978, p. 2-A; William F. Miller, "Mayor Surprises Businessmen, to Study E. 17th," *Plain Dealer*, February 22, 1978, p. 26-A; William F. Miller, "A Downtown Booster Bows Out," *Plain Dealer*, May 25, 1980, p. 4-A.

76. Tom Green, "Diners Keep Moving for a Square Meal," *Plain Dealer*, July 2, 1976, p. 4-C.

77. Jindra, "Bouncing Back."

78. Cheryl Jensen, "The Shadow of Crime Downtown," *Plain Dealer*, November 5, 1978, Sunday PD magazine, p. 36.

79. Stanley Ziemba, "That 'Great' State Street to Be a Mall," *Plain Dealer*, September 26, 1976, sec. 1, p. 25.

80. Wadsworth interview, p. 21.

81. Strawbridge, *Remembering Higbee's*, 225; William F. Miller, "The Cabaret Theater Is Alive and Well and Thriving in Playhouse Square," *Plain Dealer*, June 1, 1973, Friday PD weekend magazine, p. 3.

82. Michael Kelly, "Halle's Plans Changes at Its Euclid Ave. Store," *Plain Dealer*, May 2, 1979, p. 1-F.

83. Emerson Batdorff, "Lights On!" *Plain Dealer*, April 22, 1979, sec. 7, p. 1.

84. Emerson Batdorff, "The Shaker Theater Is Third Down in Six Months," *Plain Dealer*, April 16, 1978, sec. 5, p. 8.

85. Bill Doll, "Shed No Tears for Music Hall," *Plain Dealer*, April 23, 1978, sec. 6, p. 6.

86. William F. Miller, "Playhouse Square Inches to Another Victory," *Plain Dealer*, May 28, 1979, p. 3-D.

## CHAPTER 6

1. Daneen Fry, "Ohio City Tour Will Reflect 19th Century," *Cleveland Press*, September 10, 1971; Marjorie Alge, "A Party for Ohio City," *Cleveland Press*, September 13, 1971; Mary McLaughlin, "Party on a Bridge; Salutes Ohio City," *Plain Dealer*, September 13, 1971, p. 3-B.

2. Andrew Hurley, *Beyond Preservation: Using Public History to Revitalize Inner Cities* (Philadelphia: Temple University Press, 2010), 4–9.

3. Untitled notice, *Cleveland Herald*, June 29, 1835; "Columbus Street Bridge," *Encyclopedia of Cleveland History*, https://case.edu/ech/articles/c/columbus-street-bridge/; City Plan Commission, *Territorial Growth of the City of Cleveland* (map), ca. 1922, Cleveland Public Library (hereafter CPL), Cleveland, OH.

4. Carol Poh Miller, "Ohio City: A Proposal for Area Conservation in Cleveland" (M.A. thesis, George Washington University, 1975), 67–71.

5. Ibid., 89.

6. Eugene Segal, "$46,290 U.S. Grant Assures Monroe Area Facelifting," *Plain Dealer*, June 29, 1956, p. 6; "Launch Test Program for Monroe Area," *Plain Dealer*, March 22, 1957, p. 10.

7. Eugene Segal, "West Siders Give $12,000 for Planning; 13 Eye Neighborhood Redevelopment," *Plain Dealer*, July 4, 1957, p. 38.

8. Klein and Hodne Associates, *Ohio City—Central Park West Planning Project, Technical Report on a Preliminary Plan for the Future Development of the Area* (Cleveland: n.p., April 1958), WRHS.

9. "West Side Renewal Urged in 20-Yr. Plan," *Cleveland Press*, April 11, 1958; "Attack Ohio City Proposal," *Cleveland Press*, January 19, 1959; Bob Siegel, "Planners Urge Revitalization of Near West Side," *Cleveland Press*, December 2, 1960.

10. U.S. Bureau of the Census, *Census of Population*, 1960; Eugene Segal, "Councilmen Clash over W. 25 Zoning," *Plain Dealer*, March 17, 1961, p. 1; "Franklin Circle Urban Renewal Aid up to U.S.," *Plain Dealer*, February 17, 1962, p. 5.

11. "Big Renewal Plan Unveiled; On West Side," *Plain Dealer*, October 19, 1963, p. 1; "Be Sure to Vote No on Issue 8" (advertisement), *Plain Dealer*, November 4, 1963, p. 26; Eugene Segal, "Issue Fails to Capture 55% Vote," *Plain Dealer*, November 6, 1963, p. 1.

12. Upshur Evans to Alfred S. Andrews, April 3, 1964, Cleveland Development Foundation Records, MS. 3514 (hereafter CDF), container 48, folder "Near West Side Development Association Correspondence," WRHS.

13. "West Siders Blast City Hall; Renewal Plan Deplored," *Plain Dealer*, March 1, 1967, p. 26; "Near West Side Plan for Renewal Is Stalled," *Plain Dealer*, April 21, 1967, p. 6.

14. Roldo Bartimole and Donald Sabath, "Pockets of Poverty Pepper Near West Side Area," *Plain Dealer*, September 30, 1965, p. 96.

15. On the advantages enjoyed by blue-collar ethnic white neighborhoods that escaped rioting in the 1960s, see Jon C. Teaford, *The Rough Road to Renaissance: Urban Revitalization in America, 1940–1985* (Baltimore: Johns Hopkins University Press, 1990), 245.

16. James M. Naughton, "Quit-City, Join-Shaker Plan Eyed by Civic Group," *Plain Dealer*, May 2, 1967, p. 33; "German Village Tour Scheduled," *Plain Dealer*, June 28, 1968, p. 29; Ethel Boros, "Stokes OKs Hungarian Village Plan," *Plain Dealer*, March 2, 1969, p. 12-A.

17. Sandy Feldhausen, "Reviving Ohio City," *Cleveland Press*, December 7, 1968; "Group Formed for Restoring Ohio City Area," *Cleveland Press*, January 4, 1969.

18. Suleiman Osman, *The Invention of Brownstone Brooklyn: Gentrification and the Search for Authenticity in Postwar New York* (New York: Oxford University Press, 2011), 11–13; Bruce W. Hedderson to James Kirby, April 24, 1968, CDF, container 49, folder "Ohio City Restoration"; "Big Renewal Plan Unveiled."

19. Bruce W. Hedderson to Thomas J. Miller, February 7, 1968; M. Riemer, memorandum, Ohio City Restoration meeting, February 21, 1968, CDF, container 49, folder "Ohio City Restoration."

20. William B. Hammer to Fr. James Kirby, February 7, 1968; Hedderson to Kirby; Upshur Evans to John H. Burt, February 27, 1968; Alan J. Eichenberger to Upshur Evans, February 28, 1968, CDF, container 49, folder "Ohio City Restoration."

21. M. Riemer, memorandum, Ohio City Restoration Luncheon, February 27, 1968; Upshur Evans to Allen Fonoroff, March 1, 1968; Richard N. Campen to Bruce Hedderson, March 15, 1968; Bruce Hedderson to Thomas J. Miller, March 18, 1968; Thomas J. Miller to Bruce Hedderson, April 2, 1968; Frank Fetch to Bruce W. Hedderson, April 2, 1968, CDF, container 49, folder "Ohio City Restoration."

22. Mary Hooper, "Renewal Unit Stirs Doubt," *Cleveland Press*, March 15, 1968.

23. Linda Freyer, "The 1970s Hit Old Ohio City with a Bang," *Plain Dealer*, October 9, 1970, p. 12-A.

24. Sandy Feldhausen, "Spooky Home Doesn't Scare Restorers," *Cleveland Press*, January 18, 1969; Freyer, "The 1970s Hit Old Ohio City with a Bang."

25. "Group Formed for Restoring Ohio City Area."

26. "West Side Federal Savings and Loan Assn.," *Encyclopedia of Cleveland History*, https://case.edu/ech/articles/w/west-side-federal-savings-and-loan-assn/; Miller, "Ohio City," 79; William F. Miller, "Old Ohio City Gets a Clean New Face," *Plain Dealer*, May 5, 1974, p. 1-AA.

27. "May Company and Small Savings Will Add Up" (advertisement), *Plain Dealer*, May 29, 1971, Better Living, pp. 15, 18; West Side Federal Savings advertisement, *Plain Dealer*, June 28, 1973, p. 7-C.

28. Dan Coughlin, "Plan Grid Shrine for Heisman House; Born on Bridge Avenue," *Plain Dealer*, December 9, 1973, p. 1-C; Christopher Busta-Peck, *Hidden History of Cleveland* (Charleston, SC: History Press, 2011), 93–94.

29. Mary Strassmeyer, "Eskimo Art Finds Nook in Restored Ohio City," *Plain Dealer*, February 20, 1973, p. 2-B.

30. Jason Thomas, "Ohio City," *Plain Dealer*, August 17, 1974, Saturday Home Magazine, p. 1; Freyer, "The 1970s Hit Old Ohio City with a Bang"; Tom Green, "Shackled Spirit; Bicentennial Planners Ignore Ohio City," *Plain Dealer*, September 21, 1975, sec. 4, p. 1; "Mary Hirschfeld Hears . . . ," *Plain Dealer*, August 29, 1972, p. 13-A. On the rise of antiques shops in conjunction with gentrification, see Osman, *Invention of Brownstone Brooklyn*, 214.

31. William F. Miller, "Old Ohio City Gets a Clean New Face," *Plain Dealer*, May 5, 1974, p. 1-AA; Judy Sammon, "Restaurant Has Heck of a Note," *Plain Dealer*, July 9, 1974, p. 8-A; Cleveland City Directories, 1960–1970, CPL.

32. William F. Miller, "Chauvinism, Cleveland-Style; Because He Believes, an Eastsider Goes West with Rose-Colored Glass," *Plain Dealer*, July 30, 1973, p. 12-A; Judy Sammon, "Minister to Try 'Happy Hour,'" *Plain Dealer*, October 3, 1974, p. 8-A.

33. Michael A. Hobbs, "West Side Blacks Form New Group," *Plain Dealer*, April 11, 1971, p. 5-Z; W. Dennis Keating, *The Suburban Racial Dilemma: Housing and Neighborhoods* (Philadelphia: Temple University Press, 1994), 57.

34. On ethnic depictions at expositions, see Robert W. Rydell, *All the World's a Fair: Visions of Empire at American International Expositions, 1876–1916* (Chicago: University of Chicago Press, 1984), 60–62; Robert W. Rydell, John E. Findling, and Kimberly D. Pelle, *Fair America: World's Fairs in the United States* (Washington, DC: Smithsonian Institution Press, 2000), 90. For examples of international pageantry surrounding the "Seaway Year," see "Seaway," *Clevelander*, May 1959, p. 12.

35. Mark Tebeau, "Sculpted Landscapes: Art and Place in Cleveland's Cultural Gardens, 1916–2006," *Journal of Social History* 44, no. 2 (2010): 336.

36. Teaford, *Rough Road to Renaissance*, 283; Aaron Cowan, *A Nice Place to Visit: Tourism and Urban Revitalization in the Postwar Rustbelt* (Philadelphia: Temple University Press, 2016), 97; Joseph A. Rodriguez, *Bootstrap New Urbanism: Design, Race, and Redevelopment in Milwaukee* (Lanham, MD: Lexington, 2014), chap. 3; *Detroit: City on the Move*, directed by James T. Slayden (1965; Detroit: Jam Handy Organization), http://archive.org/details/DetroitC1965. For broader historical context on the ethnic revival in 1970s America, see Matthew Frye Jacobson, *Roots Too: White Ethnic Revival in Post–Civil Rights America* (Cambridge, MA: Harvard University Press, 2006).

37. Robert H. Holden, "Perk's Name, in Large Letters, Launches Festival Promotion," *Plain Dealer*, August 3, 1973, p. 1-C; Mary Strassmeyer, "A Bit of Old Europe Is Going on Display," *Plain Dealer*, June 27, 1976, sec. 4, p. 5.

38. See, for example, *Wonderful World of Cleveland* (Cleveland: State of Ohio; Greater Cleveland Growth Board, 1967), CPL.

39. Thomas, "Ohio City." Historian David Glassberg relates a similar desire by gentrifiers to erase almost a century of intervening history that separated the Victorian period from their own in one Springfield, Massachusetts, neighborhood; see David Glassberg, *Sense of History: The Place of the Past in American Life* (Amherst: University of Massachusetts Press, 2001), 155–156.

40. George E. Condon, "Happy Homecoming in Ohio City," *Plain Dealer*, July 21, 1974, p. 4-AA.

41. Miller, "Old Ohio City Gets a Clean New Face"; Thomas, "Ohio City."

42. Jason Thomas, "Ohio Citified," *Plain Dealer*, August 23, 1974, p. 6-C.

43. Condon, "Happy Homecoming in Ohio City."

44. Bartimole and Sabath, "Pockets of Poverty"; Joseph Eszterhas, "Puerto Ricans Quietly Fighting for Ethnic Dignity," *Plain Dealer*, April 25, 1971, p. 1-AA.

45. Notice of meeting at West Side Community House, October 2, 1969, CDF, container 49, folder "Ohio City Community Development Association."

46. Shirley Montgomery, "Residents Ask Involvement by Ohio City Association," *Plain Dealer*, September 13, 1971, p. 4-A; "Near West Side Group Seeks Protection for All Residents," *Plain Dealer*, September 18, 1971, p. 16-A.

47. Warren Davis, "Ohio City . . . Rebuilding or Displacing?," *Plain Press*, May 21, 1971, p. 6; "OCCDA Digs Inner City," *Plain Press*, September 17, 1971, p. 2.

48. OCCDA, Minutes of meeting, March 27, 1970, CDF, container 49, folder "Ohio City Community Development Association"; William F. Miller, "Changing; Street Groups Promote Interests of Ohio City," *Plain Dealer*, April 18, 1976, sec. 7, p. 26.

49. Mathew Librach, "Ohio City Assn. Plan Is Ready to Aid Area," *Cleveland Press*, January 19, 1977; Bob Brennan, "Plans for 'Downtown' Ohio City Are Unveiled," *Cleveland Press*, October 11, 1975.

50. Fred McGunagle, "Dilemma: The Gentry Moves in and Poses a Problem for Near West Side," *Cleveland Press*, August 3, 1978.

51. Krumholz's equity-planning focus is well-documented. See, for example, Norman Krumholz and John Forester, *Making Equity Planning Work: Leadership in the Public Sector* (Philadelphia: Temple University Press, 1990); Norman Krumholz and Pierre Clavel, *Reinventing Cities: Equity Planners Tell Their Stories* (Philadelphia: Temple University Press, 1994).

52. "Ohio City Funds Sought," *Plain Dealer*, February 28, 1977, p. 7-A.

53. Deena Mirow, "Neighborhood Savers or Boondoggles?," *Plain Dealer*, August 6, 1978, sec. 1, p. 30.

54. Harry Stainer, "Crime, Neglect Start Secession Talk in Ohio City Area," *Plain Dealer*, March 19, 1978, sec. 1, p. 15.

55. William F. Miller, "Market Square Park Finally Wins Approval," *Plain Dealer*, July 6, 1978, p. 16-A; "City Refuses $25,000 Grant to Ohio City Project Group," *Plain Dealer*, January 4, 1979, p. 10-A.

56. Bob Schlesinger, "There's Big Trouble in Ohio City; Fight Rages between Well-to-do Renovators and Low-Income Residents," *Cleveland Press*, April 8, 1981.

57. Ibid.

58. U.S. Bureau of the Census, 1970, 1980; City of Cleveland Neighborhood Fact Sheets: Ohio City, http://planning.city.cleveland.oh.us/census/factsheets/spa10.pdf. Ohio City is defined here as the Cleveland City Planning Commission's Ohio City Statistical Planning Area, which corresponds to census tracts 1033.00, 1036.02, 1039.00, and 1041.00.

59. *15 Minutes* (Cleveland: Cleveland Convention and Visitors Bureau, 1974), verti-cal file, Cleveland State University Library Special Collections (hereafter CSU); *Cleveland: A New Generation* (Cleveland: Greater Cleveland Growth Association, 1978), CSU; *Are There Any Civilized Cities Left? A View from Cleveland* (Cleveland: New Cleveland Campaign, 1982), CPL.

60. William F. Miller, "Polish Pride; Renovation Giving New Life to Fleet Ave. Neighborhood," *Plain Dealer*, April 16, 1978, sec. 1, p. 25.

61. Michael Rotman and Chris Roy, "The Landscape of Tremont," *Cleveland Historical*, http://clevelandhistorical.org/items/show/102.

62. Raymond L. Pianka, interview by Becky Solecki, December 9, 2005, Cleveland Regional Oral History Collection, interview 400023, http://engagedscholarship.csuohio.edu/crohc000/57.

63. William F. Miller, "Buckeye Merchants Get 2 Remedies for Recovery," *Plain Dealer*, July 27, 1975, sec. 1, p. 25.

64. "Ohio City's Restoration No Quick Fix," *Plain Dealer*, August 28, 1983, p. 26-A; Miller, "Old Ohio City Gets a Clean New Face."

65. Mary Strassmeyer, "Mary, Mary" (column), *Plain Dealer*, October 17, 1983, p. 4-D.

## CHAPTER 7

1. "When Cleveland Took Its Story to the Nation" (booklet of advertisements from *New York Times Magazine*), ca. 1975, in author's possession. The original ad appeared in *New York Times Magazine* on July 14, 1974.

2. Lizabeth Cohen, *A Consumers' Republic: The Politics of Mass Consumption in Postwar America* (New York: Knopf, 2003).

3. Jon C. Teaford, *The Rough Road to Renaissance: Urban Revitalization in America, 1940–1985* (Baltimore: Johns Hopkins University Press, 1990), 204.

4. Untitled document attached to Frank Maris, memo to R. DeChant and J. Sheehan, May 20, 1977, Daniel J. Marschall Papers, MS. 4561 (hereafter DJM), container 1, folder 19, Western Reserve Historical Society, Cleveland, OH (hereafter WRHS); Teaford, *Rough Road to Renaissance*, 213.

5. David Stradling and Richard Stradling, "Perceptions of the Burning River: Deindustrialization and Cleveland's Cuyahoga River," *Environmental History* 13, no. 3 (2008): 517–518.

6. George E. Condon, "Cleveland? What's So Funny?," *Plain Dealer*, November 24, 1970, p. 15-A; Hal Erickson, *"From Beautiful Downtown Burbank": A Critical History of Rowan and Martin's Laugh-In, 1968–1973* (Jefferson, NC: McFarland, 2000), 163; Joe Walders, "The Man Who Made Cleveland a National Joke," *Cleveland Magazine*, January 1, 1976, https://clevelandmagazine.com/in-th-cle/the-read/articles/the-man-who-made-cleveland-a-national-joke; James Semsak, interview by J. Mark Souther, July 23, 2014, Cleveland Regional Oral History Collection, interview 999121, http://engagedscholarship.csuohio.edu/crohc000/739.

7. "Cleveland: The Friendly City to Negroes," *Jet* 7, no. 3 (1954): 10–13; Charles L. Sanders and Alex Poinsett, "Black Power at the Polls: Stokes, Hatcher Victories Point Way for Other Cities," *Ebony* 23, no. 3 (1968): 26.

8. Lois K. Dawson, letter to the editor, *Cleveland Call and Post*, May 2, 1964, p. 3B; "1,000 Add Zest to Holmes' Melancholy," *Call and Post*, August 1, 1964, p. 3A; George V. Hooper, letter to the editor, *Plain Dealer*, May 16, 1965, p. 7-AA.

9. Among the many published black critiques of the slogan in the 1950s and 1960s,

see especially "Best Location in the Nation?," *Call and Post*, December 19, 1953, p. 2C;
Marty Richardson, "Rate-Hate Suburbs Surround Cleveland," *Call and Post*, July 10, 1954,
p. 1A; Ralph Matthews, "Thinking Out Loud," *Call and Post*, February 11, 1956, p. 2D;
"This One Smells Real Bad," *Call and Post*, December 2, 1961, p. 2C; William O. Walker,
"Downtown Cleveland, a Victim of Prejudice and Selfishness," *Call and Post*, February
24, 1962, p. 10; "The Best Location in the Nation?," *Call and Post*, March 24, 1962, p. 2C.

10. George E. Condon, *Cleveland: The Best Kept Secret* (Garden City, NY: Doubleday, 1967), 319–322.

11. *Plain Dealer Historical, America's Historical Newspapers* (NewsBank), accessed
via Cleveland Public Library Research Databases, http://cpl.org/research-learning/
researchdatabases/.

12. Repr.: "What Your Wife Knows About Finding a Plant Site" (Greater Cleveland
Growth Board advertisement), *Wall Street Journal*, April 8, 1964, GCGA, container 133,
folder 2. On the rise of promotion of culture in older industrial cities, see Aaron Cowan,
*A Nice Place to Visit: Tourism and Urban Revitalization in the Postwar Rustbelt* (Phila-
delphia: Temple University Press, 2016), 132–133; Mark Goldman, *City on the Edge: Buf-
falo, New York* (Amherst, NY: Prometheus, 2007), 239; Roy Lubove, *Twentieth-Century
Pittsburgh: Government, Business, and Environmental Change*, vol. 2: *The Post-Steel Era*
(Pittsburgh: University of Pittsburgh Press, 1996), 31.

13. Cowan, *A Nice Place to Visit*, chap. 5; Miriam Greenberg, *Branding New York:
How a City in Crisis Was Sold to the World* (New York: Routledge, 2008), chap. 5.

14. *15 Minutes* (Cleveland: Cleveland Convention and Visitors Bureau, 1974), vertical file, Cleveland State University Library Special Collections, Cleveland, OH (hereafter
CSU); "Accentuate the Positive," *Call and Post*, February 2, 1974, p. 2B; "Perk Now Hopeful on 'Instant Hotel'; Pact Near on Ship," *Plain Dealer*, September 10, 1972, p. 24-A.

15. *15 Minutes*; Andrew Wiese, *Places of Their Own: African American Suburbanization in the Twentieth Century* (Chicago: University of Chicago Press, 2004), 227–228.

16. *15 Minutes*.

17. "When Cleveland Took Its Story to the Nation."

18. William F. Miller, "Growth Group's Drive Won't Hide Problems," *Plain Dealer*,
January 23, 1974, p. 4-B.

19. "The Best Things in Life Are Here" (Greater Cleveland Growth Association
advertisement), *Plain Dealer*, March 21, 1974, p. 10-E.

20. Ibid.

21. "You Can Sing TV Ditty and Praise Life in City," *Plain Dealer*, June 6, 1974, p.
9-F; Judy Voelker, "For City's Well-Wishers," *Plain Dealer*, August 14, 1974, p. 1-E; "Tyr-
anny of the Few" (editorial), *Plain Dealer*, June 6, 1974, p. 4-B; Roy W. Adams, "Let's All
'Rally Around Cleveland'; The Best Things in Life Are Here!" *Plain Dealer*, August 15,
1974, p. 1-D.

22. Clifford W. Allen, letter to the editor, *Plain Dealer*, June 17, 1974, p. 4-B.

23. Carol Ann Poh, letter to the editor, *Plain Dealer*, September 22, 1974, p. 3-A.

24. Thomas W. Mooney, letter to the editor, *Plain Dealer*, October 19, 1974, p. 6-B.

25. Edmund Morris, "Cleveland—Good Living; Best Things Are Here, New York
Times Says," *Plain Dealer*, January 13, 1976, p. 10-A [reprinted from Edmund Morris,
"Cleveland Offers a Cultural High," *New York Times*, January 11, 1974, p. 21]; Semsak
interview.

26. William F. Miller, "Construction Activity Downtown Headed for a Lull after 10
Years," *Plain Dealer*, January 27, 1975, p. 1-A; Edward W. Hill, "The Cleveland Economy:
A Case Study of Economic Restructuring," in *Cleveland: A Metropolitan Reader*, ed. W.

Dennis Keating, Norman Krumholz, and David C. Perry (Kent, OH: Kent State University Press, 1995), 54; Campbell W. Elliott, "Growth Group Cites Gains in Tough Year," *Plain Dealer*, January 13, 1975, p. 9-D.

27. Murry Frymer, "The Best Struggles in Life Are Right Here," *Plain Dealer*, September 20, 1975, Sunday PD magazine, p. 54.

28. Ralph J. Perk, Speech to Cleveland Rotary Club, n.d. [ca. 1976], Ralph J. Perk Papers, MS. 4456 (hereafter RJP), container 31, folder 429, WRHS. Hugel was the president of Ohio Bell Telephone; Weir was the president of Cleveland Trust; Coy was the chairman of May Company; and Blair was the chairman of National City Bank.

29. George Barmann, "On the Couch: Jokes about Cleveland," *Plain Dealer*, September 14, 1975, Sunday PD magazine, p. 6.

30. Perk to Rotary Club; Ralph J. Perk, Remarks to Land Use Conference, December 4, 1976, RJP, container 31, folder 429. The pro-growth ethos that celebrated demolition is explained as spanning much of the twentieth century in Andrew R. Highsmith, *Demolition Means Progress: Flint, Michigan, and the Fate of the American Metropolis* (Chicago: University of Chicago Press, 2015), 6.

31. "Cleveland: What Most Cities Want, It Already Has," Greater Cleveland Growth Association advertisement, *Forbes*, June 15, 1977, DJM, container 1, folder 19.

32. Norman Krumholz to Frederick E. J. Pizzedaz, November 9, 1977, Seth Taft Papers, box 7, folder "Population 1972–1978," Cuyahoga County Archives, Cleveland, OH (hereafter CCA). What Krumholz considered a "pessimistic" projection of 515,000 people by 2000 would instead ultimately turn out to have been wildly optimistic. Cleveland's population tumbled to 505,616 by 1990 and 478,403 by 2000.

33. The best and fullest account of the Kucinich mayoralty remains Todd Swanstrom, *The Crisis of Growth Politics: Cleveland, Kucinich, and the Challenge of Urban Populism* (Philadelphia: Temple University Press, 1985).

34. Hill, "The Cleveland Economy," 54.

35. Stefanie Chambers, *Mayors and Schools: Minority Voices and Democratic Tensions in Urban Education* (Philadelphia: Temple University Press, 2006), 67–70.

36. Teaford, *Rough Road to Renaissance*, 220, 221–224.

37. Associated Press, "Cleveland Story Like Soap Opera; Snowed Under," *Register-Guard* [Eugene, OR], January 19, 1978, p. 5E, accessed via Google News, http://news.google.com/newspapers.

38. *Quality of Living in Cleveland–Northeast Ohio* (Cleveland: Cleveland Electric Illuminating Company, n.d. [1977]), DJM, container 2, folder 53.

39. Roldo Bartimole, "Who Governs: The Corporate Hand," in *Cleveland: A Metropolitan Reader*, 167.

40. Donald L. Bean, "Hongisto Lashes Out at 'Puppet' City Hall," *Plain Dealer*, March 26, 1978, sec. 1, p. 11; "Kucinich Responds," *Plain Dealer*, March 26, 1978, sec. 1, p. 25.

41. Frederick E. Freeman, "City Bonds Down-Rated Again," *Plain Dealer*, July 12, 1978, p. 1-A; "Recall Diary: Dates, Events," *Plain Dealer*, August 14, 1978, p. 11-A.

42. Joseph D. Rice, "Grass-Roots Approach Marks Recall Nucleus," *Plain Dealer*, April 29, 1978, p. 23-A; Thomas Campbell, "The Case for the Recall," *Plain Dealer*, August 7, 1978, p. 19-A.

43. Joseph D. Rice and Joseph L. Wagner, "Kucinich Recall Move over the Top; 47,537 Petitioners Set Stage for First Removal of Mayor Here," *Plain Dealer*, April 29, 1978, p. 1-A.

44. Joseph D. Rice, "Recall Drama Ends with 236 Votes as Kucinich's Margin," *Plain Dealer*, August 20, 1978, sec. 1, p. 4.

45. "Vote Breakdown" (table and map), *Plain Dealer*, August 14, 1978, p. 11-A; Joseph D. Rice, "Suburbanites Top List of Donors Backing Kucinich Recall," *Plain Dealer*, September 28, 1978, p. 14-A. On racial dimensions, see Larry Bivins, "Confrontation: Choosing Sides at City Hall," *Call and Post*, July 22, 1978, p. 1A; William O. Walker, "Racism Puts the Spotlight on the Black Voter," *Call and Post*, August 12, 1978, p. 14A.

46. "Public, Private Sectors," *Northern Ohio Business Journal*, June 12, 1978, p. 6, County Administrators Files, AC(1)85-368, box 30, folder "W.E.C.O. 1972–1980," CCA; Robert Lever, "The Forgotten Triangle; New Industry Has Raised the Hopes of This Long Blighted Area," *Plain Dealer*, April 8, 1979, Sunday PD magazine, p. 43. WECO was started in 1971 by the Van Dorn Manufacturing Company, a long-standing holdout in East Woodland, to revitalize its surroundings by encouraging reindustrialization.

47. Jacqueline V. Jones and Joseph D. Rice, "Steelworkers Leave Kucinich Speech to Protest Dock Delay," *Plain Dealer*, June 21, 1978, p. 6-A; David T. Abbott, "Finances, Politics Blend as Backdrop for Ore Dock Hassle," *Plain Dealer*, July 9, 1978, p. 1-A.

48. Jones and Rice, "Steelworkers Leave Kucinich Speech." On Youngstown's so-called Black Monday, see Terry F. Buss and F. Stevens Redburn, *Shutdown at Youngstown: Public Policy for Mass Unemployment* (Albany: State University of New York Press, 1983), esp. chap. 2.

49. Teaford, *Rough Road to Renaissance*, 211–212; "Economic Transition and Opportunity: Corporate Headquarters and the Future of Cleveland" (Greater Cleveland Growth Association report, ca. 1973), Public Administration Library Subject File, Cleveland Public Library, Cleveland, OH.

50. Editors, "How to Rebuild the Cleveland Economy," *Cleveland Magazine*, August 1977, p. 75, DJM, container 1, folder 19, WRHS.

51. Donald Sabath and Frederick E. Freeman, "Moving-Out Plans: Harris Corp. May Shift HQ to Florida; A-T-O Admits Studying Transfer," *Plain Dealer*, July 20, 1977, p. 4-F; Frederick E. Freeman, "Harris Moving HQ Out of Town," *Plain Dealer*, August 25, 1977, p. 1-A.

52. "How to Rebuild the Cleveland Economy," 76.

53. "AM International, Inc.," *Encyclopedia of Cleveland History*, https://case.edu/ech/articles/a/am-international-inc/; Thomas W. Gerdel, "A-M's Corporate Base Will Move to California in the Spring," *Plain Dealer*, November 22, 1977, p. 1-A; Marshall Berges, "Roy Ash," *Plain Dealer*, October 23, 1977, Sunday PD magazine, p. 31; N. R. Kleinfield, "AM's Brightest Years Now Dim Memories," *New York Times*, April 15, 1982, p. D1.

54. Timothy W. Kenworthy, letter to the editor, *Plain Dealer*, December 9, 1977, p. 12-C; Larry Robinson, "Scoreboard Dismays a Civic Cheerleader," *Plain Dealer*, February 10, 1978, p. 15-B.

55. David T. Abbott, "New Feuding Perils Deal on Muny, Dock," *Plain Dealer*, September 1, 1978, p. 1-A; "The Dock Accord" (editorial), *Plain Dealer*, September 9, 1978, p. 20-A.

56. Stephen A. Blossom, "Republic Plans $200 Million Fixup; Slab Caster Set Here; Lorain Gets Dock," *Plain Dealer*, December 20, 1978, p. 1-A.

57. Frank J. Valenta, letter to the editor, *Plain Dealer*, December 29, 1978, p. 6-B.

58. Davita Silften Glasberg, *The Power of Collective Purse Strings: The Effects of Bank Hegemony on Corporations and the State* (Berkeley: University of California Press, 1989), 128.

59. Thomas F. Campbell, "Cleveland: The Struggle for Stability," in *Snow Belt Cities: Metropolitan Politics in the Northeast and Midwest since World War II*, ed. Richard M. Bernard (Bloomington: Indiana University Press, 1990), 125.

60. Glasberg, *The Power of Collective Purse Strings*, 128–129, 141.

61. Campbell, "Cleveland: The Struggle for Stability," 126.

62. W. Dennis Keating, Norman Krumholz, and David C. Perry, eds., "The Ninety-Year War over Public Power in Cleveland," in *Cleveland: A Metropolitan Reader*, 145–146.

63. Bartimole, "Who Governs," 169.

64. Michael Kelly, "Cleveland Jokes Are Target of Plan to Change Image," *Plain Dealer*, January 25, 1978, p. 9-D; "Cleveland's New Image-Boosting Termed More Attuned to Times," *Plain Dealer*, January 29, 1978, sec. 2, p. 3.

65. *Cleveland. A New Generation* (Cleveland: Greater Cleveland Growth Association, 1978), vertical file, CSU.

66. Thomas V. H. Vail, interview by John P. DeWitt, tape 2, June 20, 1990, transcript pp. 25–28, Thomas Vail Papers, MS. 4852 (hereafter TVP), container 4, folder 92, WRHS.

67. Joseph A. Rodriguez, *Bootstrap New Urbanism: Design, Race, and Redevelopment in Milwaukee* (Lanham, MD: Lexington, 2014), 1–2; Goldman, *City on the Edge*, 236.

68. Vail interview, tape 7, August 8, 1990, transcript p. 2, TVP, container 4, folder 94; B. Drummond Ayres, Jr., "Kansas City Says Its Time Is Here," *New York Times*, March 23, 1973, p. 39; William Robbins, "No Surprise, Kansas City Is Surprising," *New York Times*, October 20, 1985, p. 26; William Worley, *Prime Time—A History: Kansas City's Prime Time*, Charles Newton Kimball Papers, KC0055, folder 1856, State Historical Society of Missouri Research Center, Kansas City, MO.

69. John Nussbaum, "County Pledges $100,000 to Polished-Image Drive," *Plain Dealer*, April 18, 1978, p. 1-A; Amos A. Kermisch, "Perk and Modell Agree on Stadium Lease Plan," *Plain Dealer*, July 13, 1973, p. 1-A; "Sheraton-Cleveland Mortgage Bought for $2.8 Million," *Plain Dealer*, May 11, 1977, p. 3-A; "Vail Outlines Effort to Boost City Image," *Plain Dealer*, May 17, 1978, p. 7-E.

70. "'Selling' Cleveland; A $4 Million Drive Will Tell Nation of Good Things Here," *Cleveland Press*, June 22, 1978; "Ad Drive Will Push Highlights of City," *Plain Dealer*, June 23, 1978, p. 2-A.

71. Michael L. King, "Cleveland Resumes Bid to End Its Status as a National Joke," *Wall Street Journal*, May 6, 1980, DJM, container 1, folder 23; Jack Nicholl, "Unabated; City Hall's Priorities for Economic Growth," *Plain Dealer*, March 10, 1979, 3-B.

72. Gary Clark and Ann Skinner, "Split Image; Losers Discover Winning City ... but It's a Tough Sell for Recruiters," *Plain Dealer*, April 9, 1979, p. 1-A; Jules Wagman, "Image Problem: Cleveland Firms Have Trouble Recruiting Executives," *Cleveland Press*, July 26, 1979, p. A1; "Diamond Shamrock Leaving Cleveland," *New York Times*, May 30, 1979, p. D10.

73. "City Shoulders Push Against Closing SEC Door," *Plain Dealer*, June 5, 1979, p. 1-C; Michael Kelly, "White Motor HQ Going to Detroit," *Plain Dealer*, September 27, 1979, p. 1-A; Donald Sabath, "CleveTrust Votes Change of Name to AmeriTrust Corp.; Shareholders Hit Loss of Cleveland Identity," *Plain Dealer*, October 19, 1979, p. 10-D; "Headquarters Cleveland," *Clevelander*, August 1980, p. 5, Commissioners File, box "Miscellaneous," folder "Greater Cleveland Growth Association," CCA.

74. Myron Magnet, "How Business Bosses Saved a Sick City," *Fortune*, March 27, 1989, http://archive.fortune.com/magazines/fortune/fortune_archive/1989/03/27/71774/index.htm.

## EPILOGUE

1. James Semsak, interview by J. Mark Souther, July 23, 2014, Cleveland Regional Oral History Collection, interview 999121, http://engagedscholarship.csuohio.edu/crohc000/739; Thomas W. Gerdel, "Cleveland Is Now on the North Coast," *Plain Dealer*, August 26, 1979, sec. 2, p. 3; J. Mark Souther, "'The Best Things in Life Are Here' in 'The

Mistake on the Lake': Narratives of Decline and Renewal in Cleveland," *Journal of Urban History* 41, no. 6 (2015): 1107.

2. *Will the U.S. Economy Still Lead the World in 1990? An Emphatic YES from Cleveland* (Cleveland: New Cleveland Campaign, 1982), 15, Cleveland Public Library, Cleveland, OH; "Cleveland Ads Put on a Happy Face," repr. of advertisement, *Clevelander* 9, no. 2 (February 1980): 14, Commissioners File, box "Miscellaneous," folder "Greater Cleveland Growth Association," Cuyahoga County Archives, Cleveland, OH.

3. Souther, "'The Best Things in Life Are Here,'" 1106–1107.

4. John Herbers, "A New Cleveland Fears Budget Cuts," *New York Times*, March 1, 1986, p. 8; Leon Harris, "Cleveland's Come-Around: The Overnight Municipal Success Story the Country Is Cheering About," *Town and Country*, October 1981, repr. by New Cleveland Campaign, in author's possession.

5. Patricia Atkins et al., "Responding to Manufacturing Job Loss: What Can Economic Development Policy Do?," *Brookings*, June 2011, p. 7, http://www.brookings .edu/~/media/research/files/papers/2011/6/manufacturing-job-loss/06_manufactur ing_job_loss.pdf; "Housing Values Rising Faster within City Limits vs. Suburbs," *Cleveland Today*, October 1983, George V. Voinovich Papers, MS. 5048, container 4, folder 11, Western Reserve Historical Society, Cleveland, OH.

6. Daniel R. Kerr, *Derelict Paradise: Homelessness and Urban Development in Cleveland, Ohio* (Amherst: University of Massachusetts Press, 2011), 205, 222.

7. Iver Peterson, "Boom and Bust Overlap in Cleveland," *New York Times*, February 5, 1982, p. A10.

8. On the national office boom, see Bernard J. Friedan and Lynne B. Sagalyn, *Downtown Inc.: How America Rebuilds Cities* (Cambridge, MA: MIT Press, 1989), 265.

9. Ruth Ratner Miller is another figure whose deep devotion to Cleveland's revitalization merits much more detail but falls outside the focal period for my study. For insights into her connection to Forest City Enterprises, the developer of Tower City Center, and her personal role as a catalyst for the project as an instrument of downtown revitalization, see Sheehan Hannan, "Tower Struggle," *Cleveland Magazine*, November 1, 2016, https://clevelandmagazine.com/in-the-cle/the-read/articles/tower-struggle.

10. For the reference to "municipal vaudeville," see James Barron, "Cleveland Mayoral Race: Voinovich vs. Kucinich with a Twist," *New York Times*, October 31, 1985, p. A18.

11. On Gaslight Square's decline, see Alison Isenberg, *Downtown America: A History of the Place and the People Who Made It* (Chicago: University of Chicago Press, 2004), 281–283. On Underground Atlanta's decline, see Harvey K. Newman, "Race and the Tourist Bubble in Downtown Atlanta," *Urban Affairs Review* 37, no. 3 (2002): 309.

12. Alison Isenberg offers an alternative perspective to that of dismissive white suburbanites. She points out that a similar transformation of James Rouse's Gallery at Market East in Philadelphia "proved that downtown retail could revive even without suburbanites, with the help of nonwhite customers." Such a revival in Cleveland was, at best, very limited in scope. See Isenberg, *Downtown America*, 272.

13. Les Christie, "Where Cleveland Went Wrong," *CNNMoney.com*, November 14, 2007, http://money.cnn.com/2007/11/12/real_estate/Cleveland_foreclosure_factors/; Alex Kotlowitz, "All Boarded Up," *New York Times*, March 8, 2009, Sunday magazine, p. 28; George E. Condon Jr., "How a Community Demolished Its Way Out of a Crisis," *National Journal*, December 10, 2012, http://www.theatlantic.com/politics/archive/ 2012/12/how-a-community-demolished-its-way-out-of-a-crisis/443166/.

14. Atkins et al., "Responding to Manufacturing Job Loss," 7–8. The national growth of what some call a "third sector" (eds and meds) is becoming a focus in scholarship. See,

for example, Carolyn T. Adams, *From the Outside In: Suburban Elites, Third-Sector Organizations, and the Reshaping of Philadelphia* (Ithaca, NY: Cornell University Press, 2014).

15. Atkins et al., "Responding to Manufacturing Job Loss," 2, 7–8.

16. Michael Gill, "Cleveland on the Couch," *Cleveland Free Times* 12, no. 1 (2004): 16; Regina Brett, "A Counterattack on 'Tourism' Videos," *Plain Dealer*, May 13, 2009, p. B1; Kurt Badenhausen, "America's Most Miserable Cities," *Forbes*, February 18, 2010, http://www.forbes.com/2010/02/11/americas-most-miserable-cities-business-beltway-miserable-cities.html.

17. Janet Cho, "Remaking the City into a Tourist Destination, Positively Cleveland Builds on Slogan of 'Never Conventional' to Change Image," *Plain Dealer*, March 20, 2014, p. A4; Susan Glaser, "Positively Cleveland Now Destination Cleveland," *Plain Dealer*, October 29, 2014, p. A7.

18. Clevelandthundercat [Mike Polk], "The Factory of Sadness (A Cleveland Browns Fan's Reaction to Today's Game against Houston)," *YouTube*, November 6, 2011, https://www.youtube.com/watch?v=tRBDMMVctu8.

19. On the role that Cleveland sports teams played in shaping white male identification with the city, see Andrew D. Linden, "Blue-Collar Identity and the 'Culture of Losing': Cleveland and the 'Save Our Browns' Campaign," *Journal of Sport History* 42, no. 3 (2015): 340–360.

20. Matt Bonesteel, "ESPN's '30 for 30' on Cleveland's Sad Sports Fans to Get New Happy Ending," *Washington Post*, June 21, 2016, https://www.washingtonpost.com/news/early-lead/wp/2016/06/21/espns-30-for-30-on-clevelands-sad-sports-fans-to-get-new-happy-ending/.

21. Richey Piiparinen, Jim Russell, and Charlie Post, "Downtown Cleveland: The Dynamic Engine of a Talent-Driven Economy" (2016), *Urban Publications*, Paper 1349, http://engagedscholarship.csuohio.edu/urban_facpub/1349; Steven Litt, "Landscape of Reinvention," *Plain Dealer*, July 24, 2016, p. A11; Richey Piiparinen, Jim Russell, and Charlie Post, "The Fifth Migration: A Study of Cleveland Millennials" (2016), *Urban Publications*, Paper 1338, http://engagedscholarship.csuohio.edu/urban_facpub/1338; Michelle Jarboe, "Progress Seen in Downtown's Revival," *Plain Dealer*, May 13, 2016, p. A1; Scott Suttell, "List of Cuyahoga County's Largest Employers Proves Cleveland Is a Health Care Town," *Crain's Cleveland Business*, August 25, 2014, http://www.crainscleveland.com/article/20140825/FREE/140829853/list-of-cuyahoga-countys-largest-employers-proves-cleveland-is-a; Walter Wright, Kathryn W. Hexter, and Nick Downer, *Cleveland's Greater University Circle Initiative: An Anchor-Based Strategy for Change* (Washington, DC: The Democracy Collaborative, May 2016), http://democracycollaborative.org/greater-university-circle-initiative.

22. Richey Piiparinen, "Cleveland Getting Better, Worse at the Same Time," *Plain Dealer*, March 20, 2016, p. E3.

23. See, for example, Global Insight, *U.S. Metro Economies* (Washington, DC: United States Conference of Mayors, July 2012), 110, http://usmayors.org/metroeconomies/0712/FullReport.pdf.

# Bibliography

**ABBREVIATIONS**

CCA    Cuyahoga County Archives, Cleveland, OH
CPL    Cleveland Public Library, Cleveland, OH
CSU    Cleveland State University Library Special Collections, Cleveland, OH
WRHS    Western Reserve Historical Society, Cleveland, OH

**PRIMARY SOURCES**

Manuscript Collections

Board of Cuyahoga County Commissioners. Proposed Subway System for Downtown Cleveland, 1953–1960. CCA.
Bohn, Ernest J., Papers. Special Collections. Kelvin Smith Library. Case Western Reserve University. Cleveland, OH.
Celebrezze, Anthony J., Papers. Series II. MS. 4046. WRHS.
Centerior Energy Corporation Records, MS. 4791. WRHS.
Cleveland Development Foundation Records. MS. 3514. WRHS.
Cleveland Mayoral Papers, MS. 4276. WRHS.
Commissioners File. CCA.
County Administrators Files. CCA.
Greater Cleveland Growth Association Records. MS. 3471. WRHS.
Klain, Maurice, Research Papers. MS. 4219. WRHS.
Locher, Ralph S., Papers. MS. 3337. WRHS.
Marschall, Daniel J., Papers. MS. 4561. WRHS.
Murtaugh, Larry, Papers. CCA.
Perk, Ralph J., Papers. MS. 4456. WRHS.
Public Administration Library Subject File. CPL.
Stokes, Carl B., Papers. MS. 4370. WRHS.

Taft, Seth, Papers. CCA.
University Circle, Inc., Records. MS. 3900. WRHS.
Voinovich, George V., Papers. MS. 5048. WRHS.

## Newspapers, Periodicals, and Other Media

*Cleveland Call and Post*
*Clevelander* (Cleveland Chamber of Commerce/Greater Cleveland Growth Association)
*Cleveland Magazine*
*Cleveland Plain Dealer*
*Cleveland Press*
*Council Action* (Hough Area Council, Cleveland, OH)
Google News (http://news.google.com/newspapers)
*New York Times*
*Plain Press* (Cleveland, OH)
*Point of View* (Cleveland, OH)

## Oral History Recordings

Hadden, Mrs. John A., Jr. (Elaine). Interview by Jeannette Tuve. January 26, 1985. Transcript. Cleveland Families Oral History Project. MS. 4345. Container 1. Folder 5. WRHS.

Hemsath, John. Interview by Andreana Somich and J. Mark Souther. May 10, 2006. Audio recording. Cleveland Regional Oral History Collection. Interview 319003. http://engagedscholarship.csuohio.edu/crohc000/16.

Pianka, Raymond L. Interview by Becky Solecki. December 9, 2005. Audio recording. Cleveland Regional Oral History Collection. Interview 400023. http://engagedscholarship.csuohio.edu/crohc000/57.

Rosenheim, Jacob. Interview by Patrick Miller. December 6, 2005. Audio recording. Cleveland Regional Oral History Collection. Interview 400019. http://engagedscholarship.csuohio.edu/crohc000/44.

Semsak, James. Interview by J. Mark Souther. July 23, 2014. Audio recording. Cleveland Regional Oral History Collection. Interview 999121. http://engagedscholarship.csuohio.edu/crohc000/739.

Vail, Thomas V. H. Interview by John P. DeWitt. June 20, August 8, 1990. Transcript. Thomas Vail Papers. MS. 4852. Container 4. Folders 92 and 94. WRHS.

Van Dijk, Peter. Interview by Nina Gibans. August 31, 2006. Audio recording. Cleveland Regional Oral History Collection. Interview 951011. http://engagedscholarship.csuohio.edu/crohc000/224.

Wadsworth, Homer C. Interview by Jeannette Tuve. April 10, 1985. Transcript. Cleveland Families Oral History Project. MS. 4345. Container 2. Folder 12. WRHS.

## Additional Primary Sources

Adams, Howard and Greeley. *University Circle: A Plan for Its Development.* Cambridge, MA, 1957.

*Are There Any Civilized Cities Left? A View from Cleveland.* Cleveland: New Cleveland Campaign, 1982. CPL.

Atkins, Patricia, Pamela Blumenthal, Adrienne Edisis, Alec Friedhoff, Leah Curran, Lisa Lowry, Travis St. Clair, Howard Wial, and Harold Wolman. "Responding to Manufacturing Job Loss: What Can Economic Development Policy Do?" *Brookings*, June 2011. http://www.brookings.edu/~/media/research/files/papers/2011/6/manufactur ing-job-loss/06_manufacturing_job_loss.pdf.

Badenhausen, Kurt. "America's Most Miserable Cities." *Forbes*, February 18, 2010. http:// www.forbes.com/2010/02/11/americas-most-miserable-cities-business-beltway-mis erable-cities.html.

City of Cleveland Neighborhood Fact Sheets: Ohio City. http://planning.city.cleveland .oh.us/census/factsheets/spa10.pdf.

City Plan Commission. *Territorial Growth of the City of Cleveland*. Ca. 1922. CPL.

*Cleveland: City on Schedule*. Cleveland: General Pictures Corporation/Cleveland Devel- opment Foundation, 1962. http://flash.ulib.csuohio.edu/cmp/general/cmp-cleveland cityonschedule.html.

Cleveland City Planning Commission. *Cleveland Today . . . Tomorrow: The General Plan of Cleveland*. 1950. CPL.

———. *Downtown Cleveland 1975*. 1959. CPL.

Cleveland Electric Illuminating Company. Annual Report, 1953–1954, 1956–1959. CPL.

*Cleveland Subway: Operating and Engineering Feasibility*. Cleveland: Board of County Commissioners, Cuyahoga County, 1955. CPL.

"Cleveland: The Friendly City to Negroes." *Jet* 7, no. 3 (1954): 10–13.

Cleveland Transit System. *The Future of Metropolitan Cleveland Depends on the Subway: Report to the Cleveland Transit Board Covering Pertinent Facts Relating to the Down- town Distribution Subway, April 1957*. 1957. CPL.

Condon, George E. *Cleveland: The Best Kept Secret*. Garden City, NY: Doubleday, 1967.

*Detroit: City on the Move*. Directed by James T. Slayden. 1965. Detroit: Jam Handy Orga- nization. http://archive.org/details/DetroitC1965.

Ernst and Ernst. *Development Program, Downtown Cleveland: Guidelines for Action*. 1965. CPL.

*Executives Talk about Business Climate in the Cleveland Area*. Cleveland: Special Surveys, 1963. CPL.

*15 Minutes*. Cleveland: Cleveland Convention and Visitors Bureau, 1974. Vertical file. CSU.

Gill, Michael. "Cleveland on the Couch." *Cleveland Free Times* 12, no. 1 (April 28–May 4, 2004): 14–17.

Global Insight. *U.S. Metro Economies*. Washington, DC: United States Conference of May- ors, July 2012. http://usmayors.org/metroeconomies/0712/FullReport.pdf.

Greater Cleveland Growth Association. *Cleveland: A New Generation*. 1978. Vertical file. CSU.

Halprin, Lawrence, and Associates. *Cleveland Take Part Workshop: Objectives for Down- town; Report and Recommendations, May 31, June 1, 2, 1973, Cleveland, Ohio*. Cleve- land: Greater Cleveland Growth Association and the City of Cleveland, 1973. CSU.

———. *Concept for Cleveland: A Strategy for Downtown*. Cleveland: Greater Cleveland Growth Association and the City of Cleveland, 1974–1975. CPL.

Harris, Leon. "Cleveland's Come-Around: The Overnight Municipal Success Story the Country Is Cheering About." *Town and Country*, October 1981. Repr. by New Cleve- land Campaign. In author's possession.

"History of Gateway Center." Records of Gateway Center. MSS#130. Historical Society of Western Pennsylvania. Senator John Heinz Pittsburgh Regional History Center. Pittsburgh, PA.

"It's Still Yesterday in Cleveland." *Montage* (WKYC-TV 3, Cleveland, Ohio), February 3, 1967. http://flash.ulib.csuohio.edu/library/montage/still-yesterday.html.

Klein and Hodne Associates. *Ohio City—Central Park West Planning Project, Technical Report on a Preliminary Plan for the Future Development of the Area.* April 1958. Pamphlet Collection. WRHS.

Magnet, Myron. "How Business Bosses Saved a Sick City." *Fortune,* March 27, 1989. http://archive.fortune.com/magazines/fortune/fortune_archive/1989/03/27/71774/index.htm.

*More Land for Industry: A Basic Planning Survey for the Best Location in the Nation.* Cleveland: Cleveland Electric Illuminating, 1960. CPL.

Parsons, K. C. *A Report on the Preliminary Plan for the Hough Community.* Cleveland: City Planning Commission, 1957.

Piiparinen, Richey, Jim Russell, and Charlie Post. "Downtown Cleveland: The Dynamic Engine of a Talent-Driven Economy." *Urban Publications,* 2016. Paper 1349. http://engagedscholarship.csuohio.edu/urban_facpub/1349.

———. "The Fifth Migration: A Study of Cleveland Millennials." *Urban Publications,* 2016. Paper 1338. http://engagedscholarship.csuohio.edu/urban_facpub/1338.

Rotman, Michael, and Chris Roy. "The Landscape of Tremont." *Cleveland Historical.* http://clevelandhistorical.org/items/show/102.

Sanders, Charles L., and Alex Poinsett. "Black Power at the Polls: Stokes, Hatcher Victories Point Way for Other Cities." *Ebony* 23, no. 3 (January 1968): 23–35.

Suttell, Scott. "List of Cuyahoga County's Largest Employers Proves Cleveland Is a Health Care Town." *Crain's Cleveland Business,* August 25, 2014. http://www.crainscleveland.com/article/20140825/FREE/140829853/list-of-cuyahoga-countys-largest-employers-proves-cleveland-is-a.

Uzzle, Burk. "A Bitter and Insistent Plague." *Life,* December 24, 1965, pp. 106–117.

"When Cleveland Took Its Story to the Nation." *New York Times Magazine,* ca. 1975. In author's possession.

*Will the U.S. Economy Still Lead the World in 1990? An Emphatic YES from Cleveland.* Cleveland: New Cleveland Campaign, 1982. CPL.

*Wonderful World of Cleveland.* Cleveland: State of Ohio/Greater Cleveland Growth Board, 1967. CPL.

Worley, William. *Prime Time—A History: Kansas City's Prime Time.* Charles Newton Kimball Papers. KC0055. Folder 1856. State Historical Society of Missouri Research Center. Kansas City, MO.

Wright, Walter, Kathryn W. Hexter, and Nick Downer. *Cleveland's Greater University Circle Initiative: An Anchor-Based Strategy for Change.* Washington, DC: Democracy Collaborative, May 2016. http://democracycollaborative.org/greater-university-circle-initiative.

## SECONDARY SOURCES

### Books

Abbott, Carl. *The New Urban America: Growth and Politics in Sunbelt Cities.* Austin: University of Texas Press, 1981.

Adams, Carolyn T. *From the Outside In: Suburban Elites, Third-Sector Organizations, and the Reshaping of Philadelphia.* Ithaca, NY: Cornell University Press, 2014.

Anderson, Martin. *The Federal Bulldozer: A Critical Analysis of Urban Renewal, 1949–1962.* Cambridge: Massachusetts Institute of Technology Press, 1964.

Apel, Dora. *Beautiful Terrible Ruins: Detroit and the Anxiety of Decline.* New Brunswick, NJ: Rutgers University Press, 2015.

Bankoff, Greg, Uwe Lübken, and Jordan Sand, eds. *Flammable Cities: Urban Conflagration and the Making of the Modern World*. Madison: University of Wisconsin Press,
2012.

Barber, Alicia. *Reno's Big Gamble: Image and Reputation in the Biggest Little City*. Lawrence:
University Press of Kansas, 2008.

Baugh, Joyce A. *The Detroit School Busing Case: Milliken v. Bradley and the Controversy
over Desegregation*. Lawrence: University Press of Kansas, 2011.

Bauman, John F., Roger Biles, and Kristin M. Szylvian, eds. *In Search of an Urban Housing
Policy in Twentieth-Century America*. University Park: Pennsylvania State University
Press, 2000.

Bayer, Ronald H. *Race and the Shaping of Twentieth-Century Atlanta*. Chapel Hill: University of North Carolina Press, 1996.

Beauregard, Robert A. *Voices of Decline: The Postwar Fate of U.S. Cities*. 2nd ed. London:
Routledge, 2002.

Berman, Lila Corwin. *Metropolitan Jews: Politics, Race, and Religion in Postwar Detroit*.
Chicago: University of Chicago Press, 2015.

Bernard, Richard M., ed. *Snow Belt Cities: Metropolitan Politics in the Northeast and Midwest since World War II*. Bloomington: Indiana University Press, 1990.

Bloom, Nicholas Dagen. *Merchant of Illusion: James Rouse: America's Salesman of the Businessman's Utopia*. Columbus: Ohio State University Press, 2004.

Bloom, Nicholas Dagen, and Matthew Gordon Lasner, eds. *Affordable Housing in New
York: The People, Places, and Policies That Transformed a City*. Princeton, NJ: Princeton University Press, 2016.

Buckholz, Marjorie. *Twenty-Three Years of Work to Improve the Hough Area*. Cleveland:
n.p., 1966.

Buss, Terry F., and F. Stevens Redburn. *Shutdown at Youngstown: Public Policy for Mass
Unemployment*. Albany: State University of New York Press, 1983.

Busta-Peck, Christopher. *Hidden History of Cleveland*. Charleston, SC: History Press, 2011.

Campanella, Richard. *Bourbon Street: A History*. Baton Rouge: Louisiana State University
Press, 2014.

Chambers, Stefanie. *Mayors and Schools: Minority Voices and Democratic Tensions in Urban Education*. Philadelphia: Temple University Press, 2006.

Cocks, Catherine. *Doing the Town: The Rise of Urban Tourism in the United States, 1850–
1915*. Berkeley: University of California Press, 2001.

Cohen, Lizabeth. *A Consumers' Republic: The Politics of Mass Consumption in Postwar
America*. New York: Knopf, 2003.

Countryman, Matthew J. *Up South: Civil Rights and Black Power in Philadelphia*. Philadelphia: University of Pennsylvania Press, 2006.

Cowan, Aaron. *A Nice Place to Visit: Tourism and Urban Revitalization in the Postwar
Rustbelt*. Philadelphia: Temple University Press, 2016.

Cowie, Jefferson, and Joseph Heathcott, eds. *Beyond the Ruins: The Meanings of Deindustrialization*. Ithaca, NY: ILR Press, 2003.

Darden, Joe T., Richard Child Hill, June Thomas, and Richard Thomas. *Detroit: Race and
Uneven Development*. Philadelphia: Temple University Press, 2010.

Darden, Joe T., and Richard Walter. *Detroit: Race Riots, Racial Conflicts, and Efforts to
Bridge the Racial Divide*. East Lansing: Michigan State University Press, 2013.

Davis, John Emmeus. *Contested Ground: Collective Action and the Urban Neighborhood*.
Ithaca, NY: Cornell University Press, 1991.

Doody, Colleen. *Detroit's Cold War: The Origins of Postwar Conservatism.* Urbana: University of Illinois Press, 2013.

Dudley, Kathryn Marie. *The End of the Line: Lost Jobs, New Lives in Postindustrial America.* Chicago: University of Chicago Press, 1994.

Elfenbein, Jessica I., Thomas L. Hollowak, and Elizabeth M. Nix, eds. *Baltimore '68: Riots and Rebirth in an American City.* Philadelphia: Temple University Press, 2011.

*Encyclopedia of Cleveland History.* https://case.edu/ech.

Erickson, Hal. *"From Beautiful Downtown Burbank": A Critical History of* Rowan and Martin's Laugh-In, *1968–1973.* Jefferson, NC: McFarland, 2000.

Frieden, Bernard J., and Lynne B. Sagalyn. *Downtown Inc.: How America Rebuilds Cities.* Cambridge: Massachusetts Institute of Technology Press, 1989.

Gallagher, John. *Reimagining Detroit: Opportunities for Redefining an American City.* Detroit: Wayne State University Press, 2010.

Galster, George. *Driving Detroit: The Quest for Respect in the Motor City.* Philadelphia: University of Pennsylvania Press, 2012.

Galster, George C., and Edward W. Hill, eds. *The Metropolis in Black and White: Place, Power, and Polarization.* New Brunswick, NJ: Rutgers University Center for Urban Policy Research, 1992.

Gillette, Howard, Jr. *Camden after the Fall: Decline and Renewal in a Post-industrial City.* Philadelphia: University of Pennsylvania Press, 2005.

Glasberg, Davita Silften. *The Power of Collective Purse Strings: The Effects of Bank Hegemony on Corporations and the State.* Berkeley: University of California Press, 1989.

Glassberg, David. *Sense of History: The Place of the Past in American Life.* Amherst: University of Massachusetts Press, 2001.

Goldman, Mark. *City on the Edge: Buffalo, New York.* Amherst, NY: Prometheus, 2007.

Gordon, Colin. *Mapping Decline: St. Louis and the Fate of the American City.* Philadelphia: University of Pennsylvania Press, 2008.

Greenberg, Miriam. *Branding New York: How a City in Crisis Was Sold to the World.* New York: Routledge, 2008.

Gregory, James N. *The Southern Diaspora: How the Great Migrations of Black and White Southerners Transformed America.* Chapel Hill: University of North Carolina Press, 2005.

Hamilton, Paula, and Linda Shopes, eds. *Oral History and Public Memories.* Philadelphia: Temple University Press, 2008.

Hardwick, M. Jeffrey. *Mall Maker: Victor Gruen, Architect of an American Dream.* Philadelphia: University of Pennsylvania Press, 2004.

Hartigan, John, Jr. *Racial Situations: Class Predicaments of Whiteness in Detroit.* Princeton, NJ: Princeton University Press, 1999.

High, Steven C. *Industrial Sunset: The Making of North America's Rust Belt, 1969–1984.* Toronto: University of Toronto Press, 2003.

High, Steven C., and David W. Lewis. *Corporate Wasteland: The Landscape and Memory of Deindustrialization.* Ithaca, NY: ILR Press, 2007.

Highsmith, Andrew R. *Demolition Means Progress: Flint, Michigan, and the Fate of the American Metropolis.* Chicago: University of Chicago Press, 2015.

Hill, Laura Warren, and Julia Rabig, eds. *The Business of Black Power: Community Development, Capitalism, and Corporate Responsibility in Postwar America.* Rochester, NY: University of Rochester Press, 2012.

Hirsch, Alison Bick. *City Choreographer: Lawrence Halprin in Urban Renewal America.* Minneapolis: University of Minnesota Press, 2014.

Hirsch, Arnold R. *Making the Second Ghetto: Race and Housing in Chicago, 1940–1960.* Chicago: University of Chicago Press, 1983.

Hurley, Andrew. *Beyond Preservation: Using Public History to Revitalize Inner Cities.* Philadelphia: Temple University Press, 2010.

Isenberg, Alison. *Downtown America: A History of the Place and the People Who Made It.* Chicago: University of Chicago Press, 2004.

Jackson, Kenneth T. *Crabgrass Frontier: The Suburbanization of the United States.* New York: Oxford University Press, 1985.

Jacobson, Matthew Frye. *Roots Too: White Ethnic Revival in Post–Civil Rights America.* Cambridge, MA: Harvard University Press, 2006.

Johns, Michael. *Moment of Grace: The American City in the 1950s.* Berkeley: University of California Press, 2002.

Keating, W. Dennis. *The Suburban Racial Dilemma: Housing and Neighborhoods.* Philadelphia: Temple University Press, 1994.

Keating, W. Dennis, Norman Krumholz, and David C. Perry, eds. *Cleveland: A Metropolitan Reader.* Kent, OH: Kent State University Press, 1995.

Kenyon, Amy Maria. *Dreaming Suburbia: Detroit and the Production of Postwar Space and Culture.* Detroit: Wayne State University Press, 2004.

Kerr, Daniel R. *Derelict Paradise: Homelessness and Urban Development in Cleveland, Ohio.* Amherst: University of Massachusetts Press, 2011.

Klemek, Christopher. *The Transatlantic Collapse of Urban Renewal: Postwar Urbanism from New York to Berlin.* Chicago: University of Chicago Press, 2011.

Koistinen, David. *Confronting Decline: The Political Economy of Deindustrialization in Twentieth-Century New England.* Gainesville: University Press of Florida, 2013.

Kolson, Kenneth. *Big Plans: The Allure and Folly of Urban Design.* Baltimore: Johns Hopkins University Press, 2001.

Krsolovic, Ken, and Bryan Fritz. *League Park: Historic Home of Cleveland Baseball, 1891–1946.* Jefferson, NC: McFarland, 2013.

Krumholz, Norman, and Pierre Clavel. *Reinventing Cities: Equity Planners Tell Their Stories.* Philadelphia: Temple University Press, 1994.

Krumholz, Norman, and John Forester. *Making Equity Planning Work: Leadership in the Public Sector.* Philadelphia: Temple University Press, 1990.

Kruse, Kevin M. *White Flight: Atlanta and the Making of Modern Conservatism.* Princeton, NJ: Princeton University Press, 2005.

Lemann, Nicholas. *The Promised Land: The Great Black Migration and How It Changed America.* New York: Knopf, 1992.

Linkon, Sherry Lee, and John Russo. *Steeltown U.S.A.: Work and Memory in Youngstown.* Lawrence: University Press of Kansas, 2002.

Logan, John R., and Harvey L. Molotch. *Urban Fortunes: The Political Economy of Place.* Berkeley: University of California Press, 1987.

Lubove, Roy. *Twentieth-Century Pittsburgh: Government, Business, and Environmental Change.* Vol. 2: *The Post-Steel Era.* Pittsburgh: University of Pittsburgh Press, 1996.

McKee, Guian A. *The Problem of Jobs: Liberalism, Race, and Deindustrialization in Philadelphia.* Chicago: University of Chicago Press, 2008.

Michney, Todd M. *Surrogate Suburbs: Black Upward Mobility and Neighborhood Change in Cleveland, 1900–1980.* Chapel Hill: University of North Carolina Press, 2017.

Miller, Raymond Curtis. *The Force of Energy: A Business History of the Detroit Edison Company.* East Lansing: Michigan State University Press, 1971.

Moore, Leonard N. *Carl B. Stokes and the Rise of Black Political Power.* Urbana: University of Illinois Press, 2002.

Morley, Judy Mattivi. *Historic Preservation and the Imagined West.* Lawrence: University Press of Kansas, 2006.

Neumann, Tracy. *Remaking the Rust Belt: The Postindustrial Transformation of North America.* Philadelphia: University of Pennsylvania Press, 2016.

Nickerson, Michelle, and Darren Dochuk, eds. *Sunbelt Rising: The Politics of Space, Place, and Region.* Philadelphia: University of Pennsylvania Press, 2011.

O'Connor, Thomas H. *Building a New Boston: Politics and Urban Renewal, 1950–1970.* Boston: Northeastern University Press, 1993.

O'Mara, Margaret Pugh. *Cities of Knowledge: Cold War Science and the Search for the Next Silicon Valley.* Princeton, NJ: Princeton University Press, 2005.

Osman, Suleiman. *The Invention of Brownstone Brooklyn: Gentrification and the Search for Authenticity in Postwar New York.* New York: Oxford University Press, 2011.

Puckett, John L., and Mark Frazier Lloyd. *Becoming Penn: The Pragmatic American University, 1950–2000.* Philadelphia: University of Pennsylvania Press, 2015.

Rodriguez, Joseph A. *Bootstrap New Urbanism: Design, Race, and Redevelopment in Milwaukee.* Lanham, MD: Lexington, 2014.

Rohe, William M. *The Research Triangle: From Tobacco Road to Global Prominence.* Philadelphia: University of Pennsylvania Press, 2012.

Rydell, Robert W. *All the World's a Fair: Visions of Empire at American International Expositions, 1876–1916.* Chicago: University of Chicago Press, 1984.

Rydell, Robert W., John E. Findling, and Kimberly D. Pelle. *Fair America: World's Fairs in the United States.* Washington, DC: Smithsonian Institution Press, 2000.

Sawers, Larry, and William K. Tabb, eds. *Sunbelt/Snowbelt: Urban Development and Restructuring.* New York: Oxford University Press, 1984.

Scarpaci, Joseph L., with Kevin J. Patrick, eds. *Pittsburgh and the Appalachians: Cultural and Natural Resources in a Postindustrial Age.* Pittsburgh: University of Pittsburgh Press, 2006.

Self, Robert O. *American Babylon: Race and the Struggle for Postwar Oakland.* Princeton, NJ: Princeton University Press, 2003.

Seligman, Amanda I. *Block by Block: Neighborhoods and Public Policy on Chicago's West Side.* Chicago: University of Chicago Press, 2005.

Simon, Bryant. *Boardwalk of Dreams: Atlantic City and the Fate of Urban America.* New York: Oxford University Press, 2004.

Smith, Fraser. *William Donald Schaefer: A Political Biography.* Baltimore: Johns Hopkins University Press, 1999.

Sorkin, Michael, ed. *Variations on a Theme Park: The New American City and the End of Public Space.* New York: Hill and Wang, 1992.

Souther, J. Mark. *New Orleans on Parade: Tourism and the Transformation of the Crescent City.* Baton Rouge: Louisiana State University Press, 2006.

Stokes, Carl B. *Promises of Power: A Political Autobiography.* New York: Simon and Schuster, 1973.

Stradling, David, and Richard Stradling. *Where the River Burned: Carl Stokes and the Struggle to Save Cleveland.* Ithaca, NY: Cornell University Press, 2015.

Strawbridge, Herb. *Remembering Higbee's.* Cleveland: Western Reserve Historical Society, 2004.

Sugrue, Thomas J. *The Origins of the Urban Crisis: Race and Inequality in Postwar Detroit.* Princeton, NJ: Princeton University Press, 1996.

———. *Sweet Land of Liberty: The Forgotten for Civil Rights in the Urban North.* New York: Random House, 2008.

Swanstrom, Todd. *The Crisis of Growth Politics: Cleveland, Kucinich, and the Challenge of Urban Populism.* Philadelphia: Temple University Press, 1985.

Teaford, Jon C. *The Rough Road to Renaissance: Urban Revitalization in America, 1940–1985.* Baltimore: Johns Hopkins University Press, 1990.

Thomas, June Manning. *Redevelopment and Race: Planning a Finer City in Detroit.* Detroit: Wayne State University Press, 1997.

Thompson, Heather Ann. *Whose Detroit? Politics, Labor, and Race in a Modern American City.* Ithaca, NY: Cornell University Press, 2001.

Tittle, Diana. *Rebuilding Cleveland: The Cleveland Foundation and Its Evolving Urban Strategy.* Columbus: Ohio State University Press, 1992.

Van Tassel, David D., and John J. Grabowski, eds. *Cleveland: A Tradition of Reform.* Kent, OH: Kent State University Press, 1986.

Walter, Richard. *Detroit: Race Riots, Racial Conflicts, and Efforts to Bridge the Racial Divide.* East Lansing: Michigan State University Press, 2013.

Wiese, Andrew. *Places of Their Own: African American Suburbanization in the Twentieth Century.* Chicago: University of Chicago Press, 2004.

Wilson, James Q., ed. *Urban Renewal: The Record and the Controversy.* Cambridge: Massachusetts Institute of Technology Press, 1966.

Wilson, William Julius. *The Truly Disadvantaged: The Inner City, the Underclass, and Public Policy.* Chicago: University of Chicago Press, 1987.

Wolcott, Victoria W. *Race, Riots, and Roller Coasters: The Struggle over Segregated Recreation.* Philadelphia: University of Pennsylvania Press, 2012.

Zipp, Samuel. *Manhattan Projects: The Rise and Fall of Urban Renewal in Cold War New York.* New York: Oxford University Press, 2010.

## Articles

Bloom, Nicholas Dagen. "The Federal Icarus: The Public Rejection of 1970s National Suburban Planning." *Journal of Urban History* 28, no. 1 (2001): 55–71.

Borchert, James, and Susan Borchert. "Downtown, Uptown, Out of Town: Diverging Patterns of Upper-Class Residential Landscapes in Buffalo, Pittsburgh, and Cleveland, 1885–1935." *Social Science History* 26, no. 2 (2002): 311–346.

Carriere, Michael. "Fighting the War against Blight: Columbia University, Morningside Heights, Inc., and Counterinsurgent Urban Renewal." *Journal of Planning History* 10, no. 1 (2011): 5–29.

Jenkins, William D. "Before Downtown: Cleveland, Ohio, and Urban Renewal, 1949–1958." *Journal of Urban History* 27, no. 4 (2001): 471–496.

Linden, Andrew D. "Blue-Collar Identity and the 'Culture of Losing': Cleveland and the 'Save Our Browns' Campaign." *Journal of Sport History* 42, no. 3 (2015): 340–360.

McKee, Guian. "Urban Deindustrialization and Local Public Policy: Industrial Renewal in Philadelphia, 1953–1976." *Journal of Policy History* 16, no. 1 (2004): 66–98.

Michney, Todd M. "White Civic Visions versus Black Suburban Aspirations: Cleveland's Garden Valley Urban Renewal Project." *Journal of Planning History* 10, no. 4 (2011): 282–309.

Newman, Harvey K. "Race and the Tourist Bubble in Downtown Atlanta." *Urban Affairs Review* 37, no. 3 (2002): 301–321.

Souther, J. Mark. "Acropolis of the Middle-West: Decay, Renewal, and Boosterism in Cleveland's University Circle." *Journal of Planning History* 10, no. 1 (2011): 30–58.

———. "'The Best Things in Life Are Here' in 'The Mistake on the Lake': Narratives of De-
    cline and Renewal in Cleveland." *Journal of Urban History* 41, no. 6 (2015): 1091–1117.
———. "A $35 Million 'Hole in the Ground': Metropolitan Fragmentation and Cleveland's
    Unbuilt Downtown Subway." *Journal of Planning History* 14, no. 3 (2015): 179–203.
Stradling, David, and Richard Stradling. "Perceptions of the Burning River: Deindustri-
    alization and Cleveland's Cuyahoga River." *Environmental History* 13, no. 3 (2008):
    515–535.
Tebeau, Mark. "Sculpted Landscapes: Art and Place in Cleveland's Cultural Gardens,
    1916-2006." *Journal of Social History* 44, no. 2 (2010): 327–350.
Vitale, Patrick. "Decline Is Renewal." *Journal of Urban History* 41, no. 1 (2015): 34–39.


### Theses and Dissertations

Miller, Carol Poh. "Ohio City: A Proposal for Area Conservation in Cleveland." M.A. thesis,
    George Washington University, 1975.
Richter, Cynthia Mills. "Integrating the Suburban Dream: Shaker Heights, Ohio." Ph.D.
    diss., University of Minnesota, 1999.
Vitale, Patrick. "The Atomic Capital of the World: Suburbanization, Technoscience, and the
    Remaking of Pittsburgh during the Cold War." Ph.D. diss., University of Toronto, 2013.

# Index

J. MARK SOUTHER is a Professor of History at Cleveland State University and the author of *New Orleans on Parade: Tourism and the Transformation of the Crescent City.* Visit him online at https://marksouther.org.